The Indigo Bunting

and 365 other ways to experience God in your life

A Daily Devotional

by
Pastor Charlie Chilton

Trinity **R**ivers

Manassas, VA

It is with gratitude that we, the author and publisher, acknowledge the many word combinations used herein that were first spoken, penned, typed, or translated by others. We have made every reasonable effort to give proper credit and obtain permission for using their work. When that has not occurred, we ask that they accept our thanks and grant us an opportunity to obtain permission to be noted in future editions. We trust that everyone contributing to this work for the Ultimate Creator will receive both temporal and eternal blessings for using their gifts for good.

Unless otherwise noted, Scripture taken from the HOLY BIBLE: NEW INTERNATIONAL VERSION®. NIV®. Copyright © 1973, 1978, 1984 by International Bible Society. Used by permission of Zondervan Publishing House.
The "NIV" and "New International Version" trademarks are registered in the United States Patent and Trademark Office by International Bible Society.

Scripture quotations marked "NKJV" are taken from the New King James Version. Copyright © 1979, 1980, 1982 by Thomas Nelson, Inc. Used by permission. All rights reserved.

Scripture quotations used in this publication marked "CEV" are from the Contemporary English Version. © American Bible Society 1991, 1995. Used by permission.

Scriptures quoted marked "EB" are from The Everyday Bible, New Century Version, copyright © 1987, 1988 by Word Publishing, Dallas, Texas 75039. Used by permission.

Scripture quotations marked "KJV" are taken from The Holy Bible, King James Version.

Other permissions and credits are stated at the back of this book when indicated by an asterisk* within the daily devotion.

Foreword

Much of the pastoral ministry is a seed-sowing ministry. Writing devotionals is certainly under that heading. For more than ten years I have written a weekly devotional column for a local newspaper, never knowing who might read it. I share insights that God gives me about ordinary things. I'm encouraged when, from time to time I meet someone in a public place who mentions to me that a particular column was helpful to them. Many have suggested that these short inspirations should be published for a wider audience. That's how *The Indigo Bunting* came to be (see August 20). I pray that it blesses your life.

Along with the little messages, I have included a plan for reading the Bible through in one year. Many courageous souls have attempted this feat but were defeated in the process, for various reasons. I'm calling the plan I've devised, *"THE ONE YEAR CHALLENGE."* This plan mixes together the Old and New Testaments, which should help prevent getting bogged down in any one part. You'll find the O.Y.C. at the end of each day's devotion. Let the devotion help you focus your mind on God's presence and then move into the rich experience of reading the Bible (which is God's Word to you) yourself. It can be done in a year, and it will change your life, for the better! If you don't yet have a Bible, or would like a different translation, browse in some bookstores until you find one to buy that speaks to your heart, or ask someone to give you one.

I have referred to God in masculine terms using masculine pronouns. I don't believe that God is just all male, but our culture traditionally refers to God in this way.

Charles A. Chilton

Acknowledgments

A project like this leaves the writer with many debts of gratitude.

I am grateful to God for giving me insight into what He is doing in our daily experiences.

I am grateful to my secretary friends, JoAnn McConnell and Brenda Drennan, for working so diligently to get this material ready for the publisher.

I am grateful to all of those people who have read my weekly column in the *Potomac News* and urged me to put it together in book form.

I am grateful to Trinity Rivers for accepting the manuscript for publishing.

And I am grateful to you, the reader, for purchasing this book.

Publisher's Credits:

    Initial page design concept: Dan Ciocan
    Editing (September devotions): Bob Clark
    Proofreading: Kathy Clark
    Final page design and composition, editing, photography (back cover): Ric Clark
    Cover art (front and back): Winifred Coolbaugh

To:
Ilana & Eliza
Let God speak to your
life daily! He has news for you!

Pastor Charlie Chilton
John 1: 12

**To my prayer partner
of 40 years—
Fay White Chilton**

Dedication

Another New Year

HUNDREDS OF YEARS AGO JOSHUA SAID TO THE ASSEMBLED ISRAELITES, *"YOU HAVE NEVER BEEN THIS WAY BEFORE"* (Joshua 3:4-5). Then he went on to challenge the people (Joshua 3:5), *"Consecrate yourselves, for tomorrow the LORD will do amazing things among you."* The two prongs of his challenge sound good to me—something I need to hear on New Year's Day. Regardless of how bad the past year has been, or how many troubles I have had, or how many good opportunities I have squandered; there is a brand new year today. It has possibilities unknown. I don't have to hold a negative point of view. Hope is reborn. The other idea is: *"consecrate* (dedicate) *yourself to God because he wants to do something great in your life."* God is prepared to work in your life. He wants to use your life. He wants to bless your life. He wants to do something new in your life in the new year. But he needs a prepared person.

Sad to think that God has good things in store for people but can't give them to some folks because they refuse to prepare for the blessing. Like the old saying, *"do not throw your pearls to pigs"* (Matthew 7:6), unprepared people wouldn't know what to do with blessings from God if they received them—probably just waste them. For myself, I am excited about the New Year. I don't know what God has in store for me but I can hardly wait to receive it. I believe the Bible when it says *"no good thing does he withhold from those whose walk is blameless"* (Psalm 84:11). The world is bent on self-destruction and so are many people unawares. But that will not keep Almighty God from blessing and helping a prepared people. I prefer a God-blessed New Year to a happy one!

> **Dear God, open my eyes to see where You are going in this New Year and give me the grace to follow You. Amen.**

ONE YEAR CHALLENGE—Read:
Genesis 1-3

January 1

All New

ONE CAN'T HELP BUT BE ENTHRALLED BY THE IDEA OF THE *"NEW,"* regardless of what the *"old"* was like. The *"old"* may have been horrible, disappointing, heartbreaking—something you would never want to go through again. Or the *"old"* may have been exciting, money-making, successful, enlightening. Whatever the lasting effect of the *"old"* in your life, the possibility of the *"new"* has to grab you with some expectancy. This is a good time for us to consider new things—whether it's a new year or new job or new classes or new friends. The idea of the *"new"* can quicken your step, increase your heartbeat, pump your adrenaline, revive your hope, and resuscitate your reason for living. Some of you are perhaps thinking by now, *"I don't want to go through that again. I got excited about the 'new' once before and nothing came of it. I just don't believe it's worth the gamble to try it again."* Just a minute! Try this one on for size: *"if anyone (you) is in Christ, he is a new creation; the old has gone, the new has come!"* (2 Corinthians 5:17). Christian or non-Christian, atheist or agnostic, philosopher or searcher—This is for you! This means that if you are coming from a bad situation, there is a radical change possible for you. If you are coming from an acceptable situation, there is a revolutionary event waiting for you. Lamentations 3:23 says that God's compassions *"are new every morning."* And Revelation 21:5 records God as saying, *"I am making everything new!"* We are creatures of habit. We get in ruts and routines. We bore ourselves to death with repetition. We feel comfortable in our ruts, even when we are actually miserable, fearing the unknown of the *"new."* Seek God's *"NEW."* Today is a good day.

Please God—today, restore a sense of newness in my relationship with You. Help me to repeat this request daily as I spend time with You. Amen.

ONE YEAR CHALLENGE—Read:
Genesis 4-6

January 2

A Spiritual Direction

ARE YOU LOOKING FOR A NEW YEAR'S DIRECTION? In Joshua Chapter 3, there is a great story for this time of year. The Israelite slaves have come out of Egypt. Now free from a terrible experience of pain and humiliation, they stand on the banks of the Jordan River ready to go into the Promised Land of hope, freedom and possibility. Joshua is their leader and he says in verse 5, *"Consecrate yourselves, for tomorrow the LORD will do amazing things among you."* What a challenge he gives them! Don't look back! Don't think about the past anymore! You can't change it! Just *"consecrate yourself"* today (that is, dedicate yourself completely to the Lord) and watch God work in your life in this new year. I like that, especially at this point. The *"yesterdays"* of your life are behind you. You can leave them; they are excess baggage for the future. They are too heavy for you to drag around. So many people are miserable be-cause they refuse to release past burdens, hurts, and failures. How can you escape the burden and guilt and anger of your past? By dedicating your life to God and the things of the Spirit. You have tried many roads to success and real joy in life, but they have all been dead end streets. Don't start out the New Year by going back and walking in the same old ruts that lead nowhere. I'm not talking about a New Year's resolution. You made one of those (or several) and you have already lost sight of it, right? No, this is turning in a spiritual direction to meet the needs of your soul. The physical will take care of itself if you get your spiritual direction set. It's a New Year! Great! Brand new! With new tomorrows! Listen to Joshua!

Dear Father, I need a destination for my life. Keep me from wandering around in circles. I want your direction in my life. Amen.

ONE YEAR CHALLENGE—Read:
Genesis 7-9

January 3

Build a New and Rich Tradition

IN A TELEPHONE CONVERSATION WITH A FRIEND, she said, *"Let's start a new tradition for the new year."* I agreed that would be nice. Many people like the idea of the New Year because it suggests the possibility of something new and different. Perhaps we'll escape from the dull and boring routine. Perhaps we've recognized that some old habits and traditions have outlived their usefulness. Perhaps we're admitting that the current rut is getting deeper and the possibility of being trapped someday and not being able to escape is frightening. Obviously, people come from different experiences—positive and negative—when they say, *"Let's start a new tradition."* But did you notice the choice of words: *"New tradition"*? We desire something new and different, but yet want assurance that it will be worthwhile and meaningful—not something new just for the sake of newness. Many have been trapped in that well-camouflaged snare. With all the change and newness, we crave stability and sameness. We need some unchanging, solid base for new experiences to be really satisfying. So, while we are in the mood for change (making New Year's resolutions is an example), let's sort out the old and meaningless and throw it away. Do away with it! Now, let's build a new and rich tradition. Let's begin a new and more meaningful relationship with God. The foundation for this is already prepared: *"For no one can lay any foundation other than the one already laid, which is Jesus Christ"* (1 Corinthians 3:11). The hymn writer said, *"On Christ the Solid Rock I stand, all other ground is sinking sand."* Here is newness: in Christ all things become new. This is not kinky, fruitless newness. Here is a new life, new attitude, new mindset that is based solidly and squarely on God's love for you. A new tradition? Indeed.

God of all Creation, take the stuff of my life and make something new and usable to You. I give You permission to bring newness to my life. Amen.

ONE YEAR CHALLENGE—Read: Genesis 10-12

January 4

On Being Resolved

WE ARE FAR ENOUGH REMOVED FROM IT NOW THAT I THINK IT'S SAFE TO TALK ABOUT IT. *"What's that?"* you ask. A New Year's resolve! Yes, it's different from a New Year's resolution, which usually isn't worth the breath expelled saying it. Generally, people smile when they say, *". . . New Year's Resolution."* It's like an insider's joke. Everyone winks; everyone understands, but no one takes it too seriously. But there are those people who take a clear-eyed look at things, evaluate what they see, then **Resolve** to act accordingly. George Burger aptly said it for me when he commented, *"By God's grace I will forget those things which are behind and press forward to new heights. I will, like David, lift up my eyes unto Him from whence cometh my help; like Abraham, trust implicitly in His guidance; like Enoch, walk in daily fellowship with my Heavenly Father; like Moses, choose to suffer affliction rather than to enjoy the pleasures of sin for a season; like Daniel, commune in prayer with God regularly; like Job, be patient under all circumstances; like Caleb and Joshua, refuse to be discouraged; like Andrew, strive to lead my brother into a closer walk with Christ; like John, lean upon the bosom of the Master and partake of His spirit; like Stephen, manifest a forgiving attitude to all who seek my hurt; like Timothy, study the Word of God; and like my Lord himself, overcome all earthly allurements by refusing to succumb to their enticements."* Realizing that we cannot hope to achieve these objectives by ourselves, we should cling to the promise that *"I can do everything through him (Christ) who gives me strength"* (Philippians 4:13). This to me is genuine resolve. Serious, to the point, and with an expected result. I AM RESOLVED! This sense of determination has to bear good fruit.

> *Patient Father, You who have heard my promises and resolutions for many years, now hear my resolve to follow You. In your strength, I will not turn back. Amen.*

January 5

ONE YEAR CHALLENGE—Read:
Genesis 13-15

Helping Sufferers

From time to time someone stands out who has shown great faith and courage in adversity and shine as an inspiration to many. Recently the former major league pitcher Dave Dravecky joined that group. In his prime, cancer caused the surgical removal of one arm and ended a fine baseball career. In his book, **When You Can't Come Back**,* he wrote: *"In America, Christians pray for the burden of suffering to be lifted from their backs. In the rest of the world, Christians pray for stronger backs so they can bear their suffering. It's why we look away from the bag lady on the street and to the displays in store windows. [It's] why we prefer going to the movies instead of to hospitals and nursing homes."* I find that quite an indictment, don't you? Did Dravecky have to experience suffering to learn that truth? Do I? Do you? On Mother's Day a group from our church went to a nursing home for a worship service. Our group's turn just happened to fall on Mother's Day. I was surprised at the small number of visitors there and the large number of senior ladies alone in their rooms. One of the obvious things that Jesus did in His ministry was to search out sufferers to encourage them. Many people suffer alone from a variety of physical, mental, and emotional pains. People who are healthy should make the effort to comfort them. Jesus said: *"For I was hungry and you gave me something to eat, I was thirsty and you gave me something to drink, I was a stranger and you invited me in, I needed clothes and you clothed me, I was sick and you looked after me, I was in prison and you came to visit me."* (Matthew 25:35-36). His explanation to his shocked listeners was if you did this for anyone you did it for Him.

> **Patient Father, we don't like to suffer and oftentimes we are not comfortable around those who are suffering. Tenderize us. Amen.**

One Year Challenge—Read: Genesis 16-18

January 6

Epitaph

ONE OF THE MOST UNUSUAL EPITAPHS I ever heard is written on a gravestone down in Appalachia. It said, *"The dogs barked at him."* I don't know if they barked from joy or fear, but they barked. Did you ever consider your epitaph? Imagine some of the things people might say about you. Scary, huh! There is one that is really terrible in 2 Chronicles 21:19-20. It says about Jehoram: *"His people made no fire in his honor, as they had for his fathers. . . . He passed away, to no one's regret."* Wow, what an epitaph! No one honored him in death, no one regretted his dying! That was really a wasted life, the uselessness of it became particularly obvious when he died. What kind of impact is your life making? Will people miss you when you are gone? Will they be sad because you are no longer around? We can be careless about life and our relationships with others or we can be sensitive as to the effect we are having on people. I'm sure some would say, *"I don't care what people say after I'm dead,"* but that is a surface reaction. Our influence on people is important. Consider carefully what power your life has for the building up or tearing down of other persons. The greatest memorials are living memorials. The best epitaphs are those written on human hearts because of some positive thing you did. When Jesus talks about us being *"the salt of the earth"* and *"the light of the world"* (Matthew 5:13-14), He is talking about our potential to give help and direction to people. There are several people that I would like to honor by writing their epitaph. They have had a powerful influence on me. Don't waste your life. God gives us fifty, or sixty, or seventy years on earth, but we can influence others for eternity.

> *In my time, O God of Eternity, You have made yourself known to me. Help me to use my time wisely before I join You in eternity. Amen.*

ONE YEAR CHALLENGE—Read: **Genesis 19-21**

January 7

"Off Loading"

I DON'T KNOW MUCH ABOUT COMPUTERS. I know enough to type and print my sermons every week. Recently, one of the computer-smart people in our church came by to "off-load" some material from one computer to my personal computer. It only took a few moments and it was completed. The more I thought about what had happened, the larger became the spiritual lesson I gained from it. When Jesus died on the cross for my sins—literally—all of my sin was "off-loaded" onto Him in just a short moment. "We all, like sheep, have gone astray, each of us has turned to his own way; and the LORD has laid on Him the iniquity of us all" (Isaiah 53:6). The Apostle Peter grasped this great truth when he wrote, "He himself bore our sins in his body on the tree, so that we might die to sins and live for righteousness; by his wounds you have been healed" (I Peter 2:24). Because of this great transaction in eternity you are free on this day to experience the "off-loading" of your sins. Through a simple process of repentance (turning from going your way and instead, toward God's) and confession (agreeing with God about your sinful condition and His unique remedy), you can be relieved of an unbearable burden. Many can testify to the feeling that a great burden was lifted from their back the day they received Jesus as Savior. In fact, I used to sing a little chorus as a child, "burdens are lifted at Calvary."* Need to off load? Try it. Johnson Oatman, Jr. wrote, "Yes, Jesus took my burden, I could no longer bear; yes, Jesus took my burden, in answer to a prayer; my anxious fears subsided, my spirit was made strong, when Jesus took my burden and left me with a song."

I thank You for Your kindness, Father, in receiving the burden of my sin and all of its guilt. I have felt "light" since that day. Amen.

ONE YEAR CHALLENGE—Read: Genesis 22-24

January 8

Moving to a New House

WE'VE RECENTLY MOVED TO A NEW PLACE. It was fun! We had lots of help. Friends are such good support at times like that; they like to share the experience with you. It doesn't matter where you live if you use the place in the right way. Joshua challenged his neighbors by saying, *"as for me and my household, we will serve the LORD"* (Joshua 24:15). Some houses or apartments are noted for dirt and discord. Screams and shouts come from the place, the people who come out from the place are not pleasant. How different it is when a house or apartment is noted for the spirit of Christian love and gentleness. Everyone who enters there leaves feeling better. Everyone is treated with kindness. A house ought to be a reflection of all that is good about the people who live there. How is it at your house? Are people welcomed there, especially children? Does it do people good to come to your house? There should be a very short bridge between your house and your church. One reason teenagers from church families sometimes shock us with their actions is because they have not clearly seen the bridge. What was it about the house of Mary, Martha, and Lazarus that made Jesus always want to go there (John 11:5)? What was it about the house of the single parent Lois and her mother Eunice, that made it such a healthy place for Timothy to grow up (2 Timothy 1:5)? What was it about deacon Philip's house that made it conducive for all of his daughters to become ministers (Acts 21:9)? It had to be related to the commitment in the house. Deuteronomy 6:9 says the direction of the home should be set by writing the word of God on the door frame. How's your house?

> *Dear God, I like the phrase You used in your New Testament, "the church in Your house." I want my place to be centered on You, and I want Your Spirit to dominate it. Thank You! Amen.*

January 9

ONE YEAR CHALLENGE—Read:
Genesis 25-27

Do You Know Me?

Have you seen that TV ad that features a well-known personality's face and a voice speaking, but you don't know the true identity until you see it printed on a certain credit card? *"Do you know me?"* is the question. I might ask that now. I know you are reading this book so you know how I think about several subjects, but do you know me? You may even see my picture and you might recognize me, but do you know me? It's hard to get to know someone. The only people who really know me are my family and the people to whom I minister. Most of us don't know many people and few people know us. Many people confess to me that they have many acquaintances but few friends. Generally, life is lived at a surface level. You may work in an office with someone for 10 years and still not know them. Conversation is usually idle chit-chat, stuff that has no depth. While all of us long for community and relationships, we fear taking the initiative about being open and vulnerable. Sometimes people divorce because they finally got to know their mate and didn't like what they found. Lasting relationships can only develop when we let people know us heart to heart, how we think and feel. In the Old Testament a man named Jehu met a friend named Jehonadab and said, *"Are you in accord with me, as I am with you?"* (2 Kings 10:15). In current slang, we would say, *"Are you and I on the same wave-length?"* Jehu went on to say, *"If so, give me your hand."* I like the way Jesus invited two men to come where He was living and get to know Him (John 1:30). Why don't you let someone get to know you this week?

> *O God, sometimes I feel so isolated and alone, even like an island in a sea of humanity. I know You have something better for me. Help me to experience it. Amen.*

One Year Challenge—Read:
Genesis 28-30

January 10

Post-Christian Era

ARE YOU A CHURCH PERSON? Are you related to a local church? Does it have a significant place in your life? I am! If you are a church person, we have something to talk about. As you may know, the last few years have been described as the *"post-denominational"* era for the church. That is, denomination isn't as important now as it was in the past. People no longer feel they must stick with the denomination of their parents. Today there are more important considerations than doctrines or denominational distinction: the minister, style of worship, location, services offered, to name a few. Like folks moving from one supermarket to another, folks change churches. That's okay. I think there's a bigger question to answer: how do we minister in the *"post-Christian"* era? Denominationalism may be no more than the reflection of the culture where we were born and raised. *"Post-Christian"* says to us that the majority of our culture today couldn't care less about the Christian church. With an individualistic, Lone Ranger *"belief in God,"* the majority are not interested in setting aside any time for church. Besides, if even half of the population decided to go to church on Sunday (like Easter), there would be no room to accommodate them. Don't expect any sympathy for the church or don't expect people to automatically come to a church building. We must attract people with the *"good news"* where they live and work; then they might follow us to the place where they can learn more about it. In the *"pre-Christian era,"* Acts 4:13 relates, *"When they saw the courage of Peter and John and realized that they were unschooled, ordinary men, they were astonished and they took note that these men had been with Jesus."* That's what draws people to the *"church house,"* even in the *"post-Christian"* era.

Make me a magnet for You, O God. So fill my life with Your sweet Spirit that others will want to know You. Amen.

ONE YEAR CHALLENGE—Read: Genesis 31-33

January 11

On Helping Folks

I'VE JUST LEARNED AGAIN, IN A VERY PAINFUL WAY, HOW IMPORTANT IT IS TO HELP people. Our youngest daughter was caught in a two-hour back-up of traffic on the interstate, near midnight, in a pouring-down rainstorm. Her car's engine died. She couldn't get it started. She asked for help from several people and received none. She was cursed by several people for breaking down in the road. Do you understand her helplessness and feeling of powerlessness? Finally, God sent a man from out-of-state, on temporary duty, in a rental car, who stopped to help. I suppose God always has a Good Samaritan (Luke 10:29-37). I am sure many church-going people, highly visible in their religious community, saw her distress and passed by on the other side. It was late. She could have been armed. She could have been immoral. I'm sure all the religious folks who passed by had a rational explanation to themselves for the next couple of miles after they passed her. So did the priest and choir director in the story Jesus told. To be sure, some situations are too dangerous for a single person to deal with adequately. (If that is your gut feeling, you can stop at the next exit and call the police and inform them). I know nothing of mechanical things, but I have stopped and taken people to a garage or went to look for help for them. The stranger who helped my daughter said he had a young daughter back home and that's what made him stop. The Bible says *"Do not forget to entertain strangers,* (homeless, powerless) *for by so doing some people have entertained angels without knowing it"* (Hebrews 13:2). Jesus said, *"whatever you did for one of the least of these brothers of mine, you did for me"* (Matthew 25:40). Help somebody when you have the opportunity, for Heaven's sake!

> **Dear Jesus, did I pass You today, or yesterday? Please forgive me, I am so sorry; I will be looking for You tomorrow. Amen.**

ONE YEAR CHALLENGE—Read: Genesis 34-36

January 12

A Trip to the Zoo

WE TOOK THE GRANDCHILDREN TO THE ZOO today. I always enjoy going to the zoo, especially one that I haven't visited before; it's fun to see new animals. But while it's fun for us, my wife pointed out to me that it was sad for the animals. They were not created to be in cages; they were created to be free, like us humans! There's something revealing about that: even if they have wonderful care, food, and shelter, they can never realize the best, for they are not free. There is more to life than having your physical needs provided. Some years ago I visited South Africa; it felt like a giant, outdoor prison. Why? People were not free. Do you know someone who has the best of everything but yet they have a prisoner mentality? Someone said something once about *"stone walls do not a prison make or iron bars a cage."* How true! What a shame that many do not experience liberty. As limited in the apprecia- tion of life as animals in a cage, many have made their own cages, trapping themselves. Paul said in Colossians 2:8 (we are warned) *"See to it that no one takes you captive through hollow and deceptive philosophy, which depends on human tradition and the basic principles of this world rather than on Christ."* Sometimes they capture monkeys for the zoo by placing a small coin in a gourd just big enough for the monkey's hand. When it grasps the coin, it can't extract it's hand and is trapped because it refuses to release the coin. It is trapped by it's own selfish desires and becomes enslaved. It's easy to trap monkeys, they say. The next time you see some attractive bait, remember the zoo.

> *Set me free, God, from all negative things that have entrapped me. Give me freedom to turn loose to You all bad habits, views, and negative feelings. Amen.*

January 13

ONE YEAR CHALLENGE—Read:
Genesis 37-39

Sanctity of Life

MANY CHURCHES AND RELIGIOUS groups are observing a *"Sanctity of Life"* day this month. It is an important truth that should be emphasized all the time. Parents should teach their children that life is sacred. All life is sacred, from the cradle to the grave. From the womb to the tomb, we must recognize that life is sacred. The first reason is because God created the human race: *"The LORD God formed the man from the dust of the ground and breathed into his nostrils the breath of life, and the man become a living being"* (Genesis 2:7). Secondly, because Jesus died for the human race: *"For Christ died for sins once for all, the righteous for the unrighteous, to bring you to God"* (1 Peter 3:18). There may be a thousand other philosophical, sociological, or ethical reasons to say human life is sacred, but if it were not for the biblical reasons presented, I doubt that the other reasons would hold much water. Let us not throw in our lot with vote-craving politicians who would make this a single issue question. Pro-life speaks to such issues as nuclear arms, hunger, environment, racism, euthanasia, abortion, smoking, alcohol abuse, AIDS, suicide, homelessness, capital punishment, and aging. Pro-life refuses to tunnel-vision on only one issue. Anything that does not respect the gift of life and enhance it for all does not deserve to be called pro-life. The human rights of women and children who are sexually and physically abused and exploited are pro-life issues. When Jesus said in John 10:10, *"I have come that they may have life, and have it to the full,"* he was covering the whole spectrum. The Bible has much to say about the conception of life, the preservation of life, and the fulfillment of life's potential as a stewardship from God. Life is short. Each person should be able to enjoy it.

> *You surprise me, God, when You point out to me all of the issues You are concerned about. Broaden my views; save me from tunnel vision. Amen.*

ONE YEAR CHALLENGE—Read:
Genesis 40-42

January 14

A Matter of Perspective

IT'S THE TIME FOR OUR ANNUAL "MAD-NESS." At no time during the year are we victim to such all-out promotion as we are during Super Bowl Week. Television rates for advertisers, already unreal, become *"totally unreal."* It's almost like being the chosen few or the 144,000 (Revelation 7:4) to actually go there. Everybody gets into it, even non-football fans. Like those who read only the last chapter in a book, millions of us only watch the Super Bowl to see how it all turns out. The other 16 games a team plays are thought to be unimportant preliminaries. I understand the feeling. I feel that way about professional basketball. If I'm not preaching, I will no doubt be watching. Wait! It's important to keep things in perspective. If this many people get this excited and spend this much money for something that is only a game, what would happen if this kind of concentrated energy was focused on something of lasting value, like eradicating hunger, or war, or poverty, or race prejudice, or drug use? Suppose there was the same kind of concern to let the unknown, poor, and powerless people be heard on big political issues? Sure, I know—games give us release or escape from the real problems of life. They're a safety valve. But the difference between *"the haves"* and *"the have nots"* is obvious, too. It's a matter of perspective. How great if we could have this kind of focus on a real issue! For instance, this Super Bowl is a small battle when compared to the one fought on Calvary's cross for the salvation of the world. What is your perspective on this statement: *"This is love; not that we loved God, but that he loved us and sent his Son as an atoning sacrifice for our sins"* (1 John 4:10)? Do you believe this? Are you committed to this truth? If you will commit yourself, it will give perfect balance to your life.

> **O God, shake me loose from my preoccupation with what's happening now while not seeing the big picture. Help me to look at this time from a timeless point of view. Amen.**

January 15

ONE YEAR CHALLENGE—Read:
Genesis 43-45

Handling Disappointment

THE REALIZATION THAT THINGS HAVE NOT CHANGED has now settled in on some friends of yours—maybe you, too. Christmas and New Year's celebrations revived hope. With the holidays and parties as an interruption of the routine, there had been a rebirth of hope. "Maybe the worst is over," we thought. Maybe the promise and resolution would stick this time. Maybe the kindness shown, though small, was a glimmer of hope of better things to come. Maybe the old flame had not totally died. But things have settled down to the way they were before and it is harder to deal with disappointment. How many times can a person build themselves up, only to be let down again? How can I handle disappointment? As a believer, I can say, *"I can do everything through him who gives me strength"* (Philippians 4:13). Or I can say, *"in all things God works for the good of those who love him,"* (Romans 8:28). Or I can say as Joseph did to his brothers who had dealt disappointment to him, *"You intended to harm me, but God intended it for good"* (Genesis 50:20). We cannot allow disappointment to defeat us. One day a large group of followers turned their backs on Jesus and left him and Jesus said to the 12 disciples, *"You do not want to leave too, do you?"* Peter said, *"Lord, to whom shall we go? You have the words of eternal life"* (John 6:67-68). Jesus was disappointed that some left but was heartened by the fact that the others stayed. If you know who you are and you know with assurance your relationship with God and God's plan and purpose for your life, you are equipped to handle disappointments. This doesn't mean you won't feel the emotion of disappointment, it simply means you won't sink in it and allow it to swallow you. Faith can defeat disappointment!

ONE YEAR CHALLENGE—Read: Genesis 46-48

> **Thank you God, that You have never disappointed me. It is hard for me to deal with disappointments. But I feel good knowing that you will never disappoint your children. Amen.**

January 16

Unusual Situations

LIVING IN THE COMMUTER WORLD creates a lot of unusual situations. One of the interesting sites we see are those areas designated *"Kiss and Ride"* at the subway stops. The object is to get your loved-one close to transportation without the cost of parking and send or receive them with a kiss. Certainly not a bad idea! Maybe even an improvement on the Dagwood Bumstead kiss-on-the-run-out-of-the-front-door style. At least it requires the lovers to spend some time together in the car on the way to the commuter station. There is the possibility of morning communication when both are alert and later afternoon communication when both may need encouragement. Probably, though, the *"Kiss and Ride"* picture is symbolic of the way many couples think a quick kiss ought to fix everything. *"Kiss it and make it better"* might work for a two-year old who has stubbed his toe but it's not as good for adults. The stress and strain on marriage in our society can be endured a little better if there are lots of tender kisses, but there is no substitute for an enduring effort to make the marriage work and make the love endure. Marriage and family relations is one place where quick and easy answers won't work. That's why the permanence of Genesis 2:24 (until death) is so vital. In the security of a permanent relationship, current problems can be solved and questions answered. The beautiful picture of Jesus (husband) and the church (bride) forms a beautiful portrait of total and permanent commitment (Ephesians 5:21-33). This kind of setting for a marriage gives the wife the opportunity to put on display daily her *"inner beauty"* and the husband to develop a *"considerate"* attitude as he lives with his wife, his respect for her growing continuously (1 Peter 3:1-7). *"Kiss and Ride"* is just icing on the cake.

> *Thank You for secure marriage and family and home life, or the potential for it. Tell me several times today that commitment is the key. Amen.*

ONE YEAR CHALLENGE—Read: Genesis 49-50, Matthew 1

January 17

Losing is not Fun

We RECENTLY HAD AN UNUSUAL PHENOMENON: the media gave as much publicity to a basketball team's losing streak as is generally given to winning. Maybe it was just another typical bandwagon to jump on, a cause to celebrate, or doing something different. Losing is not fun! People who see themselves as losers or those who experience loss a lot know how hard it is. You are the butt of jokes, people look at you with questioning eyes, people feel sorry for you; but who needs that? How do you feel about the *"lost"* column of your life? (Generally speaking, we say we can handle the *"win"* column.) David said during one of his losing streaks, *"Though my father and mother forsake me, the LORD will receive me"* (Psalm 27:10). Losing streaks can help you know if you have true friends or pretend. Paul, in jail, said that everyone except Luke had deserted him (2 Timothy 4:10-11). God gave Paul special insight in how to handle the situation when you are on the losing side. In Philippians 4:11-13 he said, *"I have learned to be content whatever the circumstances. I know what it is to be in need, and I know what it is to have plenty. I have learned the secret of being content in any and every situation, whether well fed or hungry, whether living in plenty or in want. I can do everything through him who gives me strength."* You see, Paul had been in a career like a Federal Judge (a winner—powerful) but got kicked out when he became a Christian (a loser, it seems). Then he became a famous Christian preacher (a winner) but ended up in jail for preaching about Jesus (a loser, it seems). But a life anchored by faith in God through Jesus Christ can handle either situation with equal ability, and is definitely going to show up in God's *"Win"* column!

> *Lord, how does my box-score of life look today? I know that whether I win, lose, or tie; it will be all right through Your Presence. Amen.*

ONE YEAR CHALLENGE—Read:
Matthew 2-4

January 18

Cameras don't Lie

WHY DO PEOPLE GET IRRITATED WITH PHOTOGRAPHERS? Across the years, in different churches, we have made a pictorial directory of the church members to aid in fellowship and getting to know everybody's name. When the photographer returns with the proofs for folks to choose their pictures, some folks get irritated. What do you expect from a picture? The camera can only give back what it sees. Do people naturally see themselves as younger, sexier, or more dramatic than they really are? There are probably three images of all of us: as we think we appear, as we really appear, and how other people view us through their prejudice about us. What area demands the most work? Obviously, we can't change others' eyes and we can't change what we have been, so, we are left to work on the real me of today and tomorrow. I remember the poet Robert Burns once remarked on how great it would be to see ourselves *"as others see us."* That might bring us down to reality! So, how to make the real me more pleasing? I must start on the inside: *"Create in me a pure heart, O God, and renew a steadfast spirit within me"* (Psalm 51:10). That was where David started. Until we like ourselves on the inside, we are not going to appreciate the outside appearance. Inner doubt, fear or guilt will automatically make us feel negative about ourselves. In fact, Jesus based the second great commandment on self-love: *"love your neighbor as yourself"* (Matthew 19:19). Realize that you are made in the image of God and as a current slogan goes, *"God don't make trash."* I'm just suggesting to you that if you are tempted to get mad at your camera, take an inner photo first. When that picture is good, you can smile at the glossy prints.

Lover of my soul, thank You for loving me "warts and all." I couldn't love me unless You loved me. Amen.

ONE YEAR CHALLENGE—Read: Matthew 5-7

January 19

Breaking Old Patterns

BOY, IT'S HARD TO CHANGE! When you have done something the same way for a long time, it is really painful to do it differently. Almost every religious denomination in America today is struggling with change. The hymns are changing; many complain that they *"don't sing the old songs anymore."* There are so many different translations of the Bible that some complain about not hearing the *"beauty of the King James."* With a more relaxed style of dressing, many are offended by those who don't *"get dressed for church."* Even though Jesus said *"No one sews a patch of unshrunk cloth on an old garment,"* and *"Neither do men pour new wine into old wineskins"* (Matthew 9:16-17), many people still try. Some of us enjoy the heady taste of our *"new wine"* but we really hate to give up our old wineskins. Like children at a party, we want to eat our cake and keep it too. It can't be done. There's only one solution; if the old pattern is no longer satisfying, lay it down and move on to the more satisfying. It will only hurt for a while. Read in the Book of Acts and you will struggle with Peter and Paul as they move from *"legalistic religion"* to a *"grace relationship in Christ."* This is probably why Jesus describes Christian conversion as a new birth (John 3), meaning an abrupt surrender to Jesus. The idea many have of gradually bringing their lives in line with a Christian pattern seldom ever works. To decide to follow Jesus is radical. Once the basic commitment is made, other things will have to come in line. If my security is in my relationship with Jesus Christ, then I can go wherever that relationship takes me. I am no longer limited to previous patterns of conduct. God's power makes big changes happen easily.

Thank You God, for shaking me up. Thank You for turning my world upside down. Thank You for the excitement of the Christian life! Amen.

January 20

ONE YEAR CHALLENGE—Read: Matthew 8-10

Disappointment

On my way to the hospital, I passed by where my friend used to live. What a disappointment! The grass was tall; there was trash in the yard. The place looked terrible! In such a little while it had deteriorated. Have you ever gone back to a place where you used to live? Were you hurt by what you saw? Reality hardly ever measures up to memory. That's why it's not always wise to return to a honeymoon spot or a favorite restaurant years later unless you are prepared to deal with disappointment. The *"good old days"* might not have been so good, but our memories often chose to only retain the pleasant parts only. Disappointment can be a spirit-killer. Many people have developed the negative philosophy of *"don't ever trust anybody, they will always let you down or disappoint you."* Have you heard the tongue-in-cheek Beatitude, *"Blessed is the man who expects nothing, for he will never be disappointed"*? There may be a grain of truth in there somewhere, but what a terrible way to live! Without hope and expectancy, life will be a drag. Sure, people and careers and vacations sometimes disappoint us, but the hopeless attitude on life is worse. Pessimism is almost always a self-fulfilling prophecy. If I am expecting the day to be bad, it almost certainly will be. If you are a Christian, you need to remember the promise of Jesus, *"I will not leave you as orphans; I will come to you"* (John 14:18). Disappointments should never be allowed to destroy us, for *"the peace of God, which transcends all understanding, will guard your hearts and your minds in Christ Jesus"* (Philippians 4:7). On the other hand, if you are a person without faith, disappointments may lead you to the One who never disappoints. *"He has never broken any promise spoken, He will keep His promise I know,"* wrote a songwriter. *"I am still confident of this: I will see the goodness of the LORD,"* said David (Psalm 27:13). Remember, your disappointment can be His appointment to bring good to your life.

ONE YEAR CHALLENGE—Read: Matthew 11-13

> *Dear Jesus, I give to You my disappointments. They have hurt and hindered me too long. Let my disappointment be a new appointment with You. Amen.*

January 21

Building a Church Building

IT'S FUN TO BE A PART OF A GROWING CHURCH FAMILY. It's really exciting as the church grows and buildings have to be built for worship and study and training. I'm glad to be a part of something like that. So much of what we humans do is for the now; it has no long range implications. THINK: Building houses or stores, cooking food or shopping for it, making cars or airplanes, etc.; these are things that won't outlast our own lifetime. But building a church building is different; it's like investing in eternity. It will live long after you are gone. The lives of the people who discover the truth there will be changed for eternity. We really experience I Corinthians 3:9, *"For we are God's fellow workers."* No Christian could help being challenged by this opportunity. Giving financially comes easy for many Christians when it comes to building a church building; it is a time to invest in eternity, being a part of God's on-going ef-fort to redeem the world. Mark 16:20 talks about the first Christians going out preaching after the Resurrection and says, *"the Lord worked with them and confirmed his word by the signs that accompanied it."* What a reward—seeing God's hand confirm your actions! When people begin to stream into a new building dedicated to teaching the Bible, everybody who had a part in it experiences that confirmation. Paul describes himself as God's fellow worker (2 Corinthians 6:1) and Timothy as *"God's fellow worker"* (I Thessalonians 3:2). What a great description! The Bible says that *"in all things God works for the good of those who love him"* (Romans 8:28). You can get out of the rut you are in and plug in to eternity. Give your life to Jesus Christ. Find a reason for living. Discover eternity. Become an active part of the work crew that is changing lives for eternity.

ONE YEAR CHALLENGE—Read: Matthew 14-16

> *God of Eternity, in You my life has found lasting value. I know now that my short life has a lasting purpose and that is so good. Amen.*

January 22

Earth Watch

From time to time I see a little blip on television called *Earth Quest*. It is always a short commentary on the environment. It has to do with ecology, which is the *"science concerned with the interrelationship between organisms and their environments"* according to the dictionary.* Whenever I have seen any of the Moody Institute's science films or browsed through **National Geographic** magazines and looked at the pictures, I have thought of Genesis 1. Perhaps you have read it and remember the lines: *"Then God said, 'Let the land produce vegetation . . . Let the water teem with living creatures, and let birds fly . . . Let the land produce living creatures according to their kinds: livestock, creatures that move along the ground, and wild animals,' . . . And it was so. . . . And God saw that it was good."* What a beautiful, moving picture of this beautiful earth! I'm not sure if I can, but David the Psalmist could wax eloquent when he thought of God *"the Maker of heaven and earth, the sea, and everything in them"* (Psalm 146:6) and expressed the beauty of it all. It's enough to make you weep now when you see the rain forests being denuded or the latest bulldozer starting a new subdivision in your area. The trees are disappearing! When the wastewaters poison more and more water life, and exhaust fumes of all types poison people and plants, you would think the general population would be alarmed. But no one's surprised. Many consider it no big deal; *"We don't have to worry about the greenhouse effect,"* they say, *"because we will be dead by the time it's full-blown. Another generation will have to deal with it."* Man must stop thinking he is the center of the universe and thinking only of his selfish comforts. It's time to start listening to the environmentalists; they are our friends, trying to get our attention. Preserving the earth for the next generation and the one after that is the wise path to take. The implications of our responsibility as *"earth-keepers"* are many. Do your part.

OneYearChallenge—Read: Matthew 17-19

> *Even though this world is not my home and I am just passing through, help me, O My God, to be a good caretaker while I am here. Amen.*

January 23

Meeting Expectations

SOMETIMES IN LIFE, WE HAVE THE OPPORTUNITY of fulfilling expectations. Have you ever spontaneously gone to someone's house and when they answered your knock on the door, they said, *"Come on in. I've been expecting you"*? It's usually followed by an explanation, *"I just had a feeling you were coming today"* or *"I need to talk to someone and I know that you care about me and I wanted you to come."* When you are in either of the roles, it is a very satisfying experience. God works that way with responsive people. If you want to help someone and you make your life available to God, He will send you to someone who needs an encouraging word or a listening ear. That is another truth that we learn about God: He has great timing. I believe that's why the world responded so quickly to Jesus when He came and even one of His detractors observed that He had *"turned the world upside down"* (Acts 17:6 KJV). Paul said in Galatians 4:4, *"when the time had fully come, God sent his Son, born of a woman, born under law, to redeem those under law."* It was at just the right time. World religions had all proven to be empty. Political systems had risen and fallen. Human hearts were crying out to God to do something—to come closer, to be visible, to save the world. The Bible relates an instance where two people said in effect, *"Thanks, we have been waiting for you."* I'm referring to Anna and Simeon who are introduced in Luke 2:25-38. A great thing about God is that He never fails to meet those who are waiting for Him. If we lack sensitivity we may miss knowing that certain people need us and that God is prompting us to go and minister for Him. Think of the unfulfilled (or delayed) expectations! What a great opportunity for every Christian! Make yourself available to God daily and He will use you.

ONE YEAR CHALLENGE—Read: Matthew 20-22

> *O God, who is waiting for me to call or visit or write or witness today? I don't want to lose any opportunity to be a blessing to someone. Amen.*

January 24

Caring for Others

ONE OF THE SIGNAL MARKS OF OUR FAITH IS THE ABILITY TO CARE for others: The sequence of seeing others in need and acting to meet their needs. In the pattern of Jesus, we go outside ourselves to help others. Paul describes it in Romans 15:2, *"Each of us should please his neighbor for his good, to build him up."* The world tends to *"beat-up"* on people. Many people collapse in their homes at night feeling put upon by family, co-workers, the boss, the government, neighbors or even the church. What they need is someone to say an encouraging word or do an encouraging act. Christians could validate their faith before many non-believers simply by caring. We have the perfect example in Jesus as He picked out the people who were hungry for someone to care. I am reminded of Proverbs 25:11, *"A word aptly spoken is like apples of gold in settings of silver."* A simple expression of care can blast away the despair of depression in a heartbeat. Many people have become followers of Jesus Christ just because they heard the challenge to *"Cast all your anxiety on him because he cares for you"* (I Peter 5:7). What a marvelous discovery when you find out there is Someone who really cares for you. For Christians reading this, I offer this challenge: *"Cast your cares on the LORD and He will sustain you; He will never let the righteous fall"* (Psalm 55:22). In this way, we are equipped for the business of caring. It requires no special training. Once a person has been healed of loneliness and isolation, that person can begin to think about others and their feelings of abandonment. For non-believers reading this, I offer this caring word: *"Commit your way to the LORD; trust in him"* (Psalm 37:5).

Thank You Jesus, for caring for me. No one has ever cared for me and expressed it the way You do. Thanks again! Amen.

ONE YEAR CHALLENGE—Read: Matthew 23-25

January 25

One Grey Eyebrow

IF SOMETHING IS DIFFERENT OR BECOMES DIFFERENT FROM THE ORDINARY, PEOPLE REALLY NOTICE it. And they ask questions, or say something should be done about it. Recently, one of my eyebrows turned grey. Almost overnight. Slowly but surely people started asking questions. I rediscovered that people do not like to deal with unusual or different things. Or change from the routine. That's not totally bad, of course. For example, the reason the newspaper headlines stories about murder, rape, or arson is because they are not ordinary; they are not what we expect normal people to do. How do you deal with the different; with change? The world is so transient, everything seems to be in a state of flux. We can refuse to accept change. Do you know women who still wear their hair in a 50s style or men who wear ties that were *"in"* when they were young? Or we can try to keep up with change. There are occa-sional lists in magazines of what is thoroughly modern and we can respond in kind, as much as possible. In a transient world, we must discover some non-negotiables—truths that can never change—and fix our lives firmly on them. Having done that, we can be flexible enough to change where we should, and not be harassed by the rest. Learning to be flexible and learning to compromise are not bad things to do. Growth and development can take place in the tension between what we are today and the change that we are challenged to confront. Dealing with constant change Paul said, *"I have learned to be content"* (Philippians 4:11). Or, we can be like Jesus, and be a *"change-agent." "I am making everything new!"* He said (Revelation 21:5). Some things need to be changed for the better. Look for them and do it.

> **Help me, God, to change in my life the things that need to be changed. Enable me to deal with change through Your unchanging love. Amen.**

ONE YEAR CHALLENGE—Read: Matthew 26-28

January 26

Loneliness

"*NO ONE IS CONCERNED FOR ME*" (Psalm 142:4). So lamented David in the Old Testament. Some considered him an outlaw and a rebel. Some considered him the greatest man alive. He was always in the center of things! He always had an admiring group around! But in this Psalm, he is feeling absolutely cut-off and lonely, isolated in life, sick with loneliness! How often we hear that refrain. Surely loneliness is the number one soul sickness. Go to the church house or the meeting of Alcoholics Anonymous, you hear the same refrain! It's not isolated in the hospital or nursing home. Every person who feels secure and loved and surrounded has a mission to attack this enemy of mankind. For me, the real terror of hell is loneliness. Indeed, being in a place where "*no one is concerned for me*" is hell; isolated from God and any real community with other people. I know people who would take a chance on the fire of hell if they thought it meant being with people who understood them. There are a couple of steps to get out of the bowels of loneliness. First, hear God's invitation through the lips of Jesus: "*Come to me, all you who are weary and burdened, and I will give you rest* (satisfaction)" (Matthew 11:28). The second is to reach out to some people. Call someone! Visit someone! Just go and drop in (leave your pride at home) and admit your loneliness and ask to talk for awhile. Whoa! Stop that rebuttal! You are already saying, "*They're busy,*" "*I'm not worth it,*" "*I don't want to be a cry-baby,*" etc. God made us to need each other. Give someone the opportunity to help you. Don't just sit and stare and wait for an answer to your loneliness to be delivered by the United Postal Service. With God's help and taking a piece of the responsibility yourself, you can escape.

ONE YEAR CHALLENGE—Read: Exodus 1-3

Lord Jesus, you were often left alone but you never suffered from loneliness. Teach me your secret. Give me your presence. Amen.

January 27

Signs of Nature's Winter

HAVE YOU BEEN COMPLAINING about the weather? Well, what do you expect? It's winter, isn't it? It's time for cold wind, and thick frost on the windshield, and uncomfortable weather. It's winter! Winter is often hard for people. Remember when Paul was in prison and he wrote to Timothy, *"Do your best to get here before winter"* (2 Timothy 4:21). Winter can be especially hard and we need reinforcement. Of greater dread than the season of winter is the winter-time of the soul and spirit—the days of spiritual coldness—days when all signs of spiritual life are gone; spirituality is non-existent. Prayer has fallen from the life because it seemed the skies were always brassy cold and unresponsive. Bible reading is no longer attempted because the pages of Holy Writ seemed too puzzling and there was no one to give a word of enlightenment. Church-going has ceased because you don't feel at home. Christian standards of morality and right were left behind climbing up the ladder of success. Yes, just as clearly as you see the signs of nature's winter when you look out the frigid kitchen window you can look at the lives of friends and associates (even family members) and see the signs of spiritual winter in their lives—or perhaps your life. And seeing that should send a chill up the spine! It's deathly, seeing no true life, and it mutely prophesies even darker days. Just as we prepare and defend ourselves against nature's winter, so we need to defend against spiritual winter. In Romans 12:11, we are told *"Never be lacking in zeal, but keep your spiritual fervor, serving the Lord."* Later, in verse 21, Paul says, *"Do not be overcome by evil, but overcome evil with good."* Don't let winter defeat you! Spring can come, if you let it.

God of all seasons, I want to love your winter time. Please be my constant companion and pour your warmth into my spirit. Amen.

ONE YEAR CHALLENGE—Read:
Exodus 4-6

January 28

Super What?

HOW MANY TIMES HAVE YOU HEARD THE WORD "SUPER" this week; or read it in an advertisement? Since communication is so highly developed in our country, we are saturated on every level by promotion. Because of the countless repetitions of the theme *"Super,"* many people can hardly wait for that Monday when they won't have to hear the word again until advertisers get brave enough to use it for the next *"Super Big Sale."* The big problem here is that we get jaded after a while. We know we are getting manipulated. If you are a true sports fan, you don't need the hype; the game itself carries enough interest for one to not miss it. If you are not a fan, you may hate it and couldn't care less what happens. So the advertisements are aimed at *"hooking"* the vast in-between group who can be temporarily excited or just want to be able to talk about it next week. As an involved observer of humanity, I've noticed that the bigger the hype, the quicker the event is forgotten. Anything that is so temporary and demands so much money and effort to inflate its position, should not collapse so quickly from view. But the truly great events of history had no hype and very little media coverage: the signing of the Declaration of Independence, the Emancipation Proclamation, and the Gettysburg Address, to mention a few. In my opinion, the greatest event of history was hardly noticed in its time. Take either the birth of Jesus, His death, His resurrection, or His ascension to Heaven. No hype, just the dynamic power of God at work. In fact, what happens at your church this Sunday morning will receive little attention or community promotion. But what happens there, in the lives of men and women changed by the gospel, will be truly super!

O Father, tune me in to a true evaluation of what you are doing in this world. Give me wisdom not to be deceived by flashy advertisement. Amen.

ONE YEAR CHALLENGE—Read:
Exodus 7-9

January 29

The Size of Your Dream

WHAT WE EXPECT FROM LIFE is usually what we get. In **Winnie-the-Pooh**, Pooh and Piglet take an evening walk. For a long time they walk in companionable silence. Finally, Piglet breaks the silence and asks, *"When you wake up in the morning, Pooh, what's the first thing you say to yourself?" "What's for breakfast?"* answers Pooh. *"What do you say, Piglet?" "I say, I wonder what's going to happen exciting today?"** is the reply. Small expectations yield meager results. You can choose a *"breakfast dream"* for your life or you can chose an *"excitement dream."* How big is your dream for this year? It has been said that when Sir Christopher Wren was rebuilding St. Paul's Cathedral in London after the great fire, he passed by anonymously one day and asked a worker, *"What are you doing here?"* He answered, *"I'm hauling stone blocks."* To another he asked the same question and was told, *"I'm trying to earn a few pounds."* To a third he asked, *"What are you doing?"* and the man replied, *"I'm helping Sir Christopher Wren build a magnificent cathedral for our Lord!"* Indeed your expectation and outlook on life each day will determine your self-image and your sense of satisfaction and well-being. Paul challenges us to *"Set your minds on things above, not on earthly things"* (Colossians 3:2). What are you looking for in life? Just to get by, or to pay the bills? Life is too routine without a vision bigger than the day-to-day experience. To be just *"marking time"* or as a poet said, *"be on a treadmill to oblivion"* is sure to reduce life to meaninglessness. Don't be satisfied with existing when you could be really living! Jesus said, *"I have come that they may have life, and have it to the full"* (John 10:10). Check it out! When God created you, He had a purpose for you. Find it. Experience it. If you do, this will be the best year of your life.

> *Dear God, make me a dreamer. Give me the ability to see the potential of every situation as an opportunity to get to know you better and share with You in your work. Amen.*

January 30

ONE YEAR CHALLENGE—Read: Exodus 10-12

Morality in Government

IT HAS BEEN DIFFICULT FOR MANY SINCERE CHRISTIAN FOLKS to deal with those who politicize moral questions. Some politicians have become very good at it and been able to use religious folks for political advantage. Some religious people are surprised how little their opinions matter once the election is over and the votes are counted. As Christians, we are instructed to be *"the salt of the earth"* and *"the light of the world"* (Matthew 5:13-14). We are to be acting as yeast does in a lump of dough: slowly but surely showing people how we believe by the lifestyle we live and convictions that make a difference in our actions. Jesus never used force to get people to follow Him. Jesus never used *"majority rules"* as a way to get people to do the right thing. Jesus never led a demonstration or formed a political action group. Yet, He and His followers *"turned the world upside down"* (Acts 17:6 KJV).

Some Christians now want politicians to be *"spiritual enforcers."* Separation of Church and State has always worked in America because it has kept each side from manipulating the other for selfish reasons. Christians *"seek first his* (God's) *kingdom"* (Matthew 22:21). There are many important issues facing the citizens of our country. Christians need to look for what is morally right rather than what is politically correct. Morality cannot be legislated. Love and concern for the needs of real people cannot be legislated. Don't let anyone deceive you. If the citizens will live the moral right, the politicians would know the citizens expect morally right legislation. Evil men take the field when good men refuse to get involved. *"I have no greater joy than to hear that my children are walking in the truth"* (3 John:4). That's above politics.

Father, I want to be a good citizen. Because I am a citizen of the Kingdom of God, make me see my urgent responsibility in this earthly kingdom. Amen.

OneYearChallenge—Read: Exodus 13-15

January 31

Using the Season to Help Others

FEBRUARY—HERE IT IS AGAIN. Many people just hate February. The trees are bare; the grass is brown (if not covered with snow); the weather is cold; the children have runny noses; spring seems far off; and there are many more complaints you could make during this cold and bleak month. I remember a few years ago when a couple of people petitioned Congress to remove February from the calendar. They wanted a few more days of spring in April, and a few more for vacation in August, and a couple of more beautiful October afternoons—just do away with February. Yes, we all have a problem with the routine days, the humdrum hours, the days that come and go without fanfare. That's why so many people live in the make-believe world of television, especially in February. Their worlds keep turning in beautiful materialism, secret affairs, and other exciting events regardless of the month.

Compare your February feeling with David in Psalm 31:14-15: *"But I trust in you, O LORD; I say, 'You are my God.' My times are in your hands."* There is a profound faith written in this statement. Regardless of how bored and useless I feel, or trapped and going nowhere, I trust God. I maintain my trust. I deepen my trust and I look to see what God has for me. My time is His time: His to control, His to direct, His to sustain. It may be that He has given me February for a time of renewal and retooling. Since activity may be more limited, there is more time for reading, reflecting, meditating, or just asking myself *"why do I have to be so busy all the time to be happy?"* Perhaps there is someone close by who needs help in a way that you have been prepared. You are available. Don't hate this month, use it!

> *My Father, make this the best February of my life. Bless me, that I may be a blessing to at least one person each day this month. Amen.*

February 1

ONE YEAR CHALLENGE—Read: Exodus 16-18

Winter Barrenness

WE ARE IN THE HARD DAYS OF WINTER now in most of the United States. Daylight hours are still short; the trees are still bare; the yards are brown; the winds are cold. There is a kind of stark coldness surrounding all. It is harder to get out and around, especially if your bones are stiffened by age or arthritis. You must put out more effort to overcome the circumstances. It's harder (almost impossible) to enjoy walking or jogging or cycling when the wind is blowing in your face at a below-freezing temperature. Staying inside more and watching television more and snacking more does not make for feelings of vigor and vitality. Psalm 63 is described as a song written by David while in the desert of Judah. He writes in verse 1, *"O God, you are my God, earnestly I seek you; my soul thirsts for you, my body longs for you, in a dry and weary land where there is no water."* The winter days stretch out for the house-bound as a desert wasteland, barren of excitement. Christmas is a winter highlight, but it seems far away and nearly forgotten by the time you reach February. Actually, these dull times of winter cold are better times of spiritual instruction for us than summer's warmth. Some folks are so busy running around and working in their yards, when the days are long and comfortable that they have more trouble finding time for God. Winter barrenness can speak volumes to us about the barrenness of life without God. We can and should do some spiritual evaluation that could equip us for the spring. *"There is sunshine in my soul today, more glorious and bright, than shines in any earthly sky, for Jesus is my light."* That is the answer penned by the Christian poet Edgar Hewitt. Lift up your eyes; see God this winter day.

God of Grace and God of Beauty, shine into my soul today. Refresh me with the warmth of Your love, drive any coolness from my spirit. Amen.

February 2

OneYearChallenge—Read:
Exodus 19-21

A Wall of Fog

THE BED AND BREAKFAST MANAGER CHEERILY SAID as we left, *"Today you will see which is really the sunny side of the mountain."* We had spent the night in Luray, and the morning was beautiful. As we started to climb up the mountain to the Skyline Drive, it was a brilliant morning. We soon arrived at the top of the mountain and started down the other side and then it happened: we entered a wall of fog. Suddenly the sun was gone and we could not see. We slowed to a crawl and very slowly inched our way along down the other side. It was terrible! What a shock! How could it happen so quickly that we went from clear visibility to sudden dark shadows? I have often re-lived that experience in my mind because life is like that fog bank experience. You get up in the morning feeling great and all is well and suddenly you get a phone call about a tragedy. Your family life is happy and secure, you think, and then you get the news that something bad has happened. Things like that come in life and we suddenly feel that we are grasping in the dark trying to find the way. Some of us instinctively remember *"Even though I walk through the valley of the shadow of death, I will fear no evil"* (Psalm 23:4). We remember, *"The eternal God is your refuge, and underneath are the everlasting arms."* (Deuteronomy 33:27). There is no way to prepare for the sudden fog banks. They just come. Life is unpredictable. Deep down inside, we must discover a personal relationship with Jesus Christ that sees us through every situation. Romans 8:31-39 has helpful words about this need. You put yourself at a great disadvantage if you wait for the fog to fall and then flounder. Prepare now.

> *Father, sometimes when I pray I don't feel like I am getting through to You. The sky looks gray. You seem so distant. When that happens, gently remind me that You are still in control. Amen.*

ONE YEAR CHALLENGE—Read: Exodus 22-24

February 3

Racism and You

IT WON'T GO AWAY. I don't think it ever will. It will always demand attention. As long as we live we must fight racism and teach our children by words and actions how to combat it so they can continue the battle after we are gone. As long as there are fears and stereotypes and long memories, racism will be a problem. The people of God, the church in particular, must do all possible to root out this cancer. *"Have we not all one Father? Did not one God create us?"* (Malachi 2:10) Recognizing the common ground of our creation and our relationship to the Creator could be a good place for us to start. If we could see ourselves as human beings without a descriptive adjective stuck in front, we could make progress. I remember a picture from a newspaper account of a rally led by Dr. Martin Luther King Jr. There was a man holding a placard that simply said *"I Am A Man."* Starting from there we can build. Man was created by God. Man rebelled against God. Man needed a savior to re-establish a relationship with God. Jesus carried our sin of rebellion to the cross. Jesus brings us into a right relationship with God and gives us the freedom to relate to every other human being equally, on a person-to-person basis. These preceding words included no descriptive word about color or national origin. We are all in the same boat called humanity and we must pull the oars together or the boat is just going to float around in circles and no progress will be made. *"Dear friends, let us love one another, for love comes from God. Everyone who loves has been born of God and knows God. Whoever does not love does not know God, because God is love."* (1 John 4:7-8).

O God, we all appreciate the varieties of birds, flowers, and fishes. Open our eyes to appreciate the same thing in the human family. Amen.

ONE YEAR CHALLENGE—Read: Exodus 25-27

February 4

More Spaniel than Bulldog

I HEARD SOMEBODY SAY RECENTLY THAT WE CHRISTIANS ARE MORE cocker spaniel than bulldog. The more I think about it, the more I think it's true. Many people view evangelical Christianity as legalistic, the so called *"hell-fire and damnation"* type of religion. Many evangelical Christians just accepted that characterization, even though they didn't feel very *"bull-doggish"* in their faith. It's hard being a bulldog when you feel like a cocker spaniel. Bulldogs want everything in black and white. They want a lot of rules, *"do's"* and *"don'ts"* to fit every situation. When Jesus gave principles to be used in every situation and made relationship the key to righteousness, many went back to their old religion where they didn't have to think, pray and decide. It was this celebratory, dynamic view of righteousness that made Jesus so attractive to people from *"the other side of the tracks"*— the people who had trouble remembering all the rules. Romans 14:17-18 says, *"For the kingdom of God is not a matter of eating and drinking* (open and shut legalism) *but of righteousness, peace, and joy in the Holy Spirit, because anyone who serves Christ in this way is pleasing to God and approved by men."* Christians know what it means to be pleasing to God and they want to get along well with people also. Even with deep-seated convictions of right and wrong, they are amazingly understanding, non-confronting, and accepting at the church house where they are meeting. That's where the cocker spaniel spirit greets us with joy—showing it with smiles, open arms and outstretched hands of greeting—saying it with, *"Welcome, we're glad you're here!"* Remember how the cocker spaniel gets so excited when you come in the house where he lives? He jumps! He barks! He celebrates! What a terrible thing if the Prodigal finally comes home and is met by a bulldog rather than a cocker spaniel (Luke 15).

Thank you, Jesus, that people did not run from You in fear when You walked the earth and we don't have to do it today. Thank You for making me feel welcome. Amen.

OneYearChallenge—Read: Exodus 28-30

February 5

On Living Too Long

ANEW FEAR IS GROWING IN AMERICA. It is a very demanding fear. It takes a lot of energy from people. It is growing especially among older adults and middle-aged adults who are watching their aged parents finish out their lives. The disquieting truth is that the fear of dying too young has been replaced by the fear of living too long. Every time I visit a nursing home and see old people tied in chairs, I tell myself, *"Boy, I hope that never happens to me."* In 40 years of pastoring God's people I have heard many old people wish for death to come. I read recently the account of a woman who traveled about America disguised as an 85 year-old woman. In this disguise, she encountered almost all of the human emotions: support, helpfulness, hurtfulness, acceptance, rejection, hatred, love, anger, peace, fear, and joy. These emotions describe the heartbreak and challenge of growing older. What do we do to prepare ourselves for the eventuality of living *"too long"* or caring for those who have lived too long (in someone's opinion)? We must develope a strong sense of trust in God—A belief that God knows best and length of days is best left to Him. There is still a great mystery wrapped around the inner experience of senior citizens who are wrapped in their own private world and are unable or unwilling to communicate out of their silence or confusion. It is our place to love and make as secure as possible the aging. It is our place to deal with our own inner security. Is it based on our own ability to care for ourselves? Or is our security trusting Jesus, who said, *"I am with you always, to the very end of the age"* (Matthew 28:20)?

> *Remind me again, God, that quality of life is more important than quantity; it is not how long I live but how I live that matters. I desire eternal life through Jesus. Amen.*

February 6

ONE YEAR CHALLENGE—Read: Exodus 31-33

Getting Caught

IT WAS MY MOTHER'S REGULAR WARNING, maybe even her favorite warning to a teen-age son going out of the house, *"you may be sure that your sin will find you out"* (Numbers 32:23). It was solid advice, no young man (or anyone else) should ever get the mistaken idea that you can break God's law and no one will ever know and you will never get caught. Boy, the news has been full of that lately—from religion, to politics, to banking, to families, . . . ! People never seem to learn from this. As a man, I have always contented myself with the thought that the truth will always come out. People can think what they will but the truth will eventually speak up and be heard. Jesus said, *"For whatever is hidden is meant to be disclosed, and whatever is concealed is meant to be brought out into the open"* (Mark 4:22). In Romans 2:16 there is the reminder to each of us that *"God will judge men's secrets*

through Jesus Christ." One great possibility of hearing the truth of God is that people hearing it will feel their secrets are being exposed to all and they will repent and change their ways (I Corinthians 14:25). Some people have described times when they were listening to a sermon and it seemed the preacher had been reading their mail or talking to their mate, because he seemed to be mentioning their shameful secrets. Such it is when the burden of pretense or covering up gets heavier. One lie demands two to be hidden. David talked about *"presumptuous sins"* (Psalm 19:13 KJV). One of the biggest presumptions that people make about sin—and they are dead wrong—is that they will never get caught and no one will ever know. You can assume (no, you can know for sure) your secret sin won't always be secret.

Loving and forgiving Father, the Devil has deceived me so many times with this temptation. Will you help me be smarter the rest of my life? Amen.

OneYearChallenge—Read: Exodus 34-36

February 7

Short February

We HAVE ENTERED THE SHORTEST MONTH of the year; already it's almost one-fourth over. Before you realize it, we will be in March. One would think there would be a high level of anticipation about February, but I often detect a sense of dismay about the month. February threatens more cold weather, more snow, more virus, more time spent indoors doing unexciting things. Question: Is February suffering a bad name because she is February or is she suffering from comparison? Of course, she is not new, like January, or hot, like July. But is it fair to put her down just because she has her own unique personality among the months? Someone has said that without the contrasts of life, its beautiful color would soon fade to black and white. Certainly there is a sense in which the extremes of life help us to appreciate its quality. The day would offer little enjoyment if there was never any night and vice versa. (Try an east to west, trans-Pacific, 22 hour flight in darkness to appreciate this). Good would seem mundane if there were never any evil to contrast with it. That's why crime makes headlines. What difference whether you travel north if there is no south? It is the contrasts of life that give it color, meaning, and let us appreciate it. The contrast makes for special challenge as well. I remember that the disciples of Jesus asked Him after His resurrection, *"Lord, are you at this time going to restore the kingdom to Israel?"* And Jesus said, *"It is not for you to know the times or dates the Father has set by his own authority"* (Acts 1:6-7). That is to say: you can't limit God, or box Him in to do this or that in a certain month or year. Just live expectantly, February or not!

> *Create in me a sense of expectancy. Let me see each new morning as a new opportunity to see You. I want to see You today. Amen.*

February 8

One Year Challenge—Read:
Exodus 37-39

Giving of One's Self

THE ANNUAL EMPHASIS ON LOVING AND GIVING has begun. Saint Valentine, who was martyred on February 14, 271 A.D., became the patron saint of all lovers. We are urged to give cards, candy, and other nice things as a sign of our love. I hope all this gushy talk doesn't really portray our understanding of love. Most obvious is the fact that all the gifts in the world won't prove love if it is not already there. True love means giving yourself and when this is true, the little gifts just form the frosting. The greatest love story of all time revolves around this giving of one's self. In John 3:16 we read, *"For God so loved the world that he gave his one and only Son, that whoever believes in him shall not perish but have eternal life."* God, the greatest lover, could have no shadow of selfishness. Rationally, we could say, "Wouldn't it have been enough to give man food, or clothing or just the use of the good earth?" No, the best gift would be to give Himself, so that meant to give His son to be mankind's Savior. If you will examine the claims that Jesus makes about himself, you will notice this dedication to giving himself for mankind. He said, *"You would have no power over me if it were not given to you from above."* (John 19:11). Indeed, the Apostle John was right in saying, *"Greater love has no one than this, that he lay down his life for his friends"* (John 15:13). Jesus has made this claim for your friendship by loving you and giving himself for you. If God loves you enough to give his very best to you, what will you give to him? The hymnwriter Issac Watts wrote this suggestion: *"Love so amazing, so divine, demands my soul, my life, my all."**

Lord Jesus, I love You! I want to love You more. Does my action and speech validate what I just said? I hope so! I really hope so. Amen.

ONE YEAR CHALLENGE—Read: Exodus 40, Mark 1-2

February 9

Let's Talk about Love

DID YOU EVER THINK ABOUT HOW FAR APART the common definition of love is from the greatest living definition? To define love today on the street means roses, candy, gifts, orchids, candlelight dinners, and love letters—all things that are soft, sweet, and mushy. But the greatest definition of love is ugly, vile, loud and corrupt. That's right; love was truly defined when Jesus was put to death on a cross on a hill called *"the Skull"* (Matthew 27:33). How could the same word be used and have two such totally different meanings? How could something so self-satisfying use the same word that is so self-forgetting? Such is the strangeness of our language. Does this point to the root of so much divorce? For instance, two people decide to get married. One partner defines love in the popular way, while the other is thinking in terms of lifelong commitment. After they are married a serious problem eventually arises because one love has grown deeper and one has become more shallow. So it is vital for both the man and the woman to agree upon their definition of love before they say *"I do."* The Biblical definition of love is self-forgetting, giving, serving, and totally committed. The street definition has to do with feeling and receiving, and promoting self. Popular songs about love generally ignore the long range implications of the word, choosing rather to focus on the now. Street love is temporary and passing. Biblical love is for the duration of life. Marriage is so vital for society for it is meant to give the secure setting for love to grow and develop. Do you love someone? Who do you think about first, yourself or that person? *"May the Lord make your love increase and overflow for each other and for everyone else, just as ours does for you"* (1 Thessalonians 3:12). This was Paul's prayer for his Christian family. This is not a syrupy, feel good idea but a solid commitment to be a blessing to others.

> *O God of Love, I need to understand this word. They say You are Perfect Love. I can know You better, I think I can learn the word. Help me. Amen.*

ONE YEAR CHALLENGE—Read: Mark 3-5

February 10

Saying "I Love You" with a Hug

NOTICE THE BUMPER STICKERS THESE DAYS: *"Have you hugged your kids today?"*; *"Have you hugged your parents today?"*; *"Have you hugged your horse today?"*; etc. Possibly it's become like the greeting *"Have a nice day"*—so mechanical as to be meaningless to so many. Maybe not! I think there is more to hugging. Especially among Christian folks! You see, in the first century church, the thing that stood out about these folks was the way they loved one another. There was a special bond. They had experienced a spiritual bonding. They had experienced a spiritual rebirth. They had become children of God. They called each other brother and sister. They had everything in common. They greeted one another with a holy kiss (Romans 16:16). It was just a natural display of warmth and tenderness. Then that fell out of usefulness or got a bad reputation, or for some reason ceased to be practiced. But think of this: Jesus displayed affection by touching people. You will notice that when people came to Jesus for help, the Bible usually mentions that He touched them. There is something that says *"I love you"* or *"I care about you"* in a touch. One of the most comforting sights around churches today is the way the people hug one another as an expression of love. This is God's answer to the *"skin hunger"* that people have—the desire to feel *"community,"* or feel *"family."* No doubt you have read about the psychological testing and the results in the lives of children who are not held and cuddled. Read the gospels again. Visualize the scenes as Jesus hugs children himself or puts His arms of loving acceptance about people's shoulders. Remember that when you get with your friends again. They may need your help. Reach out and touch them; and I don't mean with just the telephone.

Jesus, is that picture of You with your arms open wide still true? I sure could use a hug from You today. Thanks! Amen.

OneYearChallenge—Read: Mark 6-8

February 11

Letting Love Enrich Your Life

"*I LOVE YOU.*" WHAT WORDS of promise! What words of joy! What words of heartbreak! Same words in each case, but oh, the difference in meaning. To sweethearts, the words promise so much. Perhaps unreal, but still promising. To a mature wedded couple, it stirs up pleasant memories of days and years spent together, struggling to make sense out of life. To the used, abused, divorced, abandoned, it is the stabbing pain that cuts the heart whenever the words are spoken; the little phrase is unbelievable and mocking. How do you react when you hear it? A secret smile warming your heart; or a cynical grin that doesn't believe anyone could fall for that line again? The phrase is overused. People love ice cream, going to the beach, little puppies; you name it and somebody loves it. Talk is cheap, and familiarity does breed contempt, and overuse of "*I love you*" may cheapen the human ideal of love. But really, don't you want to love? Don't you want to be loved? Real love, that's what I'm talking about, not imitations. Real love like "*Greater love has no one than this, that he lay down his life for his friends*" (John 15:13), or "*Love does no harm to its neighbor*" (Romans 13:10), or "*God so loved the world that he gave his one and only Son*" (John 3:16), or "*We love because He first loved us*" (I John 4:19). Let God's love enrich your life so you can enrich someone else's life. To love and receive love is a by-product of God's love to the world in Jesus Christ. Since His love was pure and totally unselfish, it provides an unchanging point of reference for your experience. All other love can be compared to Jesus' love. All other love is tested there for its genuineness. His love can inspire you to really love and care for others.

> *God of Truth, I didn't know the Bible was a love story until I started reading it. Some people think it's just religious history. I'm glad I found out the truth. Amen.*

ONE YEAR CHALLENGE—Read: Mark 9-11

February 12

Persuasion of Love

FORTY YEARS AGO JOSEPH M. DAWSON WROTE: *"There is today, as there was in the days of Roman imperialism which Jesus knew, strong tendency to rely upon coercion; yet the Christian answer is undoubtedly in the realm of persuasion. It would be an unspeakable blessing to the whole world at this time if Christians had as much faith in persuasion as they do in coercion."* God never uses coercion with His followers or would-be followers; it's always persuasion. We tend to rattle swords, threaten, boycott, place embargoes, establish blockades, cut aid, not call or write, refuse to return calls, and countless other power moves to make people come around to our point of view. It happens internationally, nationally, locally, and personally. Of course, it is our pride that makes us do it. God, acting out of love, offers us the best and then leaves us completely free to act. *"Choose for yourselves this day whom you will serve"* (Joshua 24:15). God said in Deuteronomy 30:19-20, *"This day I call heaven and earth as witnesses against you that I have set before you life and death, blessings and curses. Now choose life, so that you and your children may live and that you may love the LORD your God."* Why can't we use the persuasion of love? Are we too lazy? Surely, gains made through pressure and intimidation do not leave a lasting satisfaction. Some of the most embarrassing pages in the history books for Bible believers are days that so-called *"Christians"* used the sword to make converts. That is so contrary to the spirit of Jesus who loved people and gave the best of Himself to them and then simply called them to *"follow me"* (Matthew 4:19). The only force used was love that *"became flesh"* (John 1:14)—*"incarnated"* is another translation of the Bible word. The old saying, *"you can draw more flies with sugar, than vinegar"* has a spiritual application, too.

One Year Challenge—Read: Mark 12-14

O God of Love, I thank You for that day Your love magnet drew me to You. People had told me You were mad with me and didn't want to see me. It was a great day. Amen.

February 13

"Love Must Be Sincere"

IT JUST JUMPED OFF THE PAGE and grabbed me. A four word declaration tucked away in a long list of instructions: *"Love must be sincere"* (Romans 12:9). It's imperative! It's bold! It's explosive! It's absolutely true! *"Love must be sincere."* People can talk about love and be as descriptive or colorful as they might be but it is worthless if it is not sincere. Poetry or prose, it doesn't matter, if it isn't sincere. Environment, economics, education; none of these matter if love is sincere. A major problem children and teenagers have today is trying to define *"love."* By the time the radio music and television sitcoms and cheap novels and moral-less movies get through tossing around the word *"love,"* they are confused. The role models of adults they know, moving from one temporary relation to another, add confusion to the picture. But the Apostle Paul gives us a bottom line definition: *"Love is sincere"*! That's why Jesus is the best role model for defining love, both by His words and lifestyle. The life of Jesus was not about saying pretty words but getting involved with people in their needs and helping them change for the better. With Jesus it had to do with weeping at Lazarus' funeral, taking a leper by the hand, feeding a hungry crowd, opening blind eyes, and squatting in the dirt talking to an embarrassed prostitute. Love is sincere. Some years ago, at 2 AM, I was awakened from sleep by the telephone. The voice on the other end said, *"I'm about to commit suicide. You said on the radio today you cared. I'm calling to see if you meant it."* There is a world full of people waiting to see if we Christians love *"sincerely."* In fact, before the throne of God, we will be judged in the same way. Is our love sincere? Let love be real! (I John 3:18)

I know, dear God, that there is no pretense in Your Love for me; it is the real thing. Help me to learn how to be that kind of lover. Amen.

OneYearChallenge—Read: Mark 15-16, Leviticus 1

February 14

Love Grows from Commitment

CAN WE DO VALENTINE'S DAY WITHOUT BEING MUSHY And sentimental? There's nothing wrong with mushiness and sentimentality, in their proper place and time. Actually, with all the soap operas and other shows on television, there is plenty of that! So, let's talk about *"hard-core"* love—love that gives and doesn't care about receiving, love that serves rather than wanting to be served, love that is concerned about the other's well-being and satisfaction rather than one's own—unselfish love rather than self-centered love. You don't *"fall in"* this kind of love, so consequently, you don't *"fall out"* of it and you don't come to the place where *"I don't love him/her anymore."* Translated, that means if you don't love now, you never did. Love doesn't die! Have you been to a contemporary wedding where the bride and groom pledged to be faithful *"while love lasts"*? Love grows from commitment. Permanent marriages allow love to develop. When a baby is born, a mother and father are infatuated by a new bundle of life, so fascinating and alive. Love grows from the commitment to care for it day and night for weeks, months and years. Couples marry because of physical attraction and warmth that is potential love, but love grows from commitment to the marriage vow, *"honor and serve until death parts us."* It grows slowly and surely. It's dependable and priceless love, not cheap and exchangeable on anybody's market. The perfect example is Jesus *"who loved me and gave himself for me"* (Galatians 2:20). He *"made himself nothing"* (Philippians 2:7) or, emptied himself of heaven's glory and honor. The scripture says we don't love and follow Jesus because He is physically attractive. That would be the world's approach. No, we respond to His offer of His self-giving love to us, and in return, we give ourselves in love to Him. We gladly make a *"Burn all the bridges"* response to the greatest love we have ever known.

> **Thank You, God for the word "commitment." I don't hear it much anymore. I don't think it is a bad word. I am committed to following You. Amen.**

February 15

ONE YEAR CHALLENGE—Read: Leviticus 2-4

Lovers Anonymous

THERE ARE MANY SELF-HELP GROUPS that have the word *"Anonymous"* in their name. Anyone for *"Lovers Anonymous"*? Remember when you were a kid in elementary school? Remember the times you sent a note to a boy or girl saying *"I love you"* and signed it: *"Guess Who?"* Or maybe you received that kind of note. Made you feel good didn't it? Then you had to work hard to discover who sent it. Probably a lot of people have received a card, a box of candy, or some flowers from an anonymous lover. The classified section during Valentine's week always has some *"I love you! Guess Who?"* people. Lovers Anonymous—I don't like it! Love can't remain anonymous, it must identify itself. In Hosea 2:8 God is identifying himself as the *"anonymous lover"* of Israel. *"She has not acknowledged that I was the one who gave her the grain, the new wine and oil, who lavished on her the silver and gold—which they used for Baal."* Can you imagine? Adding insult to injury, she took the good things from the hand of one lover and gave them to another lover. Maybe that's happened to you, too. But God does not keep his love for us anonymous. He clearly marks and defines every gift of his love: *"Every good and perfect gift is from above, coming down from the Father"* (James 1:17). You see, God knows who we are, he knows all about us; there are no secrets from God, so he deals with us out in the open. Clearly he says, *"I Love You!"* Likewise, we must be open with God. No anonymity! No secret admirer! No closet Christians! If we love God for sure, let's say it out loud! Don't be shy, burst right out and go to worship Sunday, saying *"God, I Love You!"*

> **God, You have loved me personally by my name. I want everyone to know that I have fallen in love with You, too. See, I'm not even blushing about it. Amen.**

OneYearChallenge—Read: Leviticus 5-7

February 16

Let's Talk about Love!

IS THERE ANYBODY THAT DOESN'T LIKE to talk about love, and loving? Poets write about it; singers sing about it—but many people aren't experiencing it. Some grow up without enough and have a hard time coping with life. Some read about it in romance magazines and get confused. Maybe it's easier to talk about it than live it. Remember the great love poem inspired by God and given to us for our instruction by the Apostle Paul in I Corinthians 13? If you have a Bible, get it and read it before you go any further. Even if I am good with words about love but my life is not validating the words, I may as well be quiet. That is, whispering *"sweet love words"* in someone's ear isn't much if the life isn't proving it by actions. If I do great things for people in a cold, mechanical, impersonal way but don't act with a loving spirit, I will leave people feeling cold and unloved. Real love is not mushy sentiment. I know many have been deceived by mush. *"Love is patient, love is kind. It does not envy, it does not boast, it is not proud. It is not rude, it is not self-seeking, it is not easily angered, it keeps no record of wrongs. Love does not delight in evil but rejoices with the truth. It always protects, always trusts, always hopes, always perseveres. Love never fails"* (I Corinthians 13:4-8). The cost of loving is high! But it's worth the price paid in work, struggle, tears, sacrifices, and self-denial. Lives are enriched. The world is made better! For other inspiring words on the real meaning of love, continue to read God's love letter to us—the Bible.

> *My parents taught me, God, that You are love. They also taught me that Jesus loves me. O Holy Spirit of God, help me to fully understand what I was taught. Amen.*

February 17

ONE YEAR CHALLENGE—Read: Leviticus 8-10

Loving Others

WHEN JESUS SAID TO A MAN ONE DAY, *"love your neighbor as yourself"* (Matthew 19:19), he set the stage for a whole new mentality in people-to-people relationships. Two conclusions can be made relative to the current scene: (1) many people have chosen to disobey this command, or (2) many people don't love themselves very much. As to the former, quite a few folks would admit to this. For them, it is a dog-eat-dog world—every man for himself. Since every community has an *"us versus them"* mentality at some level, some grew up hating and distrusting *"them."* *"Them"* could be white, black, brown, immigrant, poor or rich—any group perceived as different. The culture of the community had racial or class prejudice. It was unthinkable to love *"them"*; it would have gone against the cultural pattern. With this background, this command of Jesus seems totally unreasonable. As for my latter observation; it's true, many people don't love themselves. Many have a low self-image and very little self-esteem. When this mental condition is complicated by people saying (by word or action) *"you're no good"* or *"you're worthless,"* self-despising sets in and you are not able to love another person. Many problems of our society are rooted here. What is the answer? I suggest that we introduce these people to Jesus who loved them so much He died for them (John 3:16) to immediately show them that they are creatures of value and worth. When self-hating folks can realize *"How great is the love the Father has lavished on us, that we should be called children of God! And that is what we are!"* (I John 3:1)—then they can know that they are people of worth. Receiving this love will create self-esteem and the freedom and ability to love others. Jesus died for us, so we must be precious in His eyes. We need to receive this love from God and then we'll be able to love ourselves. This sequence allows us to become a canal through which His love and forgiveness can flow to others.

> **O God my Creator, the Bible says you created me in Your image. I want to look like You. I want to act like You. I'm glad You are not ashamed of what You made. Amen.**

February 18

ONE YEAR CHALLENGE—Read: Leviticus 11-13

Celebrating Love

So, HOW MANY WEDDINGS HAVE YOU ATTENDED this year? How many invitations do you have for this summer? All of us will know someone who is getting married this summer. Hopefully, they have thought through all of the implications of such a decision. Many take it lightly and the marriage soon dies and divorce quickly follows. It's the same kind of reasoning some follow about pre-marital sex: if a pregnancy develops, there is always abortion. So they reason with marriage: if it doesn't work out, we can always try again with someone else. I've attended a couple of weddings where the participants laughed throughout the ceremony. They didn't last! I've been at the county courthouse in two different states on the day the *"marrying judge"* was in town. Folks lined up! Paid the fee! Five minutes, in and out, all over! With that kind of assembly line setup, no wonder there are a lot of breakdowns. I'm not appealing for expensive, formal wedding services; their rate of success is not much better, that's not my point. God created marriage! Jesus blessed marriage! I believe in marriage! The Bible teaches the importance of marriage commitment. Real love wants commitment and doesn't run from it. That wonderful statement in Ephesians 5 concludes by saying, *"each one of you also must love his wife as he loves himself, and the wife must respect her husband."* It takes years to grow that high level of relationship. Surveys show that most divorced people feel that they acted too quickly; if they had it to do over, they would have been more committed to making it work. It is a thrill for me to attend a wedding worship service and hear two Christians seriously pledge themselves to one another *"until death do us part,"* expecting the life-long help of Almighty God, who can bring it to pass.

One Year Challenge—Read: Leviticus 14-16

> *As we celebrate Your unchanging love for us, our Heavenly Father, save us from the foolishness of giving our love in bits and pieces. Amen.*

February 19

A Forgotten Word

TWO ITEMS FROM THE NEWS caught my attention: first, one fourth of the babies born in America in 1990 were born out of wedlock. The other item said 4,000 babies per day are being aborted in America. You can make any kind of social evaluation of the foregoing that you wish, but one thing is sure: *"chastity"* is a forgotten word. Either parents have neglected to teach the word and its meaning, or else young people forget the meaning too quickly. Whatever happened to virginity? Whatever happened to morality? According to the Bible, the gift of sexuality to humans is to be used in the bonds of marriage. In the animal kingdom, sexuality is a chance contact of two animals of the opposite sex with no emotional commitment or sense of responsibility. From the items I mentioned from the newspaper, it is obvious that many humans are now living by the standards of the animal kingdom! To be sure, children growing up in a television taught, soap op-era generation, would not have any idea about the sanctity of sex in or out of marriage. Popular movies and cable channels would reinforce the idea that sex is without any moral value. What is commonly referred to as *"making love"* (which, by the way, can't be made) is, in reality, making babies. The gift of sex is a powerful force that God said was *"good"* (Genesis 1:27-28, 31), certainly not to be misused without a terrible price to pay. Is this another expression of sexual abuse, where people are treated as objects or things to satisfy physical desire, regardless of the results? Date rape is not even taken seriously by many. Is the gift of sex to be just another bodily function? Let's return it to its sacred place by applying some related Biblical principles. There are Biblical principles for using every gift from God. About your sexuality, God says, *"It is God's will that you should be sanctified: that you should avoid sexual immorality"* (I Thessalonians 4:3).

ONE YEAR CHALLENGE—Read: Leviticus 17-19

It seems we have missed the point, God, on your gift to us of sexuality. Will You patiently teach me again, starting today? Amen.

February 20

Disposable People

WE LIVE IN AN AGE OF DISPOSABLES. One of the hottest ecological questions today is what to do about disposable diapers in the landfill. We make so much throw-away stuff, but most of it is not biodegradable. So we are being inundated with things that reject our disposing. Maybe we should just call a halt to the age of disposables. It seems to have entered the human arena now. The aged are disposed of in nursing homes; lonely veterans are disposed of in hospitals; troubled people are disposed of in mental institutions; criminals are disposed of in penitentiaries—the disposable list builds up. Humans who are thought to be of no more use to society are being disposed, like garbage! Disposing babies is now routine as a result of the abortion revolution; disposable marriages have skyrocketed, brought on by the divorce revolution; disposable children are now a generation of latch-key and runaway youth. On several fronts the disposable people mindset is encountered: many people just want to use you and throw you aside—most single women believe modern men are only after their body or their money. Surely the idea of disposable people must be repugnant to you! What about our homeless population? The problem here is that they are so visible. Local officials and other organizations are hard-pressed to find an acceptable (to the community—us) place to house them. But these people are unlike disposable things, in that they cannot be covered up with dirt or incinerated. What a contrast to the high value Jesus put on human life: *"Look at the birds of the air; they do not sow or reap or store away in barns, and yet your heavenly Father feeds them. Are you not much more valuable than they?"* (Matthew 6:26). Jesus came to save people, not dispose of us.

ONE YEAR CHALLENGE—Read: Leviticus 20-22

Thank You, God, that You do not waste Your creative efforts by throwing us away and starting over. Thank You for the redemption center You opened on Mount Calvary. Amen.

February 21

Removing Barriers

I HAD ENTERED THE CORONARY CARE UNIT at the hospital to visit a member of my church. In another cubicle I saw a very familiar sight: a lady lay with half-closed eyes while two daughters stood on either side of the bed. They were holding her hands very gently. I moved toward them to offer my concern, the patient heard me and opened her eyes. It was then that I discovered a frustrating truth. She was Spanish and did not understand my language. Gratefully, her daughter spoke my language and she was able to interpret for me while I prayed for her mother. I recalled again my early days as a missionary in Southeast Asia and my initial frustration caused by the language barrier. I soon learned to speak the language there and the barrier was removed. I am reminded now of the different refugees I have wanted to help in the metropolitan area, but was hindered by the foreign language barrier. A smile is the same in any language, a small deed of kindness that crosses any language gulf. But the need to communicate demands that the language barrier be removed as soon as possible. God had such a barrier to overcome to speak to us. God speaks a language of love, gentleness, kindness, forgiveness and helpfulness. We spoke a language of anger, selfishness, revenge, fear and stubbornness. Since we could not understand God's love language, we rejected him. "*All day long I have held out my hands to an obstinate people,*" God said in Isaiah 65:2. It was when God came to us and made his dwelling among us (John 1:14) that he overcame the language barrier and we were able to finally understand what he had been trying to say. Revelation 5:9 envisions a time when all tribes and languages and nations have learned God's language. Let God speak to you today, you will understand this language that speaks love in action.

Thank You for speaking our language, O God. Thank You for having something special to say and saying it so clearly. I love You! Amen.

ONE YEAR CHALLENGE—Read: Leviticus 23-25

February 22

Toward a Healthier Self Image

DID YOU READ ABOUT THE PAUNCH LEAGUE? It's a basketball league that's been organized for men over 40 who still want to play basketball. It's for those whose *"punch"* has turned to *"paunch."* (If you read Sally Forth in the comic strips, you know her husband reasons that God made men that way.) Joining a paunch league is a realistic thing to do when you realize time is marching on. It is wiser and healthier for us to compare ourselves to our peers rather than looking back at the younger set. The problem with an aging woman still trying to look and dress like the Barbie doll set is that she fools no one but herself. We are who we are! We need to accept ourselves as we are and work toward a healthy self image. When Paul said, *"I have learned to be content whatever the circumstances"* (Philippians 4:11), he was talking about physical surroundings, but it could be applied to chronological age. At every age, there are things to do and accomplish that are special for that age. There are stages of growth and development that should be enjoyed to the maximum. Don't let the advertising world sell you a bill of goods about trying to look young or being young to the point that you don't enjoy where you are right now. I remember hearing George Burns sing *"I Wish I Was 18 Again"* in his 90s. Ha—he probably didn't remember what 18 was like! Compare that to the Bible saying in Proverbs 16:31: *"Gray hair is a crown of splendor; it is attained by a righteous life,"* or God's promise to believers in Isaiah 46:4, *"Even to your old age and gray hairs I am he, I am he who will sustain you. I have made you and I will carry you; I will sustain you and I will rescue you."* The Biblical concept is healthier! With eyes of faith, enjoy your age.

Father, I thank You that I am getting older, I'm not ready for the alternative. Give me a clearer insight into Your will for every coming year of my life. Amen.

One Year Challenge—Read: Leviticus 26-27, Luke 1

February 23

Building on a Solid Foundation

DURING THE TERRIBLE BOMBINGS AND STRAFINGS OF WORLD WAR II, the city of London was practically destroyed. The beloved House of Commons, seat of their government, was a shambles, as was all else. The people set to work to rebuild the city and they wanted to rebuild the House of Commons like the original, but they couldn't find the old plans and specifications anywhere in the ruins of the official buildings. However, during this time the people were asked to collect all old newspapers and turn them in to be used in munitions factories to make explosives. As he searched out old papers in his attic, an old architect found the original plans for the House of Commons and so they were able to rebuild it. There are plenty of people who have made a shambles out of their lives. One mistake is piled on another, one wrong choice races madly after another, until the whole of life becomes a horrendous mess. The search for the original plans to build a meaningful life seems hopeless and fruitless. Can they be found? The Bible says we are built (made) in the image of God, but that *"all have sinned and fall short of the glory of God"* (Romans 3:23). So we have to start cleaning back the wreck of life and get ready for a new foundation. Jesus warned us not to put our foundation on sand because that won't hold; He said to build on a rock solid foundation. The Apostle Paul said we should choose Jesus as our foundation: *"For no one can lay any foundation other than the one already laid, which is Jesus Christ"* (I Corinthians 3:11). The truth is, this is the original pattern. In Christ we have the perfect model. Build on Him.

> *God, I thank You that You have a wonderful plan for my life. Help me not to be deceived by other architects and their offers. Amen.*

One Year Challenge—Read:
Luke 2-4

February 24

A Cheerful Heart

"**A** CHEERFUL HEART IS GOOD MEDICINE," says the Bible in Proverbs 17:22. So, how are you doing in spreading this medicine around? It is time to leave the depressing feelings of February. The first brave robins to show up and the first bold crocus to push out of the dirt say that spring is just around the corner. But it will take more than these signs for many others. The harassed look on many faces begs for relief. The rat race, the financial pressures, and the other stress factors; all of these make life a drag. Add to it unfriendly neighbors and co-workers and wow—it's hard! Haven't you thought about how good it makes you feel when someone smiles at you and says *"Hello"*? That gives me more of a lift than the mechanical *"Have a nice day."* If I may say so, what your community needs is more smiling faces, more people with the joy in their hearts that shines out of their faces. None of us knows what heavy burdens our fellow human beings are carrying. That person you describe as an *"old grouch"* may have a broken heart. I especially try to smile at and greet people at the hospital. I know they wouldn't be there visiting if something serious wasn't happening. Those new neighbors you have, don't you know they had to pull up some roots to come live near you? Have you given them some welcome medicine of a cheerful and friendly smile? Every time I think of Jesus down by the river with the fishermen or somewhere with children crawling on Him, I see Him with a smile on his face. In fact, he used the word *"happy"* nine times in as many verses in Matthew 5:1-12 (EB). In Proverbs 15:13 the truth is told: *"A happy heart makes the face cheerful."* Jesus said *"take heart! I have overcome the world"* (John 16:33). That's something to smile about!

ONE YEAR CHALLENGE—Read: Luke 5-7

> *God, You made me laugh today. Not just a chuckle, but a real laugh. I felt so much better afterward. I am grateful to You. Amen.*

February 25

How Do You Feel about Yourself?

I'VE GOT TO SAY IT, I LIKE TO SEE THE SNOW FALL. It's so quiet. It's so peaceful. So beautiful! I don't mean when you are driving home at rush hour on Interstate 95. Nor do I mean the slush of brown that splashes on you after the sand and salt truck passes your house. I am referring just to the snowfall itself and the cover of white that drops over everything. Maybe it's just that for a few hours all of the ugliness gets covered up and we are able to see the world as it was supposed to be—a place of beauty. I think that's what David had in mind in Psalm 51:7 when he said to God *"wash me, and I will be whiter than snow."* He was reflecting on the first fresh purity in his life again. (He had just been caught in an adulterous affair and had repented to God.) When you are overcome with guilt feelings or just ashamed of what you have done, there is often a desire for a purer more innocent time of life when you could face yourself in the mirror and God in prayer. In fact, in Isaiah 1:18 the prophet, as God's spokesman, invites *"Though your sins are like scarlet, they shall be as white as snow."* I think the appeal is there. It's an offer a person needing freedom from guilt can't afford to turn down. So, how do you feel about yourself today—like the purity of the snowfall, or like the slush that's been slopped around for a couple of days? What do you want to feel like? When God offers this kind of opportunity, no one should ignore it. Go for the snow! Your self-image will improve dramatically after being cleaned-up by Jesus. You will feel better about yourself. You are precious in God's sight; refuse to believe otherwise.

Loving Father, why do my enemies always attack my self-esteem? And even friends do too, sometimes. Do they know about my self-doubt? I need security that only You can give. Amen.

February 26

One Year Challenge—Read:
Luke 8-10

"Tangibilitate"

When I was a child, my father liked to listen to Father Divine preach on the local radio station. He was a colorful preacher, with lively messages. He would challenge his followers to apply his teachings in practical ways. Religious sentiment and inclination are useless unless you can *"tangibilitate."* (I never heard anyone else use that word.) The idea is that no one can understand your love for God until you make it real and touchable. All of the sermon-listening, worship-attending, mass-repeating that a person might do is useless without action. Christianity was never intended to be merely philosophical or theoretical. It is totally practical in application. It can't be said any clearer than *"faith by itself, if it is not accompanied by action, is dead"* (James 2:17). Perhaps it is slightly comforting to think religious thoughts about God and heaven, and loving your neighbor, but we cannot just content ourselves with thinking. Action is required. Human hands do God's work. Human voices spread God's word. Indeed, James goes on to challenge, in verse 18, *"Show me your faith without deeds, and I will show you my faith by what I do."* God always works through true believers. Ordinary mortals are used by God everyday as tangible evidence that He is alive and well. The Apostle John said that God knows how to *"tangibilitate."* Notice in I John 4:9: *"This is how God showed his love among us: He sent his one and only Son into the world that we might live through him." "Whoever claims to live in him must walk as Jesus did"* (I John 2:6). More people would be drawn to churches and the faith, if they could see it in action. In a pagan generation, when the truth of the Bible is not generally known, the implications of the gospel must be seen in the lives of believers before non-believers will be curious enough to ask *"Why?"* and *"How?"*. A touchable faith, a faith in action will challenge and change their status quo.

One Year Challenge—Read: Luke 11-13

> *I want to be real, O God. I want to make my faith real in my life so my friends can know that You really do control my life. Amen.*

February 27

Getting "Something for Nothing"

I BOUGHT MY CAR not too long ago. I remember how shocked I was when I went to the showroom: there were televisions everywhere. There were boxes of them! I asked the salesman what was going on, and he was glad to explain. Anyone who bought a new car would receive a *"free"* television set. I didn't believe it and said, *"No one gives away new television sets."* His reply was, *"You're right, we just add the cost of the set to the cost of the car and people pretend it's free."* So much for thinking people! But on the other hand, it's a great sales gimmick. The appeal of *"something for nothing"* has always fascinated us. If something is offered to us free, most of us would take it, whether we needed it or not. *"Buy one, get one free"* is another often used appeal. Put something in, get a little more back than you had at the start. Man seems to have no pride, sense of embarrassment, fear of being tricked, or any of the things that should make us cautious if somebody uses the magic word *"free."* This is true except in one situation: if it has to do with spiritual things. If a spiritual blessing is offered free of charge, people get afraid; they fear they are going to be tricked. The Bible says *"the gift of God is eternal life"* (Romans 6:23). Also, *"by grace (freely) you have been saved, through faith—and this not from yourselves, it is the gift of God"* (Ephesians 2:8). Any takers? Step right up! When it comes to God and Heaven, many want to pay their own way. Would you go to church Sunday if you had to pay at the door? Some would! Would they listen? Yes, if they paid first. The stumbling-block is pride. God's gift of eternal life is free. You cannot pay for it. A very high price was paid when Jesus died for you on the cross. This is one *"Free"* offer you can trust.

Heavenly Father, I know Jesus paid a price I could not pay. He is so rich in love to me. I surrender my pride, Lord. I accept your gift of salvation. Amen.

ONE YEAR CHALLENGE—Read:
Luke 14-16
(Non-leap year: Luke 17)

February 28

Fighting Regardless of Obstacles

"IT'S NOT THE SIZE OF THE DOG IN THE FIGHT, BUT THE SIZE OF THE FIGHT IN THE DOG." Years ago I saw that slogan written under a cartoon of a small dog who had just conquered a much bigger dog. There have been a lot of applications of that theme: in athletics, in recovery from illness, in handicapped individuals struggling for independence, etc. You could think of some examples, I'm sure. It says something about determination; about the inner will to fight on, regardless of the obstacles. On many fronts, there is a lack of such determination. Look at the growing number of suicides, quick marriages and quicker divorces, increasing alcoholism and drug addiction, abortion, declaration of bankruptcy. There are all kinds of indications of a lack of determination to face problems, find solutions and work it out. Look at the number of church dropouts! Many people used to be faithful in worshiping God, but they didn't have the determination to work out a problem they had with God, a minister, or someone else at church. Paul is a good example of a *"little dog"* with a big fight on the inside. In 2 Timothy 4:7, he said, *"I have fought the good fight, I have finished the race, I have kept the faith."* This is from a man who had been beaten several times, stoned by a mob, thrown in prison, nearly starved, . . . You name a major problem, he probably experienced it (2 Corinthians 6). But he was determined to be faithful to the Lord and his responsibility. Don't run from opposition. Don't be alarmed that things are going rough. Be determined. This current crisis in your life may be your greatest opportunity yet for growth. Remember: *"I can do everything through him (Christ) who gives me strength"* (Philippians 4:13). You can't experience that by giving up.

Jesus, I'm running scared in some areas of my life. Are You running with me? Okay then, I will keep running, but I won't be afraid. Amen.

ONE YEAR CHALLENGE—Read: Luke 17-18

February 29

Overcoming Evil With Good

WE CALL THEM "COMIC STRIPS" BUT THEY ARE NOT ALWAYS COMIC. Sometimes they are amusing, sometimes comical, but often they are too true to make us laugh. Like the cunning and crafty Commander Crock the other day. On the wall of the fort, Lt. Poulet asks, *"Sir, how do we know what's right and wrong in life?"* Crock replies, *"There's only a right and wrong if you get caught."** He had a sinister smile on his face. A common attitude? Sure! This is supposed to be a moral country, not a communist one, right? Communism teaches that nothing is right or wrong per se, it depends on whether or not it helps the party. Here we are in what many consider to be *"Christian America,"* and too many people have no moral standards. The important question is this: are there absolutes for right and wrong, or does it depend on the situation? Yes! Without a God-taught standard of right and wrong, we are left to our own opinions. We risk anarchy in a time when *"everyone did as he saw fit"* (Judges 17:6). Life becomes chaos; children grow up without standards; inconsistencies abound. Compare the situation where parents drink some kind of alcohol (a drug), then yell at their children about cocaine use (another drug). In Hebrews 5:14 we are told *"to distinguish good from evil."* Psalm 34:14 says to *"Turn from evil and do good."* Amos the Prophet said, *"Seek good, not evil, that you may live. Then the LORD God Almighty will be with you"* (5:14). The current philosophy which says *"If it feels good, do it"* is a dead-end road. Doing what feels good reduces you to animal morality! In Romans 8, Paul describes the civil war going on inside each of us between good and evil. The winning side should not be determined by whether we get caught or not. Overcome the world's evil with God's good.

> *Teach us, O Lord, that when we do whatever we feel like doing, someone is going to get hurt—if not us, someone we love, or that You love. Save us from that foolishness. Amen.*

ONE YEAR CHALLENGE—Read:
(Non-leap year: Luke 18)
Luke 19-20

March 1

Exercising Our Faith

SAYING YOU HAVE FAITH AND DOING something with your faith are two different matters. In Luke 8:43-48 is recorded Jesus' encounter with a woman who had a lingering illness for 12 years duration. She pushed her way through the crowd, reached out and touched the clothes that Jesus was wearing, and was healed. Jesus said to her, *"your faith has healed you."* It was not the touching of the garment that provided the healing but the exercise of faith. Anyone can grab a fistful of cloth, that's easy, but it is a different matter to have a motivating faith. In this story we have summed up the whole work of Jesus, that of bringing wholeness to people. There were many people in those days who had incomplete lives, just as now. People fill their lives with the best material things money (or credit) can buy, the best of entertainment, the best of medical care, and then discover that there is still something missing. Life still feels incomplete; something is missing. All of the things we have listed are wasted until there is an exercise of faith in the One who provides all blessings. Did God intend for us to be frustrated always because of our lack of something? The answer is an emphatic *"No!"* His master plan always included our coming to Him by faith and then He would make our lives complete, or whole. The Bible is so bold as to say that unless we have given first place in our lives to Jesus by an act of faith, we can never be a whole person. There will always be something missing. The complete life comes from the exercise of faith as shown by the woman who was healed. This may make your life complete overnight or it may begin a process that begins to bring to your life all that God has for you in one total package. Dare to exercise your faith in Jesus. You have to stretch out your hand in faith, to touch Him and receive.

> *Dear Jesus, one man said to You "Lord, I believe, help the part of me that does not believe." I want to pray that prayer today. Amen.*

ONE YEAR CHALLENGE—Read:
Luke 21-23

March 2

Spiritual Urgency

I'VE JUST COME ACROSS THE STORY OF BARTIMAEUS again (Mark 10:46-52). That man's story always impresses me. I know a lot of people who are living in bad situations. They complain about their circumstances, but they never do anything about them—even when they have the opportunity. Some seem to prefer misery to happiness, confusion to peace. Not so with Bartimaeus. It doesn't take much imagination to picture the misery and unhappiness of this poor man. He was blind, a beggar, and dirty from the traffic along the road. All of his companions were miserable. His life situation was terrible. Then they told him Jesus was coming down the road. He began to shout to Jesus and ask for help. His friends told him to be quiet, not to create a scene. They advised him not to make a fool of himself. But Bartimaeus had had enough. It was his big chance. He kept shouting. Jesus stopped and asked him what he wanted. He presented his problem to Jesus and Jesus fixed it, giving him his sight. All because he expressed his need and his faith personally to Jesus. He was one of those people who was *"sick and tired of being sick and tired."* So he acted. It's amazing how people have a sense of urgency about employment, transportation, education, and almost anything you could mention except spirituality. Too many are living with destructive bad habits, a guilty conscience, jealousy or animosity toward someone, rebellion against God. They go through life dragging a bag of spiritual garbage, while complaining daily about the smell! How unwise to reject the only one who can do anything about the situation. Bartimaeus took stock and realized he couldn't help himself, nor could any of his friends. When Jesus came his way he immediately grabbed the moment, dealt with his situation and got it resolved. Today is the day of salvation! Move quickly.

Dear Jesus, I know I take Your love for granted a lot of days. Restore to me a sense of urgency. Amen.

ONE YEAR CHALLENGE—Read: Luke 24, Numbers 1-2

March 3

Powerful People

DON'T GET TOO IMPRESSED BY POLITICAL POWER displays. They can't last very long. Many who get elected and ascend to high places never get to complete their plans because of a fickle populous. Rulers rise and fall almost daily. With the rise to power of a new strong man in many countries, there begins an immediate purge of every trace of the preceding strong man. Humans tend to be very short-sighted. We get caught up in the glitter of the moment and mistake it for permanence. We need insight into what makes for true greatness in leaders. It's easy to get deceived. In Acts 12:21-23 for example, *"Herod, wearing his royal robes, sat on his throne and delivered a public address to the people. They shouted, 'This is the voice of a god, not of a man.' Immediately, because Herod did not give praise to God, an angel of the Lord struck him down, and he was eaten by worms and died."* History moved on and the people realized they had made fools of themselves by thinking this man was so great. 2 Kings 5:1-14 relates the story of a great military commander of Syria who went to visit the preacher Elisha in Samaria, hoping for a cure from his disease of leprosy. The preacher was unimpressed by his high rank and didn't even go out to greet him. (Some modern preachers could learn from this; see March 10.) The preacher saw through the outer decorations of power and suggested God's simple answer to a dread disease. It was good for Commander Naaman that Elisha didn't lose his spiritual perspective in the face of such pomp, and was able to give the correct prescription. Fascinated as many seem to be by the private lives of the rich and famous and powerful, we need to remember *"Man looks at the outward appearance, but the LORD looks at the heart"* (1 Samuel 16:7).

ONE YEAR CHALLENGE—Read:
Numbers 3-5

Enlighten us, God, to realize that it is the media that is continuing to create our heroes of today. Remind us that Jesus is the same yesterday, today, and forever. Amen.

March 4

Wasted Daydreams

IT'S EASY TO WASTE TIME DAYDREAMING of bygone days. We look with alarm and despair about much that is happening these days. We sigh because we think there are no more worlds to conquer. We long for the past and tell ourselves that if we had lived in the founding days of our country we would have been right there involved in the excitement. We think of Washington, Lincoln, or Daniel Boone and glory in their struggles and wish for those days when there were plenty of big things to be done. But this is a weakness. We are not called upon to fight the battles of the past, they have already been fought; already won or lost. Those issues have been settled. We try to excuse our lack of dedication to the main things of importance today by pretending it might have been different in another time. Let's be truthful: it would not have been. In Psalm 118:24 the inspired writer said, "This is the day the LORD has made; let us rejoice and be glad in it." This is the positive view of history. This interprets history as being in the hand of God and finding our place of service today. As Jesus said in Matthew 25, there is physical hunger and thirst and nakedness and sickness and imprisonment in the world that cannot be ignored because it involves people. We must attack these problems today! If we keep busy fighting these battles, then we shall not have time to wish for other days. Neither science, nor philosophy, nor psychology, nor any combination of our ideas or systems has been the answer to the daily needs of the world. A spiritual base gives us a rock-solid place to stand. We have been called to change the part of the world where we live. Let's get busy!

God, it is easier to think than to act, and we tend to be lazy. Save me today from laziness. Amen.

One Year Challenge—Read: Numbers 6-8

March 5

Worst of All Sins

IN SEVERAL PLACES IN THE BIBLE, PRIDE is listed as the worst of all sins. To *"think of yourself more highly than you ought"* (Romans 12:3) is clearly defined and condemned. This may come as a shock to some people. Some people make a list of all the terrible things they don't do (murder, adultery, stealing) and then feel very proud about the things they do not do. There is a bigger picture to consider. *"Pride goes before destruction, a haughty spirit before a fall"* (Proverbs 16:18). An elevated opinion of oneself is a deadly trap. David said in Psalm 10:4 *"In his pride the wicked does not seek him; in all his thoughts there is no room for God."* That means that many people are ruining their lives today because of pride. Many are too proud to admit that they need help or to look for help. Pride can give you a *"Messiah complex"* and you begin to imagine that you can save yourself. Millions will die from addiction, because they are too proud to admit that they need help. Many people enter into a bad marriage agreement that they know will fail, even as they stand before the minister, but are too proud to call it off. Pride causes problems. *"Do you see a man wise in his own eyes? There is more hope for a fool than for him"* (Proverbs 26:12). Young people get in trouble every day, some even run away from home because they are too proud to admit their mistake. Don't stumble over your ego! The only thing that keeps many people from becoming Christians today is pride. After trying to make life meaningful without God and *"doing their own thing,"* they are too proud to confess their mistakes and come back to God and His way. Foolish pride—don't let it destroy you! Lay it down, now.

> *God, keep me from going out on a limb today dressed in my foolish pride. I might not be humble enough to crawl back and it would be a long fall. Amen.*

March 6

ONE YEAR CHALLENGE—Read:
Numbers 9-11

Declaring War on Drugs

IT STARTED IN THE '80S, AND IT GOES ON now in the '90s; we have declared war on drugs. Who declared it? Where is the battlefield? Who's winning? Maybe it gives politicians something to talk about or journalists something to write about, but have we really declared war on drugs? I think not! Recreational drugs are defined with a sugar coating as mood-altering substances. The demand for such drugs has permeated the fabric of the American society. Take tobacco for instance, a mood-altering substance. Folks say they smoke to relax, calm nerves, etc. The same goes for any alcoholic type drink like beer and wine coolers. Do folks drink them for taste? Of course not, you drink them for the mood-altering effect. Formal education, the government says, will be the key to drug control. Not so, as long as children grow up in homes where adults are using any kind of mood-altering substance. This is the education that sticks. There is such a great inconsistency between what children are told and what they see. As long as sports events are advertised by tobacco and alcoholic drugs, there are contradictory messages going out. The education needed must be based on a drug-free home environment. The best education has to do with the inner person, where inward strength needs no mood alteration to get along with people. When Jesus promised *"life, . . . to the full"* (John 10:10), *"And the peace of God, which transcends all understanding"* (Philippians 4:7), he was getting down to the nitty-gritty of life. After David came to grips with his problems being inner rather than outer, he prayed *"Create in me a pure heart, O God"* (Psalm 51:10). Government programs and funding will not win the war on drugs. Government programs can't help the inner you deal with peer pressure or insecurity, the desire to be popular, or whatever it is that gives you permission to use mood-altering substances. Jesus can! Receive His inner security; then share it with the children.

Dear God, I know that only through Jesus can I have the freedom to be me, and do what's right. I need that freedom, please. Amen.

March 7

ONE YEAR CHALLENGE—Read: Numbers 12-14

Learning from a Mobile Society

FROM TIME TO TIME THERE ARE ARTICLES ABOUT THE UNFRIENDLY NATURE OF OUR METROPOLITAN AREA. I think much of it has to do with the transient nature of life around any large city. With the unusually high concentration of military and civil service people, most don't stay very long. A family may buy a home, move in, and put up a *"For Sale"* sign all in six months. It's no wonder that people don't get to know and enjoy each other. Many of you reading this don't know the people on your street. Some don't like to make friends for a short while because we don't want to deal with the pain of losing them when one of us moves away. Since our society is so mobile, we should learn from it and make something positive. You've heard, *"If the world hands you a lemon, make lemonade."* First, can you believe that stability and security are inner conditions? They are not dependent on outward circumstances or location. Feeling at home, and comfortable in a place only depends on inner peacefulness. Paul said, *"I have learned to be content whatever the circumstances"* (Philippians 4:11). Strange as it may seem, he wrote that while he was imprisoned. Second, see how many people you can find who are more lonesome, more miserable, more needy than you. This is not to allow you to gloat and feel good because you have it better but to allow you to give yourself away as a helper. Move outside of yourself. The best way to make friends is to be a friend. There are very few people who will turn down loving help when it is needed. As you forget yourself through serving others, you will find you are not withdrawing into your cave of self-pity and loneliness. Mobility multiplies ministry opportunities.

Dear Jesus, since You are the friend that sticks closer than even a family member, show me how to become that kind of friend. Amen.

ONE YEAR CHALLENGE—Read: Numbers 15-17

March 8

Spring Training Time

IT'S THAT TIME AGAIN! The good old American pastime of baseball is about to start. When spring training starts, can spring be far behind? Spring training seems like a good idea for the church. Some churches have gotten cold and still in the winter—not much activity, and too much time spent at the dinner table. It's time for churches to wake up and come alive. After all, Easter is coming; it will be too late to prepare for it if we don't get busy. A good beginning would be to stretch your faith in prayer. An unknown poet said, "*every morning lean your arms on the window sill of Heaven.*" God's challenge in 2 Chronicles 7:14 is "*if my people . . . will humble themselves and pray.*" King David had a rigorous prayer schedule: "*Evening, and morning, and at noon, will I pray*" (Psalm 55:17 KJV). Start off with a little prayer of thanksgiving and move on into a longer time for praise. When you have expressed thanks and praise to the Lord, you can begin to bring your petitions to God. Now that you have yourself in a spiritual posture, pick up your Bible. It's not too heavy to lift. Begin to read and let your mind walk slowly through the truths. It will exercise spirit more than body. You will notice that there is strength and direction in God's word. "*I have hidden your word in my heart that I might not sin against you*" (Psalm 119:11) is David's way of describing the effect of walking in the Truth. Perhaps you are ready for some running now. This will require more concentration and determination. Hebrews 12:1 challenges us to "*run with perseverance the race marked out for us.*" I Corinthians 9:24 emphasizes the need to run to accomplish our spiritual goals. Springtime is a good time to "*train yourself to be godly*" (I Timothy 4:7). Go ahead, it won't just make your day, it will make your eternity.

ONE YEAR CHALLENGE—Read: Numbers 18-20

> *Please forgive my spiritual weakness. Change me from a spiritual weakling into one who is strong in faith. Amen.*

March 9

Small Steps to Big Faith

I HAVE JUST BEEN READING AGAIN THE STORY OF NAAMAN, A MAN with leprosy (2 Kings 5, see also March 4). Naaman was a commander in the army of Syria, a well respected man and highly valued for his military record. In his time, there was no medical cure known, so he faced an ongoing future of despair. A servant girl suggested that he should go to a preacher in Israel whose name was Elisha. When he arrived at the preacher's house, Elisha sent word out to him to go wash seven times in the Jordan River. The commander was insulted, angry, and disappointed. *"I thought that he would surely come out to me and stand and call on the name of the LORD his God, wave his hand over the spot and cure me,"* he objected (v.11). He stalked off in a rage; maybe he had watched too many of the showman style preachers, like some on TV today! A servant ventured the observation that if the preacher had told him to do some-thing spectacular, he would gladly have done it. Why not try following the simple little instruction? He finally did, and was healed, and thanked God for it. I wonder how many people today are missing out on God's blessings because they are waiting for the spectacular and missing out on the obvious. Gratefully, not everyone of us has to be struck down blind on the road like Saul of Tarsus before we will get the message and be converted to follow Jesus. In fact, Jesus said that the basic requirement was to have faith in Him, at least faith as big as a mustard seed (Matthew 17:20). Not much spectacular there! Sometimes in our culture, the cult of bigness fools us. Yes, there are enough spectacular conversion experiences to assure us it can happen, but just enough to let us know that spectacular is not the norm. Generally, it takes small steps to get to large faith!

Patient Father, I need to be reminded that small steps of faith are okay with You. Just keep me pointed in the right direction and I will make it. Amen.

OneYearChallenge—Read: Numbers 21-23

March 10

No One Came

IT HAS BEEN AN UNUSUALLY HARD WINTER in many places and there have been many sad stories in the news. The news always has this mixture. One story was especially touching. Did you read about the old widow found dead in her apartment? She had lived there a long time and the neighbors saw her regularly on the street going to and from her apartment. When some noticed that she had not been seen for several days, the police were called. They entered the apartment and found her dead. In rummaging through papers and books looking for some evidence about her, a young policeman discovered she had kept a daily diary. On 30 or 40 pages was this sad phrase: *"No one came."* Her life had been lived out in solitude and loneliness and expectation that someone might care about her. But, *"No one came."* How is it on your street? Might there be a person who has enough food, clothes and money but no other human relating to her/him on a personal basis? Have you been to their place and sat with them for a while? Have you been the answer to someone's loneliness? In a different context, David once complained to God, *"no one cares for my life"* (Psalm 142:4). Jesus talked about the importance of visiting people and concluded by saying, *"whatever you did for one of the least of these brothers of mine, you did for me"* (Matthew 25:40). The fact is anyone can meet this kind of need. No special training is required. All you need is a loving, caring heart. In this crowded world with so many churches and religious people, it is a crime against humanity for one to sit and wait and wait for someone to care. The church must minister to these lonely where they are if we ever expect them to join us where we meet.

Thank You, Hound of Heaven, that You hunted me and found me in my hiding place, so lonely and feeling isolated. Thank You for knocking at my door. Amen.

ONE YEAR CHALLENGE—Read:
Numbers 24-26

March 11

Philosophy of Despair

Is IT A SIGN OF THE TIMES? A while back I saw a new bumper sticker. Since then I've seen it several times: *"Life is a bitch, then you die."* It is a flippant heart cry of lonely, cynical people who have no reason to live. The death wish is barely hidden below the surface. It is no wonder that alcoholism and drug addiction and sexual weirdness multiplies. Have you seen the listing of movie titles lately? Check out the listing of the top-selling videos. Worse yet, read the names of the heavy-metal rock groups. The name of most sound like disillusionment and despair. *"Let's eat, drink, and be merry; Tomorrow we die"* is still the standard life-view for many. How did it happen? How did society sink to such a low level? We are created *"in the image of God"* (Genesis 1:27), with the possibility of living *"life . . . to the full"* through Jesus Christ (John 10:10). Life was meant to be long and meaningful. Indeed it can be for people if they will seek it out. And death was not to be a final stop to all the misery of existence. After a full life of living with a full faith in God through Jesus Christ, death is to be an open door into an even richer and fuller eternal life. Is your philosophy of life one of despair or hope? No wonder suicides increase yearly, especially among the youth. Despairing adults, who can't face life without a bottle or a pill, are passing on despair to the kids because they aren't able to expose their kids to the gospel (good news) that there is a better way. Paul says in Romans 8:22, *"that the whole creation has been groaning"* but in verse 24 he says we are saved by hope. Christian hope is what defeats despair! It's not too late to turn the tide of despair. Keep hope alive!

> *Dear God, David said you could restore my soul. I hope that is true today. So many of my acquaintances are depressed, I want to help them too. Amen.*

March 12

ONE YEAR CHALLENGE—Read:
Numbers 27-29

Learning to Trust One Another

TRUST IS SUCH A FRAGILE COMMODITY. So hard to earn! So easy to lose! So hard to regain when lost or broken! Healthy, trusting children learn to trust their parents from infancy in a relationship of love and support. Lovers learn to trust one another in courtship and carry it over into marriage and it grows. Public officials are chosen by the public because they have proven trustworthy in their public and private affairs. Nations trust one another because of the mutual benefit of helping one another and being honest in their dealings with each other. It really is a gift. You give me the right to trust you because you express genuine and sincere concern for me. I give you the right to trust me by an open-faced, personal concern for you. It is a precious gift; it can't be bought, Some have tried—for example, an unfaithful spouse returning from a fling bearing gifts. So many people are cut adrift today because they don't know who to trust. Where do you turn? Who is trustworthy? Have you been deceived by someone you trusted? Even Jesus is described in John 2:23 as not trusting Himself to a group of people who believed in Him just because He did miracles. The explanation given is that He knew what they were really thinking in their hearts. How can we give or receive the gift of trust? For one thing, be trustworthy. Don't fail people who trust you. You can be a positive model for others. You must also put your trust in the Lord. As the Bible says *"Trust in the LORD with all your heart"* (Proverbs 3:5). Finally, pray for wisdom to recognize the difference between hypocrisy and sincerity; you can develop a trust relationship only with the sincere. Without trust, any relationship is too fragile.

I'm so glad I learned to trust You, Jesus. You are my best friend as well as my Savior. I want You to be able to trust me, too. Amen.

ONE YEAR CHALLENGE—Read:
Numbers 30-32

March 13

Our Inability to See

A VISION PROBLEM COMMON TO MAN-KIND IS THE INABILITY TO SEE POTENTIAL. We tend to look at people as they are, rather than what they might be if challenged and encouraged. The Gospels relate story after story of Jesus looking at people and seeing their potential. His challenge was *"follow me and I will make you* [to become] ..." (Mark 1:17); it was an open-ended challenge. He looked at Zaccheus, and while others saw a physical runt, Jesus saw a man who had big possibilities (Luke 19). He looked at a hot-headed *"son of Thunder"* (Mark 3:17)—the community view—who had the potential to be an apostle of love and gentleness. We know him as John the Apostle. The list is long! Even today the list grows longer. We need to ask God to bless our vision and enable us to see what Jesus saw when He looked at people. We give up on some children, ignore some teen-agers, discount some couples simply because at first glance, they do not impress us. Or at second glance, we don't notice any improvement in looks or behavior. It requires patient looking to see potential. It could require some personal involvement on your part to help release someone's potential. Visualize someone smashing an ugly cocoon attached to a tree trunk, just because the beautiful butterfly trapped inside, working to be released, can't yet be seen! Many of us who have enjoyed some measure of success in our chosen field did it in spite of the fact that many did not see our potential early on. The Bible relates the story of one woman pushing her way through a crowd to Jesus for she reasoned, *"If I just touch his clothes, I will be healed"* (Mark 5:28). The potential was there, Jesus released it! Look at yourself, or the person near you.

One Year Challenge—**Read:** Numbers 33-35

> *In our concern about how we appear to other people, remind us to look at others with eyes of love and nurture, always giving them the benefit of Your belief in them. Amen.*

March 14

Manipulation

How DID YOU FEEL ABOUT THE REVELATION THAT A TOBACCO company was coming out with a couple of new brands: one for African Americans and one for *"virile females"*? Perhaps it was no big deal—new products are launched all the time. The interesting thing for me was the psychological studies that accompanied the launching of the products. Backgrounds, attitudes, morals, values, and related data of the target group were compiled in order to exploit these people. Without knowing why, people would buy these products because their subconscious self would be tapped, the studies suggested. We've known about subliminal advertising before in theaters and television ads and shows. That just seemed more blatant and more people got angry. It is scary, huh? Manipulation of people's feelings and actions goes on all the time. Parents manipulate their children and children manipulate their parents for selfish ends. Rewards are promised people if they will conform to a certain standard or perform certain acts. Some people use guilt as a tool to manipulate others and have their own way. Some use anger the same way. How can a person protect himself against being used? Paul said, *"Put on the full armor of God so that you can take your stand against the devil's schemes"* (Ephesians 6:11). We are also told to *"be as shrewd as snakes and as innocent as doves"* (Matthew 10:16). Practically, it says don't lose your vulnerability but be aware of the fact that people will use you. What about the other side of the coin? Do you ever manipulate people in order to get your own way? Romans 13:10 says, *"Love does no harm to its neighbor."* The Old Testament law that Jesus emphasized was *"love your neighbor as yourself"* (Matthew 19:19). When you are tempted to manipulate, remember the commandment to love, not use others, and back off.

> *O God, I know that I have been manipulated by Satan and I am tempted to do it to others. Enable me to be a helper instead. Amen.*

ONE YEAR CHALLENGE—Read: Numbers 36, John 1-2

March 15

Jogging to Keep Fit

I'VE JUST BEEN JOGGING. I used to run but now that I'm older, I jog. My knees can't take running anymore. But that's okay—I'm glad I can jog. In the Bible many comparisons are made between running and the Christian life. The Prophet Isaiah (40:31) said, *"those who hope in the LORD will renew their strength. They will soar on wings like eagles; they will run and not grow weary, they will walk and not be faint."* (Notice the contrast to running in your own strength!) In Hebrews 12:1 we are challenged: *"Let us run with perseverance the race marked out for us."* Paul is concerned in Philippians 2:16 about being faithful to Christ so that when Christ returns he (Paul) would not have been running or working *"for nothing."* Or read that big descriptive paragraph in 1 Corinthians 9:24 about runners in a race. Each of the runners uses self-control and stays on the track and competes at his very best, knowing that only one is going to win the prize. So, the comparison goes, all Christians should use the same kind of self-discipline: keeping in shape, practicing, goal firmly in mind and running as best as each one can, knowing that every runner in this race is a winner. Well, there is certainly a lot to be learned from this. I've heard that there are three groups who consider themselves runners: those who buy fancy running gear but never run (they just wear it to the shopping mall); those who buy the gear but perhaps only run on weekends; and then there are those serious runners, who run every single day, whether their gear looks good or not. You can certainly find a comparison for that in the religious community. Those who dress up and pretend the part, but don't live it; those who wear it and live it on weekends only; and those who live it daily, never mind how they are dressed. I wonder, in which category do we find ourselves today? Let's be honest, and careful to not judge others.

> *The Bible reminds me, Father, that the body accomplishes little without spiritual exercise. Now that my body is Your temple, help me keep it in good shape. Amen.*

ONE YEAR CHALLENGE—Read: John 3-10

March 16

Meeting Someone Different

IN MANY RELIGIOUS COMMUNITIES ACROSS AMERICA THIS SUNDAY, RACE RELATIONS DAY will be observed. It's still needed badly. We aren't doing too well in this area of American Life. We begrudgingly give way when someone of a different racial or cultural origin passes us going up the ladder of success and make some grumbling remark about it. When someone of a different origin steps in front of us at the drug store, or cuts us off in traffic, or insults us; we tend to assign another demerit to their racial origin. Though equal employment and equal opportunity is the law of the land, the words on the street are still derogatory. Sad to say, many of the people saying the derogatory words have recently come out of some kind of house of worship. Some folk's religion must not help them to love other people. Responsible men and women need to be seen and heard on this problem. Hate organizations are publicly condemned but they continue to exist. They are not as dangerous though as subtle racism, the quiet dislike of anyone that is different from us. Genesis 2:27 says that God created man in His own image. Not white man, black man, yellow man—just man! The color adjectives were something we created. We made color and ethnic origin a significant point; God didn't. It's about time for us to just accept what God has done in putting us all in the human family. The walls of hostility that divide people have been smashed to smithereens by Jesus Christ (Ephesians 2:14), in his humanity-changing self-sacrifice. We could take advantage of that, if we would. When was the last time you made an effort to get to know someone different from you? When people take the time to get to know someone, they are usually surprised at how much alike they are. Try it!

ONE YEAR CHALLENGE—Read: John 11-15

March 17

Creating Emotional Stress

CRYING IS A NATURAL EMOTION. When God created us, He gave us tear ducts. Their job is to help us show our emotions and feelings when we are so moved. But many see crying as weakness. They consider it unacceptable to cry tears of joy or pain, or let on anything is wrong, even in front of loved ones or friends. If someone asks, *"How are you?"* we answer, *"Fine,"* even if we feel terrible. If you have been to a funeral home, no doubt you heard some well-meaning person say *"Don't cry, it will be all right."* Many parents start early teaching their children to deny their true feelings. If the child falls and hurts himself and begins to cry, what do parents say? Something like: *"Don't cry, people are looking at you."* Thus our society has a part in creating many emotional stresses in the life of our people. Hypocrite—that was the original word to describe speaking from behind a mask. In a drama, one actor could play several parts, just by holding up a different mask. What a harmful trap when we do that with our families and friends each day! Putting on a face that is in conflict with our inner feelings causes misunderstanding. If anyone recommends you hide your feelings, they are recommending you be dishonest. How can people live together and get along if we are hiding our true feelings? Better to heed the words of Paul in Ephesians 4:15: *"speaking the truth in love, we will in all things grow up."* Lies, half-truths, pretenses and the like are hindrances to the best relationships. If you really love someone, don't you care too much to deceive them? How can a friend help you if they don't really know how you feel? Should they have to pry to get your true feelings out? It is childish and immature to hide them, not macho. The genius and beauty of the New Testament church was their openness and sharing with one another, not withholding themselves. Remember, when one is honest, that frees others to be honest also.

> *Teach us again, Great Physician, that what we try to hide from You and others only haunts us in a painful way. Help me to learn to trust a friend today. Amen.*

March 18

ONE YEAR CHALLENGE—Read:
John 16-20

Dealing with Death

SOME PEOPLE DO A GOOD JOB OF NOT THINKING ABOUT IT: they have so disciplined themselves that the unpleasant fact of life, called death, is not allowed to intrude on their thoughts—not until a senseless, unexplainable event, like a mass murder takes place. Then death becomes too real to ignore. *"I could have been in that post office, [or bank, or convenience store]"*—what a shuddering thought! Or if someone dear to you dies, and the grief comes down hard, the well-arranged life is disturbed by death coming too close. It's important for us to know how to deal with death, our own or that of someone dear to us, so it doesn't destroy or disable us. To pretend to be unconcerned is just that—pretense. Everyone can hear the hollow sound of your words. Death is a major concern. Every day we get closer to it, our own or that of a loved one. It is the last great event of life. We should want to do it well. With hope! and expectancy! This enemy should not be allowed to beat you! Your personal fear may be the fear of that great unknown. What will it be like one minute after I'm dead? And if someone close to me dies, how will I handle the loss? How will I deal with the grief that lingers after the loss? I know we all like to put off doing things; *"procrastinate"* is the word. But we can't afford to do that about death; it's destructive if you are not prepared. *"Praise be to the God and Father of our Lord Jesus Christ, the Father of compassion and the God of all comfort, who comforts us in all our troubles, so that we can comfort those in any trouble with the comfort we ourselves have received from God"* (2 Corinthians 1:3-4). You should plan today for this great event.

O God of Life, thank You for giving me so much help in the Bible to prepare for death. Give me a sense of peace about death. Take away my anxiety. Amen.

ONE YEAR CHALLENGE—Read: John 21, Deuteronomy 1-2

March 19

Living Without Windows

IN THE NATIONAL GEOGRAPHIC magazine sometime ago I read a description and saw pictures of strange, tower-like houses built somewhere in the Caucasus mountains overseas. The most peculiar feature of these odd structures is that they have no windows. As long as the people are in the house they live in darkness or artificial light. Wouldn't you hate that? A house without windows sounds like a dismal place, a dungeon rather than a house. It would be more like a prison than a home, it seems to me. When I go to minister at the jail, I think of how hard it would be to live without natural light. Too many persons live with nothing but an inward look, contemplating their own troubles and dwelling on their own petty schemes until they become morbid and disagreeable, like an un-sunned chamber. Living without windows has to be oppressive. John Bunyan wrote about the Pilgrim: "They laid him in a large upper chamber, whose window opened toward the sun rising. The name of the chamber was Peace" (**Pilgrim's Progress**). We must have the rooms of life opening toward the sun rising. While speaking at the University of Edinburgh, Viscount Haldane said, *"The way to escape from the depressions incident to the numerous reverses of life, and that deeper depression which arises from no external cause, is by acquiring a large outlook."* Have you found your way out of the dungeon? Does your life have a large window facing the sun? Jesus said that He came to give us the ability to see life: *"I am the light of the world,"* and he further said, *"Whoever follows me will never walk in darkness, but will have the light of life"* (John 8:12). Jesus gives us life with a view as wide as the horizon. Once He challenged His followers, *"open your eyes and look at the fields! They are ripe for harvest"* (John 4:35). That's it, see all the possibilities that God had placed before you with the help of The Light of the world. The view is terrific!

> *O God, Paul said that our best view of things is as if looking through a smeared mirror. Clarify our vision, both physically and spiritually. Amen.*

ONE YEAR CHALLENGE—Read: Deuteronomy 3-5

March 20

Spring: a Time of Promise

AH, REMEMBER THE BEAUTIFUL LINES FROM THE SONG OF SONGS, chapter 2, verses 11 and 12, *"See! The winter is past; the rains are over and gone. Flowers appear on the earth; the season of singing has come, the cooing of doves is heard in our land."* What a beautiful, poetic way of describing this time of year. The accumulation of snow is now forgotten. The difficulty of traveling to work is forgotten. Spring is here! The spring flowers are blooming! The birds are chattering outside my window. Such a time of promise. Many do not agree. This is also the time of the greatest number of suicides. Many who struggled through the winter with the hope that things would be better in the spring, now have given up on life because nothing changed. I agree that it takes more than beautiful weather to make a person feel good about life. I guess what impresses me today is the thought that if our loving creator could make such a beautiful world, God must have some special plan for my life and your life too! Jesus tells us, *"See how the lilies of the field grow. They do not labor or spin. Yet I tell you that not even Solomon in all his splendor was dressed like one of these. If that is how God clothes the grass of the field, . . . will he not much more clothe you?"* (Matthew 6:28-30) The winter season is hard with its freezing rain and bitter cold, but how much worse is winter in the soul, or the barren wasteland of a life without faith, or the cold storm of cynicism that swirls about the life of one who believes he is of no more value than an animal who will just die and go back to the dust? Let your life be awash with the beauty of God and let your soul leap up daily in joy in the continuing springtime of His love.

> *God, make me a springtime person. Bring to my life a newness and freshness that I have never known before. And let everyone see your beauty blooming in me. Amen.*

March 21

One Year Challenge—Read:
Deuteronomy 6-8

The Greening

Does the green seem a little greener this year? Or is it just the sharp contrast between the new green grass and the grey trees not yet budded. The fresh and new spring green is such a startling color, especially compared to the drab shades of brown and gray we've seen all winter. Whatever the reason, the new life seen in green and other bright spring colors is beautiful—even inspiring! That's the main reason so many of us cultivate small gardens. It would be cheaper (in most instances) to just buy from the bin of your favorite grocer, when you count the cost of fertilizer, seed, bug killers, and all the other costs related to home gardening. But you would miss the joy of seeing the plants come up and grow so green. It has such a pleasing effect on your emotions. David verbalizes this in Psalm 23:2, *"He makes me lie down in green pastures."* His trust in God's care for his life was so complete that he could not imagine it ever drying up or turning brown with lifelessness. In Psalm 52:8 David said, *"I am like an olive tree flourishing in the house of God; I trust in God's unfailing love for ever and ever."* God, speaking through Hosea (14:8) says, *"I will answer him and care for him. I am like a green pine tree; your fruitfulness comes from me."* I find a profound spiritual lesson here. God is the God who makes all things new and alive. In and through Him, I can enjoy this life. The beauty of the green around me is a daily reminder of God's gift of life. We love life. We hold on to life. It is precious, and priceless if it is ours or someone's who is dear to us. Let us take comfort in the thought of God's provision of life. He is always our Provider. And when we cut ourselves off from Him and life dries up and loses meaning, He will be there to restore life to us. In this greening, growing season, are you alive?

The world needs to hear a message of life and new life, my Father. Make me a person who brings good news of new life. Amen.

ONE YEAR CHALLENGE—Read: Deuteronomy 9-11

March 22

Christian Geography

HELPING SOMEBODY "IN THE NAME OF JESUS" is never done anonymously. It never occurs in isolation. It can't happen in a vacuum. What church people call ministry just means serving. That is, real people reaching out to real people and helping them with their personal needs in a personal way. Ministry in the Name of Jesus must always originate somewhere. That's why the church in the New Testament always has an address. It's always the church in Ephesus or Rome or some place. Philanthropy or charity can mean writing a check or donating usable goods without ever getting your hands dirty or being personally involved. Christian geography started in the earthly ministry of Jesus. For example, when He miraculously fed 5,000 people (Mark 6:30-44), the food was personally distributed by the hands of the disciples. This pattern was kept up with the daily food distribution out of the church in Acts 6 and the clothing distribution by Dorcas in Acts 9. The government helps people with their physical needs when the church doesn't, but government assistance is more impersonal and mechanical. The needy become a *"number"* rather than persons and that's one of the reasons it's so easy to abuse the system. But let it never be so with the people of God. When a cup of cool water is given *"in Jesus' name"* there is a loop of love thrown to draw a person closer to Jesus and His church. Note in the Gospels how Jesus dealt with individuals. He stopped crowds in their places to single out individuals who were needing help. He did not allow people to think that their physical need was the biggest problem they had. Christian service doesn't end at the person who is doing it but points away from them to Jesus and the whole family of God. Service builds up the body of Christ (in churches) so that we might more effectively minister to more people. The old adage still applies, both literally and figuratively: *"One beggar will always tell another where he has found bread."*

I am amazed, Jesus, that I can do anything in Your name. If You use me today in serving humanity, my friends will be amazed. Amen.

March 23

ONE YEAR CHALLENGE—Read: Deuteronomy 12-14

Empty Hands

AN ANCIENT SOURCE SAYS THAT ALEXANDER THE GREAT gave instructions that when he died, his body should be placed in the coffin in such a way that his hands were visible. He wanted all to see that his hands were empty. All of us depart from this world with empty hands. *"Naked I came from my mother's womb, and naked I will depart,"* declares Job 1:21. Ecclesiastes 5:15 adds, *"He takes nothing from his labor that he can carry in his hand."* Paul says in I Timothy 6:7, *"For we brought nothing into the world, and we can take nothing out of it."* If this is the bottom line, why do people work so hard for material possessions? Why isn't more of mankind wise enough to invest in spiritual things that last for eternity? I wonder if Psalm 126:5-6 speaks to this situation: *"Those who sow in tears will reap with songs of joy. He who goes out weeping, carrying seed to sow, will return with songs of joy, carrying sheaves with him."*

There is a promise of eternal fruitfulness and joy. One going out in the service of the Lord sows spiritual truth in the world with a real concern for the world. The work is hard and the ultimate benefits and harvest of fruit are in the distant future. But faithful service for the Master of the Harvest continues. Then in harvest time, we have something to present the Lord. Are you living for yourself, for others, or for the Lord? Jesus talked in Matthew 6 about those who love to pray publicly to be seen by men and receive the reward they are looking for—that is, human praise. On the other hand, those who do their spiritual duties *"in the Lord's Name"* will receive a reward from Him. Someone has suggested another possibility: Christians die with empty hands here so they can receive their reward in heaven when they meet the Lord.

Take my hand, Jesus, lead my life. If there is something for me to carry, place it in my other hand. Amen.

ONE YEAR CHALLENGE—Read: Deuteronomy 15-17

March 24

On Keeping Promises

LATE NIGHT COMEDIANS OR SITCOM CHARACTERS get a chuckle from the audience when they say *"Promises are made to be broken."* I'm currently working with a group of couples that are trying to keep their marriage vows. The promises they made on their wedding day are still precious to them. They are different from a young woman I heard about who pleaded with her mother for her blessing to marry a young man in the community. The mother would not relent; she did not approve. The daughter protested, *"But he is such a promising young man."* *"That's just it,"* the mother replied, *"He is always promising, never delivering."* We need to make only promises that we will keep. To keep your promises to God is sure to result in intense joy. Have you heard of William Booth, the founder of the Salvation Army? Asked about the secret of his spiritual power, he said *"There was a day in my life when I vowed that God would* have everything there was to have of William Booth." What an excellent vow! But, years later, his daughter gave us insight into General Booth's heart. *"The vow on it's own wasn't the real secret of father's victorious life. The real secret was that he kept the vow,"* she said. How true! What marvelous promises and vows are made to God at the altar of churches, in hospital rooms, in funeral homes, during private devotionals! Oh, God, that all of these promises were honored and faithfully kept. The Bible commands in Psalm 76:11, *"Make vows to the LORD your God and fulfill them."* Let us join together and affirm right now with David *"before those who fear you* [God] *will I fulfill my vows"* (Psalm 22:25). As you keep your promises to God, fellow Christians are encouraged to be faithful and the spiritually lost are pointed to The Truth that can be counted on.

Thank You Jesus, that You have never broken a single promise that You made to me. I want to be a promise keeper. Amen.

ONE YEAR CHALLENGE—Read:
Deuteronomy 18-20

March 25

Starting Back to Church

NOT TOO LONG AGO, I RECEIVED A CALL FROM SOMEONE WHO HAD JUST READ MY WEEKLY newspaper column. She was a regular reader. She was complimentary. Then she requested, *"Why don't you write a piece for people like me? Tell us what to do in order to start back to church. Some of us want to start back."* When I hung up the phone, I immediately thought about the young man in Luke 15:11-24 who wanted to come home. Here are his steps: (1) Accept the fact that life is better in the Father's house with the Father's children. Don't just mentally agree but emotionally place your life on it. (2) Realize how much God loves you. Regardless of how far you have roamed from *"home"* or how long you have been gone, our Loving Heavenly Father is still waiting. (3) Resolve to go back at the earliest opportunity. *"To resolve"* involves our will. Drive a stake down deep! (Verse 17 says that *"When he came to his senses,"* he made a resolve.) Call a minister and put some feet on your resolve. (4) Take the step. If you have read the aforementioned passage from the Bible, you know now that nothing changed until he took the first step. The love of the Father and the extended family (even though the older brother put up a fuss) and the welcome from the whole group was waiting for him all the time. Please remember: the New Testament Church is the only group in the whole world that exists solely for the people who don't come. The whole reason for being the church is to receive those who want to come to God and live in fellowship with him. As the church, we are a clinic to receive any hurting, lonely, broken, despairing, needy person who wants to share the Father's love. The people of God say, *"Come with us, we will do you good!"*

> **O Father, there are so many churches and imitations in the world, I sometimes get confused. Impress on my heart as to where I should invest my life. Amen.**

OneYearChallenge—Read: Deuteronomy 21-23

March 26

Exercise and Fitness

THERE IS A GREAT GAP DIVIDING THE PEOPLE of America. A large part of our population is into exercise, aerobics, athletics, health food, and physical fitness; it is a major industry and a great income producer. On the other hand, an equally large number are devoted to excessive eating, drinking, and sitting around on their duffs. Usually they do these anti-activities while watching athletes perform on TV. Of course, the second group supports a major industry, producing income also, for someone earns money selling the snacks, television sets, and sofas and bleacher tickets on which this group practices its art. Hopefully, these two groups will never boycott each other! But it does raise a question or two: when the Bible says that physical exercise had little value unless there is spiritual exercise (I Timothy 4:8), does that mean God isn't really concerned about how we care for our bodies? Or can a

spiritual man be truly spiritual if he is not concerned about his physical condition? The Bible does teach the Christian that his body is the temple of God and residence of the Holy Spirit (I Corinthians 3:16 and 2 Corinthians 6:16). A kind of morality question arises regarding the extremes in either direction. Certainly there is a reminder here that the physical body (whether in shape or not) is a very temporary piece of equipment, but it does house the human soul-spirit—the real you—that was created for eternity and someday will return to God who created it. While physical fitness is important for a short time, spiritual fitness is an eternal proposition. Have you checked your spiritual pulse rate lately? What is the spiritual condition of your heart? Let's clean up both body and spirit!

Jesus, when You said I should love you with all my heart, mind, body, and spirit, You meant total surrender, didn't You? I thought so. Amen.

One Year Challenge—Read:
Deuteronomy 24-26

March 27

Streams in the Desert

THERE IS A BEAUTIFUL STATEMENT ABOUT GOD'S CARE in Isaiah 43:20 that describes God as giving *"water in the desert and streams in the wasteland."* On so many days, we need refreshment. Problems build up. Pressures mount. Difficulties seem insurmountable. Friends or family members aren't close by when we need them. We cry out for help but no one answers. Where do we turn? For His children, God provides *"water in the desert"* and a reminder of His presence and peace. For seekers of faith, God introduces *"streams in the wasteland"* of love and forgiveness. To be sure there are many mirages. Satan takes advantage of our *"desert times"* also, and attempts to deceive with false promises of relief and empty cups that hold no satisfaction. Or, we may even be tempted to dig our own oasis, not realizing that we are deluding ourselves and the self-generated relief will only be temporary. Go for streams in the desert from the Lord Himself! I remember that in another place in the Bible God talks about people who dig cisterns for themselves, cisterns that won't hold water, while rejecting Him as *"the spring of living water"* (Jeremiah 2:13). In this highly pressured time, people don't take the time to know and love each other. Many think they are too busy to get involved in other people's lives. But the human spirit can't live like that. We must have real satisfaction in life or we dry up on the inside. Spiritual and emotional drought will be ended by the God who gives *"water in the desert."* How do you feel today? How has this week been to you? He who gives *"streams in the wasteland"* will give you *"streams of living water* [that] *will flow from within"* (John 7:38), or in another way of saying it, He will give His Holy Spirit to refresh you.

I am ready for a stream experience, Water of Life. I feel dry and parched in several parts of my life. Amen.

ONE YEAR CHALLENGE—Read:
Deuteronomy 27-29

March 28

Physically Healthy? Spiritually Healthy?

How DO YOU READ THE PAPER? You know, what's your order of priority? Surely you have a plan for reading; we all do. Want to know mine? I pick up the paper, scan the headlines, read the sports section, then the comics, then go back to the heavy stuff. (Unless it's Friday, then I read the religion page to see what's happening in all the churches.) Is that just me? Or am I a product of my culture and environment? Sometimes I ask myself, "Why are you so interested in sports? Forget me. Why do Americans generally spend so much time doing, viewing, discussing or reading about athletics? Almost everybody is into some kind of sports. I have a friend who likes to quote the Bible verse "bodily exercise profits little" to excuse his lack of physical activity, but even he likes baseball. Did you hear about the man who said he gets his exercise by being pallbearer for all his friends who like exercise? Many

hours can be spent on sports activity, whether profitably or wasted, depending on your point of view. One thing is obvious though, we spend more time on physical care than spiritual care. Many who make great effort to be physically trim are spiritually out of shape. It's a question of emphasizing what is most important. Like Jesus said in the Sermon on the Mount, "Don't store your profits here on earth where they can erode away or may be stolen. Store them in heaven where they will never lose their value, and are safe from thieves! If your profits are in heaven your heart will be there, too" (Matthew 5-6). Of course, we should care for our physical bodies, and exercise is one good way to do that. But keep it in proper perspective. Give time each day to spiritual exercise, also.

My scale of life needs to be balanced. Show me what needs to be added and what needs to be subtracted. Thank you! Amen.

One Year Challenge—Read:
Deuteronomy 30-31

March 29

Disappointments

YOUR FAVORITE BASKETBALL TEAM IS NOW out of the playoffs. Your favorite baseball team is off to a terrible start. The person you expected to take you to the senior prom took someone else. Your child's teacher just said your child will have to repeat this grade. Oh, no! What a disappointment! Some weeks seemed filled with disappointments, worse than that, some days do! How can we deal effectively with disappointment? One day Jesus spelled out clearly the cost of discipleship and *"many of his disciples turned back and no longer followed him"* (John 6:66). Jesus simply turned to the rest and said, *"You do not want to leave too, do you?"* When they said that they wouldn't, he went on teaching them. There were many times he could have given up in discouragement, but where would we be if he did? The other day someone was driving me to the airport and it was raining. She asked, *"Do you mind flying in bad weather?"* I replied, *"As soon as we take off, we will climb above this rain and fog."* We need to get on top of discouraging times like that; we can get grounded or rise above it. Jesus said, *"take heart! I have overcome the world"* (John 16:33). I like to think that includes these times of disappointment. What's that old saying? *"If the world hands you a lemon, make lemonade."* Disappointment can make you bitter, but why allow it? The Apostle Paul stated his philosophy for handling disappointments in Philippians 4:11-13, *"I have learned to be content whatever the circumstances. . . . I have learned the secret of being content in any and every situation, . . . I can do everything through him who gives me strength."* Letting Jesus give balance to your life will help you handle both the surprises and the disappointments in healthy ways.

> *Father, why did I think I should never have a disappointment? Show me reality and make my disappointments stepping stones to You. Amen.*

ONE YEAR CHALLENGE—Read:
Deuteronomy 32-33

March 30

Cleansing the Soul

WHY DO YOU SUPPOSE, CHILDREN COME to a certain point in life where they hate to take a bath? When they are very small, most of them love it. Grinning and kicking, they love to splash in the warm, sudsy water. I guess coming from the warm, clean environment of the womb, they like getting their supple and soft skin clean again from the dirt that's rubbed off on them. Then all of a sudden, they come to the day when they don't want to bathe or be bathed. They run from it, put it off as long as possible, and sometimes even lie about it. Check for evidence on the towel! Then they go through a certain transformation, during which they learn that being dirty is not the most desirable state, and they begin to enjoy being clean again. There are similar stages in the soul of an individual. Originally created good in the image of God, we enjoyed the good fellowship with God and we enjoyed a "clean" feeling of peace with God. Then, all of a sudden, the day of rebellion came, and man didn't want to be "clean" anymore and so he rebeled. He dirties himself mentally and emotionally. Some of us get tired of the dirt and come home saying, "purify us from all unrighteousness" (1 John 1:9). Titus 2:13-14 says, "Jesus Christ, . . . gave himself for us to redeem us from all wickedness and to purify (cleanse) for himself a people that are his very own, eager to do what is good." After this cleansing, usually one of the first things a person asks is, "Why did I run from this so long?" When David got tired of being dirty he prayed, "Create a clean heart in me, O God" (Psalm 51:10). You see, when you clean your inside, the outer will follow, not the other way around. What stage of life are you in? Take a look in God's mirror; what do you see?

Yes, Lord, I want to be clean, all the time, mentally, emotionally, and spiritually. You can do it. Do It now. Amen.

ONE YEAR CHALLENGE—Read:
Deuteronomy 34,
Joshua 1

March 31

The Season of Hope

MAYBE YOU HAVE HEARD IT BEFORE, but recently I seem to have heard more discussion about people suffering from light starvation. This is a new description of the phenomenon of winter depression in people who have been deprived of light during the short daylight hours of winter. The suggested cure for many people is to sit in front of a bright light or work in a brightly lighted room. Well, the days are getting longer now, and all who have suffered through the long gloomy days of winter can take heart. This is the season of hope, not just because spring is near and the days are longer, but because of a bigger event. Many people have indeed suffered from light starvation and light deprivation. Wandering around in a kind of midnight of the soul, they grasp to find the door that leads to walking in the light. The Prophet's message *"Arise, shine, for your light has come"* (Isaiah 60:1) found a very responsive people when he said it. As Jesus began His ministry,

Matthew said of Him: *"the people living in darkness have seen a great light; on those living in the land of the shadow of death a light has dawned"* (Matthew 4:16). It was later said about the dawn of resurrection day that *"On the first day of the week, very early in the morning, the women took the spices they had prepared and went to the tomb. . . . but when they entered, they did not find the body of the Lord Jesus"* (Luke 24:1,3). The whole message of the Bible is a message of hope. It shines a beacon of light for those tired of shadows and darkness. Yes, this is the season of hope. The symbolic message (for the person of faith) behind the events of spring is fantastic. Every natural phenomenon represents a deeper, more powerful spiritual message. Indeed, as the old hymn goes, *"when through the woods I wander and hear the birds singing in the trees . . . How Great Thou Art!"**

O God, my hope is in You. Whenever I am down, help me to look up to You. Please let this month be a month of renewal for me. Amen.

ONE YEAR CHALLENGE—Read:
Joshua 2-4

April 1

A Living Hope

DID YOU HEAR ABOUT THE LITTLE GIRL WHO WENT FOR A WALK WITH HER MOTHER after a spring rain? As they walked, they passed a puddle where the water had mixed with the oil on the pavement, giving off a variety of colors. Said the little girl, *"Look Mommy, a rainbow gone to smash!"* Why are there so many suicides and suicide attempts? Why are there so many divorces? Why so many alcoholics and addicts? Because, so many rainbows have gone to smash. We lose hope, give up, get tired of waiting; hopelessness takes many faces. Just observe the faces of folks in psychiatric care or maybe a family member battling despondency. The Bible talks much about the gift of hope that Jesus gives. In Hebrews 6:19-20, the gospel writer says, *"We have this hope as an anchor for the soul, firm and secure. It enters the inner sanctuary behind the curtain, where Jesus, who went before us, has entered on our behalf."*

The comparison here is inspiring. In the old days of shipping, if a storm was blowing, a ship searched for a refuge. Finding a cove, it would enter it until the storm passed. But sometimes, because the big ship demanded deep water, it could not enter the cove. The anchor was then put in a small boat, carried into the peaceful cove, and the ship could be securely anchored—safe from the storm. As long as the anchor was securely planted, deep in the cove, there was no reason for the sailors to fear. When a person plants his faith firmly in Jesus, plenty of storms still come and rainbows still get smashed, but there is always that anchor of hope that never releases us to the torrents and whirlpools trying to dash us and drag us down. The songwriter said, *"We have an anchor, that keeps the soul, steadfast and sure while the billows roll."** About to give up? Wait, grab the anchor of faith and place it in Jesus.

> *O God of Hope, You are my hope. I will not let the disappointments of my past rule over my life any longer. Amen.*

ONE YEAR CHALLENGE—Read:
Joshua 5-7

April 2

Daylight-Saving Time

HOW DID YOU MAKE OUT ON "SPRING FORWARD" DAY? It has now become an annual rite for all of us. Some amusing things always happen, being late on arrival at church not the least of them, since we always save that hour between Saturday night and Sunday morning. By the way, how have you used the daylight time you saved—yard work, or softball practice? Or are you just being a couch potato while it is still light, trying to keep the glare from the windows off the TV screen? Actually, saving time is not a bad idea if you are wise in your use of time. So many things are advertised for the home as *"time savers"*: frozen dinners, microwave ovens, cake mixes, etc. It's amazing how much time we save in this generation and yet everyone complains about how busy they are and about the shortage of time. From a Biblical perspective we should be *"making the most of every opportunity, because the days are evil"* (Ephesians 5:16). Colossians 4:5 reiterates, *"make the most of every opportunity,"* while David says in Psalm 90:10, *"The length of our days is seventy years—or eighty, if we have the strength; . . . they quickly pass."* I believe this raises the real value of time. Until we begin to see the days of our lives reflected in God's Eternal Clock, we are in for a lot of frustration. *"Perspective"* is the word that should guide you. As a responsible creation of God, I know that I am a steward (caretaker) for the time I have. I know I will give account to God for my use of my time. Resolving that before God, I can work on my priorities. When I chose to receive *"eternal life"* through Jesus Christ, then my daily use of my time changes dramatically. Daylight or dark, I want to use my time in the best way to bring glory to God and help to those around me.

ONE YEAR CHALLENGE—Read: Joshua 8-10

> *Eternal God, I cannot imagine the length of eternity. Teach me moment-by-moment to live in fellowship with you. Amen.*

April 3

A Love of Its Kind

My friend, Jim, shared with me a principle for living: *"Love demands a love of its kind."* In a world where people enthusiastically say, *"I love ice cream,"* or *"I love the Redskins,"* or *"I love God,"* it's hard to sense the difference in the depth of feeling expressed. The religious-like fervor that some people give to their favorite recreation far exceeds the fervor they express in their religion. In fact, with divorce rates being what they are, many people obviously *"love"* their career or business more than the mate they vowed to *"love, honor, and cherish until death do us part."* *"Love demands a love of its kind"* reveals how little is invested in the overuse of the word *"love."* Americans tend to talk very glibly about *"loving God"* around Thanksgiving, Christmas, and Easter. But the love is non-demanding, non-restrictive, and non-committal. It is unfortunate that English only has one word for *"love"*; the Greeks are more fortunate. When Jesus was challenging Peter in John 21:15-17, He was trying to clarify how Peter stood on the question of loving His Savior. Was it selfish love? That is, did He want to receive Jesus as His Savior but not submit to Him as Lord of his life? Was it a bargaining love, like: *"I'll scratch your back if you scratch mine"*; *"I'll serve you, if you will give me what I want"*? Or was it an unselfish, self-giving love? You see Jesus, in His teaching and living, expressed only self-giving love. His love for me challenges me to love Him in the same way. That's why Jesus said one day, *"You are my friends if you do what I command"* (John 15:14). Just suppose: what if Jesus loved you only as much as you love Him?

Thank You for loving me so totally and completely. I need the freedom to love You in the same way and not hold back. Amen.

ONE YEAR CHALLENGE—Read: Joshua 11-13

April 4

One Generation Gap, Then What?

I READ THAT THE DESERT IS SPREADING. Every year the sand spreads a bit further and kills a little more vegetation. The thought is scary because it's hard to turn the desert back to life. What about spirituality? That concerns me because I've noticed a lack of discipleship and training in our churches. Christianity is always but one generation from extinction. Paganism and godlessness could regain the country if one generation did not work faithfully at discipling believers. Churches are very concerned about membership roles and the number of converts they baptize each year. Some feel they have failed if they have not baptized more this year than last. But the Bible is clear; baptism is the front end of the Christian experience, not the back end. In the same command where Jesus said we should baptize believers, He also said we should be *"teaching them to obey everything I have commanded you"* (Matthew 28:19-20). Yes,

baptism is important, but where are they now? Have those who were baptized in your church last year continued to faithfully worship and serve the Lord? Discipling believers is hard. It takes commitment on the part of the discipler and the student. Religious poll takers may give impressive statistics of the people who say they believe in God but the lifestyle of many of those same people is practical paganism—that is, living as if God does not exist. We read Psalm 119:11, *"I have hidden your [God's] word in my heart that I might not sin against you."* How does this work? By the churches faithfully equipping all of their believers in the teachings of the Bible. Acts 2:42 says the first Christians devoted themselves to studying doctrine. Someone said, *"It's not how high you jump when you get religion that counts, but how fast you run when you hit the ground."* The difference? Discipleship: *"hold to my teaching,"* Jesus said in John 8:31.

ONE YEAR CHALLENGE—Read: Joshua 14-16

> *God, help me to do all I can to stop the desert of disbelief from spreading. Remind me daily to be faithful. Amen.*

April 5

My Favorite Verse

Let me tell you my favorite verse in the Bible. It's found in the Gospel of John, chapter one, verse 12: *"Yet to all who received him, to those who believed in his name, he gave the right to become children of God."* This verse says it all. Every non-Christian in the world needs this verse of truth. Every church-going religious person, operating on a second-hand religion, needs to memorize it; take it to heart! This promise is for anyone who will receive Jesus—not those who want to read about Jesus or think about Jesus or argue about Jesus. The key is to receive Jesus. Notice: not receiving sacraments or ordinances of the church but receiving Jesus. Many have stumbled on this point and ended up miserable. You need to receive Jesus the same way you would any other guest who would come to your door; you open the door and invite Him—welcome Him, into your life. Another way of saying this is *"to believe in the name of his Son, Jesus Christ"* (1 John 3:23). The word *"believe"* means to trust with all your heart. When all of the historical facts about Jesus have been assimilated in the intellect, you transfer all of this to a faith commitment to Jesus. Or, when you believe enough in what you know about Jesus, then you can choose to trust your life to Him. Instantly, He will make you His child and give you the right to be called a child of God. This experience is also called the *"new birth"* (1 Peter 1:3) or *"the second birth"* (John 3:3-4). This is a spiritual birth in the inner person that will be evidenced by a new lifestyle. I don't remember the day I was born the child of my mother and father, but I will never forget the day I was born the child of my Heavenly Father. Now you know why I love John 1:12.

> *Thank You, Father, for the clarity of your salvation offer. Thank You that this life-changing offer is not complicated. Amen.*

One Year Challenge—Read: Joshua 17-19

April 6

Easter Preparations

"**Y**OU HAVE GOT TO BE KIDDING ME! A DONKEY? Jesus is riding into town on a donkey? And people are following him? What will he think of next?" When the news of King Jesus entering the city that day reached the city officials and his enemies, I'm sure some of them thought it was funny. Or perhaps he had lost his sanity. The Bible tells us that at one point his family even thought so. If you were indeed a king, this was a strange way to claim your kingdom. If you were a king making a triumphal entry, your conquered captives should be following you in subdued shame. Didn't he know that kings ride white stallions and show off their might with disciplined ranks of soldiers? This event might remind us of the passage in the Bible where God says, *"my thoughts are not your thoughts, neither are your ways my ways"* (Isaiah 55:8). In fact, God goes on to say that his way of doing things is easier and better.

God's way of doing things doesn't require a big budget and a public relations team, right? You see, Jesus had been preparing for this for three years. During that time, he had preached and taught about the Kingdom of God. He said that kingdom ways and standards were totally different from the world and proven that they are more effective. So, when the time was prophetically right, (Jerusalem was filled with pilgrims attending Passover) Jesus made his move as the king to reign and rule in the kingdom of men's hearts. When the leaders objected and commanded Jesus to tell the people to stop worshiping him, he replied, *"if they keep quiet, the stones will cry out"* (Luke 19:40). Even the coolest, most blasé, worldly-wise and nonchalant were confronted by his proclamation of his kingship. Have you surrendered and paid homage to the humble, servant King of kings?

Dear God, if religion keeps us from accepting Your surprises, take our religion and give us a dynamic relationship with You. Amen.

ONE YEAR CHALLENGE—Read: Joshua 20-22

April 7

"Who Killed Jesus?"

THERE IS A VERY PENETRATING SONG that I like to sing at this season of the year. It's called "Who Killed Jesus?"* Its message is very personal. The question that theologians and historians have debated for many years is asked on a personal basis. Several are mentioned as possible culprits. The Roman soldiers are obvious candidates; they actually drove the nails in his hands and feet. The Jewish religious leaders are accused as being to blame because they put the pressure on the Roman government. Or, was it a mixed bag of enemies that got together and forgot their differences long enough to get Jesus killed? And then the song comes to the point of personal examination and it becomes clear that I cannot blame any group or individual because Jesus died for my sins. I killed Jesus! My rebellion, my lostness, my separation from God caused a situation so desperate for me, and so important to God, that my only hope was for someone to die for my sinful situation.

It's called the "Vicarious Atonement" in theology books, or you might hear it called the "Substitutionary Sacrifice" in a sermon. The Bible puts it plainly: "when we were still powerless, Christ died for the ungodly" (Romans 5:6); "he was pierced for our transgressions, he was crushed for our iniquities," Isaiah had prophesied (53:5), and when Matthew looked at the cross, he saw it all fulfilled. "Christ Jesus came into the world to save sinners" is the simple statement of I Timothy 1:15. Human nature does not like to take blame for her actions. We like to sow wild oats but we don't like to reap the harvest. We tend to cop out on responsibility and blame someone else for our actions and what happens as a result, but it won't work. So what do we do? Admit it and confess it and repent of it and be declared justified by God the Righteous Judge. He's already paid (His Son) for you! It's the ONLY way out of a "Guilty!" conviction.

Lord of every Easter, may I experience a deepening of my spiritual life this year? Add excitement to my spiritual routine. Amen.

ONE YEAR CHALLENGE—Read: Joshua 23-24, Acts 1

April 8

The Day of Triumph

WE CALL IT *"THE TRIUMPHAL ENTRY."* Hindsight allows us that privilege. It was not perceived that way by all who were there. Some would have called it a bold political move. Some would have called it pure foolishness. Some would have called it a religious demonstration. I think history can accept the Christian's definition of a *"triumphal entry."* When Jesus entered Jerusalem that day, during the Feast of Passover, riding on a donkey with the crowds acclaiming Him as Messiah and Savior, it certainly was an open, public declaration by the carpenter from Nazareth that things would never be the same again. He claimed Himself to be the King of the Kingdom of God. He dramatically fulfilled prophecies that described the servant Messiah. By doing so, He forever thereafter forced every human being who would ever hear His name to decide if He was just a mad man and a fool, or the Savior of mankind. The world has never been the same. The marriage of religion and government was exposed as empty and corrupt. Material success and status was declared phony. Individual soul freedom was lifted up. The list is long, but what many had questioned or feared was boldly declared: God had invaded Main Street. I'm talking about the account in Matthew 21. With all of the beautiful music and celebration in the churches on Palm Sunday, let us not so domesticate the celebration that we remove the implications. Jesus still rides down the Main Street of our lives and lays claim to the place of King of our lives. He still dares people to follow Him heart, mind and soul. He still leads His followers in an unending attack on lies, oppression, political foolishness, or any other enemy of man. His resurrection from the grave verified everything He said on Palm Sunday! Come, join the Triumphal procession this week.

> *Lord, there have been so many personal defeats in my life, I have lost many battles. Please let me join You in triumph. Amen.*

April 9

ONE YEAR CHALLENGE—Read:
Acts 2-4

Who Killed Jesus?

LET ME TELL YOU AGAIN THAT ONE OF MY FAVORITE SONGS at this season of the year asks the question: *"Who Killed Jesus?"* The haunting melody raises the questions: was it the work of Roman soldiers? Or Jewish traditionalists? Or the Emperor who passed the sentence? Or the religious establishment? Some debate the question still today. Occasionally, deep-seated religious prejudice breaks out as some group expresses the anger over *"Christ killing."* The song comes to the shocking (and Biblical) conclusion that I was responsible for the death of Jesus. I rebelled against God and broke his commandments in every conceivable way. He sent his son to convince me of my mistake, but I would have no part of it and even rejected the Son of God. As Isaiah the Prophet described it *"We all, like sheep, have gone astray, each of us has turned to his own way; and the LORD has laid on him the iniquity of us all"* (Isaiah 53:6). When the naturalists are getting excited about spring and its fresh beauty at this season of the year and the reincarnationists are using spring rebirth as a launching pad for their teaching, there is a need for a sober reminder about the seriousness of Easter time. Had there been no death on the cross, there would have been no empty tomb! Every Christian knows that there is more involved in this season of the year than the anticipation of new clothes to wear in the Easter Parade. Maybe I like to sing the song because I need to hear the message. I join Paul in his letter to Timothy, *"Christ Jesus came into the world to save sinners—of whom I am the worst"* (I Timothy 1:15). *"Christ died for our sins"* (I Corinthians 15:3).

O Loving Father, there has never been a day like the day when Your Son died for my sins. I will be eternally grateful. Thank You! Amen.

ONE YEAR CHALLENGE—Read:
Acts 5-7

April 10

The Week that Was

MANY YEARS AGO THERE WAS A TELEVISION PROGRAM called **The Week That Was**. It was very entertaining, done with a British flair. When I come to this week on our calendar, I get that *"this is the week that was"* kind of feeling. This is the week that we pull out all the stops. There is no reason to hold back. Take off the long face, put away the somber religion look—this is a time for celebration! Many people are turned away from weekly Christian services because too many people going in and out of the church houses look like they just swallowed something very sour! Easter time is the time for smiling! *"Up from the grave he arose!"** is the chorus that will be heard in almost every church, regardless of denomination. This is the week of true ecumenicity. We members of the body of Christ acknowledge our common roots, we claim our common heritage and unity. There is no place to engage in doctrinal debate and division as we gather around the empty tomb. Many communities will actively portray this oneness in a joint worship service of all their churches. The seven last words from the cross are in every Bible; we claim their meaning in every church. That great prayer of our Lord recorded in John 17:11 can be visualized more clearly on Resurrection Day: *"I will remain in the world no longer, but they are still in the world, and I am coming to you. Holy Father, protect them by the power of your name—the name you gave me—so that they may be one as we are one."* As we share Easter week in one spirit of thanksgiving for His gift of life over death, let us in one spirit share together the expectancy of His return. Acts 1:11 says He will also return again! Maranatha (O Lord, come)!

God of All Joy, I often laugh and I sometimes feel happy but I don't have lasting joy. Through Your love, grant me that joy. Amen.

ONE YEAR CHALLENGE—Read:
Acts 8-10

April 11

Extra! Extra! Read all about It!

WONDERFUL EASTER! IT REALLY IS a beautiful celebration! So pregnant with meaning! I so hope that you don't let it be a one day occasion for you and the people you love. Sunday will be colorful. The Easter lilies that will decorate the Christian houses of worship will shine. The bright colors of spring in the newest fashions, that many feel compelled to display, will glow. (By the way, that's American culture, not Christianity; don't be confused.) The church choirs will all be doing triumphant anthems. There will be the sound of victory in the air. Many will be greeting friends they haven't seen for a year. All in all, you watch and see, it will be a very special day of worship on Sunday. Actually, churches should be like that every Sunday. If you follow the New Testament, we have 52 Resurrection Sundays in a row. The resurrection of Jesus is the reason we celebrate on Sunday anyway and not on Friday or Saturday. The impact of this particular Sunday should be like the 25th of December—it's the reason for all the rest. Determine now: *"I will not return to 'business as usual' next week. Furthermore, I will not allow my church to return to 'business as usual,' so help me God."* Maintain the excitement, expectation and electricity of this Sunday each Sunday of the year. *"Christ the Lord is risen today, Alleluia!"** *"Up from the grave He arose, With a mighty triumph o'er His foes; He arose a Victor from the dark domain, And He lives forever with His saints to reign: He arose!"*** *"I know that my Redeemer liveth, ... I know that Jesus lives!"**** These are the phrases we will voice together during this season. But don't you realize, your neighbor needs to hear this from you daily in word and deed? This is the one answer with any weight, to despair and meaninglessness.

> *I am so grateful for the good news that Jesus arose from the dead. That's the best news I have ever heard. Amen.*

ONE YEAR CHALLENGE—Read: Acts 11-13

April 12

In a Nutshell

YOU MAY BE IN A HURRY AS YOU READ THIS. Most people around here seem to be in a hurry. So here is the gospel in a nutshell: *"For God so loved the world that he gave his one and only Son, that whoever believes in him shall not perish but have eternal life"* (John 3:16). As people like to say, *"Give me the bottom line."* Well, there it is. This verse sums up the whole Bible. Everything in the Old Testament points to this verse. Everything in the New Testament that follows this verse is a reflection of its impact on the world. So if you are in a hurry today to understand the Bible or to get to know God, this is the place to start. The first thing you discover is that you are important to God. Wow! Maybe hard to believe, but believe it! He loves you! He sees you in all of your spiritual, mental, emotional, and physical need and His heart goes out to you. Loving you, He must give to you. (You've heard the old saying, *"You can give without loving but you can't love without giving."*) So God offers you His very best, His only Son. It's up to you to receive The Gift. The gift is available; it is the most precious gift ever offered. It remains *"potential"* until received. It's hard to imagine anyone rejecting this gift. I once had a friend in Maryland who waited for God to force him to accept the gift. God never did force him, nor anyone else. No, the gift is freely given, so it must be voluntarily received. No one else can receive it for you, either. So if you are looking for eternal life today, either in quality or in quantity, here is an offer you can't afford to turn down. Amazing, isn't it, that something so clear should be so misunderstood by so many. Anyway, there you have it, in a nutshell.

Father, some say the story of Jesus is the greatest love story ever told. I totally agree. Amen.

ONE YEAR CHALLENGE—Read: Acts 14-16

April 13

Good Friday: Commemorating History

Has this been a good Friday or a T.G.I.F. (Thank God It's Friday) kind of day? How did weekdays get to be so dreaded? Why does Friday arouse such different reactions, especially the one called *"Good Friday"*? It probably depends on how you feel about THE Good Friday. Some people look at today just as they do any other day—they don't realize that today commemorates one of the special days of history. Of course, on that particular Friday (2,000 years ago), only God knew how that day would turn out. One of the Roman soldiers might have said, *"T.G.I.F."* The teacher from Galilee was causing quite a stir in the metro area! Jerusalem already had plenty of excitement because the city was packed with people celebrating Passover. No one there was quite prepared to handle the shock waves of the brutal execution of the man from Nazareth. The significance of His death would become clear only to His followers a short three days later. In fact, that's how it got to be called Good Friday. For some, Good Friday means a vacation from school. For some, an abundance of jelly beans. For some, it means new clothes. A recent poll revealed that three out of ten high school students in America don't know what Easter means. Probably their parents don't either. Every Friday can be a *"good"* Friday if you accept what God did for you on a certain *"bad"* Friday (that God made Good) to change the meaning for you. Isaiah the prophet said, *"he was pierced for our transgressions, he was crushed for our iniquities; the punishment that brought us peace was upon him, and by his wounds we are healed"* (Isaiah 53:5). Sure, it might be Friday, and maybe so far, all you could say was T.G.I.F. But Sunday is coming! Good Friday signals the coming of victory over defeat, life over death, hope over despair. It's the tip-off! A Good Friday indeed!

Father, You are so powerful to make bad things good. You can do anything in my life if I will allow You. Lift me up. Amen.

One Year Challenge—Read: Acts 17-19

April 14

Unique and Spectacular

WHEN I FIRST SAW THE PARTHENON in Athens, it took my breath away. When I first saw the Coliseum in Rome—again, I gasped for breath. When I saw my first sunrise over the Pacific from an airplane window, that too was breathtaking. But after the first time, it wasn't breathtaking anymore. When I first heard of Jesus rising from the dead, it was breathtaking to me. When I sat alone in an empty tomb in a garden in Jerusalem, it was breathtaking, imagining that I was in *"that"* empty tomb. On Easter morning, when I join with Christians all over the world celebrating the resurrection of Jesus, it will be breathtaking again. That one event never loses its lustre. It is as exciting today as it has ever been. This is THE SINGULAR EVENT OF HISTORY. We know the burial places of all the other founders of religions. We even honor the burial sites of many of our great leaders. But THE FACT THAT JESUS, WHO WAS KILLED ON A CROSS, CAME ALIVE FROM THE GRAVE THREE DAYS LATER, stops us in our tracks. WOW! There were too many eye witnesses to truthfully discount it, or reject it as false. In one of his post-resurrection appearances, Jesus said, *"This is what is written: The Christ will suffer and rise from the dead on the third day, and repentance and forgiveness of sins will be preached in his name to all nations"* (Luke 24:46-47 [Hosea 6:2, Jeremiah 31:34]). That is what will make Easter Sunday a breathtaking (or maybe breath-overflowing) day for everyone in whom His Holy Spirit dwells. In this pagan world, if they are hearing this for the very first time, they will be so amazed that it will take their breath away and they will receive it as good news. The scars and pain of war, and even the lingering hatreds of war beg to hear the proclamation, *"He is Alive!"* He who gives life and peace IS ALIVE!

Father, I thank You for the day that I invited Jesus into my heart. It will make Easter Sunday so special. Amen.

April 15

OneYearChallenge—Read: Acts 20-22

Easter Sunday

THE GREAT CELEBRATION OF THE CHRISTIAN FAMILY is here. There are celebrations galore in the faith, and indeed, reason to celebrate every Sunday. But this weekend is the linch-pin that holds it all together. It is as the gospel writer said, *"After he was raised from the dead, his disciples recalled what he had said. Then they believed the Scripture and the words that Jesus had spoken"* (John 2:22). All parts of life wait on the resurrection to give it meaning. The cement that holds the whole evangelical (good news) story together is the resurrection. The enemies of Jesus have always understood this; that's why the resurrection is attacked more than anything else. The interesting footnote to this is how many agnostics have been converted to Christianity after setting out to disprove the Resurrection. The evidence is too heavy. But that leads me to ask you, what will you celebrate Easter weekend? Or how will you celebrate? Don't get so involved in the new clothes and Sunday dinner and egg rolling that you miss the *"AWE-FULL"* significance. Think about the first Easter when a couple sat down to eat with Jesus and didn't recognize Him. Don't you let it slip by. Luke 24:32 records them saying afterward, *"Were not our hearts burning within us while he talked with us on the road and opened the Scriptures to us?"* They had to go back to Jerusalem and relate the historical fact of seeing the resurrected Jesus, but could only kick themselves for missing out on all the possibilities of this *"holy day."* If you just allow it to become a *"holiday"* that is a shame. Easter weekend could be the dawning of a new day or better yet, a new eternity. Go to church Sunday. Listen with your ears and your heart. Respond as Thomas the Doubter did when he saw the risen Jesus: *"My Lord and my God!"* (John 20:28). Hallelujah! He's alive!

God, sometimes You seem too mighty and powerful for me to talk to personally. You have power to raise the dead. Wow! I'm amazed. Amen.

ONE YEAR CHALLENGE—Read: Acts 23-25

April 16

The Winning Side

LET'S HEAR IT FOR THE WINNER! High fives! Celebration slaps! Congratulatory handshakes! Grins to beat the band! Why? Didn't you hear? Jesus is ALIVE! Came alive out of the grave! In the battle with sin and death and Hell and the grave, He won! The *"gates of Hades will not overcome it"* (Matthew 16:18). He went to the strong man's house and robbed him (Satan) of his prey (Matthew 12:29). The old hymn proclaims, *"Up from the grave, He arose!"* This was no hocus-pocus sleight-of-hand. This was no TV charlatan pulling a slick trick and deceiving people. This is fact. Verified! He *"appeared to more than five hundred of the brothers at the same time"* (I Corinthians 15:6), as well as the eleven apostles coming in from a fishing trip (John 21). Many people talked to Him and touched Him after the Resurrection, like a man named Thomas. Listen, if you didn't know this, you must have thought that the Christians were acting strange during Easter week. Boy, it feels good to be on the winning side! We have victory songs! Paul wrote one of them in I Corinthians 15:54-55: " *'Death has been swallowed up in victory. Where, O death, is your victory? Where, O death, is your sting?' The sting of death is sin, and the power of sin is the law. But thanks be to God! He gives us the victory through our Lord Jesus Christ."* Or, *"This is the victory that has overcome the world"* (I John 5:4). The victory rally will be going on for some time. If you want to watch or participate, go to the nearest New Testament church. I'm sure they will let you enter. If you think the celebration is big here, you should read about the one going on in Heaven. In Revelation 5:11-12, it says that thousands are shouting this victory song: *"Worthy is the Lamb, who was slain, to receive power and wealth and wisdom and strength and honor and glory and praise!"* Great song! Get on The Winning Side. Join the Celebration.

> **God, I've been a loser so many times. Some of my friends even called me a loser. Thanks for not giving up on me. Amen.**

April 17

ONE YEAR CHALLENGE—Read:
Acts 26-28

The Empty Tomb

WHETHER YOU READ MATTHEW, MARK, LUKE OR JOHN's account in the New Testament, they all hit with sledge-hammer power when they relate the resurrection of Jesus: *"Early on the first day of the week, while it was still dark, Mary Magdalene went to the tomb and saw that the stone had been removed from the entrance. So she came running to Simon Peter and the other disciple, ... and said, 'They have taken the Lord out of the tomb, and we don't know where they have put him!'"* (John 20:1-2). You can argue, debate, proclaim all you want about creation, evolution, the church, the Bible, world religions, denominationalism, TV evangelists, etc., and it will pale into insignificance before awesome meaning of the empty tomb. All of the doctrinal debates seem like small stuff up against the empty tomb. Until the impact of the first Easter morning hits you, forget it—you haven't re-

ally lived! Every religious philosophy under the sun compares to chasing a feather in the wind if you haven't dealt with the empty tomb. Paul was right in 1 Corinthians 15:14, *"if Christ has not been raised, our preaching is useless and so is your faith."* Amazing and wonderful are our belief in the Incarnation and the Substitutionary Atonement, but it is the Resurrection that gives it all meaning. Many men have died on a cross, even good men, but none of those rose from the dead on the third day after paying for your sins. The Resurrection as the key can be seen in the words of Peter after the Passion (death and burial of Christ): *"I'm going out to fish"* (John 21:3). It was going to be *"business as usual"* again until he was confronted by the living Christ and then he really was a changed man!

The empty tomb—fiction or fact? Your life from now on, to eternity, will reflect your answer.

OneYearChallenge—Read: Judges 1-3

> *God, I've been to so many funerals. Most of them were so sad! Maybe they couldn't imagine an empty tomb. Thank You for showing me the one. Amen.*

April 18

Reflecting on Easter

SOME EXPERIENCES LEAVE NO AFTER EFFECT; when it's over, it's over. Some experiences leave a pleasant memory; it was a nice experience and remembering it leaves us with a warm feeling. Then there are experiences so special and powerful in effecting us that we can never be the same again. Such is the reality of the experience we had on Easter. Some will remember that they were in church on Easter Sunday morning, but it made no difference on Monday morning back in the *"real world."* Others will remember the beauty of the choir singing and the reassurance of dinner at *"Momma's house"* again, but that's about as far as it goes. But then others are allowing the full miracle of Jesus' coming alive to dawn on their lives just like the sun (and Son) coming up on the first Easter. Their whole world has had to readjust to their *"newness"* this week. Old attitudes have changed, old habits dropped (some with difficulty), old despairs given up; a newness has come and is lasting. Will they be in church again this Sunday? You better believe it! It's like a thirsty person finding an oasis in the desert, they will definitely go back to the spring, the source of living water. What will be the aftereffect of Easter for you? I remember reading long ago: *"two men looked through prison bars, one saw mud, the other saw stars."* What did you see on Easter—ordinary things or extraordinary? In some way, how you act on other days will reflect what you really experienced on Easter Sunday. I heard about a person who looked at the Grand Canyon and called it *"a big ditch."* Could that have been you? If so, I'd like to give you a second chance today if you did not take it on Easter Sunday. Sit still for a few moments. Reflect on this; say it and let it sink in: Jesus rose from death for me.

ONE YEAR CHALLENGE—Read: Judges 4-6

> *Father, I still get goose pimples and the warm fuzzies just thinking about Jesus rising from the grave. I hope I always feel this way. Amen.*

April 19

Looking Out for Others

WHEN I WAS A CHILD READING THE BIBLE, I always puzzled over what the Bible was trying to say to me in Philippians 2:4: *"Each of you should look not only to your own interests, but also to the interests of others."* It seemed to be telling me to be nosey and curious about my neighbor's life, which, I reasoned, was none of my business. Then I matured some and realized that the Bible was teaching me not to be so selfish and self-centered. Christians ought to be other-oriented instead of ego-directed. As the population multiplies, our responsibility gets larger. I am *"my brother's keeper"* (Genesis 4:9), and I ought to care what happens to him. Color, class, or culture should not be a determining factor. To see a brother or sister in any kind of need and not care is a terrible sin (James 2:16). *"Carry each other's burdens"* (Galatians 6:2) is a picture of mutuality and interdependence. In Romans 14:19, we are instructed to *"make every effort to do* what leads to peace and to mutual edification." We have much to learn on this subject, or perhaps, unlearn. The Bible says in I Corinthians 10:24, *"Nobody should seek his own good, but the good of others."* The implications are clear: if we look out for the well-being of others, our well-being will be secure. Many people's prayers are selfish: *"Lord, bless me and my wife, my son, John and his wife, us four, and no more."* Perhaps you think no one would ever be so selfish? Listen closely to your prayers next time. Learning to care for others may be the next major life test for you. Selfish people are never satisfied and self-centered people are never good friends. There is no satisfaction in multiplying material possessions. True friendship always has a measure of mutuality. When I give myself away in concern for others, the blessing of a purposeful life outranks all else. The Kingdom of God is noted for its new value system.

Dear Father, there have been so many people who have helped all of my life. Many of them were Your good friends. Thanks for sending them. Amen.

ONE YEAR CHALLENGE—Read:
Judges 7-9

April 20

"I Can Forgive Anything You Can Forget"

WHY IS FORGIVENESS SO HARD? This problem has plagued mankind from the Garden of Eden. Cain killed Abel because he was not able to forgive the grudging feeling he had against his brother. And then there are those times when someone comes to us and asks our forgiveness and we say, *"I can forgive you but I can't forget."* What kind of forgiveness is that? Simply put, it's not forgiveness. Sad thing is, we sometimes say those words with a kind of spiritual smugness. Peter tried to talk to Jesus about forgiveness in terms of a mathematical formula. *"Lord, how many times shall I forgive my brother when he sins against me? Up to seven times?"* Jesus had an instant answer: *"seventy-seven times"*! (Matthew 18:21-22) In other words, *"Who's counting?"* We are talking about forgiveness here, about breaking down barriers, about recovering oneness, about restoring unity, about rediscovering sweetness in a relationship—who's counting?

Proper spiritual motivation doesn't nit-pick, as if in a game of *"winner take all."* In an unresolved personal dispute between friends, there are no winners, only losers. I heard someone say recently, *"I can forgive anything that you can forget."* That makes forgiveness a shared responsibility. We help each other achieve forgiveness as we work for the same goal. A spirit of humility gives us freedom to admit our part in any broken relationship. Necessity places it on the heart of every true believer to work hard for reconciliation. Remember, the Bible says so. There is a very exact, step-by-step plan that Jesus gave for seeking reconciliation. It's in Matthew 18:15-20. Have you tried it? It ends with a neat promise from Jesus: *"where two or three come together in my name, there am I with them."* Conclusion: working out a forgiveness is Jesus-like and Jesus-blessed and guarantees His presence. It's a win-win situation.

ONE YEAR CHALLENGE—Read:
Judges 10-12

> *Father, how could You forgive me? I did so many hateful things to You. Help me to reflect Your attitude. Amen.*

April 21

Fear in the Church

WHEN WAS THE LAST TIME YOU went to the church house and were afraid? Or what was the last time you became afraid in a worship service? Probably never! Sometimes when people first go to a worship service or Bible study, they may feel a little nervous or anxious, but fearful? No! Maybe that's the difference in church today and in the first century. In Acts 9:31, the Bible says, *"Then the church through-out Judea, Galilee, and Samaria enjoyed a time of peace. It was strengthened; and encouraged by the Holy Spirit, it grew in numbers, living in the fear of the Lord."* The first churches had a great impact on the world because when they came together there was a sense of awe and reverence for God. They knew they were in the presence of a Holy God. They knew they were handling *"holy"* things when they dealt with God. They did not come to worship to be happy. They did not come to Bible study to make new friends. They did not go to hear preaching of God's Word because they liked the choir. Church is for many people a diversion, a social action, a neighborhood political rally; anything but a confrontation with the Living God. Church will be a boring experience until there is a recovery of a sense of the Holy. In Acts 5, there is an account of Ananias and Sapphira dying while at a church service be-cause they lied to God. Again, the record says, fear filled the church. But, please note this fact: when this sense of fear was in the church, the church had her greatest impact on the world. When the church recovers a core of people who *"have heard, . . . have seen with our eyes, . . . and our hands have touched . . . the Word of life"* (I John 1:1), she will recover fear and won-der. A second-hand Chris-tian experience knows no fear of God Almighty.

ONE YEAR CHALLENGE—Read:
Judges 13-15

> *Dear Lord, they say familiarity breeds contempt. Don't let me get trapped in that and take You for granted or ignore you. Amen.*

April 22

In-Between Times

THESE ARE DIFFERENT TIMES, BUT REALLY PLEASANT! Cool nights and warm days! Then warm days followed by cool ones! Windy days! Winter is leaving the scene and spring is coming on stage. You can't be sure of the weather during the in-between times. Whenever the seasons change, we have this good time that flips us back and forth—good tastes of what we are leaving and what we are entering. In our lives also, we have these "seasons" of the soul, transition times of great importance. For example, there is the kindergarten child who wants to explore the big world but hates to leave the security of home; the high schooler who wants independence but holds on to the benefits of childhood; the college student who likes to go back and visit his old high school because it was a simpler time—it goes on and on with us. The Apostle Paul wrote of it near the end of his life. In Philippians 1:23-25 he said, "I am torn between the two: I desire to depart and be with Christ, which is better by far; but it is more necessary for you that I remain in the body. Convinced of this, I know that I will remain, and I will continue with all of you for your progress and joy in the faith." His faith and expectancy gave him a good feeling about what the future held while he still remembered what the Lord had helped him accomplish. I think he was enjoying the transition. So should we, and live this transition time to the fullest. We too can look forward and back. Some people seem to shift into neutral and live in a "no-man's land" with no joy in what has passed and no excitement about what will follow. Some even spend a lot of time grumbling about how things are always changing. Rather than moaning about the change, grasp it and grow with it. By God's grace, you could be standing at the edge of the greatest growth opportunity in your life. Hear Jesus say: "Come, follow me" (Mark 1:17).

Some days, O God, I really feel like the citizen of two worlds. Deep down, I know this world is not my permanent address. Amen.

April 23

ONE YEAR CHALLENGE—Read: Judges 16-18

Watching Baby Grow

NOTHING GROWS AS FAST AS A HEALTHY BABY, (especially if it's a grandchild, niece, or nephew that lives out of town). It is a beautiful sight to see a baby fed and well-cared for as it responds to nurturing with such vigor. (Truly it is a tragedy that all the babies of the world don't have this privilege.) The kind of vigor we observe in a healthy baby is what makes so understandable the biblical injunction: *"Like newborn babies, crave pure spiritual milk, so that by it you may grow up in your salvation"* (I Peter 2:2). Yes, we enter the Kingdom of God as babies. We are *"born again"* (John 3:7), and every Christian starts the new life at the same place. Then there is the expectation that we will *"grow in the grace and knowledge of our Lord and Savior Jesus Christ"* (2 Peter 3:18), even as Jesus is described in his pre-teen years as growing *"in wisdom and stature, and in favor with God and men"* (Luke 2:52). Growth is what's programmed, whether in the physical or spiritual world. The baby grows and begins to smile and interact with other people and then begins to develop his own personality. First he crawls, then walks, and then runs. First he is fed by loving care-givers, then he learns to feed himself, then he can even feed someone else. There are so many comparisons to the Christian life. What a thrill to see spiritual growth! That is a work of God. Paul said that he and Apollos planted and watered the gospel *"seed"* in Corinth, but *"God made it grow"* (I Corinthians 3:6). Just as God's grace makes our conversion possible, it is God's grace that continues the growth process. How much scripture have you mastered or memorized this year? How much have you improved in your prayer life? How much more do you want to grow?

Father, am I growing or just getting flabby? I want to grow more and more like my Savior, Jesus. Amen.

ONE YEAR CHALLENGE—Read:
Judges 19-21

April 24

The Courage to Protect

Mr. AND MRS. BLUEBIRD MOVED into our bird house a few weeks ago. They worked hard building the nest and then Mrs. Bluebird produced the eggs to start the family. That's when the protection started. Both of them began to invest their energy protecting the eggs and then the newborns. They have been so courageous. When the neighbor's cat gets near or the big woodpecker or the starlings get close, they attack. They are not afraid to attack enemies twice their size. Parents need the courage to protect. Sometimes Mother's Day, Father's Day, and Grandparent's Day stress nothing but the warmth of the parent's role. But this role of protection is vital. It takes courage to stand up against the pressure of *"everybody's doing it."* It takes courage to protect your children from certain television programs and certain movies. The path of least resistance requires no courage. It takes courage in this permissive society to give your children a curfew. Many parents have abdicated this role of protector. Having fed and clothed your child does not free you from the need to put your life on the line for the well-being of your child. Build protection into your home by keeping tobacco, drugs, and alcohol out; you would do as much with any other poison. The best antidote to the poison of half-truths is to have the courage to take your children often to a house of worship. *"Bring them up in the training and instruction of the Lord"* (Ephesians 6:4). In the pattern of Deuteronomy 6:8, this protection starts at the front door. Perhaps children would not grow up to be such a *"pain"* to their parents as young adults if parents endured a little more pain of providing protection while they are teenagers. Perhaps a child raised with the security of limits wouldn't feel the need to act out lovelessness later on.

Father, I am ashamed of my cowardice in spiritual things. I'm afraid some days people don't know where I stand with You. Help me. Amen.

April 25

One Year Challenge—Read: Ruth 1-2

Where Do Wars Come From?

A NEW QUESTION IS BEING RAISED BY CHILDREN today. The question is: *"Where do wars come from?"* In the old days, they asked simpler questions like, *"Where do babies come from?"* In the era of *"saturation news coverage"* of wars going on around the world, little children are being forced to see a real world that they do not understand. Parents may try to teach their children to not fight with brothers, sisters or playmates, but then they're seeing grown-ups fighting every day, either on TV news or shows, or in their own home. So, children (being naturally inquisitive) ask their parents, who sometimes fumble for an answer. The Bible poses this question and then gives the answer, in James 4:1-2, *"What causes fights and quarrels among you? Don't they come from your desires that battle within you? You want something but don't get it. You kill and covet, but you cannot have what you want. You quarrel and fight. You do not have because you do not ask God."* Then war comes from inside people. The desire for power or property or position becomes so overpowering and consuming that individuals, special interest groups, or nations are willing to do anything to get it, regardless of who gets hurt. Rather than being submissive to God and accept personal or national boundaries, man asserts his rebellion against God by asserting himself against his fellow man. History is bloody with the accounts of men's striving against one another. Is war inevitable? Yes! As long as mankind lives by lust rather than love, conflict is inevitable. The same kind of heart condition rejects mediation or reconciliation for fear of losing face or place. If the question is, "How do we stop wars?", the answer is to submit to the *"Prince of Peace"* (Isaiah 9:6). When that happens, *"the peace of God, which transcends all understanding, will guard your hearts and your minds in Christ Jesus"* (Philippians 4:7). Are you in peacetime or war?

> *Father, I hate war. It scares me and the little ones I love. I want to be a peacemaker. Show me how. Amen.*

April 26

ONE YEAR CHALLENGE—Read: Ruth 3-4

Gymnasium of the Soul

I HAVE HEARD PRAYER DESCRIBED as a *"gymnasium of the soul."* One thing that war causes is an increase of prayer. In time of international conflict, churches are filled with people attending prayer vigils. People who have never prayed before begin to pray. People who don't know how to pray try it anyway. People who used to insist that they didn't believe in prayer request prayer. What is happening? They are going to the spiritual gymnasium. When people pray, they *"exercise"* faith or put their faith *"muscles"* to work: *"anyone who comes to him must believe that he exists and that he rewards those who earnestly seek him."* So wrote the man of God in Hebrews 11:6. When people pray, they *"stretch"* their belief in God. *"I do believe; help me overcome my unbelief!"* is related in Mark 9:24 as the prayer of the man with a sick child. It was as if the man were saying, *"Jesus, I want to believe in your power but I have so many doubts attacking me."* The end of that story is a good one because

Jesus answered his *"stretching"* prayer. When people pray, they take a *"leap of faith"* (Kierkegaard coined the phrase). This jump is best exhibited in the story of the *"professional religionist"* versus *"the sinner"* at prayer in Luke 18:13. While one boasted self-righteously in his perverted prayer, the other beat himself on the chest, praying, *"God, have mercy on me a sinner."* All prayer must begin here; this particular prayer lays the foundation for all other prayers. In other words, God can't provide for your needs until you admit to God how needy you are. Hear it this way: a satisfying prayer relationship with God is based on a personal closeness to God, through God's son Jesus, who bridges the gap between (imperfect) us and (perfect) God. John 16:24 says, *"Until now you have not asked for anything in my name. Ask and you will receive, and your joy will be complete."* In order to build up your spiritual strength, you need to spend more time in the gym.

> *Father, You beat me to the prayer room again today. You always do. I know I will never be alone there. Thanks! Amen.*

April 27

ONE YEAR CHALLENGE—Read:
1 Samuel 1-3

Throwing a Beanball

Do YOU KNOW WHAT A "BEANBALL" IS? It's when a baseball pitcher intentionally tries to hit the batter in the head with the baseball. Seriously! We are talking about grown men doing something that they would spank their sons for doing. It is a way to intimidate the opposition. It has bad consequences because then the opposing pitcher throws at your players. It's bad because the aim is to intentionally hurt someone. But then, to intentionally do something bad is another definition of the word "sin." Sin is rooted in our attitude. For instance, when David began his prayer of confession in Psalm 51:1-2, he said, "Have mercy on me, O God, according to your unfailing love; according to your great compassion blot out my transgressions. Wash away all my iniquity and cleanse me from my sin." The meaning of "transgressions" is: open and intentional going away from God; having a stiff-necked, rebellious attitude. One definition of iniquity is: our natural fallen tendency toward perversion and doing what is displeasing to God. A definition of sin is: missing the mark of godly behavior; aiming at that target and falling short of our goal. Here are three different aspects of living contrary to God's Word. But regardless of the root or intent of our contrary acts and nature, there are always unpleasant repercussions, just like with the beanball. The batter will be hurt, and maybe the pitcher and others, if the batter's teammates retaliate. The Bible says, "the wages of sin is death" (Romans 6:23). And sin is a faithful paymaster; it always pays off: No IOUs! No idle threats! No empty promises! It pays off in death. That is worse than painful. You might get by with a slight physical injury from a beanball, but not with sin; it always results in the worst consequence. My conclusion: avoid a beanball contest; and avoid all sin (I Thessalonians 5:22). Pray David's prayer and be cleansed by God's response—his son Jesus.

> *Surely Father, people who make jokes about Hell don't know what it is about. Show me how to be serious about judgment and joyful about salvation. Amen.*

April 28

ONE YEAR CHALLENGE—Read:
I Samuel 4-6

"Something for Nothing"

P.T. BARNUM SAID THERE WAS AT LEAST ONE fool born everyday. I really think he was underestimating. From all the advertisements and promotions I get in the mail and hear on the radio and see on the television, there must be dozens. Suckers still bite on the bait of *"getting something for nothing."* People are tempted to gamble the money they've earned, or maybe received in the form of a welfare check, on the possibility of being an overnight millionaire. It really could be more accurately stated of the gambler that he/she gets *"nothing for something."* The odds are always stacked against the gambler. Like someone said, *"There ain't no free lunch!"* Even when the government gets into the lottery business using taxpayers' dollars in advertising to attract folks to gambling on their future, it is with the calculated plan of enticing people to part with their money on a long shot. Sometimes you hear someone say about the lottery or bingo or some other game of chance, that it's *"for a good cause."* Pardon me while I adjust my cynical smile, but sinning for a good cause is still sinning. It's a sin to intentionally manipulate people and use them for selfish ends. The only real *"something for nothing"* I ever knew about was described in the Bible in Ephesians 2:8-9, *"For it is by grace you have been saved, through faith— and this not from yourselves, it is the gift of God— not by works, so that no one can boast."* Millions around the world have trusted and tested this truth and found it to be absolutely true. When this happens, people trust in Christ and not in chance. You don't need good luck when you are trusting God. Paul could affirm triumphantly *"my God will meet all your needs according to his glorious riches in Christ Jesus"* (Philippians 4:19). No gamble!

OneYearChallenge—Read: I Samuel 7-9

> *Father, this has been an amazing month. I have met with You on a regular basis and every meeting has blessed me. Amen.*

April 29

Converting to Christianity

IT IS A BEAUTIFUL SIGHT TO SEE and I have been privileged to see it happen several times in my life: immediate conversion to Christianity the first time a person hears the good news (gospel) about Jesus. I remember an old man in the Philippines who said, *"All my life I have believed there must be somebody like Jesus and now I know there is."* On our mission campaign into Chalco, Mexico, people who had never seen or read the Bible in their lives, prayed to receive Jesus as Savior and Lord the first time they were introduced to Him. Such is the amazing power of this good news to the receptive hearer! It's too bad that in about every community in America there are many *"gospel-hardened"* folks; that is, they have heard the gospel so many times that they can't hear it anymore with any spiritual perception. If only these people could hear it again for the first time. First-time hearers of the gospel are excited to hear it. First-time hearers usually aren't antagonistic to the gospel. They honestly admit that they have a spiritual vacuum in themselves. They have tried the world's answers to their search for meaning and purpose in life. They are like the soil Jesus described as *"good soil, where it produced a crop—a hundred, sixty or thirty times what was sown"* (Matthew 13:8). My own belief is that people locked in the prison of spiritual darkness will go for the freedom gates opened by Jesus when they hear his offer. I remember a man in Bataan Province, Philippines, who said, *"If my father could have heard your message, he would have believed too."* If you are a Christian and you want to see a miracle, find someone who hasn't read the Bible and tell them about Jesus. As surely as Peter and Andrew *"At once . . . left their nets and followed him"* (Matthew 4:20), there is a good possibility that you will participate in a miracle.

> **God of Miracles, thank You that we can be born again, be forgiven, and start life over as Your child. Give us new life, not religion. Amen.**

April 30

ONE YEAR CHALLENGE—Read:
I Samuel 10-12

May Flowers

NOW THAT THE APRIL SHOWERS ARE GONE, we can begin to look for abundant *"May flowers"* everywhere. Actually, in April we had more than showers—we had some rain storms, so we are doubly expectant. On the other hand, to be truthful, April displayed many beautiful flowers, like azaleas and tulips. It's a pleasure to be able to live with this *"May flowers"* expectancy. Sometimes when the storm clouds get so thick, we can't see the sun. It's good to know flowers are coming! As that famous sermon about Easter says, *"It's Friday, but Sunday is coming!"* Living with an air of trust in God's future blessing is sweet. The Psalmist said, *"weeping may remain for a night, but rejoicing comes in the morning"* (Psalm 30:5). Grieving people need that handle of hope. How about this challenge from 2 Corinthians 4:16-17: *"we do not lose heart. Though outwardly we are wasting away, yet inwardly we are being renewed day by day.*

For our light and momentary troubles are achieving for us an eternal glory that far outweighs them all?" I am not proposing a *"pretend it ain't so"* philosophy. By standing on the reality of faith in God and living in a daily prayer fellowship with God, we *"can do everything through him who gives me strength"* (Philippians 4:13). Why do people commit suicide? Because they have convinced themselves that the May flowers are not going to bloom this year; there is only going to be an unbearably long rainy season. Despair and despondency will be the constant travelling companions of those who can't see or hang in there to see the May flowers. Goodness and Mercy, the sheep dogs of Psalm 23:6, are much better company on the road of life. Some spend a lot of time planting, fertilizing and watering in April, just to be sure they are doing their part for May. The flowers will not disappoint them. Look around you. God will give you beauty.

> *Holy God, God of all creation, I know that you have some special plans for me this month. I am hopeful. I want to do Your will. Amen.*

May 1

OneYearChallenge—Read: I Samuel 13-15

Telling Lies

I CAN DEAL WITH ALMOST ANYTHING EXCEPT people telling me lies. Maybe it is an occupational hazard for a minister. People lie voluntarily before you even ask them to do so. *"Pastor, I will see you in church on Sunday,"* but they never come. In the hospital, recovering patients often say, *"I will be back in church as soon as I get home."* They still haven't been to church. Some lie with such sincerity. Perhaps practice makes perfect in the sport of lying? Promises are broken, appointments are not kept, hearts are broken, lives even ruined because of lies. Why do people lie? It's not necessary. It creates more problems. Jesus said liars belong to their father, the Devil, and learned their trade naturally. All lies originate in Satan (John 8:44). When you lie, you reveal your family tree. It must be total truthfulness, all the time, for the followers of *"the truth"* (John 14:6). *"Speaking the truth in love, we will in all things grow up into . . . Christ"* (Ephesians 4:15). You see, you can say the truth, the whole truth, to anyone, in a spirit of love. It will not hurt but be a blessing in the long run. We are directed, *"each of you must put off falsehood and speak truthfully to his neighbor"* (Ephesians 4:25). It is inexcusable for a Christian to ever lie. The court system has people to raise their hands and promise to tell the truth and yet many are guilty of perjury while under oath. A Christian's truthful lifestyle should be so obvious that a simple *"Yes"* or *"No"* will be sufficient and always believable (Matthew 5:37). You will be a much better person if you don't exaggerate, stretch or withhold the truth, add to the story, or in any way manipulate the facts. Anyway, the truth always comes out. Save yourself getting caught in a lie.

Father, being with You makes me want to be truthful. I know I can't fool You and You are always listening. Amen.

ONE YEAR CHALLENGE—Read:
I Samuel 16-18

May 2

Being Locked Up

THE SOUND OF STEEL DOORS CLANGING SHUT and locks falling into place is a terrible sound. Even though I have heard it for many years in jail visitation ministry, I still don't like it. Men and women were not made to be locked up, but to be free. Because of crime, many forfeit the right to be free so society can be protected from their harmful acts. We must never forget those who are imprisoned. We must never allow them to be so stripped of personality that they lose their own self-image as valuable human beings. Jesus focused on those in prison throughout his ministry. In his first recorded speech in a synagogue, he chose a passage from the Prophet Isaiah where it was foretold that the Messiah (Savior) would *"proclaim freedom for the prisoners"* (Luke 4:18). At the close of his ministry, he told the parable about the Day of Judgment when one of the evidences of true discipleship was visiting those who were in prison (Matthew 25:36). It is obvious to me that all of us have a continuing responsibility for those who are locked-up, we simply cannot wash our hands of them with an *"out-of-sight, out-of-mind"* attitude. It is equally true of our responsibility for those who are free to walk around in society but are spiritually and emotionally locked up. Someone said, *"stone walls do not a prison make, nor iron bars a cage."* That was just a poetic way of saying that not all prisoners are locked up within physical prison walls. Just as one has to make a definite effort to visit in a jail or prison, effort is required to minister to those people who are emotionally or spiritually locked up. The idea of intentionally helping people experience freedom is a pattern we need to follow. Jesus said, *"I have come that they may have life"* (John 10:10). The freedom that Jesus offers will lift us above our life situation, enabling us to minister to one another.

Thank You, Jesus, for saying that if I knew the Truth, the Truth would make me free. Thank You more for letting me experience that. Amen.

May 3

ONE YEAR CHALLENGE—Read:
1 Samuel 19-21

Coming Up Blank on a Big Question

THE QUESTION IS ROOTED IN A SAD LAMENT. A certain woman had grown up going to Sunday School and worship services. She had learned about God. But when she married, it was to a young man who wouldn't help her get their small children ready and take them to church. She soon stopped going. Then she got involved in a Sunday bowling league. Now, she sits in a courtroom and hears the judge sentence her baby boy, now 20 years old, to 20 years in prison. Drunk driving and robbery had almost taken the life of a victim. She had watched as her son had defiantly sneered at every police officer and officer of the court. She was humiliated when the judge asked the defiant young man, *"Young man, don't you believe in God?"* And he gave a long, loud laugh and said, *"God? Who's that?"* She felt like everyone was looking at her. But the son's question: can you answer it? Can your spouse answer it? Can your child answer it? If you know the answer, rather, if you know God, have you introduced Him to the person closest to you in life? How sad to think that many people do not know the most significant One in the whole universe. Philip said to Jesus, *"show us the Father and that will be enough"* (John 14:8). I believe that could be true for every person in the world. The Bible's answer to that big question is in John 1:18, *"God the only Son is very close to the Father. And the Son has shown us what God is like"* (EB). There, you can meet Him and know Him and introduce Him to someone else. Why come up blank on such a big question?

Thank You, God, that the hardest questions have the clearest answer. Who said simple truth isn't deep? You didn't! Amen.

ONE YEAR CHALLENGE—Read:
I Samuel 22-24

May 4

Rainy Days

WHAT DO YOU DO ON A RAINY DAY? No, I don't mean to ask a childish question. If you listen to the weather people on radio or television, the worst thing that can happen is have a rainy day, especially on a weekend. But then these same people will, during a late summer drought, talk about the need for rain. Maybe they are just making conversation when they fuss about rain, or the lack of it! Rain is such a blessing to the earth, whenever it comes, that we need to be totally grateful. I know, sometimes it seems like too much, like during floods, but we couldn't live without it. All of the beauties of our world depend upon it. Gratefully, God doesn't play favorites with the rain but sends it *"on the righteous and the unrighteous"* (Matthew 5:45). If it's not too cold or windy, walking in the rain is a good experience. Smelling it and feeling it helps you appreciate it. Rainy days are also good for forc-ing us to sit down and think, something we might not do if it were sunny. Some people get despondent and despairing when it rains. People who grow up on a part of the earth where there is an extended *"rainy season"* have a positive attitude when it rains. They have learned to be content with and accepting of this blessing. When Paul and Barnabus went to Lystra on a missionary journey, Paul used the gift of rain as a proof of the existence of a loving God: *"He has shown kindness by giving you rain from heaven"* (Acts 14:17). James uses the hope for rain that a farmer has as an object lesson for the kind of expectancy that a Christian has for the Second Coming of Christ (James 5:7). Rain is obviously a physical gift from God that we need. Try being a little more spiritually perceptive the next time it rains. You may learn some spiritual lessons.

> *Dear God, we need showers of blessings. No, make that a downpour. We get dried out too quickly. Amen.*

OneYearChallenge—Read: I Samuel 25-27

May 5

Wanting to be First

IT'S CRAZY THE WAY WE ACT! Have you made a plane trip lately? The plane lands and taxis to the airport. Before the seat belt light is turned off, everyone is on his feet and trying to be the first one off. Why—to be the first at the luggage carousel? Been to a sports event lately? Did you rush to be the first to get in your car to get out of the parking lot? The desire to be first makes us do so many strange things. Even in unimportant areas. And after achieving first or second place, what have you accomplished? Marriages and families have been destroyed by one member of the family who always had to be first. Some parents make nervous wrecks of their kids by pushing them to be first in everything. It's inherent in human nature. Jesus had to deal with the same problem in teaching His disciples. They came from a "me first" culture and wanted to carry that pattern over into the Kingdom of God. On one occasion Jesus heard them arguing about who was first among them. Jesus said, *"If anyone wants to be first, he must be the very last, and the servant of all"* (Mark 9:35). *"But,"* you ask, *"where goes the good old competitive spirit"* with this attitude? There's nothing wrong with a competitive spirit but if being *"number one"* depends on putting someone else down, you are using people for selfish reasons. Ask yourself, *"Why do I want to be first? What insecurity drives me to have to prove myself?"* Jesus said in another place, *"whoever humbles himself like this child is the greatest in the kingdom of heaven"* (Matthew 18:4). The key to being first is a humble attitude. It depends on your value system. Do you want to be first in worldly things or spiritual things? First before man or God? You can't have it both ways. Think about what Jesus said and did: the humble, servant, King of Kings.

Today I want to make You first in my life. Discipline me when I try to take Your place. I know You are the only God. Amen.

OneYearChallenge—Read: I Samuel 28-30

May 6

A Clean Environment

WHAT DO YOU THINK ABOUT THE WAY WE ARE POISONING ourselves in the environment? We're driving toward national suicide if you think about it. We poison the waters and then eat the seafood that lives in the water. We spray the plants and fruit trees with poison and then eat the contaminated fruit. We cut down all the trees for lumber and paper, and so do away with the natural system of purifying the air. Where will it end? The hospitals have more and more patients that give evidence of environmental poisoning. Soon we must take this business seriously. *"This is the day the LORD has made, let us rejoice and be glad in it"* (Psalm 118:24). It's time to put that into action and do what I can to protect it. I am not as excited as some about exploring outer space until we use more of our vaunted know-how to do a better job taking care of Planet Earth. One of these days there will be no more places to put a landfill and bury our garbage—what then? When Paul wrote in Romans 8:22, *"the whole creation has been groaning as in the pains of childbirth right up to the present time,"* he didn't know half as much as we know now about environmental problems. We need to be called back to Genesis 2:15 where the Bible relates, *"the LORD God took the man and put him in the Garden of Eden to work it and take care of it."* We may never restore America to the lush perfection of the garden of Eden but we still need to remember that God appointed us the stewards (caretakers) of this earth and we have a responsibility for it. We also owe a debt to the next generation to pass it on to them in an acceptable condition. *"The earth is the Lord's and everything in it, the world, and all who live in it"* (Psalm 24:1).

> *Thank You, God, for recycling my life; I was really in a "throw away" state. Thank You for making my life usable in the Kingdom of God. Amen.*

May 7

ONE YEAR CHALLENGE—Read:
1 Samuel 31,
2 Samuel 1-2

A Christian Mother

LET'S GET DOWN TO THE NITTY-GRITTY on this subject. There's no need for a philosophical debate between yesterday's nostalgia and today's position on women's rights! The bottom line for us today is about the effect of a Christian mother. The Bible says, *"Her children arise and call her blessed"* (Proverbs 31:28). Why? Obviously, a Christian woman is going to see her task as a stewardship, that is, a caretaker role. As she prepares for the birth of her child, she begins to understand that God has entrusted this child to her to protect and raise until the time the child can be responsible for himself (or herself). She knows the child is not hers to possess and control for a lifetime, but to nurture and train until the child discovers *"the way he should go"* in life (Proverbs 22:6). This is a very special role. To do this takes time. She will be there for the child as much as possible. She will be there to teach, train, discipline, listen, and encourage! More important than *"presents"* is *"presence"*. Some mothers spend so much time working in order to buy presents that they neglect the importance of their presence—being there for the kid! A Christian mother knows that her child needs her more than things. A Christian mother is going to be as concerned about her child's spiritual growth as its physical growth. It's a significant part of her stewardship! She will read the Bible daily for her own personal growth and then she will read the Bible to her child to build a solid moral base in the child's life. A Christian mother doesn't see child-rearing as a burden, or irritation, or the frustration of a another career. A Christian mother can be what she wants to be and do what she wants to do; she will just have a sound grasp of her priorities. And if she is a single mother, her church family should do all possible to help her do this job. May God bless those seriously involved in the profession of motherhood.

> *God, thank You for giving me a Christian Mother. She knew You so well and taught me so much about You. I am grateful. Amen.*

ONE YEAR CHALLENGE—Read:
2 Samuel 3-5

May 8

About Mom

I HEARD AN INTERESTING STATEMENT the other day. Someone said that the greatest power in the world today is the power of God and that the second greatest power in the world today is a godly mother. That sounds realistic to me. It certainly puts a different slant on this celebration we call *"Mother's Day."* Instead of a time for sentimentality, it is a time for serious thought. Instead of being a time for nostalgia, let it be a time for self-examination. None of the advertising you will ever hear or read this week will focus on that, so let me fill the void. Some of us have the mistaken idea that you can't support ERA or be a liberated woman and still think highly of being a mother. Wrong! Being a good mom builds a woman's self-esteem. We suffer more from our ignorance of a biblical view of motherhood. Some people claim that mothers are just *"baby-factories"*. That's really too bad. Take a census at your local high school and ask the girls what they know about God's plan for womankind. You will probably get no answer or the wrong answer. In the Genesis account of creation, you will find that God gave men and women equality in the sharing with Him of the creation process and gave them equal responsibility as parents. This double standard that exists in our country about male freedom and female submission certainly isn't biblical. Begin to study your Bible. Let God speak to you from your Bible. Indeed, *"a woman who fears the LORD is to be praised"* (Proverbs 31:30) and, *"Her children arise and call her blessed; her husband also, and he praises her"* (Proverbs 31:28). In every country in the world where Christianity establishes a beachhead, godly women will be in the forefront. Don't underestimate God's work in women's lives. One of our national treasures is the sensitive Spirit of Godly women.

> **Thank You, Father, for the godly women at the core of every church. Their courage and commitment far exceeds their recognition. Amen.**

May 9

One Year Challenge—Read:
2 Samuel 6-8

Motherhood

Is MOTHERHOOD A BIOLOGICAL FUNCTION (planned or accidental), a mechanical role, or a Divine plan? The morning news reported that the Washington, D.C. metropolitan area leads the nation in abortions; so many view motherhood as a biological accident, thinking it's okay to back out of it if at will. Remember when there used to be a lot of sweet poetry about *"Mother"*? Remember when one of the main subjects of country/western music was breaking Mother's heart with wild living and sin? Remember when Motherhood was upheld as honorable, maybe even the most honorable role for a woman? Remember when women were not put down for making no greater contribution to society than staying home and raising their children? The only thing that seems the same is the business community's push to capitalize on Mother's Day! After all, more people will eat out on Mother's Day than any other Sunday of the year. When the place of the mother is not respected in society, all women suffer. The place of women and their role in God's plan for mankind is clear in the Bible. They have special ministries, also. The contempt with which women are held by the pornographic industry and the people who buy it is obvious. Yes, when respect for motherhood started to slide, the shock waves were felt in a lot of places. I quote Peter with this word to mothers in I Peter 3:3-4, *"Your beauty should not come from outward adornment, such as braided hair and the wearing of gold jewelry and fine clothes. Instead, it should be that of your inner self, the unfading beauty of a gentle and quiet spirit, which is of great worth in God's sight."* This is practical advice to a woman taking seriously her role before God. God gave her qualities that make for lasting relationships; she's not a mechanical *"rent-a-womb"* or short order cook.

One Year Challenge—Read: 2 Samuel 9-11

> *Father, it was no accident that You chose a woman as the vehicle to bring Your Only Son into the world. Give us insight into that. Amen.*

May 10

A Mother's Influence

I HAVE HEARD IT SUNG ABOUT IN COUNTRY AND WESTERN MUSIC all my life, but I had never heard a personal story of a mother's memory keeping someone from gross sin before. A man was relating to me his experiences in World War II. Stationed overseas, he and his friends were living a very debauched lifestyle. Booze was cheap, and he was spending many hours just drinking whiskey and wasting his life. And then he thought of his mother and how disappointed this godly woman would be if she could see him. He put down his bottle, went through three days of torture in a self-imposed, drying-out experience and didn't drink again. Maybe all the stories aren't that dramatic, but some of you reading this now are thinking back to the powerful influence for good your mother had on your life. I don't write this to glorify motherhood, for frankly, there's not much glory in scrubbing floors, washing diapers, and all the other distasteful duties moms have. No, I write this to salute and commend the influence of a godly mother. In the grind of the ordinary, my mother powerfully shaped my life. Both in this culture and another culture, my wife influenced our children to be well-developed, spiritual human beings. Mothers should be alert to this and challenged by the possibilities. Being a mother should not be taken lightly. No one can take a mother's place in child development. Proverbs 31 is devoted to praising a godly wife and mother. She is devoted and industrious, faithful and helpful, and *"Her children arise and call her blessed; her husband also, and he praises her: 'Many women do noble things, but you surpass them all.' Charm is deceptive, and beauty is fleeting; but a woman who fears the LORD is to be praised. . . . let her works bring her praise at the city gate"* (Proverbs 31:28-31). The issue is far greater than women's rights and equality—the issue is women seeking motherhood as a God-given opportunity and stewardship. Bless them!

Lord, call godly men and godly women to form spiritual training grounds for their children. Remind parents today of their spiritual responsibility. Amen.

ONE YEAR CHALLENGE—Read: 2 Samuel 12-14

May 11

Like a Child

THE GOSPEL WRITERS AGREE that there was a certain day when people were bringing their babies and small children to Jesus to have Him touch them and let them feel His hand of blessing. When Jesus' companions saw this, they chided those bringing the children and started to shoo the little ones away. They felt that Jesus' time was too valuable to be wasted on children; they assumed adults needed Him more. Then Jesus stopped them in their tracks saying, *"Let the little children come to me, and do not hinder them, for the kingdom of God belongs to such as these"* (Luke 18:16). Mothers of children in their *"terrible twos"* have a hard time believing this! Also day care providers who struggle with the self-centered little ones fighting over toys may raise an eyebrow at this. Just what did Jesus have in mind? What is the characteristic in little ones that Jesus identified and made a *"Kingdom quality"*? After a week at the beach

with my grandchildren I know the answer. The key is trust! Why else would a pre-schooler accompany an adult into the ocean surf with the waves three feet tall? Why else would a 2-year old, fearful of heights, suddenly jump from the top of the stairs to the outstretched arms of a grandfather? Trust! It is as simple as that! The three short years of Jesus' public teaching ministry was a repetition of the lesson *"trust me."* Trust me to forgive your sins, trust me to change your life, trust me to give meaning to your life, trust me to take you to heaven when you die, and so on. The kids trusted Jesus! They ran to Him. They didn't know Him personally. But they looked at Him and knew He could be trusted. That's why He used a little child as an object lesson. The word *"believe"* in your Bible means *"trust."* Question: will you trust Him?

O God, You are trustworthy. I am going to take another step of faith and trust this whole day to You. Amen.

ONE YEAR CHALLENGE—Read:
2 Samuel 15-17

May 12

What Is Woman?

WHAT'S OUR COUNTRY THINKING ABOUT WOMEN? It seems that the place of women has gotten mixed up. Why such ill-will toward women? Statistics say that every few seconds in America a woman is sexually or physically abused. This doesn't make sense. Can this many men have had such a terrible relationship with their mothers that they are angry with all women? What kind of sick satisfaction is derived from abusing someone weaker than yourself? Whether it happens in the market place, paying a woman less than she is worth, or behind closed doors by punching her—abuse is abuse. I don't think the church has a good record in supporting women either. Although the church pays lip-service to the role of women (after all, Jesus was born to a virgin woman), at church, women are often given secondary roles. Some churches forbid women to preach or teach or express any form of "authority" over the male members. The message is subtle, but obvious, that women are second-class. The fact is that from the time a group of women accompanied Jesus and the disciples until now, women have played an absolutely essential role in the life and development of the Christian church. Yet today, in some churches, a woman divorced from a destructive marriage is not welcomed and is told to go elsewhere. My Bible still says in Genesis 2:22 that *"God made a woman"*; she was not an accident. In Galatians 3:28, the Bible emphasizes that in Christ there is no male or female discrimination but *"you are all one in Christ Jesus."* Contempt for these for whom Christ died is a sin and that includes women. Yes, Jesus gave women status in his kingdom. The Christian faith is clear on that. Let the church be faithful to that teaching!

> *Thank You, God, that our maleness or femaleness is not a barrier to our relationship with You. You made us and know us best of all. Amen.*

ONE YEAR CHALLENGE—Read:
2 Samuel 18-20

May 13

Feeling Sorry for Oneself

My WIFE AND I OFTEN GET A CHUCKLE FROM THE ADVENTURES OF **HI AND LOIS** in the Sunday comics. Some of their situations remind us of ourselves. Have you ever been tempted to feel sorry for yourself? In one strip the baby complained that the only fun for that day might be to do just that. Dad goes off to work; siblings to school; Mom to the laundry room, while the dog just sleeps. Baby feels trapped I guess, with nothing to do and no one paying any attention. Well, in such circumstances, feeling sorry for yourself could seem like the thing to do. Most of us occasionally get the opportunity to wish we were elsewhere, with someone or something different perhaps. Why do we enjoy having a *"pity party"*? Did you ever know someone who *"enjoyed poor health"*? That's absurd, right? How could you enjoy feeling bad? Many do! Some folks seem to be gifted in putting a dark lining on every silver cloud. There is al-ways some kind of fly in their ointment. There is a better way to live. Life has too much to offer for us to get caught in that trap. Knowing *"I can do everything through him who gives me strength"* (Philippians 4:13), I am *"Forgetting what is behind and straining toward what is ahead"* (Philippians 3:13-14). I can do all this by working on the principle that *"Everything is possible for him who believes"* (Mark 9:23). It has a lot to do with self image, self respect, and self love to be sure, but better than all that is the rock-solid foundation of trusting faith in a Living God. Like the song says, *"I don't know what the future holds but I know who holds my future."** As long as the world tries to tear me down I can know that God is alive and that lifts me up. Feeling sorry for yourself can't be fun, can it? Jesus died on the cross for you. You are valuable and special to God!

> *Forgive me for feeling sorry for myself when there are so many people who need my genuine sympathy. Help me to look beyond myself. Amen.*

May 14

ONE YEAR CHALLENGE—Read:
2 Samuel 21-23

Getting Good at What We Practice

MANY PEOPLE HAVE TOLD OF THE FUTIL-ITY OF WAR. Perhaps you have heard the sad statistic that in the last 3,000 years of history, there have been less than 300 years of peace in the world. I can't verify those numbers but they're probably not far off. We constantly train and equip our military forces for war. It seems to me that mankind has over-practiced this vocation. Shouldn't we practice peace more? The Bible says so: "seek peace and pursue it" (I Peter 3:11). Let's work harder toward applying this command. We get good at what we practice. We celebrate a National Day of Prayer for Peace. Some churches observe it; some don't. Some people think it is a great idea that needs support; others suspect it indicates a sign of weakness. Why is it we spend so little time training for peace? Fighting wars comes naturally to humans; for little or no reason the urge comes out of us. To work for peace takes more effort. For years a grass-roots group worked in Washington, connecting people around the country, to establish a peace academy just like the Army, Navy, and Air Force academies. It did become a reality finally, in 1984, when Congress passed legislation and a relatively small appropriation, which President Reagan signed. Maybe someday The United States Institute of Peace will be as well known and attended as the war academies. Jesus said, *"Blessed are the peacemakers, for they will be called sons of God"* (Matthew 5:9). The implications for us are obvious: There is more lasting joy in making peace than in making war. War brings pain, sorrow, hurt; nothing of lasting value comes from war, just death and the seed-bed for another conflict. *"Returning hate for hate multiplies hate, adding deeper darkness to a night already devoid of stars,"* wrote M.L. King, Jr. International issues are beyond you, you say. Perhaps, but living peacefully with the white, black, alien, or native in your community, or even those in your house isn't beyond you. Practice peace, not war!

> *Jesus, Paul said that You came to make peace in the world. It is exciting to see you bringing people together by breaking down walls of hostility. "Peacemaker" is a good name for You. Amen.*

May 15

ONE YEAR CHALLENGE—Read: 2 Samuel 24, Romans 1-2

Intensive Care Waiting Room

As A PASTOR I HAVE SPENT A LOT OF TIME in the intensive care waiting room. Have you ever been there? It is different from any other place in the world. The people you meet there, waiting for news from the doctor or nurse, are different too, at least temporarily. Those folks can't do enough for each other. They buy coffee and soda for all and ask if anyone is hungry. No one is rude. No one is racist. The distinctions of color and class disappear. A person is a father first, an African American second. Another person is a mother first, an ethnic second. The garbage man loves his wife as much as the bank president loves his, and the maid loves her child as much as the nurse loves hers. Everyone understands that! The ground is level in intensive care, and there is equality of concern. Vanity and pretense vanish. The universe is focused on the doctor's next report. Everyone there knows that loving someone else is what life is all about. Wes Seelinger asks, "Why does it take the intensive care waiting room to drive home the brotherhood of man?" Genesis 4:9 implies that I am my brother's keeper. We are told to "Love each other" (John 15:17). "By this all men will know that you are my disciples, if you love one another," Jesus said (John 13:35). Obviously, if the common good works in the intensive care waiting room, it can work anytime and in any place. Don't wait for a crisis in your life (like having someone in intensive care) to begin to look around and accept your fellow man. People need you and you need them. Be sensitive to other people all the time, not just in their crisis time or yours. Begin to practice acceptance and concern wherever you meet people.

Remind us, Loving Savior, that the ground was level at the foot of the cross. Give us some tools we can use to keep it that way. Amen.

OneYearChallenge—Read:
Romans 3-5

May 16

Loving Flowers

DON'T YOU JUST LOVE FLOWERS? Boy, God did a great thing when He created flowers. They add so much to life. FTD florists advertise a *"Pick-me-up"* bouquet and that is a fitting description. The most depressed person has to feel momentary relief in the presence of flowers. The springtime is special because the flowers begin to literally *"burst out"* in loveliness. Because flowers have this impact on me I have always been interested in the way the Bible uses flowers. Flowers are an object lesson in the Bible, primarily to teach us the temporary nature of things. Earthly beauty is described as a fading flower, the length of life is compared to a cut flower, the passing glory of man is likened to a falling flower, etc. Let's consider the nature of the flower; it is beautiful, but it's beauty is so tender and fragile and momentary and then it is thrown away. (Ever notice the day after a funeral how the grounds-keeper at the cemetery has thrown away most of the flowers?) So what can we learn from all this? We can accept every beautiful gift from God, enjoy it to its fullest, and be grateful for it and not grieve over its passing. That song about taking time to smell the roses may be saying the same thing. Eight hundred years before Jesus, the Prophet Isaiah expressed the right perspective when he said, *"the flowers fall, but the word of our God stands forever"* (Isaiah 40:8). Let's gain an insight into reality and a proper perspective: invest in what lasts, that's the issue. Many people are peddling posies of their pet philosophy, in fashion for a season. Jesus' advice was to put your heart into heavenly things that don't fade (Matthew 6:20-21). Love the flowers, but love the Flower Maker more!

> *Creator God, You have such a sense of beauty. You have brought color into my life. Help me to keep the colors from fading. Amen.*

May 17

ONE YEAR CHALLENGE—Read: Romans 6-8

A Spoken Word is Comforting

"**A** WORD APTLY SPOKEN IS LIKE APPLES OF GOLD IN SETTINGS OF SILVER" (Proverbs 25:11). Ever heard that? Maybe you didn't know it was from the Bible. It's a grand comparison from the wise man Solomon. That truth was recently made very real for me. When my oldest brother died, many people offered "*aptly spoken words.*" They wrote or spoke words of encouragement, comfort, direction, concern, support, help—you know the kind of words they said. And it was so important, so needed! The effectiveness of saying something good at the appropriate time cannot be measured. It doesn't have to be profound! It doesn't have to be unusual! But it has to be genuine and it needs to be said. Some people are hung up by the thought that they "*don't know the right thing to say,*" so they think good thoughts but don't express them. When a person is grieving, worried, pressured, excited or whatever, the power of the spoken word from a concerned individual is truly great. Indeed, like golden apples on a silver tray, beautiful to behold and valuable! Don't miss the possibilities here. Look around you today and every other day. See that person, go up to them, express your concern in a word. If you don't know what to say, ask God. Have you noticed the life of Jesus as recorded in the Bible? There are long discourses and sermons recorded but so much of the impact of Jesus on individuals was His coming up close to people in a particularly difficult time and saying a caring word: To a grieving Mary, "*Why are you crying?*" (John 20:15); to a crippled man, "*Do you want to get well?*" (John 5:6); to a terrified and embarrassed woman who had been caught in adultery, "*neither do I condemn you, . . . Go now and leave your life of sin,*" to mention a few. Each situation and its meaning changed for these people. Try it. You'll like it! So will the other person.

Father, we are made to communicate and live in community. May we use our words to strengthen relationships. Amen.

One Year Challenge—Read: Romans 9-11

May 18

Quiet Fanaticism

WHAT IS A FANATIC ANYWAY? When the word is used, it's usually in a derogatory way. It tends to introduce a sense of fear and revulsion. However, there are some areas where it is okay to be a fanatic. The dictionary defines a fanatic as a person possessed by an excessive and irrational zeal. In the founding of our country, we had several men who were considered fanatics. They said such things as, *"Give me liberty or give me death," "I only regret that I have but one life to give for my country,"* and *"We must all hang together or it is assured that we will all hang separately."* Their fanaticism was praiseworthy because it brought good results. Some people are described as *"football fanatics"* or *"softball fanatics"* or *"racing fanatics,"* etc. (especially by members of their families who regret seeing them overindulging.) This kind of fanatic is considered basically harmless and irritate only the people who live with them. Religious fanatics may create the most problems for society. Again, I may be raising unpleasant images in your mind. Was it someone selling flowers on a street corner in sub-freezing weather, someone stopping you in an airport, or a brother-in-law who was always browbeating you with the Bible? Often the media publicizes terrible events caused by a religious fanatic. I raise the question with you today about your own personal convictions. Do you have any? Are they worth giving your life, devoting all your energy? I am thinking that what the world needs today are some quiet, clear-eyed, determined people who will hear the challenge of Jesus: *"If anyone would come after me, he must deny himself and take up his cross and follow me"* (Matthew 16:24), and do just that! And not turn back!

> *Lord, help me to be a quiet fanatic, deeply in love with You and deeply committed to patiently sharing the truth. Amen.*

ONE YEAR CHALLENGE—Read: Romans 12-14

May 19

Seeking Inspiration

WHY ARE YOU READING THIS? Did this page happen to catch your eye? Are you looking for help or inspiration? Perhaps there is a spiritual struggle going on in your life? Did you wonder if God might have some special word for you today, so you sought it in these lines? As we meet on these lines, our motivation for being here is probably quite different, but, no doubt, there is a basic spiritual motivation. We search for truth and the help it gives us. John said to a group in John 5:39, *"You diligently study the Scriptures because you think that by them you possess eternal life. These are the Scriptures that testify about me."* But then he went on to say that not all who receive spiritual instruction act on it. A group of people in Berea were commended by Luke in Acts 17:11 as noble people, *"for they received the message with great eagerness and examined the Scriptures every day."* It would be good if our meeting here would lead you to look more closely into the Book (Holy Bible) that is quoted here for additional inspiration and direction. A man recently made a very interesting observation. Being an avid reader, he suddenly realized that he was reading more books about the Book than he was spending time reading the Book. Our hunger for spiritual truth can be satisfied; Jesus promised that: *"Ask and it will be given to you; seek and you will find; knock and the door will be opened to you"* (Matthew 7:7). Even if you are reading this strictly by chance, God has *"butted in"* on your thought process to speak a challenging word to your heart. Thank God for that. *"He has not left himself without testimony"* (Acts 14:17). Even if it is on this page.

> *Father, many people are going down today because they lack inspiration. The Bible commands us to proclaim good news to every person. Remind us again. Amen.*

May 20

ONE YEAR CHALLENGE—Read:
Romans 15-16, 1 Kings 1

The AIDS Menace

THE LITTLE CLOUD ON THE HORIZON has now loomed large and foreboding. What formerly instigated snickers about homosexuals, now threatens the whole community. Many fear blood transfusions who formerly welcomed them for lifesaving. Wedding day bliss is clouded by the unspoken fear concerning the stranger coming into the family: Is he/she a carrier? Will their children have AIDS? How do we deal with this? How do we treat the victims? Regarding the threat of sexual transmission, we can obey the Bible. Look there for the standard God established for sexual relationships. Sex is to be enjoyed only by a man and a woman whom God has brought together in God's covenant of marriage. Jesus reiterated His Father's will in Matthew 19:4-6: "Haven't you read, . . . that at the beginning the Creator 'made them male and female,' and said, 'For this reason a man will leave his father and mother and be united to his wife, and the two will become one flesh'? So they are no longer two, but one. Therefore what God has joined together, let man not separate."

With regard to our attitude toward the victims of AIDS, it must be unconditional love. Sadly, according to statistics, most will not live past one year. Their last days will be miserable; we should minister to them, not judge or fear them. Christian love is always in order. Just as we would visit a cancer or diabetes victim with a message of God's forgiveness, mercy and hope, we should do the same for AIDS victims. Again, our model is Jesus. In John 5, He is described going to a place where there were many sick people. He picked out the most desperate, a man who hadn't walked in 38 years, and went to him with a message of love and help. So we should go to the most desperate and not leave them only to more impersonal, public care. We may hate and despise the sickness and whatever produced it, but we cannot be trapped into hating the sick person. The church must not withdraw from this field of opportunity.

> **Jesus, You offer physical and spiritual healing. While we are anxious to tell everyone about the spiritual help, I pray we will not ignore the physically needy. Amen.**

May 21

ONE YEAR CHALLENGE—Read:
I Kings 2-4

When My World Stopped

I HAD AN AUTOMOBILE ACCIDENT, A HEAD-ON collision. When I did, my world stopped. I realized it immediately. When I tried to get out of the car and couldn't move, I realized my world had abruptly changed. Strong, healthy, active, independent, busy, now I was no longer in control; other people took over. Strangers! The rescue squad came; they were in control. I was then taken to the emergency room where skilled people took over my life. Later, my care was transferred to nurses on the floor, my world had stopped! I was told when to sleep and when to wake up, was given medicine by someone else's orders. Well, you can imagine the rest. Did you notice the emphasis I made on *"my world"*? You see, the rest of the world was not directly affected and continued on its merry way. It happens like that to all of us from time to time. Things go smoothly for a long time, then a crisis comes and disrupts our control of our situation and that is difficult for many of us to handle. It is certainly a good time to say with David, *"But I trust in you, O LORD; I say, 'You are my God.' My times are in your hands; deliver me"* (Psalm 31:14-15). Sometimes we react to crisis as if God did not know that it was happening. The poet, Whittier, once affirmed, *"I only know that I cannot drift beyond His love and care."* Christians can find great encouragement in the face of an upside-down world in the words of Psalm 84:11, *"the LORD bestows favor and honor; no good thing does he withhold from those whose walk is blameless."* One old saint observed, *"I like the statement in the Bible 'it came to pass'."* Regardless of how bad it is, it will pass. It may be poor exegesis, but it's rich trust.

From my self-centered point of view, I think the world can't get by without me. From time to time You remind me of my place. Thank You, I needed that. Amen.

ONE YEAR CHALLENGE—Read: I Kings 5-7

May 22

Weekend Exhaustion

WHY NOT BE GOOD TO YOURSELF THIS WEEKEND? Early Friday morning the local disc jockeys start blaring from the radio, *"It's T.G.I.F."* or *"Thank God It's Friday."* The newspaper has a weekend supplement with suggestions for you to follow on the weekend. By the end of Friday afternoon's commute, weekend plans are often made: working in the yard, painting the house, going on a trip, watching a soccer game, visiting the shopping mall, etc. All of this and more in one weekend. The result: scientific surveys have shown that the majority of the American work force returns to work on Monday morning more exhausted than they were on Friday afternoon. Why do people wear themselves out on weekends? Do people keep busy so they won't have to talk and get to know one another? What force drives people on weekends? Surely, all aren't workaholics. The Bible clearly says we need rest and lays out a plan for it. *"Remember the Sabbath day by keeping it holy. Six days you shall labor and do all your work, but the seventh day is a Sabbath to the LORD your God. On it you shall not do any work"* (Exodus 20:8-10). It makes good sense and it is practical. A rested employee certainly will do better than a tired and exhausted one; thoughts are clearer and response is sharper. I often think that driving on the freeway is a lot like the rolling, barrel-like exerciser in a gerbil cage. After five days running the same treadmill, why not get off for a couple of days? Take the time to enjoy the beauty of the world around you. *"Gaze upon the beauty of the LORD"* (Psalm 27:4) that He has made. Take time to worship. A full hour of singing praise to God and studying His Word and just being with others in the worship experience will be a real *"spring tonic"* for your mind, body, and soul.

God, did you create weekends, too? Why is it so hard to see You active on my street on Sunday? Help us understand. Amen.

OneYearChallenge—Read: I Kings 8-10

May 23

Rising Expectations

MANY YEARS AGO, I HEARD A DR. SAM HILL speak, and in his talk, he described people who were caught up in a *"wave of rising expectation."* I have never forgotten that phrase, although I have long ago forgotten what the man looked like. In looking at the world scene, much of what is good and positive in our world today is a result of that wave. When minority Americans began to see on television what the rest of Americans were enjoying, they could no longer be satisfied in their oppressed state. When satellites began to beam television signals behind iron and bamboo curtains, oppressed Europeans and others began to raise their expectations. Out of the Persian Gulf War, another group of people woke up with rising expectations because the N.A.T.O. forces gave them freedom. Christianity has always thrived on that kindling of inner hope. When Jesus said, *"you will know the truth, and the truth will set you free"* (John 8:32), and when he said, *"Follow me, . . . and I will make you fishers of men"* (Matthew 4:19), he struck a chord that spiritually oppressed people had been wanting to hear. People who are enslaved and oppressed by man-made religions long for the good news of a real Savior with a real salvation that will come soon. When Jesus said, *"I am the resurrection and the life. He who believes in me will . . . never die"* (John 11:25-26), He rang a bell of hope that stirred the whole world. It cannot be hushed. Christians have been killed and the Bible forbidden in many countries but *"God's word is not chained"* (2 Timothy 2:9), and millions ride the *"wave of rising expectations"* right into the Kingdom of God. It's like that man, crippled for 38 years, sitting forlornly by the Pool of Bethesda, having *"no one to help me"* suddenly seeing the outstretched hand of Jesus (John 5:5); you just have to respond to the opportunity.

Help me never to just accept things as they are but to always expect things to get better, especially the spiritual condition of my neighbors. Amen.

May 24

ONE YEAR CHALLENGE—Read: 1 Kings 11-13

Warning: Watch Total Lifestyle

MANY PEOPLE HAVE SUFFERED GREAT DISAPPOINTMENT lately. Believing words of certain very visible individuals they built up a great trust and respect and even invested their hard-earned money to support those individuals who then let them down. It does no good to say, *"I told you so."* So, I want to make a suggestion: next time, check their lifestyle. No matter the words, if the music (lifestyle) isn't right, it can't be good for you. Jesus taught and lived by openness, honesty, humility, self-forgetfulness, righteousness; He was always the same, day by day, in word and deed. Whether your fallen hero was in the world of religion, politics, or the business world, their lifestyle was revealing the truth about them all the time. Paul said in Philippians 3:17-19, *"Join with others in following my example, brothers, and take note of those who live according to the pattern we gave you. For, as I have often told you before and now say again even with tears, many live as enemies of the cross of* Christ. *Their destiny is destruction, their god is their stomach, and their glory is in their shame. Their mind is on earthly things."* It's not a new problem and the answer is old too. To keep from being deceived, watch a person's total lifestyle. When Paul wrote the Christians in Thessalonica, he told them he had tried to give them a lifestyle to imitate (2 Thessalonians 3:9). If you want a hero or someone to look up to as a role model, look for someone who has the right words to say (coming from the Bible) and the right lifestyle to emulate (according to the Bible). Of course, no human being is perfect and can't be a perfect example; we all fail at times. But I know many wonderful, consistent Christians who read the Bible and live by it seven days a week with the help of the Holy Spirit; it is their lifestyle. They're not fake, or putting on different behavior for certain people or places; they just live a Godly lifestyle consistently.

> **Make me a consistent Christian. Help me to "talk the talk" and "walk the walk." Amen.**

ONE YEAR CHALLENGE—Read: 1 Kings 14-16

May 25

Pornography: Growing Sickness

A GROWING SICKNESS RESULTING IN PAIN and even death goes untreated all around us: pornography. Small battles have been won against this malady of society, but it seems that as soon as we make a step of progress somewhere, pornography makes two giant strides forward elsewhere. As with other diseases, some seem to have been inoculated (brainwashed) to the point where it does not disturb them. Do you see a difference between hard-core and soft-core pornography? What was considered by the public and courts as hard-core during the 1960s is now classified as soft-core, so it's obvious that we have compromised our standards. Did you know that there are now more hard-core pornographic outlets in America than McDonald's restaurants? Pornography is cloaked hatred—of self, other people, even children. For a price, you can use and abuse people. Hatred knows no limits in degrading the human mind and body. It's big business now! The dollars are rolling in from marketing the flesh of men, women and children! What's the difference between this and the slave trade of another century? Many people who would oppose buying and selling slaves today, on grounds that it is too barbaric, will buy porno magazines and watch lewd videos. Everyone knows, at some level of their consciousness, that it's shameful! For many, their shameful sickness is only indulged under cover of darkness or in secret. A recent poll of newsstands says 90 percent of the people who buy soft-core pornography ask that it be put in a bag. Mr. Gallup says that pornography is the largest social problem facing America today. We have sunk low from the lofty view God bestowed on men and women according to the Bible: *"You made us a little lower than you yourself, and you have crowned us with glory and honor. You let us rule everything your hands have made"* (Psalm 8:5-6 CEV). Seeing every person as a creature of worth forbids pornography. If you have even the slightest touch of this sickness, ask God to heal you.

It is sin, O God, that draws us to pornography like some kind of unseen magnet. Break that attraction, God, each time I feel it. Amen.

May 26

ONE YEAR CHALLENGE—Read: I Kings 17-19

Greater Airline Safety

PERIODICALLY IT HAPPENS AND WHEN IT DOES, we all get shook up. The dimensions of a plane crash are always too large. Strange, but it seems we can deal easier with a dozens being killed daily in auto crashes than the large casualty list we get once in a while from an airline crash. Right after the crash, the cries for greater airline safety come, and I am sure everyone concerned is a little more careful for a while. But let's face it, there is a limit to human-made security. There is no absolutely safe situation when human beings are involved. *"No king is saved by the size of his army; no warrior escapes by his great strength. A horse is a vain hope for deliverance; despite all its great strength it cannot save"* (Psalm 33:16-17) was the Psalmist's word for those who thought military preparedness made people feel safe. In fact, the Bible has much to say about safety and where to find it. *"you alone, O LORD, make me dwell in safety"* (Psalm 4:8), David said. God promised His people safety in Hosea 2:18

when He said, *"Bow and sword and battle I will abolish from the land, so that all may lie down in safety."* You could be paralyzed by fear if you listened to every warning against your personal safety. Safety may have a lot to do with our inner condition. When we went as missionaries to a developing Third World country, many people asked if I was not concerned about the safety of my wife and children. My reply was that when you are where God wants you to be and doing what God wants you to do, you are in the safest place in the world. When the peace of God is promised as a fortress built around your life, there is all the safety you need (Philippians 4:7). I was impressed recently by the futility of people canceling tickets on one airline and purchasing tickets for another airline hoping for more safety; the planes were still piloted by humans. Humans can never guarantee security. As Gene MacLelland wrote in the song: *"Just put your hand in the hand of the man who calmed the sea."**

Father, when I was a child I used to sing the song, "Safe In the Arms of Jesus." I had almost forgotten its comforting message. Amen.

May 27

ONE YEAR CHALLENGE—Read:
I Kings 20-22

Brand Names: Sign of Affluent Society

DO YOU BUY BRAND NAME PRODUCTS only when you go to the store, or do you buy whatever is on sale, or just the cheapest you can find? One of the signs of an affluent society is that those who can afford it buy only brand names—that which is perceived as the best. Well, it's not always the best. Sometimes, things are advertised as the most expensive or exclusive just in order to entice those who are impressed with labels. You probably see this in clothing often. What kind of shirt, shoes, or jacket does your child ask for? Children have been known to steal in order to be able to wear brand names and fit in with a certain clique in school. Some have been caught cutting the brand name labels out of clothing in department stores to take home and sew it in what they wear. This is how powerful the appeal of brand names is! I listened with interest to the radio the other day to a list of the current "What's In" and "What's Out." Is there any way to determine true value? Yes! The Bible says in Philippians 4:8, *"whatever is true, whatever is noble, whatever is right, whatever is pure, whatever is lovely, whatever is admirable—if anything is excellent or praiseworthy—think about such things."* Somehow we must move away from a superficial way of looking at things. Going by outward appearances is meaningless. Jesus was speaking to this when He warned about searching for value in material things: *"treasures on earth, where moth and rust destroy, and where thieves break in and steal"* (Matthew 6:19). We also need to deal with what Samuel said to Jesse, *"Man looks at the outward appearance* (labels), *but the LORD looks at the heart"* (1 Samuel 16:7). What determines your sense of value?

> *Thank You, God, that Your Holy Spirit gives us discernment about what is truly valuable. Increase our sensitivity to the Spirit's revelation. Amen.*

May 28

ONE YEAR CHALLENGE—Read: 2 Kings 1-3

Precious Memories

I REMEMBER AS A CHILD HEARING SOMEONE SINGING on the radio, *"Precious memories, how they linger! How they ever flood my soul!"** No doubt that old country tune is descriptive for many people on Memorial Day weekend. Good memories of some good person who did something good that helped a lot of people; those memories will be stirred by this season of the year. Have you noticed how selective our memories become? We tend to remember the good things and good times more than the bad, it's better that way. There is danger in forgetting certain things. Some things must not be forgotten, we can't afford to forget. Jesus recognized this when he ate the Last Supper with his friends. And he told them, *"For whenever you eat this bread and drink this cup, you proclaim the Lord's death until he comes"* (I Corinthians 11:26). Certainly every Sunday should be a Memorial Day for Christians, a day to stir up a precious memory. Maybe if all professing Christians woke up on Sunday morning realizing it was Memorial Day they would jump up and go to worship with more excitement. What a joy to remember his work on Calvary's cross for me! *"Praise the LORD, O my soul, and forget not all his benefits"* (Psalm 103:2). Forget not, means to remember; memorialize the best on this Memorial Day. I remember the father of Proverbs 3:1 saying, *"My son, do not forget my teaching, but keep my commands in your heart."* What a meaningful Memorial Day it could be if the many people who have strayed from the biblical teachings of their youth, could be refreshed in memory of the great truths once taught them. A fitting memorial to the past is the reviving of precious truths! Remembering in an active and significant way will mean a Memorial Day worth remembering. Let yourself go back to church and remember.

Help us to make a fitting memorial to those who have died. Perhaps a living memorial of a life lived for God would be the best memorial for those who influenced us for good. Amen.

May 29

OneYearChallenge—Read:
2 Kings 4-6

Childhood Cop Out

YOU CAN HEAR A PERVERTED LOGIC all over America when people excuse themselves from attending worship in a church building. *"My parents forced me to go when I was a child, so I don't go now and I don't make my children go."* That's perverted, I say, because that same logic doesn't extend to going to public school, the doctor's office, or any other place that was helpful to a growing child. Whenever I hear that excuse, I picture an adult-child on the floor having a temper tantrum, making no sense at all. Having delivered their performance, at least two things are wrong with this childhood cop out: first, as bad as they may have been, childhood experiences do not release us from adult responsibility and, secondly, shirking parental responsibility to children leaves them pagans. So many people today are being robbed of any kind of spiritual heritage because their parents are still striking back at their grandpar-

ents. The philosophical approach of *"I wanted my children to find their own religion"* should impel parents to introduce their children to several religions, if they really feel that way. Paul said in I Corinthians 13:11, *"When I was a child, I talked like a child, I thought like a child, I reasoned like a child. When I became a man, I put childish ways behind me."* If you are one of those people excusing your current actions and attitudes because of your childhood upbringing, why don't you drop it? The Bible says, *"each one of us will give account of himself to God"* (Romans 14:12). It's an old trick. Many have been deceived by it. Adam and Eve, in the Garden of Eden, tried to cop out on taking responsibility for their actions before God. You know what happened to them, don't you? It never works.

> *I know I am responsible to You, God. I know that I will someday give an accounting of my life to You. Help me to be ready. Amen.*

ONE YEAR CHALLENGE—Read:
2 Kings 7-9

May 30

Living Memorials

I, FOR ONE, PREFER LIVING MEMORIALS. We are just completing another American celebration—Memorial Day. It is rightly celebrated by a small percentage of faithful citizens who remember the high cost of liberty. It is used by the majority of folks to do things that have varying degrees of meaning from visiting relatives to causing accidents on the highways. Rather than an occasional orgy of celebrating our precious freedom (July 4th is coming) why not a continuous, living memorial? Better to do things like register to vote, vote in party primaries and all other elections, attend PTA, obey the laws of the land, pay everything you honestly should on your income tax, write letters to your congressman and the local newspaper editor, run for public office, etc.? These are the kinds of living memorials that will make a difference for everyone. Christian readers would do well to read Romans 13:1-7 regularly as a reminder of your citizenship responsibilities. Among other things Paul says, *"Do you want to be free from fear of the one in authority? Then do what is right and he will commend you. . . . it is necessary to submit to the authorities, not only because of possible punishment but also because of conscience."* While we are in this world, Jesus said we should be *"the light of the world"* (Matthew 5:14). This certainly applies to citizenship. One news source reports that more than 100 people who have been entrusted with high responsibility in the government of our country have been jailed or are awaiting trial or have resigned in shame. In one four year term! This was within one presidential administration. These were public figures who were very visible on public days of celebrating our debt to the past. Privately they had a different agenda. Christian citizenship is a great inheritance to pass to the next generation. Plan to do it.

One Year Challenge—Read: 2 Kings 10-12

> *I remember Jesus today. I remember His death on Calvary. I remember His resurrection. I want my life to be a living memorial to Him. Amen.*

May 31

Too Pooped To Parent

BETWEEN MOTHER'S DAY AND FATHER'S Day, there is a five-week window in our culture for some good things to happen in your family. Granted, it is highly commercialized and advertisers try to manipulate your guilt or sentimentality. But is does raise some important issues. It frees up some families to move toward reconciliation or building bridges. A hazard of living in a commuter generation is that many Moms and Dads are *"too pooped to parent."* When eight hours of work is sandwiched between fighting morning and evening traffic, emotional drain is inevitable. Extra effort must be made to do effective parenting. Christian fathers don't want to *"exasperate your children; instead, bring them up in the training and instruction of the Lord"* (Ephesians 6:4). Christian mothers want their children to grow up *"and call her blessed"* (Proverbs 31:28). How to do it? With intentionality—it will not be automatic. Parents must agree with the need and resolve to be effective Christian parents. Inspired and empowered by the Holy Spirit, parents need to discipline themselves to carry out God's teaching for parents and pass along (by example) to their children this same self-discipline to be able to "disciple" others. Riding in a van pool or similar group transportation allows an opportunity for Bible reading and spiritual self-feeding. Using your lunch hour for devotional reading will give you spiritual vitamins to strengthen you for sharing with the family when you get home. (Probably help your waist line, also!) Parents need to verbalize to each other and to their children their desire to be a consistent Christian parent. Ask the children to pray for you. Acknowledge your weaknesses and vulnerability. Affirm the children's ministry to you. They know you are not perfect. Joshua 24:15 has Joshua saying *"as for me and my household, we will serve the LORD."* That's a great goal. To accomplish it, every member of the family must give it priority.

> *O God, you are creator of the family and source of our inspiration. Regardless of our present family situation, give us the desire to make it better for everyone. Amen.*

June 1

ONE YEAR CHALLENGE—Read: 2 Kings 13-15

Lies That Kill a Marriage

APART OF OUR CULTURE IS THE MYTH OF THE "JUNE BRIDE." Scenes of beautiful weddings come to mind, but statistics take some of the glow away. Why is it that at least one-half of the marriages will not last? What has happened to marriage that the seeds of divorce seem to be there from the first day? I think it's because of dishonesty. For cultural, traditional, or family reasons, most want to be married in a church. You see, right away those marriages are demanding an untruth. There is only one reason to have a church wedding: A Christian man and a Christian woman want to make promises to God and to one another in a place dedicated to religious vows. If bride and groom aren't both Christians, why do it there? In the traditional ceremony, the promises and vows made to God are heavier than the ones the couple make to each other. If the couple (or one of them) has no intention of keeping holy vows to God, how can you expect faithfulness to a human being? Even though the minister may emphasize the spiritual urgency, the couple will blithely make promises to God in the service and go on the honeymoon and forget them. How many people do you know who got married on Saturday and then stopped on Sunday morning and went to church to thank God for what had happened the day before. Promising God to *"love and cherish"* your mate until you are parted by death is a heavy promise. Do you remember the minister saying, *"I require and charge you both, as you will answer on the dreadful day of Judgment"*? As long as marriage is just secular, it will die as all things secular do. The goal of oneness in marriage (Genesis 2:24) cannot be experienced if there is a mixture of untruth.

> *O God of Truth, deliver us from lies and half-truths. Help us to build channels of open and honest communication. Be our Guide. Amen.*

ONE YEAR CHALLENGE—Read: 2 Kings 16-18

June 2

June Brides

THE BRIDAL SECTION OF THE NEWS-PAPER has all the business it can handle now. In fact, there is a waiting list to get your picture and story in print. Folks still believe in love and marriage! In spite of the threats: AIDS, divorce, abortion, etc. A generation of young is coming along and saying that choosing one person and making a commitment to be faithful to that person for the rest of life is still a possibility. I certainly believe that. God said in the Bible that's how it should be and that's the way I've experienced it for more than 30 years. That's the way I teach it (I require about three months of study and counseling with a couple before I marry them). If pastors, churches, Sunday school teachers, and all other spiritual figures taught that and lived that, things would be different, but we don't have agreement and consistency. Our church tries to honor marriage and expects accountability while a sister church sticks out her hand and takes marriage fees as quick as a Las Vegas wedding chapel. Since so many people still believe in marriage, let's not hold out on them this month. Let's tell them what the Bible says: *"For this reason a man will leave his father and mother and be united to his wife, and the two will become one flesh"* (Ephesians 5:31). Let's tell them that *"Marriage should be honored by all, and the marriage bed kept pure, for God will judge the adulterer and all the sexually immoral"* (Hebrews 13:4). Let's teach and encourage the highest standard of pre-marital and post-marital chastity so that the June marriage epidemic will be lived in hope and not disappointment and heartbreak. Want an ideal to pattern your marriage after now? Try Jesus as the groom and the church as the bride as described in Ephesians 5 in the Bible.

Surely, O God, your plan for once-and-for-all marriage is best; we have not been able to improve on it. Statistics prove that your way is best. Thanks! Amen.

June 3

ONE YEAR CHALLENGE—Read:
2 Kings 19-21

Good Marriages

THERE ARE A LOT OF UGLY STATISTICS spread around about marriage. Regretfully, many are trapped in situations that are going to get worse. I won't add any commentary and woe; how about a few words of encouragement for the good marriages and the people who want to make them better? Every marriage can be better, regardless of how good it is. Marriage bonds can be strengthened, satisfaction can grow deeper, fulfillment can move to another plateau. Good marriages are reaffirmed from time to time with something as simple as a couple holding hands and saying to one another *"I will never divorce you."* Taking seriously God's feeling about marriage permanence is an important step. In Malachi 2:16; God says *"I hate divorce."* God describes divorce as an act of violence. Another truth is that long years of marriage security and stability are built on a thousand little affirmations. After all, the Bible wisely says that it's *"the little foxes that ruin the vineyards"* (Song of Songs 2:15). Marriages go sour not because of some big calamitous event but because of a lot of little opportunities missed and choice words that were not spoken. The description of a man nourishing and cherishing his wife in Ephesians 5:28-29 is a picture of a man continuously working at a growing relationship with his wife. Presenting his wife to God as evidence of his stewardship and faithfulness demands an ever-alert and sensitive husband. The principle of mutuality keeps a marriage balanced and growing. Likewise, the responsibility of respecting her husband (Ephesians 5:33) involves a daily and continuous effort on the part of the wife to help her husband be all he can be and do all he can do. Both partners would be aware daily of the other's constant attention to improving the relationship. This kind of encouragement builds a good marriage.

> *Remind us, O God, that it is more important to plan for a marriage than just planning a wedding. We tend to think more about impressing our friends than pleasing you and our mate. Amen.*

June 4

ONE YEAR CHALLENGE—Read:
2 Kings 22-24

Weddings

"*Marriage should be honored by all, and the marriage bed kept pure, for God will judge the adulterer and all the sexually immoral*" (Hebrews 13:4). The Bible has such a high view of marriage, it stands out in such contrast to prevailing ideas on the contemporary scene. If there is one arena where the *"Christ versus Culture"* conflict is seen today, it is about marriage. Marriage is such a beautiful ideal and reality in the Bible. In fact, it was so dynamic a picture that Jesus often compared the very best life scenes and heavenly scenes in *"wedding"* terms. Check out Matthew 22 and 25, and Revelation 19 for instance. Biblical marriage projects commitment and faithfulness and selflessness. These are words that form the basis for real joy and deep, lasting relationships. Therefore, it is a cause for celebration. So much emphasis on weddings now is on show and frivolity and expense—a total lack of seriousness. Even though familiar Bible-based words of the tradi-

tional wedding ceremony of America are being used, the words and thoughts are so strange and unfamiliar to the participants that even the wedding party giggles. Religious ceremonies for people who are not religious have a hollow ring to them. I have noticed that in any service where I have a short message stressing the Christian values necessary for a lasting and permanent marriage that some people begin to squirm. Obviously, they came for a short ceremony and a quick exit to the reception. Here's a suggestion: during the next wedding you attend, pay attention to the words. Evaluate yourself. If you are a spiritual person, you have two special opportunities to give witness to your faith: your wedding and your funeral. Your friends will be there for both: one is an early declaration to live by God's word faithfully, the other is a declaration that you lived up to your intentions.

O God, You describe the return of Jesus as the coming of the Bridegroom to claim his bride, the church. May we be ready for that great day. Amen.

One Year Challenge—Read:
2 Kings 25,
1 Chronicles 1-2

June 5

Marriage: a Commitment

I WENT TO A 40TH WEDDING ANNIVERSARY PARTY recently. I liked that! Lately it seems some are not making that kind anymore. Words have been changed in the wedding service: " 'til death do us part" has become "while love lasts" or "while we feel like it." Commitment is a rarely used word today. Folks fear real commitment; it might interfere with something they want to do. So when the kids are born into this kind of temporary arrangement, they grow up thinking the same thing. If there is a lack of commitment at the basic and fundamental area of life, the rest of the life will be adversely affected. A lack of commitment in marriage means a lack of commitment in parenting. Without commitment, couples don't have the strength to work through problems. Without commitment, folks don't work toward understanding. Without commitment, children do not have a secure base in the home setting. (It is no wonder they are vulnerable to drug dealers and pornography pushers even at the elementary level.) The best marriage manual ever written says *"For this reason a man will leave his father and mother and be united to his wife, and they will become one flesh"* (Genesis 2:24). That's where the " 'til death do us part" comes from in the marriage vows. To be sure, some situations are unbearable, and self-preservation literally drives some people out of the marriage bond. But a marriage of 40 or 50 years duration stands to prove the truth that if a couple is genuinely committed to making it happen, it will! A full and thorough commitment will offer excitement and joyful experiences from anniversary to anniversary. Commitment bears fruit in vitality, not boredom. Committed love is growing love. Some areas of life don't need a variety of experience. Marriage is one of them!

Thank you, Jesus, for showing us the meaning of commitment when you died on the cross for us. Help every Christian to be so committed to the Biblical plan of marriage. Amen.

ONE YEAR CHALLENGE—Read:
I Chronicles 3-5

June 6

A Marriage of Masks

I JUST HEARD A FASCINATING description of the reason for broken marriages in America: the problem can be traced to the time of the marriage ceremony—it was a *"marriage of masks."* Everyone wants to make a good impression. Therefore, when we go out into the community, we put on our most attractive mask. Man meets woman and they are attracted to one another. In order to increase their attractiveness, each puts on their most attractive mask. The urgency of escaping a lonely life, or boredom filled life or an isolated life makes wearing the mask seem legitimate. And so a relationship begins to build, or at least the attempt is made. Neither realizes at that point that it is doomed. Perhaps the relationship is secure enough during the courtship so the second mask comes off and there is some feeling of security while getting to know the person. Seldom does the first mask come off until after the wedding ceremony. Warning: Some people realize during the final wedding preparations that they are making a mistake but family pressure and money spent won't let them stop. I remember a certain alcoholic who wore a sober mask for two years of courtship and then got drunk at the wedding reception and stayed drunk for the entire honeymoon. Of course, destruction followed. There are many illustrations of the *"marriage of masks"* problem. If you are in the courting stage of life, check behind the mask. If you and your mate realize today that you married a mask, don't run to the divorce court. Check out honestly the good qualities of your mate. Apologize for the mask. Renew your vows as the real you. In Revelation 21:5 Jesus said, *"I am making everything new!"* That includes marriage relationships. Take off your mask. You're tired of holding it in place anyway. Don't waste another day.

Free us of our insecurity, Lord. We need to be open to you and open to the people we live with at home. Take away our masks, help us to be honest! Thank you for accepting us as we are. Amen.

ONE YEAR CHALLENGE—Read:
I Chronicles 6-8

June 7

Blind Trust

I RECENTLY TOOK AN AIRLINE TRIP and I was amazed at what happened. We did not board the plane on time because some necessary work was being done. After boarding, we sat for a while and then the pilot announced that another problem had been discovered. The oil would have to be changed and a new filter installed and then all should be well. Another 20 minutes passed and then the pilot announced that the warning light had gone off and we would be departing immediately. The plane was fully loaded, more than 100 people, and not a single person asked, *"Are you sure it is safe?"* Everyone, including myself, was willing to trust a pilot we had never seen and could not see, with our very lives—blind trust! (We just assumed he would not place himself in danger.) In society, we constantly trust people and do just what they tell us to do. Just because we read it in a paper or hear it on the radio, we assume it is true. Politicians make promises and get elected because people don't ask questions. Dictators rise to positions of unbelievable power because no one questions their motives. Military leaders take their nations into conflict in the name of national defense and the majority are willing to accept what they say. Some even follow religious charlatans on the assumption that these people must be speaking the truth; they seem so sincere and successful. I'm glad that Jesus challenged us to think out the implications of following Him. Challenging us to count the cost of discipleship meant we would have to give serious thought to His challenge and teaching. Acts 17:11 describes the people of Berea who *"examined the Scriptures every day to see if what Paul said was true."* I'm glad Jesus said the truth would make us free, not blind (John 8:32). Examine His words and His life. He is trustworthy.

We need sight and insight God or we will be blinded by the glitter and glamour of this world. Help us see through false promises. Amen.

OneYearChallenge—Read:
1 Chronicles 9-11

June 8

Unity of the Church

IT DAWNS ON ME TODAY THAT THERE IS ONE AREA in particular where churches are sending out a mixed message. The non-Christian, or non-church community doesn't understand denominationalism, and perceives this as division among the church as a whole. Because the churches have different names out front, some even assume that these are private religious clubs vying for supremacy in the community. Sad to say, some churches add to this confusion by promoting an exclusivistic attitude. This is in great contrast to the prayer of Jesus for this church, *"that they may be one as we are one: I in them and you in me. May they be brought to complete unity to let the world know that you sent me"* (John 17:22-23). Churches need to rediscover this truth! When the Greeks came to Andrew at Jerusalem, they said, *"Sir, . . . we would like to see Jesus"* (John 12:21). When the outside world—the lost and wandering and seeking world—comes to a church today, they are seeking the same thing. They want to see Jesus. They are not saying, *"We want to see the baptism"* or, *"We want to hear you speak in tongues"* or, *"We want to observe your Holy Communions"* or, *"We want to check the quality of your church music."* They are saying, *"We want to see Jesus!"* Until searching folks are introduced to the Savior, pointing out to them the doctrinal differences of all the churches is a waste of time and a stumbling block. Many people today are not rejecting Jesus as Savior, but are offended by an attitude that smacks of religious pride. It's time for churches to realize that we are not competing with one another for the souls of mankind, but with the devil. The original Biblical confession of faith is still the best: *"Jesus is Lord"* (Romans 10:9).

Dear Jesus, we love your church and we know that you do. May we dream the dream of a united and unified people. Use us to achieve it. Amen.

ONE YEAR CHALLENGE—Read: 1 Chronicles 12-14

June 9

Execution

TWO NEWS RELEASES CAUGHT MY ATTENTION and made me cringe inside. The first had to do with the execution of two drug dealers by a rival gang. Their hands and feet were bound, they were gagged, their heads were wrapped in duct tape, they were placed in the back seat of a car and then people from outside the car riddled them with bullets. What a bloody picture! The other one had to do with the execution of a murderer in the state penitentiary. The article said the man's hands and feet were bound, a bag was placed over this head as he was seated in a special chair in a special room. Then the observers moved outside the room to view through glass as a switch was thrown and the man's body was riddled with electricity. It was reported that the bag was suddenly bloody and blood dripped down on the chest of the corpse. I'm glad there were no pictures of this. Watching an execu-tion must be a strange and moving event. Nearly two thousand years ago the daily news reported an execution on a cross. In fact, three men were executed that day. It was bloody too, as blood dripped from the hands and feet of the condemned. It was recorded (Luke 23:49) that there was a group of observers. It would seem from this that some things have not changed in 2,000 years. Angry and offended people still demand death for the one who seriously offends them. The death of the guilty party satisfies the desire for revenge but nothing else. Although man has made great strides in understanding himself, he so easily steps back to the edge of the uncivilized jungle when he executes another human being. Whether refined or crude; whether done by outlaws or the state, execution is execution. Romans 12:19 says, *"Do not take revenge."*

God of mercy and forgiveness, take away our desire for vengeance. Help us to trust you to repay all who need to be punished. Amen.

ONE YEAR CHALLENGE—Read:
1 Chronicles 15-17

June 10

A Plum or a Prune

I HEARD SOMEONE QUOTE ED FRIEDMANN the other day as saying churches are composed of *"plums or prunes."* Are you a member of a church? Do people consider you a plum or a prune? It is very easy to tell if you will just look in the mirror. The Apostle Paul likes to mention church *"plums"* in his letters. In Romans 16, he devotes a whole chapter to them. Also, he mentions Stephanas and others, who refreshed his spirit (I Corinthians 16:17); Onesimus, who was a *"faithful and dear brother"* (Colossians 4:9); Epaphras, who was *"always wrestling in prayer"* (Colossians 4:12), Philemon, a *"dear friend and fellow worker,"* is commended in (Philemon 1:1), and the godly mother, Eunice, and the godly grandmother, Lois (2 Timothy 1:5). The list is long! Yes, a prune or two is mentioned. He talks about Demas, the deserter (2 Timothy 4:10) and Alexander, the metal worker, in the same passage (2 Timothy 4:14). He also talks about two women, Euodia and Syntyche (Philippians 4:2), who can't get along and others, who act like little dogs, always chewing people up and spitting them out (Philippians 3:2). Now, which are you? The plums are described in Philippians 4:8 as thinking about *"whatever is true, whatever is noble, whatever is right, whatever is pure, whatever is lovely, whatever is admirable."* Since they aim to think good thoughts all the time, the sweetness shines out of their faces and they are a blessing to the whole church. Their aim is to always encourage others to keep their Christian brothers and sisters from being afflicted with a hard heart (Hebrews 3:13). Prunes have a way of spreading their ill will too. Nothing is pleasing to a prune: the sermon was too long, the prayer too short, the music too loud, the ushers too friendly, the air conditioning too cold. The prunes would much prefer weeping with those who weep rather than rejoicing with those who rejoice. Plums of the church: **Unite!** The prunes need your sweetness.

God, Some of us need a make over. Our frown wrinkles don't look good on us and our scowl lines look unfriendly. Loosen us up, O God. Amen.

June 11

ONE YEAR CHALLENGE—Read:
I Chronicles 18-20

School's Out

IT'S STARTING TO BE OBVIOUS NOW. If you're in an area using the traditional school calendar, it started when the college students began to come home. Then the private school kids started appearing on the streets. Then the nursery schools, now the public schools take a big yawn and give up their multitudes. School's out! Vacation, sunburn, summer job, getting in Mama's hair—all of these things happen when school is out. *"No more school, no more books . . . etc."* What about you? It's OK for kids to get a three month break; then they will go back to studies. But you, when was the last time you read a good book? So many people seem to flaunt it as a badge of honor, to say they haven't read a book since they graduated. Much of television programming is geared to be understandable by second grade children. If you watch two or more hours of TV per day, that says something about the state of your brain. Somebody said, *"A mind is a* terrible *thing to waste."* Christian folks are challenged to *"Do your best to present yourself to God as one approved, a workman who does not need to be ashamed and who correctly handles the word of truth"* (2 Timothy 2:15). There is no vacation from studying the Word of God or taking a vacation from growing in the truth. The Bible says to *"Love the Lord your God with all your heart and with all your soul and with all your mind"* (Matthew 22:37); you can't love God with your emotions if you are not loving Him intellectually and learning about Him. In fact, 2 Timothy 2:2 is more precise. It says that what has been taught to you should then be taught to other faithful believers, who can teach other people as well. School's out! More time is available with Daylight Savings Time to study the truths of God. The truth can make you free but it won't be poured into your head from a pitcher. Study for it!

Jesus, you said if we would hunger and thirst for righteousness, we would find satisfaction. May that be one fruit of this summer. Amen.

ONE YEAR CHALLENGE—Read:
I Chronicles 21-23

June 12

Loss of Discipleship

IF YOU HAVE BEEN TO CHRISTIAN WORSHIP very much, I'm sure you have heard of the *"Great Commission."* Found in Matthew 28:19-20, Jesus is giving our marching orders, *"go and make disciples of all nations, baptizing them in the name of the Father and of the Son and of the Holy Spirit and teaching them to obey everything I have commanded you."* Then, after Jesus gave this command, He went up into heaven. The church took seriously the part about baptizing people. The vast majority of people in America have been baptized into some form of religion, even if they don't comprehend the ritual. But the Church has lost sight of the command to make disciples who obey all of the commands. Baptism is an easy ritual to perform and experience. Church members feel good when they have a service of baptism. Discipling people or teaching them to understand the responsibility of living the Christian life is hard work however, so churches tend to let slide, or do it haphazardly. Yes, churches, too, tend to take the easy way out. The result today is an impotent church. The church is not bearing fruit by winning many new converts because most of the people there don't have a faith to share or the courage to share it. Many do not understand what is supposed to have radically changed their lives. Biblical ignorance is rampant in the contemporary church. How did the church get this way? She lost obedience to the command to *"disciple and teach."* The excuses are that folks are too busy or don't have time to be taught. How absurd! The glow of the television can be seen in almost every home on your street every night. The church must return to the basic *"things you have heard me say in the presence of many witnesses entrust to reliable men who will also be qualified to teach others"* (2 Timothy 2:2). Churches: Disciple or Die!

Yes Jesus, You gave us a Great Commission and showed us how to implement it by duplicating our new life in someone else. We must multiply if we desire to see the world evangelized. Amen.

ONE YEAR CHALLENGE—Read:
I Chronicles 24-26

June 13

Father's Day

A GOOD FRIEND GAVE ME SOME INSIGHT into the role of a father. When he was small, he was taught to be quiet around adults because kids didn't have anything to say that adults needed to hear. *"Adults are too busy for small stuff"* was the message. Now, as a man, this childhood teaching has made him hesitant with male authority figures. Also, as a Christian man, this childhood teaching has affected his prayer life. Is God too busy today? Does God have time for me? Will God think what I have to say is silly, or juvenile? I have long known that many people cannot think of God in a positive way because of a negative father image. Fathers: Be alert! Be sensitive to the fact that what you say and how you say it will either help or hinder your child in their relationship with God. *"As a father has compassion on his children, so the LORD has compassion on those who fear him"* (Psalm 103:13). But if a child has a father who shows little or no pity and tenderness to the child, what groundwork will be laid for the child's future relationship with his or her Heavenly Father? *"Fathers, do not exasperate your children"* (Ephesians 6:4), is another Biblical injunction. The jails and detention centers are filled today with men and women who have only anger and disgust for their fathers. They feel their fathers never loved them. How good to know on Father's Day that *"Though my father and mother forsake me, the LORD will receive me"* (Psalm 27:10); even better to learn today the spiritual responsibility of fatherhood. If all fathers would submit to God today and learn from Him how to behave as an earthly father, there would be a new blanket of peace to settle over the world. Boys especially, will grow up imitating their fathers. Does that scare you or bring a prayer of thanks to your lips?

Thank You, God, for loving earthly fathers. Help every father to take you as a role model. Every child needs a godly father. Amen.

ONE YEAR CHALLENGE—Read:
1 Chronicles 27-29

June 14

Pleasing "Dear Old Dad"

ONE OF THE MOST POINTED VERSES IN THE BIBLE FOR FATHERS is Ephesians 6:4: *"Fathers, do not exasperate your children; instead, bring them up in the training and instruction of the Lord."* Evidently, it has been largely ignored because there are a lot of folks angry with their father. It's natural to transfer this anger over toward God and be angry at God for giving them the father they had. Maybe their father deserted the family, or played favorites, or abused his kids, or drank or gambled away the family's money, or didn't love the mother. The list goes on. There is a long trail of heartbreak following some men who have fathered children. Many of the problems of youth today would not exist if there were strong fathers to give support and encouragement and be healthy role models. A lot of children will make another attempt this week to please Dad or at least get his attention and will suffer a letdown when he still doesn't come through. If a man wants to be a good father, the Bible has an excellent picture of a model father in the description of God as Father. *"As a father has compassion on his children, so the LORD has compassion on those who fear him"* (Psalms 103:13). *"How great is the love the Father has lavished on us, that we should be called children of God!"* (I John 3:1). *"The Lord disciplines those he loves, and he punishes everyone he accepts as a son"* (Hebrews 12:6). The image builds up and challenges every man, not in macho terms or material terms but in the personal qualities of strength, tenderness, understanding and self-control. It takes a lot of time to be a good father. It is the one gift to give your kids that doesn't have a price tag in dollars. Fathers need to give *"quantity time"* and *"quality time"* to their children. Make a commitment to do it.

Father, You are forcing us to think about this important question for a couple of days. Why? Do you have a special blessing waiting? Amen.

ONE YEAR CHALLENGE—Read: 2 Chronicles 1-3

June 15

Time for Socks and Ties

IT'S THE DAY OF TIES AND SOCKS AND AF-TER-SHAVE lotion—it's Father's Day! I just heard a country song, *"There Should Be a Hall of Fame for Mamas."* Maybe there should be one for Dads also. Although, come to think of it, father-hood is not enjoying the best reputation these days. Many families are suffering the pain of Dad's mid-life crisis. Men are deserting their wives and children! Every time I read in the Bible about the young man we have dubbed *"The Prodigal Son,"* I ask myself: Could there have been a Prodigal Son without a Prodigal Fa-ther? (Luke 15). The son was rather typically hard-headed and rebellious; maybe the Father was fed up and was glad to give him money to get him and his mouth out of the house. A lot of fathers are like that, thinking money can buy anything. I'm sure the father spent many worried, sleepless, teary nights after the son left, wondering what the son was doing and whether he was dead or alive or in jail. I'm sure he repented of his mistake of financing the son's rebellion, for when the son returned home the father openly loved him and forgave him and welcomed him back. But what would have hap-pened on that rebellious day if the father had lovingly but firmly sent him back to his family responsibility rather than giving him money and sending him out? Inherited money has ruined lots of children! Fathers: Give **yourself** to your children. Take off your mask. Show them some real feeling. They don't expect you to be any-thing more than human. Someone wrote, *"No man is so tall as when he is on his knees."* Let your children see you in prayer. Pray with the chil-dren and their mother. Honor the gift of father-hood that God has entrusted to you.

Clarify for us, O Heavenly Father, the true values of fatherhood. Help us understand that it is not in macho strength but spiritual strength that fatherhood is fulfilled. Amen.

June 16

ONE YEAR CHALLENGE—Read:
2 Chronicles 4-6

Being Helpless

MANKIND IS SO HELPLESS. We are! I guess that's why many of us make so much noise and try to appear strong and boisterous. I remember, as a child, walking home at night on a dark country road. I had to whistle, shout, or sing to keep from being afraid. We are fragile! I have watched news reports of people attempting to rescue others from earthquake rubble; feverishly they dig with their fingers to free the trapped ones. Other natural calamities reveal our helplessness, also. Many find it hard to honestly accept our condition. In no place is our helplessness more obvious than in the spiritual realm. In fact we probably overdo in other areas just to compensate for the place of our greatest vulnerability. Pretending above normal physical ability as compensation for spiritual helplessness is what we see in macho types. Thank God for Romans 5:6 that says, *"You see, at just the right time,* *when we were still powerless* (helpless), *Christ died for the ungodly."* When we recognize our spiritual weakness, we are at the door of spiritual strength. God has made a provision for us, that's the Good News. One of the paradoxes of the faith is that when we are weak, then we are strong in Christ (2 Corinthians 12:10). People who think they are holy, righteous or good on their own get this response from Jesus: *"It is not the healthy who need a doctor, but the sick. . . . I have not come to call the righteous, but sinners"* (Matthew 9:12-13); so He focuses his love on those willing to admit their true condition. Depending totally on yourself to save yourself can lead to more frustration. Pulling yourself up by your own bootstraps won't gain you eternal life. *"It is by grace you have been saved, through faith—and this not from yourselves, it is the gift of God—not by works, so that no one can boast"* (Ephesians 2:8-9).

> *Reveal to us again that man's helplessness is God's opportunity, and that our weakness makes possible our best view of God's strength. Save us from egotistical foolishness. Amen.*

ONE YEAR CHALLENGE—Read:
2 Chronicles 7-9

June 17

Hidden Beauty

A WHILE BACK, WE VISITED THE BEAUTIFUL CAVERNS of Luray. There are many caverns scattered around that whole area of Virginia. It's amazing that you could be riding through this mountainous area and be totally oblivious to the beauty hidden away underground. To be sure, the Skyline Drive has its own special beauty, a beauty that is truly breathtaking in the fall when the leaves are changing. But that's my point. Sometimes we get so caught up in the obvious (surface) beauty that we do not look deep enough to see hidden beauty. Are the colorful leaves more beautiful than the colorful stalactites and stalagmites? That would be a hard choice if you saw what I saw today. The beauty of a grand cathedral is wonderful but is it more beautiful than a humble wayside chapel filled with worshipers? The beauty of a great oration is magnificent but is it more beautiful than a simple gospel song raised by people of faith? If we looked at the obvious, we might be too quick to answer questions like these. In the so-called *"beauty contests"* of the summer months, the only type of beauty judged is outward, obvious physical attractiveness. There are many beautiful people who might not gain your second notice but their beauty is deep and true. Look below the surface and beyond the obvious. God, who makes *"everything beautiful in its time"* (Ecclesiastes 3:11), may have a surprise in store for you. In 1 Peter 3:1-5, we are challenged not to be concerned with outer beauty but to have the *"unfading beauty of a gentle and quiet spirit, which is of great worth in God's sight."* Obviously a lot of marriages die because people marry on a basis of physical attraction and then can't stand to stay with the hidden person. Look for inner beauty; it never deceives.

> *God, I'm glad that You don't look at outward appearances but straight into our private heart. May I be beautiful on the inside for You? Amen.*

ONE YEAR CHALLENGE—Read:
2 Chronicles 10-12

June 18

Keep Pure Thoughts

FROM TIME TO TIME THE QUESTION HITS THE FRONT PAGE OR THE MAGAZINE COVER: *"WHAT IS ART?"* Well, what is pornography? What is lewd? What is obscene? The questions never seem to be answered satisfactorily for all. This is because there are always folks pushing the boundary of decency farther and farther. One guideline has been to ask if it has redeeming social value. That seems fair to me. Dirt for the sake of dirt helps no one. I once lived in Southeast Asia in what many people considered *"the sin city"* of the world. Recently, I visited Bourbon Street in New Orleans, Louisiana. When the human body is exposed, abused, and violated for public entertainment, that type of display certainly has no redeeming social value. Something destructive is happening to the fabric of society when our amusement and entertainment has to come from extreme abuses of common decency. Others will argue that if the majority morality is not offended, it's accept-able. But, let's not forget, when some lines are crossed you can never go back again. Titus 1:15 says, *"To the pure, all things are pure, but to those who are corrupted and do not believe, nothing is pure. In fact, both their minds and their consciences are corrupted."* The pure in heart not only see God (Matthew 5:8), but they look for purity around them. Impure hearts and consciences don't know about purity unless someone shows them the alternative. The Christian commitment to purity ought to be crystal clear. How to experience it, or attain it? In 1 John 3:3, the gospel writer says that everyone who has the hope of meeting Jesus when he returns purifies himself continuously just as Jesus is pure. *"Keep yourself pure"* (1 Timothy 5:22) is not just a command for Pastor Timothy, but for all of us. The end of pornography as a problem in society won't come until a majority of our citizens are committed to purity. Don't wait for our lawmakers to decide.

> *Father, King David once asked You to create a clean heart within him. I need a clean heart, also. Make me pure for Your glory. Amen.*

June 19

ONE YEAR CHALLENGE—Read:
2 Chronicles 13-15

Awards and Rewards

JUNE IS NOT JUST A MONTH OF WEDDINGS, but also a month when people receive awards and recognition. I saw a story on television the other night of a small school that had only one graduating student, so he was the recipient of all of the awards and scholarships presented. It certainly was a unique situation. But the fact that he was alone took something away from it all. What does it mean to get an award if there is no competition? Or, of what value are some awards? I once received a formal letter asking me if I would like to be listed in **Who's Who in America?** Just fill out the form and send a check! Same thing happened when I was at the university. So I realized, some awards or recognitions mean absolutely nothing. Maybe you have seen the advertisements for ministers to purchase "graduate degrees" for a price? Don't worry about it if you feel that you are not getting proper recognition and reward for what you are doing. People around you know who you are if you are doing something worthwhile to help your fellow man. There is going to be a big day for all of us, when each will receive what is due, and not what can be bought with money or artificial influence peddling. Read 2 Corinthians 5:10: *"For we must all appear before the judgment seat of Christ, that each one may receive what is due him for the things done while in the body, whether good or bad."* That's the day to think about! So, it's all right if you don't buy your way into **Who's Who?** as long as your name is *"written in the Lamb's Book of Life"* (Revelation 21:27). *"The Lord knows those who are his"* (2 Timothy 2:19). What a blessed assurance and release!

> *Remind me again today, God, that the only reward that is worth receiving is hearing You say, "Well done, good and faithful servant," when I die. Amen.*

June 20

One Year Challenge—Read:
2 Chronicles 16-18

Constitution Celebration

WE ARE CELEBRATING A MOST IMPORTANT BIRTHDAY for our country. On June 21, 1788, the Constitution of our United States became official when New Hampshire became the ninth state to ratify it. Four days later, Virginia's General Assembly ratified the document, while recommending that a Bill of Rights be added to ensure to the people certain *"unalienable rights"* for which the American revolution had been fought and the new nation formed. When in 1791 Virginia ratified the first 10 amendments to the new Constitution, the Bill of Rights became part of that historic document, and religious liberty was guaranteed in the fundamental law of the nation. Pause to give thanks for religious liberty. The freedom to be religious or not to be religious is very precious. Jesus said, *"Give to Caesar what is Caesar's, and to God what is God's"* (Matthew 22:21). When the Bible says we are created in the image of God, it is talking about our freedom to make choices. From the first book—Genesis, to the last book—Revelation, there is never a hint or suggestion that the people should follow the Lord by force or governmental decree; it is always a free choice. Religion is a matter of the soul and each person's soul is free to reject God or surrender to Him. Church and state have both prospered in America with the system of religious freedom and separation of church and state. Our celebration this week should be tempered by re-dedicating ourselves to maintaining such vigilance that we do not lose this freedom. Other countries torn by warring religious factions could learn from us. We can sing loudly, and gratefully, the last stanza of **My Country, Tis of Thee**: *"Our Fathers' God, to thee, Author of liberty, To Thee we sing: Long may our land be bright With freedom's holy light; Protect us by Thy might, Great God, our King!*

> *Thank You, God, that prayer is a relationship with You that does not request governmental permission or affirmation. Remind us that a government approved prayer is no prayer, just recitation. Amen.*

ONE YEAR CHALLENGE—Read:
2 Chronicles 19-21

June 21

Yard Work

ISN'T IT DIFFICULT TO HAVE A WELL-GROOMED YARD? Spring comes and it looks good. As weeks pass, you notice there are bare spots so you start patching. Some places you patch twice. You fertilize and water; the weather gets warmer; some spots start turning brown. Then you discover a big rock, board, or discarded concrete just under the surface, so you dig out the trash and patch again. Then the summer really turns hot and with all your watering, it still doesn't look perfect. You go on vacation and return to bare spots and brown spots so you try to revive it in frustration. Have you experienced that? Working a yard is a parable on life. A person is born into a family of privilege, things go fairly easy growing up; it looks like they have everything in the spring of life. As they go along, they become aware of bare and empty spots. They begin the cosmetic *"make it pretty"* stage. Things look fine again for a while, then comes some *"hot"* situation, pressure in some area, and brown spots reappear. We apply more cosmetics! Dead spots keep surfacing and more effort is made to make everything turn out just right. Then a larger pressure appears and they discover that the hidden garbage in their life is causing the problem, so an attempt is made to clean that up, but it only works for a while. The spring beauty seems lost forever. At this point there is one solution. When I got to this point with my yard, I gave up on my past efforts and started over. I plowed it up, cleared out all the garbage, and began again. In your personal life, when you get to this spiritual state, God offers you the opportunity to start again. Clean out all the old garbage and begin a new life the same way. Check out John 3:16.

> *Make me new, God; please, make me new! I am tired of carrying the guilt of the past. Amen.*

ONE YEAR CHALLENGE—Read:
2 Chronicles 22-24

June 22

Ritual of Suburbia

THE WEEKLY RITUAL IN AMERICAN SUBURBIA IS MOWING GRASS. Sometimes it seems like a religious service: up and down, up and down. It's like religion in a different way for some folks. They only do it when they absolutely have to, or seasonally. Either way, did you know the Bible talks about grass cutting? It compares God's care for us in Matthew 6:30 in this way: *"If that is how God clothes the grass of the field, which is here today and tomorrow is thrown into the fire, will he not much more clothe you, O you of little faith?"* Then there is Peter the Apostle, reiterating (I Peter 1:24-25) what Isaiah the Prophet recorded in God's word: *"All men are like grass, and all their glory is like the flowers of the field; the grass withers and the flowers fall, but the word of the Lord stands forever."* On the one hand, man's life is as temporary as the grass growing on your front lawn. On the other hand, if you realize the shortness of your life span and anchor your life in the work of God, you can have eternal life. Not just length of days, but long and quality type days. There was another thought that came to my mind earlier while cutting grass: *"What would my community be like if everyone spent as much time, money, and effort on caring for their souls as they do caring for their lawns?"* What do you think about while going round and round with the mower? *"Why spend money on what is not bread, and your labor on what does not satisfy?"* (Isaiah 55:2). Don't get me wrong, I love a beautiful yard. But some folks have their priorities mixed up. A lot of broken lives come from homes with beautiful yards.

O Father, let the beauty of Jesus be seen in me. I need to know that unless Jesus beautifies my life, it is unattractive. Amen.

One Year Challenge—Read: 2 Chronicles 25-27

June 23

The Oratory of Action

I WAS RECENTLY TEACHING the people in our church about the place of spiritual gifts in the life of the church. In this particular service, I was talking about nonverbal gifts and their importance. (Some misguided folks think verbal gifts reign supreme.) I was talking about Dorcas, who is described in Acts 9:36-42. As far as we know, she never preached a sermon or taught a lesson or sang a solo but she impacted the whole town of Joppa. Her witness was by the *"oratory of action."* What powerful messages she preached by doing good! What marvelous lessons she taught by helping the poor! What Christian truths she proclaimed by giving clothing to those who needed it! There is no stopping or silencing that message. Take away the microphone or television camera or even the pulpit stand from some *"verbal"* Christians and their lifestyle would say absolutely nothing. What's the old saying: *"What you*

are, is shouting so loud, I can't hear a word that you are saying"*? That can certainly be true. That's what James was trying to get across in chapter 2, verses 14-19: *"What good is it, my brothers, if a man claims to have faith but has no deeds? . . . faith by itself, if it is not accompanied by action, is dead. . . . Show me your faith without deeds, and I will show you my faith by what I do."* Who was it that said, *"I would rather see a sermon than hear one any day"*? Listen, as a preacher, I certainly can't put down the use of words and speech. It has its special place, but all of us need to use *"oratory of action."* The world needs to see our words *"fleshed out"* and our verbs take on feet. People who don't know Jesus should be attracted to Him by my lifestyle and yours, if we are true believers.

Heavenly Guide, someone taught me that actions speak louder than words. I hope that I never forget that lesson. Amen.

ONE YEAR CHALLENGE—Read: 2 Chronicles 28-30

June 24

Knowing about God and Grass

THERE ARE ALWAYS WAYS TO EXPRESS NONCONFORMITY, right? I mean, we notice things like long hair or pot parties or loud music, and they have been written up in newspapers by social commentators. What about not cutting your grass? With the amount of time people spend every week working in their yards, you would really be considered an oddball if you didn't. Can you fathom the amount of man and woman hours spent in clipping, edging, raking, etc., during the growing seasons? Observers from other planets might wonder about us following a noisy toy back and forth over a little plot of green stuff! I wondered if the wisdom of the Bible had anything to say about our preoccupation with grass. Well, it does say that God *"makes grass grow on the hills"* (Psalm 147:8). I suppose that includes your town. It also says, *"The grass withers and the flowers fall, but the word of* our God stands forever"* (Isaiah 40:8). We are also told that people are like grass: *"in the morning it springs up new, by evening it is dry and withered"* (Psalm 90:6). But maybe the most direct statement was from Jesus in Matthew 6:30: *"If that is how God clothes the grass of the field, which is here today and tomorrow is thrown into the fire, will he not much more clothe you?"* In fact, if you read everything that the Bible says about grass, you will learn a lot about the love and care of God, the Judgment of God, and the shortness of life. What amazes me is that people can know all about grass and nothing about the God who makes the grass. Maybe one of these Saturdays or Sundays when you are out sweating in the yard, you can help me figure that one out! But right now, please excuse me. I have to cut my grass!

Thank You, that every good and perfect gift is from above; that keeps me from putting too much emphasis on money and things that I struggle to possess. Amen.

OneYearChallenge—Read:
2 Chronicles 31-32

June 25

The Many Potentials of Summer

"NO MORE SCHOOL, NO MORE BOOKS, NO MORE TEACHER'S DIRTY LOOKS." That's a June song, if your area uses the traditional school calendar. Did you ever sing it? I think I learned it in Miss Robinson's fourth grade class. (Fourth grade is the year you start learning songs like that.) Anyway, school's out, and the kids don't know what to do with themselves. Neither do a lot of parents, sad to say. Summer has such potential. Everything is so beautiful now. Vacation expectancy is running high. Some even want to take a vacation from God. What? Some want to take a vacation from God? Really? Well, let's look at the evidence. Many churches reduce their worship schedules. They are supposed to be God's folks, but on they're on vacation! Many people who are actively church-going from September to June pull a disappearing act from June to August. Church budgets take a beating for three months if there is not a surplus built up to carry through summer ex-penses. Many congregations even forget their denominational difference for three months and pool their resources, getting together to form one decent-size congregation. It's either a vacation from God or the god that many people serve is a laid-back sort of god who snoozes a lot himself in the summer heat and doesn't notice that many of his troops are AWOL. This attitude is contrary to the instruction, *"be prepared in season and out of season"* (2 Timothy 4:2). As far back as Genesis 1:14 we are told that God said, *"Let there be lights in the expanse of the sky to separate the day from the night, and let them serve as signs to mark seasons and days and years."* God's good purpose in giving us the seasons of the year is thwarted if we leave Him out of one season. *"There is a time for everything, and a season for every activity under heaven"* (Ecclesiastes 3:1). Why summer, God?

ONE YEAR CHALLENGE—Read: 2 Chronicles 33-34

> *Thank You for the warmth of summer, I am reminded of the warmth of your love for me. Warm my heart, too, O God; warm my heart. Amen.*

June 26

Affirming Our Honesty

I'VE HEARD PEOPLE WHO WANTED TO AFFIRM THEIR HONESTY SAY, "WHAT YOU SEE IS WHAT YOU GET." This is supposed to imply that there is no dishonesty, deceit, guile, or falsification in their lives. Their words and deeds always match. But so many of us have been deceived by smooth talkers that the expression itself gives us reason to wonder. Maybe it's just me, but when someone says, *"I swear it's true,"* automatically, a caution flag pops up in my mind. I think it's because early in my life I was taught the words of Jesus in Matthew 5:33-37, *"You have heard that it was said to the people long ago, 'Do not break your oath, but keep the oaths you have made to the Lord.' But I tell you, Do not swear at all: either by heaven, for it's God's throne; or by the earth, for it is his footstool; or by Jerusalem, for it is the city of the Great King. And do not swear by your head, for you cannot make even one hair white or black. Simply let your 'Yes' be 'Yes,' and your 'No,' 'No'; anything beyond this comes from the evil one."* You have seen what goes on in court. Again, people raise their hand (and sometimes even put their other hand on a Bible) and swear to tell the truth, but many lie in spite of this public promise. In another place Jesus said, *"out of the overflow of the heart, the mouth speaks"* (Matthew 12:34). Regardless of the swearing, the mouth will express the true condition of the heart. Proverbs 23:7 (KJV) says, *"as he thinketh in his heart, so is he."* Lifestyle is the key; that's what really matters. Many people talk a lot about religious experiences and beliefs. Don't listen to the words too much until you have been able to examine the lifestyle. If the words are true, the life will broadcast plenty of confirmation.

I want my life to be truthful, O God; I want to be transparent, crystal clear with everyone. Let my life be an open book. Amen.

ONE YEAR CHALLENGE—Read:
2 Chronicles 35-36

June 27

Ceiling Fan

W E HAVE JUST INSTALLED A CEILING FAN. It's a very interesting piece of equipment. I have learned some lessons from a ceiling fan. Did you know a ceiling fan takes the environment that it encounters and makes a change? If it's hot, it can cool things down. But on the other hand, in winter, you can reverse it and warm air can be brought from the ceiling down to the level of people. I like that. It's like the saying, *"If life hands you a lemon, you can suck it sour or you can make lemonade."* You can do something about your circumstances. Same idea in, *"Are you a thermometer or a thermostat?"* You can reflect back the current situation or you can change it. So many people just complain about their lives, but make no effort to change the situation. You can wring your hands, or you can turn your hands, and do something positive. Some people complain about *"what the world is coming to,"* while others rejoice in *"who has come to the world"* (the *"who"* being Jesus). What is your attitude about your situation? Is your head bowed and your shoulders stooped as you trudge along bemoaning the terrible hand that fate has dealt you? Or are your shoulders squared with the realization that no matter how much the world and life in general dumps on you, *"I can do everything through him (Christ) who gives me strength"* (Philippians 4:13)? Are you convinced that *"neither death nor life, . . . nor anything . . . will be able to separate us from the love of God that is in Christ Jesus our Lord"* (Romans 8:38-39)? If your situation is hot, turn on the cooling fan. If your situation is cool, turn the fan in a warming direction. *"In all things God works for the good of those who love him, who have been called according to his purpose"* (Romans 8:28).

It is so good to know, Heavenly Friend, that you are with us regardless of the time or temperature. I am glad to know that You are here, and not silent. Amen.

ONE YEAR CHALLENGE—Read: 1 Corinthians 1-3

June 28

Comfort in the Familiar

HAVE YOU EVER BEEN SEATED COMFORTABLY, alone, in perhaps your living room when a family member enters and asks, *"What is that smell?"* Or, *"What's that noise? Don't you hear it?"* You were shocked. You hadn't noticed anything. All seemed well and fine to you. There is something to be said for the familiar—that to which we are accustomed. There is a certain comfort in it. We often hear about people being released from prison after an extended sentence, who right away, do something to get themselves back inside. Some just ask to be sent back! Change does hold a threat for many of us. The familiarity of the rut we are in feels good. Or, even if the situation is not good, many people don't want out of their ruts because, at least, they know where the sides of the rut are found. Drinkers wonder who their friends would be if they didn't drink, gamblers wonder who their friends would be if they didn't gamble, sports addicts wonder what they would talk about if they didn't talk about sports, and so forth. Some even get stubborn about it, like the pig said, *"It's my dirt. If you don't like the way I talk, act, dress, etc., I don't care."* There was a guy like that in the Bible. He was doing his own thing. He didn't care how it affected or hurt anyone else; besides, he liked it. But it finally got old. He ended up isolated from everything beautiful. We call him *"The Prodigal Son"*. (Luke 15) You see, there simply is no future in dirt! Be careful of doing what you want, not considering other people and their feelings, or what they can add to your life. Don't just live for yourself. We are not condemned by fate to live an unhappy life. Check the positive possibilities of making a change.

God, I will leave all the filthy familiarities of this world assured of the fact that You will give me victory in that change. Amen.

ONE YEAR CHALLENGE—Read: I Corinthians 4-5

June 29

A Sense of Humor

DOES GOD HAVE A SENSE OF HUMOR? Did you ever look a donkey in the face? Or hear him bray? Do they laugh in Heaven? Do they tell jokes there? I'm sure of it. With all of the joy and happiness promised in Heaven, humor must be distributed from a bountiful supply. Sometimes the most appropriate thing we can do is tell a joke and give everyone a good laugh. What's the first thing you read in **Reader's Digest**? Me, too: **Laughter, The Best Medicine**! If and when you let God speak to your heart you will have much to laugh about. In Genesis 21:6 the old woman Sarah said, *"God has brought me laughter, and everyone who hears about this will laugh with me."* You see, people can laugh with you or laugh at you. It's okay if God gives you a good laugh, especially at the little men who set themselves up on positions of authority and try to ignore Him (Psalm 2:4). The ability to laugh is precious. If you are at peace with God and men, you are free to laugh. Wards are filled in mental hospitals with people who cannot laugh. Laughing and joking is fitting in each life (Ecclesiastes 3:4). Just be careful with teasing; it can hurt. I love the promise of Job 8:20-21, *"Surely God does not reject a blameless man or strengthen the hands of evildoers. He will yet fill your mouth with laughter and your lips with shouts of joy."* That's what David must have had in mind in Psalm 126 when he thanked the Lord that *"Our mouths were filled with laughter, our tongues with songs of joy."* The worst advertisement for God in the world today is Christian people who don't know how to laugh, who have no sense of humor. If you can't enjoy good humor, ask God to teach you how to laugh.

God, You have given me joy, it's great. Your spontaneous joy has infected my heart. Ha Ha! Thank You very much! Amen.

ONE YEAR CHALLENGE—Read: I Corinthians 6-7

June 30

Let Freedom Ring!

IT'S TIME FOR OUR ANNUAL SALUTE TO FREEDOM. How do I know? The fireworks stands are popping up like mushrooms around the area. Like all good things in our country, the idea of freedom can be commercialized. What about this *"big bang"* for democracy? Why is personal freedom such an *"explosive"* idea? Around the world there will be a new set of dates celebrating freedom. Iron curtains and bamboo curtains have fallen, many without a shot being fired or a bomb being dropped. Why? Because freedom is a better idea than slavery; democracy is better than oppression. Those countries that have recently overthrown oppressive government have a fresh appreciation of freedom. The horror stories of their recent past flames their desire for all to be free. They want all segments of their society to be free and they want to defend the rights of all. They are forming their governments anew to be sure there is help for the helpless and powerless. Where did they get these ideals? What is the spring of their inspiration? Be sure to notice that one of their first requests of the established free world is to send Bibles. Although their churches had been closed and their Bibles taken away, in small groups and in underground churches they had prayed and sought to maintain their personal soul freedom with God. Soul freedom with God drives people to freedom in every area of life. It's true, *"if the Son (Jesus) sets you free, you will be free indeed"* (John 8:36). Freedom of the soul or spirit is such a powerful idea that it asks *"why not"* about every area of life. Soul freedom is the root of Democratic freedom and justice and equality for all.

> **God, I want to be free. From all the chains that bind. From all the thoughts that limit me. From all the failures that threaten me. Lord Jesus, I want to be free. Amen.**

ONE YEAR CHALLENGE—Read:
1 Corinthians 8-9

July 1

Freedom of Worship: Don't Forget

THIS MAY BE THE MOST JOYOUS OF ALL AMERICAN HOLIDAYS. It certainly is the loudest. Some of us celebrate our freedom as a law-abiding society by buying illegal fireworks and then further break the law by exploding them. But, that's only one contradiction. We take our freedom so lightly. Stop someone on the street who was born and raised in another country and let them tell you how fortunate we are to have such freedom. The news relates stories of the struggle for democracy and freedom by the world's peoples. The gift of freedom is precious: freedom to work, freedom of self-expression, freedom to worship, or not to worship. The list is long. I may have a different opinion than you about the need to attend worship services, but I certainly want us both to have the freedom to make our own choice. Our Bill of Rights guarantees that *"Congress shall make no law respecting an establishment of religion, or prohibit-*ing the free exercise thereof."* That is basic for us. How wonderful it is to live in a country where there is no official or state religion, where everyone is not automatically baptized into a religion. How wonderful to be in a country where we are not taxed for the support of churches and ministers. When we say in our pledge, *"One nation under God,"* and print on our currency, *"In God We Trust,"* we are simply recognizing that God exists and that our nation, citizens, and trading partners are ultimately under God's dominion. The Bible says, *"Blessed is the nation whose God is the LORD"* (Psalm 33:12). This applies to many Americans, but it applies through the freedom of choice. In 1 Peter 2:16 God says, *"Live as free men, but do not use your freedom as a cover-up for evil; live as servants of God."* Let freedom ring.

> **Lord Jesus, You came to make me free. Help me not to forget Your work for me. Why is it I forget to worship and say thanks? I surprise myself. Teach me that grace means free. Amen.**

ONE YEAR CHALLENGE—Read:
1 Corinthians 10-11

July 2

A Declaration of Dependence

HERE WE ARE AGAIN AT THE TIME TO CELEBRATE OUR INDEPENDENCE as Americans. We are reminded again of our rich history, full of wonderful stories of dedicated patriots who went *"above and beyond the call of duty."* Since that ancient day of July 4, 1776, we have waved the torch of independence at all powers that would oppress us. I love America. I love freedom. I love democracy. But as I celebrate this year, there is a question nagging my consciousness: Have we gone too far? In declaring our independence, did we mean to say we were also independent of God? Some of the problems around us in society beg for us to answer this question. I fear the slide in morality and justice will pick up speed on a downward course unless we make a Declaration of Dependence on God. When man is left to himself, he is a loose cannon, he can blow from one extreme to the other. The Prophet Joshua stood before his generation and challenged them to *"choose for yourselves this day whom you will serve"* (Joshua 24:15). They could follow God and His Word and have a direction for their nation or they could *"cut loose"* from God and end up serving gods of materialism, hedonism, or anything else they could imagine. Joshua goes on to commit himself and his family: *"as for me and my household, we will serve the LORD."* Joshua didn't want a kind of independence that was divorced from God, the kind that would have him following his *"gut feeling"* or whatever emotional thing appealed to him. So, he made his *"declaration of dependence"* on God. This is one of the paradoxes of the Christian faith: you are never completely independent in this world until you are totally dependent on God. Let's declare our dependence on the Lord!

> *O God, when I depend on You, everything in my life is better. I have so much more freedom from family and friends. I don't have to depend on them or be pressured by them. I'm grateful for my God-given independence. Amen.*

July 3

ONE YEAR CHALLENGE—Read:
1 Corinthians 12-13

Freedom: It's Spiritual

WE ARE HAVING A BIG CELEBRATION this year for our Day of Independence and democracy. What are you going to do on July 4? So much nostalgia crams my thinking. *"My Country, 'tis of thee, sweet land of liberty, Of thee I sing."** *"God bless America, land that I love, stand beside her and guide her, through the night with the light from above."*** I learned all those patriotic songs in elementary school. How about the National Anthem? Hundreds of times I've croaked and strained trying to sing it before kickoffs or the first pitch! It's a wonderful song but impossible for ordinary voices to sing well. Then there's the Statue of Liberty—a symbol that says more to us inwardly than we could ever express in words. I've had the privilege of being a missionary and working with refugees from many other countries as they came to America to escape all kinds of oppression and tasted the wonderful freedom in this country. Political freedom and liberty are truly valuable possessions. What a shame that many do not know political freedom. Locked behind Iron Curtains, Bamboo Curtains, or some other kinds, they long to be free. But some of them have discovered there a spiritual freedom through faith in God while many here are still spiritually in bondage. How tragic! In this great land of freedom, many are still in spiritual shackles! Jesus said about himself, *"know the truth, and the truth will set you free"* (John 8:32). People rebutted His statement and still do, but the fact remains *"everyone who sins is a slave to sin"* (John 8:34). The evidence verifies Jesus' statement. Is your celebration of freedom complete or partial? News from mainland China reports they can't print and circulate Bibles fast enough now that people are allowed to read them again. Why not here?

> *What a freedom document You gave us God when You gave us The Bible. Every book of it offers freedom. I am captivated by spiritual liberty. Thanks. Amen.*

ONE YEAR CHALLENGE—Read: 1 Corinthians 14-15

July 4

Symbols Like the Flag

THE SUPREME COURT DECISION THAT IT IS NOT A CRIME TO BURN THE AMERICAN FLAG (as a public protest) has evoked a lot of anger and pain and disappointment. The man on the street asks, *"Why would any citizen want to burn the flag?"* Mary Q. Citizen, who often gets frustrated by some of the things *"they"* are doing in Washington, never would think of expressing her frustration in such an extreme way. Why does this evoke such feeling? Because we are a people of symbols. We use symbols daily to express our deepest feelings. Symbols are a quiet part of our lives that speak loudly to us and the community. We exchange rings in the wedding ceremony, a profound symbol. We observe Christmas, Easter, Thanksgiving, and the Fourth of July as symbols of something much deeper. We carry pictures in our wallets of our loved ones, and show them to people as symbols of realities that give our lives meaning. Thus, the flag reminds us of wars fought, sig-nificant people who died in them, teachers planting the seeds of patriotism, etc. So when someone dares to desecrate our symbol, with the strong personal meanings it evokes in us, it is as if we were personally attacked. Remember, two of the most significant acts of the Christian worship experience are symbolic. Baptism is the symbol of dying to an old way of life and starting a new one (Romans 6:4). Celebrating the Lord's Supper in Communion is our symbol of Jesus giving His very life for our salvation (Luke 22:19-20). To see these symbols used in a derogatory manner in the field of entertainment would evoke a strong response. Treasure your symbols! In the first century when Christianity was forbidden, Christians simply made the sign of the fish and they were encouraged. The empty cross is our best symbol, when God took man's worst and made a plus sign of it.

Thank You God, for the realities of our faith. Thank You for all of the rich symbolism that takes us back in time to the great experiences of our faith. I remember especially my baptism. Amen.

July 5

OneYearChallenge—Read: 1 Corinthians 16, Ezra 1-2

Celebrating History

AGAIN WE SLOW DOWN OUR REGULAR ROUTINE to pay tribute to our history. With parades, speeches, fireworks and the like, we salute our past heroes and the price they paid for liberty. Patriotism—love of country, is a special commodity for us. We are proud of the United States of America (in spite of its failures and shortcomings) and may be surprised when we see other countries celebrating their history too. They have their parades too, their national heroes, and special days to remember! We may be shocked by it, asking ourselves, *"What in the world do they have to celebrate and be happy about? No nation in history has conducted such a grand experiment as our democracy and succeeded."* National pride is good. Every nation should have it. Every person should have the opportunity to celebrate his national heritage. Those of us who were born here should celebrate our freedom by saluting everyone who paid for it. Others, who are adopting this country, can be better citizens here if they have a healthy affection for their homeland. That reminds me: we should never slow down in our zeal for celebrating our spiritual history. Again on Sunday, we will share the bread and the cup as we celebrate our spiritual freedom. We re-enact, with a sense of awe, The Last Supper, when Jesus and the 12 disciples shared that meal together and Jesus announced, *"This cup is the new covenant in my blood; do this, whenever you drink it, in remembrance of me"* (I Corinthians 11:25). And to think that all around the world, people of every tribe and tongue and nation are having the same celebration in their own national and cultural context is an exciting thought. Yes, *"God so loved the world . . . ."* (John 3:16); let us celebrate that together, too.

> *I am so glad that I'm a part of your family, God. I am glad that I am part of a spiritual family of millions who have surrendered to Jesus. Such freedom! Amen.*

ONE YEAR CHALLENGE—Read:
Ezra 3-5

July 6

Freedom From Ourselves

AN ALLEGORICAL STORY IS TOLD DESCRIBING THE DIFFERENCE BETWEEN HEAVEN AND HELL. A curious soul was taken by the Prophet Elijah to see the two realms. First, they went to Hell. It was a huge comfortable room with a large table around which sat many unhappy, sickly looking people. In front of them was a pot of steaming, rich soup, but they were not eating it, for the spoons they had been given were longer than their arms, such that these individuals were unable to feed themselves. The people around this table were doomed to starve to death while they looked longingly at this pot of nutritious, tasty soup. The visitor was then escorted to heaven. To his surprise it was a room like that in Hell. It was huge and comfortable also, with a large table around which the inhabitants sat. On the table was a pot of steaming rich soup. These people also had spoons longer than their arms, BUT they were using them to feed each other. All the inhabitants were well-fed, happy, and healthy. When we live only for ourselves, we live lives of misery. Having the bounty of the world before us, we cannot enjoy it because of our selfishness. We become prisoners of our unbridled egos. With Heaven at our fingertips, we live *"like Hell."* Jesus said that the first and greatest commandment was to love God with all your heart, soul, and mind. Then He said that the second greatest *"is like it: 'Love your neighbor as yourself' "* (Matthew 22:39). Many have discovered the joy of living and helping others. This earth will never be completely like heaven, but we can get a taste of unselfish love, given and received. Try it! It's fun! Bring a little Heaven to your house.

Thank You God, for those loving people who are always helping me. They are so special. They have increased my sense of belonging. Amen.

ONE YEAR CHALLENGE—Read: Ezra 6-8

July 7

Freedom in Slavery

"THE HARDER A MAN TRIES TO BE HIMSELF WITHOUT BEING RIGHT WITH GOD, *the less like himself he becomes and the more like everyone else he is. Man was made to have fellowship with God, and man is never himself until he submits to this divine rule. Not your talent first, or your money, or your time, or your service, but the complete 'you' is what God requests and requires—not that He might make you a slave, but that He might emancipate you.*" So said Richard Halverson. I wonder how long it will take men to learn the secret of life and freedom. Man claims his right to hate, to lust, to cheat, to be prejudiced, and in claiming these rights leads himself into an impossible slavery of the spirit. His body may be free to do certain things but the soul is an unhappy slave. It is a paradoxical teaching of Christianity that there is a way of slavery that actually is the only way to freedom. When I make Jesus Christ the Lord and Master of my life, I am tell-

ing Him that I am going to obey His commandments. Whatever they are, I will obey. Strange as it seems, when I live in complete obedience to Him, I find freedom from those sins of the flesh that had enslaved me. If you want to be free of that thing or idea or way of life that has held you for so long, give your life to Jesus and follow Him. Jesus said, *"my yoke is easy and my burden is light"* (Matthew 11:30), and, *"I have come that they may have life, and have it to the full"* (John 10:10). I am not talking about religion, for man controls his religion, man masters his religion. A personal surrender of your life to the control of Jesus is what's required; nothing less will do.

> *O God of Freedom, whet our appetite for freedom. Don't let us be content being trapped by some foolish worldly thing. We crave your freedom, O God. Amen.*

July 8

ONE YEAR CHALLENGE—Read:
Ezra 9-10, Nehemiah 1

Sweet Liberty!

WE CAN'T SAY TOO MUCH ABOUT LIBERTY AND FREEDOM, can we? How blessed we are to enjoy the freedom of speech, the freedom of press, the freedom of worship and all the rest. One only has to visit countries of limited freedom or hear about them to realize what a treasure we hold. Personal freedom is one of the fruits of Christianity. Slavery was an accepted thing in the ancient world, even the Old Testament gives direction about buying slaves and disposing of them. It was very radical when Jesus taught freedom from institutional slavery and personal slavery. The statement of our ideal in our Pledge of Allegiance: *"liberty and justice for all,"* is rooted in Jesus' teaching on freedom and equality. When people receive freedom, they receive a gift above price. Paul the Apostle found it very strange that free people would try to return to slavery. In Galatians 5:1 he wrote, *"It is for freedom that Christ has set us free. Stand firm, then, and do not let yourselves be burdened again by a yoke of slavery."* Since there is now the opportunity of total soul freedom: *"know the truth* [Jesus], *and the truth will set you free"* (John 8:32; 14:6), why do people become enslaved to alcohol, drugs, money, sex, material things? Why do people become slaves to man-made religions with their multitudes of legalistic rules? Why do some people totally abuse and misuse freedom to the extent that our jails are crowded beyond their capacity with people who don't seem to want to be free? Is it because freedom carries a burden? Yes, it is a heavy burden, called *"responsibility."* Some don't want to carry it, choosing to escape into some kind of slavery where they don't have to think freely and freely make choices. Are you free in every way? If not, this week would be a good time for all slaves to take off their chains, don't you agree?

> *O God, help us to desire freedom in every way. Help us, now, to claim from You physical, mental, emotional and spiritual freedom. Amen.*

ONE YEAR CHALLENGE—Read: Nehemiah 2-4

July 9

Forgiving Yourself

SOME YEARS AGO I MET A LADY WHO MUST HAVE BEEN IN AGONY. About five years earlier she had an argument with her 17-year-old son. As they screamed insults at one another, he ran out of the house and jumped on his motorcycle and sped down the road. She angrily shouted after him, *"I hope you get killed."* The words were scarcely out of her mouth when the motorcycle crashed and he was killed. Grief-stricken, she had continuously asked God for five years to forgive her for her words. Yet she continued to feel a heavy burden of guilt and wondered why God had not forgiven her, for she did not feel forgiven. Some people, under this type of burden, repeatedly search the Bible to find if there is something else they are supposed to do to gain God's forgiveness. I John 1:9 is very clear: *"If we confess our sins, he is faithful and just and will forgive us our sins and purify us from all unrighteousness."*

Yet some feel that their sins are too great and doubt that Christ's death on the cross was sufficient to atone for their terrible sins. Regretfully, some even swear they will never forgive themselves and keep that vow, thereby, trapping themselves into not accepting God's forgiveness. Are you one of those who has not been able to forgive yourself? When are you going to forgive yourself? *"How does one begin to forgive himself?"* you ask. The same way he forgives someone else: you will to do so. *"My grace is sufficient for you,"* Jesus said to Paul in 2 Corinthians 12:9. Will you confess your sin to Jesus and accept his forgiveness? Then, will to forgive yourself. *"We set our hearts at rest in his presence whenever our hearts condemn us. For God is greater than our hearts"* (I John 3:19-20).

> *O Forgiving God, I come to You; I am amazed that You could forgive me. Thank You! Help me to forgive myself, and go on. Amen.*

ONE YEAR CHALLENGE—Read: Nehemiah 5-7

July 10

The Beauty of the River

My WIFE AND I TOOK A CRUISE on the Mississippi from New Orleans. We rode an old paddle-wheeler, and it was fun. It was beautiful on the river, even though pollutants are constantly dumped into that great river. Rivers are one of the special beauties of God's creative work. Ask any fisherman. In Genesis 2:10 is recorded the first river that flowed through the Garden of Eden. It separated into four rivers. It has a long history that stretches from Eden's river to Revelation 22:1, where the beautiful river is seen again: clear as crystal, flowing from the throne of God, giving life and healing to all kinds of people. I think it's the same river we see in Psalm 46:4 *whose streams make glad the city of God.* Deep in the heart of every believer is the desire to see that river some day. The Jordan River is well known to Christians, because much of the great work of Jesus was done along its banks with his fishermen turned disciples. Rivers can be dangerous and foreboding waters as well. We remember the disciples in a boat, afraid that they were going to drown until Jesus calmed the storm. But mostly the river is a positive symbol. We have a chorus we sing: *"I've got peace like a river in my soul."* It's too bad that most rivers got so dirty that churches moved their baptismal services inside and lost touch with those natural waters. Some of the most expensive land in America today is riverfront property. People are looking for peaceful and beautiful settings for homes. Oh, I almost forgot! Jesus said, *"Whoever believes in me, as the Scripture has said, streams of living water will flow from within him"* (John 7:38, Isaiah 32:2). The challenge and promise of that river could change the face of America!

O Thou River of Life, flow over me. Wash me and make me clean and pure. Cleanse me, O God. Amen.

ONE YEAR CHALLENGE—Read: Nehemiah 8-10

July 11

From Theology to Doxology

SOME PEOPLE HAVE SO MUCH THEOLOGY (truths about God) they have no room for doxology (praising God). The truth is most valuable but it should never be a barrier to our enjoying God and walking in victorious fellowship with Him. When Lazarus died, Jesus was saddened and went to pay His respects to the two sisters left behind. Jesus was so touched by their grief and filled with compassion for them that He offered the opportunity to sing a song of doxology. He said in John 11:23, *"Your brother will rise again."* One sister, Martha, heard the offer but she had no room for it in her theology. Her theology had taught her that God would do wonderful things at the end of time. She gladly affirmed her theological beliefs with Jesus, understanding that her dead brother would rise later rather than sooner. But Jesus insisted on doxology for her and for a short while there was a lively discussion, even including her

sister. Finally, Jesus raised Lazarus from the dead and they all had a time of doxology together. Has that ever happened to you? Has your belief system, or what you have always heard, kept you from receiving what God has for you? Don't lock yourself up so tightly in what you have heard or read or been taught that there is no room left for doxology. God is bigger than anyone's theological system; you can't trap Him or limit Him in one. I am reminded of the account in John 20:24-29 when Thomas doubted the other followers of Jesus who testified that he had risen from death, *"Unless I see the nail marks in his hands and put my finger where the nails were, and put my hand into his side, I will not believe it."* A week later Jesus showed up and told Thomas to feel the scars in his hands and side. Thomas said to Jesus, *"My Lord and my God!"* Theology became doxology!

Lord Jesus, I believe in You. Praise You! Praise You! Praise You! Praise You! Ha! It feels so good! Amen.

ONE YEAR CHALLENGE—Read:
Nehemiah 11-13

July 12

Go for the Gold

EVERY FOUR YEARS, WE PARTICIPATE IN THE INTERNATIONAL OLYMPIC Games, most by watching on television but hundreds by striving for a gold medal. For those who participate, there is honor in their home country. For those who win a medal, there is great, world-wide recognition. For those who win a gold medal, there is great financial reward as well as world-wide praise. And then, it is over. People who have lived and worked and existed for their brief *"place in the sun"* must return to reality. The world forgets 99 percent of the participants (including the winners) until the next Olympiad. *"Going for the gold"* has a familiar ring to it; it really appeals to us. There is something about fame, fortune and the world's favor that attracts us. But it's so short-lived. That's why Jesus warned, *"Do not store up for yourselves treasures on earth, where moth and rust destroy, and where thieves break in and steal. But store up for yourselves treasures in heaven"* (Matthew 6:19-20). Paul the Apostle knew much about the Greek Games; he used examples from The Games to get his points across. In 1 Corinthians 9:24-27, he describes the training routine of the Olympic runners and their efforts, but only one gets a prize. However, he challenges Christians to run for Jesus, giving their best. Give your 100 percent effort because we know all of us will receive the *"prize,"* which is, eternal life in Heaven. So the discipline of the Olympic athlete can be a pattern for the self-discipline of the Christian life. If we are going for the spiritual gold, we can say with confidence, *"Now there is in store for me (in Heaven) the crown of righteousness, which the Lord, the righteous Judge, will award to me on that day—and not only to me, but also to all who have longed for his appearing"* (2 Timothy 4:8).

Dear Jesus, how wonderful it is to run through life with You as a running partner. Sometimes I get really tired, but You never leave me. Amen.

ONE YEAR CHALLENGE—Read:
Esther 1-3

July 13

The Batting Cage

I STOPPED BY THE BATTING CAGE THE OTHER DAY. It's fun! It's good exercise! You don't have to chase the balls! The machine will tirelessly throw you the ball. It's good practice. If you need to shorten your stride, spread your stance, or learn to hit to left field, it is ideal. It's a place to exercise discipline to improve your playing. Too bad there is not a batting cage for Christians. All Christians know their weak points but often are not willing to exercise the discipline needed to improve. *"Physical training is of some value, but godliness has value for all things,"* is Paul's instruction to Timothy in I Timothy 4:8. Further, he describes his own spiritual discipline in I Corinthians 9:26-27; *"I do not run like a man running aimlessly; I do not fight like a man beating the air* (shadow-boxing). *No, I beat my body and make it my slave so that after I have preached to others, I myself will not be disqualified."* The Apostle James has a list of things for Christians to do that are profitable for Christian growth and maturing: *"Submit yourselves, then, to God. Resist the Devil, . . . Come near to God . . . purify your hearts, . . . Humble yourselves before the Lord"* (James 4:7-10). All Christian growth and discipleship can't be dependent on public meetings with Christians. Private, self-discipline is a must. A scheduled time and place of daily devotion will bless your life. Growing in this daily quiet time of prayer and meditation, the Holy Spirit can reveal things that need to be improved. A daily, disciplined time for Bible-reading would surprise you as the Word of God speaks to your need. The blessings of spiritual self-discipline keep it from becoming drudgery or dull. If worldly people practice bowling, golf, or whatever for sport, is it too much to expect the people of God practicing to be better Christians?

> *My Father, I want to be the best possible Christian; I really do. Help me to overcome my spiritual laziness. Amen.*

One Year Challenge—Read: Esther 4-6

July 14

When Your Dream Dissolves

HOW DO YOU HANDLE IT when your dream dissolves? Or your sand castle gets washed away? Human beings, by nature, like to daydream about their own place in the world or that of their children. We want to see only the best happen to them and we work and pray in that direction. When it doesn't turn out, we ask God, *"Why?"* As Martha said to Jesus after her brother's funeral, *"Lord, . . . if you had been here, my brother would not have died"* (John 11:21). Or, there are more disturbing thoughts that come up: *"Jesus was there and He didn't stop it. He watched it happen. He didn't intervene. Why doesn't God protect my dreams?"* In the Bible, Jesus is always surrounded by people whose *"rainbow has gone to smash"* (see April 2). What do you do? First, realize He is the only one who truly cares about your broken dreams. Everyone else is too busy putting their own scattered pieces back together.

"Come to me, all you who are weary and burdened" (Matthew 11:28) is Jesus' standing invitation. Secondly, give the broken pieces to him. If he desires, he can put the pieces back together. If it is for the good of all and doesn't contradict his laws of the universe, he will fix it. Or, he can help you move to another level of trust and commitment. The man who was watching his son die and went running to Jesus had to put his dissolving dream in Jesus' hands and then go on (John 4:49). It is a difficult matter for most folks to trust the Lord when things go bad. The hymn writer, Edward Mote put it like this: *"On Christ, the solid Rock I stand—All other ground is sinking sand."** He is able to keep you. He will give you the desire to go on.

O Jesus, I give You my dreams. Keep them for me. Give them back to me, sorted out in a meaningful way. I trust You. Amen.

July 15

O${}_{NE}$Y${}_{EAR}$C${}_{HALLENGE}$—Read: Esther 7-9

"Raising the Game"

I'VE BEEN ACTIVE IN SPORTS all of my life. I am very impressed by some new phrases that have come into use in the 90s. Sportswriters and commentators talk about athletes who are able to *"raise the level of their game"* at crucial times. These are the players who can *"crank it up to another level"* if the competition is stiff. Especially during the playoffs, certain athletes are able to *"raise the level of intensity"* in their playing in order to secure the victory. It is an interesting fact that people are able to raise their concentration if they want, and thereby accomplish more. I want to transfer this notion to the spiritual arena and challenge all Christians to *"raise their game"* to another level. The Bible says, *"our struggle is not against flesh and blood"* (Ephesians 6:12), and, *"in a race all the runners run"* (1 Corinthians 9:24), so the Word of God is well accustomed to using athletics as a metaphor to teach spiritual truth. If we are going to impact our world, we cannot be satisfied with business as usual. It is time for us to *"raise our intensity level"* in Christian living. Paul, the Apostle understood this as he neared the end of his life. In prison for preaching the gospel, his life nearing an end, he wrote, *"Not that I have . . . already been made perfect, but I press on to take hold of that for which Christ Jesus took hold of me. . . . But one thing I do: Forgetting what is behind and straining toward what is ahead, I press on toward the goal to win the prize for which God has called me heavenward in Christ Jesus"* (Philippians 3:12-14). He was intense and committed to Jesus until he died and he helped people all the while. How? By his words, challenging Christians in his letters to *"raise their game."* By his lifestyle, he exemplified that being a Christian is all or nothing. Christ is Lord of all or He will not be Lord at all. Lift it up! Raise the bar!

> *Forgive me, Father, for maintaining the status quo in my spiritual life when so many need our Son. Help me to understand the term "spiritual urgency." Amen.*

ONE YEAR CHALLENGE—Read:
Esther 10,
2 Corinthians 1-2

July 16

Why Not Step Out and Enjoy the Rain

Aren't you glad it rained? And rained? And rained? The land was so dry. *"You never miss the water 'til the well runs dry"* can also be said about summer rains. How refreshing the rain, whether a drizzle, a shower, or a downpour! My daughter and I took a walk in the rain one night. There's something sweet about the rain! Maybe it's the cleansing, or the renewing, or the peacefulness—what do you think? Can you identify with the idea that rain is sweet? The Bible uses the figure of rain to describe God's dealing with us. Isaiah the Prophet said *"You heavens above, rain down righteousness; let the clouds shower it down"* (45:8). Hosea said it this way, *"it is time to seek the LORD, until he comes and showers righteousness on you"* (10:12). But I especially like God's promise of Deuteronomy 11:14, *"I will send rain on your land in its season, both autumn and spring rains."* What assurance! God gives us the *"spring rains"* or the rain for planting and cultivating. But His care for us is not partial: the *"autumn rains"* of ripening for the harvest is coming also. The promise is clear. From early to late, beginning to end, I am under His care. The spiritual implications are rich. The early rain touches all of us sometime. God's planting love is poured out on us, awakening in us thoughts of His goodness and mercy, convincing us of the need of our souls. But it doesn't stop there: the rain of His Spirit continues, until we respond to God and our lives become fruitful. Regretfully, some ground is so hard, the water runs off fast, the blessing is missed. So are some people! Why not step out and enjoy the rain?

You have refreshed my spirit and restored my soul so many times. Fall with freshness on every dull part of my life today. Amen.

One Year Challenge—Read:
2 Corinthians 3-5

July 17

Staking Out God's Quiet Place

CAN YOU BELIEVE THE BUILDING BOOM GOING ON right now in the country? Offices, shopping centers, industrial parks, subdivisions; is there any end in sight? Probably not. At least, not as long as there is a vacant lot. Some are dismayed by the amount of building. They long for the quiet past when they could get away from people. Remember the story of Daniel Boone, the frontiersman, who is said to have told his wife one day, *"Woman, we gotta move, there's folks 50 miles from here!"* Those days of quiet are gone forever from the metro areas. So how do you find space or discover a spot of solitude in a place like this? You just have to carve it out for yourself. The poet, Cleland McAfee wrote, *"There is a place of quiet rest, Near to the heart of God, A place where sin cannot molest, Near to the heart of God."** He further wrote that this is a place of joy and peace. I like what Augustine once said, *"God has made us for Himself, and our hearts are restless until they rest in Him."* That is, even if all the construction wasn't going on, some people would not attain a state of peace and quiet. How can we *"flee like a bird to your mountain"* as the psalmist asked, when we are under pressure? What mountain? Where is it? The answer is it can be any old mountain in any old place if the Lord is your retreat (Psalm 11:1). It's the secret of a hiding place with God. Find a place in your heart where you can retreat to be with Him, regardless of how crowded the area may become. Life easily gets cluttered with things, just the way a community does. God's quiet place must be staked out and guarded.

Remind me, O My Father, that a kneeling Christian can be at home anywhere and enjoy communication with You. Thank You for quiet times. Amen.

One Year Challenge—Read: 2 Corinthians 6-8

July 18

A Power Outage

WHEN HURRICANE HUGO WENT ON THE RAMPAGE through South Carolina, one of his most powerful punches was delivered to the electric power business. After he had passed, people began to realize how much they depended on electricity. Many people had never done without it before; they were totally confused about what to do. Dark had never seemed so dark and people dealt with feelings not experienced previously. Many discovered the joy of candlelight and the blessing of kerosene lamps, sources of light from bygone days. Life exists and goes on, even without television and videos and computers. Many people are suffering today from a spiritual power outage. Perhaps a storm of family crisis or economic disaster or sickness or death has plunged them into serious darkness. One day all is well, the next day is darkness and despair. The familiar is no longer there, the usual handles of life are suddenly missing. What do you do? Where do you turn? David sang, in 2 Samuel 22:29, *"You are my lamp, O LORD; the LORD turns my darkness into light."* Or consider the wise man of Psalm 119:105, *"Your word is a lamp to my feet and a light for my path."* Jesus said, *"I am the light of the world. Whoever follows me will never walk in darkness, but will have the light of life"* (John 8:12). It is really good to know that when you have a *"power outage,"* it doesn't have to be permanent. Do you feel unplugged? Is your generator broken down? Has some personal *"Hugo"* broken down the most meaningful things in your life? In the above words from the Bible, you will find your *"dark-busters." "Light has come into the world"* (John 3:19). Go ahead—hit the switch!

O God of Power and Might, I can't live without Your power. I am so weak. I need You every hour. Amen.

ONE YEAR CHALLENGE—Read: 2 Corinthians 9-11

July 19

Futility of Idols

WHY DO PEOPLE WORSHIP IDOLS? Why would anyone be foolish enough, blind enough, empty enough, searching enough, (we could go on) to worship something made by human hands? If you want to read the clearest statement that has ever been penned on the futility of idol worship, read Isaiah 44:9-20. How could people allow themselves such folly? I don't know, but Isaiah says that people who worship idols know deep down inside that they are practicing self-deception even while they faithfully go through the routine (verse 20). As Isaiah describes it, idol worship could be described as *"leftover"* religion. He says that a man cuts down a tree and uses it to cook his food and warm his body. Then he takes the *"leftover"* and forms a god and worships it. From that description, idol worship covers many religious folks. Do you use all of your time and talents and energy to serve yourself and to meet your own needs and leave the left-overs for your God? Just tipping your hat to God for a few minutes on Sunday morning or calling a minister for wedding or funeral help is a tip-off to idol worshipers. Didn't you ever wonder at the superstition of people who never go to church but then want to get married in church and wear a white gown as well? Idol worship is so subtle while taking a place in a person's life, but so obvious to an onlooker. If material things or success or popularity or any thing takes first place in your life, you are an idol worshiper. *"Worship the Lord your God, and serve him only"* (Matthew 4:10) was Jesus' reminder to Satan of the first commandment. An idol or statue or anything weaker than you cannot answer your prayer or save you. Bow your knees only to the Living Lord, Jesus Christ.

O God, save me from settling for silly substitutes when You offer me the real thing. Release me from the sin of settling for second-hand gods. Amen.

ONE YEAR CHALLENGE—Read:
2 Corinthians 12-13

July 20

Watering the Garden

I'VE HAD A SMALL GARDEN several summers. Not a *"serious"* garden but just a little place to play with the soil and watch stuff grow. All summer we patiently watered it every day, fighting the heat and drought of the summer. Then vacation came last summer. For 10 days we didn't see the garden and the garden didn't get any water. What a disappointment when we returned home! The garden had dried up. No fruit was there to be harvested, except a few tomatoes. The heat of summer defeated all of our previous efforts. My great expectations were dashed. I've known a lot of people like my garden. They got off to a good start—had a lot of potential! Had opportunities to develop and live a really productive life! Had input and care from loving and significant people. BUT, nothing came of it. Drought set in! Couldn't take the unrelenting heat of life! Basically, the life-giving water got cut off. You can't live without wa-

ter, physically or spiritually. We must faithfully water our garden of life. That's one of my concerns about people who get so busy vacationing that they don't have time for Bible reading, prayer, or worship. Jesus said in Revelation 22:17, *"Whoever is thirsty, let him come; and whoever wishes, let him take the free gift of the water of life."* Jesus is described as the Water of Life. He said to a woman whose life was parched and dried up from seeking satisfaction in men (at least six): *"whoever drinks the water I give him will never thirst. Indeed, the water I give him will become in him a spring of water welling up to eternal life"* (John 4:14). Again in John 7:37-38 *"If anyone is thirsty, let him come to me and drink. Whoever believes in me, as the Scripture has said, streams of living water will flow from within him."* Drought or refreshment? Your choice!

> *Why do my dry times attack my prayer life, Father? I need so much to have constant contact with You, O Water of My Life. Amen.*

OneYearChallenge—Read: Job 1-3

July 21

Summer Laziness

HOW OFTEN DO YOU HAVE ATTACKS of summer laziness? It's not listed in medical journals and there is no major study being done to understand it, so don't worry. But don't you get it some days? Remember those warm, balmy days when everything was beautiful outside and you just couldn't get started? You don't want to do anything but lay around and fiddle around—you just want to be lazy. It's not really serious; sometimes we get over it in a couple of hours. This is something that we can smile about later. There is a serious spiritual malady called laziness that the Bible warns us about. The book of Proverbs is the most prominent source of warning: *"Go to the ant, you sluggard; consider its ways and be wise! It has no commander, no overseer or ruler, yet it stores its provisions in summer and gathers its food at harvest"* (6:6-8). Of real insight is the statement in Proverbs 26:16 (EB): *"The lazy person thinks he is wiser than seven people who give sensible answers."* The sin of laziness, like all sins, even spends a lot of time reasoning out why the sin is acceptable. Paul said if a person is too lazy to work, he should not be allowed to eat (2 Thessalonians 3:10). In Hebrews 6:11-12 is the exhortation: *"We want each of you to show this same diligence to the very end, in order to make your hope sure. We do not want you to become lazy, but to imitate those who through faith and patience inherit what has been promised."* The matter of example and teaching is so important here. In this affluent society, children easily can grow up with little or nothing worthwhile to do, and learn laziness at an early age. The family and community has a responsibility to help children grow up without such a lazy mindset. Yes, there are spiritual implications in all of this. *"Spiritual fervor"* (Romans 12:11) will have a carry-over in all areas of life. Diligence in every area of life is commended by the Apostle Paul in I Timothy 5:10.

> **Eternal God, the summer is so good for relaxing and just doing nothing. Give me a new sense of diligence about working for You in this spiritual garden of prayers. Amen.**

ONE YEAR CHALLENGE—Read: Job 4-6

July 22

Talking about the Weather

ISN'T IT WONDERFUL THAT WE HAD SUCH A HEAT WAVE and dry spell? (You're probably thinking, *"What's wrong with this guy?"*) Imagine how quiet it would have been if not for the hot weather. The weather has been a dominant subject of conversation in carpools, radio, TV, over backyard fences, etc. The subject has really been used for days now. But, like someone once observed, *"everybody is talking about the weather but no one is doing anything about it."* Indeed, nothing can be done about it so it amounts to meaningless words! When I was a child my mother warned me about silly and meaningless speech. She often quoted Jesus from Matthew 12:36-37, *"I tell you that men will have to give account on the day of judgment for every careless* (idle) *word they have spoken. For by your words you will be acquitted, and by your words you will be condemned."* Now you may think she was being too severe on a young

boy, but she did teach me to make my words count. In Proverbs 25:11 the Bible says, *"A word aptly spoken is like apples of gold in settings of silver."* Saying the right thing at the right time can make a difference. Paul advised in Colossians 4:6, *"Let your conversation be always full of grace, seasoned with salt, so that you may know how to answer everyone."* I guess my main point is this: How many times in one day do people talk to us (many are lonely and discouraged, or confused) giving us a wonderful opportunity to say something helpful and all we can come up with is meaningless chatter about the weather or politics? You see, even writing this, I have to be very careful with my choice of words. Your coming to faith or growing in faith may hinge on the words I use!

Saying what we mean and meaning what we say is a must for our communication with you, God, and with our neighbors. Teach us to give prior thought to both. Amen.

ONE YEAR CHALLENGE—Read: Job 7-9

July 23

Grass Cutting Day

I CUT MY GRASS TODAY. DO YOU have grass to cut? If so, you may be impressed as I was by what happened. Our yard is small—it takes only one hour to mow it. When I finished, I got my rake and basket to pick up the clippings. (I don't have a grass catcher yet!) I was surprised that in the short time, the cut grass had already dried. It was as if it had been cut for a long time. At about the same time, some verses from the Bible suddenly came to mind, all of those verses that compare the shortness of life to grass. In Psalm 90:6, David said that grass flourishes in the morning, renewed by the dew, but by evening it is cut down and withered. Beautiful, but temporary! Jesus said that our Heavenly Father assuredly loves and cares for us because He gives life and beauty even to grass, although someone will cut it today and burn it tomorrow (Matthew 6:30). There are other verses in the Bible that make the same point. You have probably noticed by now that some yards on your street were quite beautiful in early spring but already have brown spots where the short-lived grass has died. I'm not suggesting that every time you cut your grass you become a shade-tree philosopher but I am saying that the Bible compares us to grass often enough that it deserves some serious attention on your part. Humans just have a way of messing up their priorities! Often, we invest time and energy into something that is going to die and be gone about the same time we are, like newly cut grass! Life is too short and eternity is too long for us to make that kind of mistake. This is a simple lesson, take a minute to let it sink into your heart.

My times are in Your hands, O God. Please direct me in a proper use of my time. Help me to see that time is very short and that eternity is very long. Amen.

July 24

ONE YEAR CHALLENGE—Read: Job 10-12

Spiritual Drought

HAS THE DROUGHT HIT YOUR LIFE? Even though we have had enough rain this summer and no particular threat of drought, many are suffering from a parching dryness in their soul. Spiritual drought may be harder to overcome than physical. David described his in Psalm 32:4, *"For day and night your hand was heavy upon me; my strength was sapped as in the heat of summer."* Guilt will throw you into spiritual drought. *"The LORD will guide you always; he will satisfy your needs in a sun-scorched land and will strengthen your frame. You will be like a well-watered garden, like a spring whose waters never fail"* (Isaiah 58:11). Has your Bible gotten a little dust on it lately? Is your praying drying up around the edges? These are sure signs of spiritual drought. Jeremiah 17:8 offers a sure shower of refreshment: *"blessed is the man who trusts in the LORD, whose confidence is in him. He will be like a tree planted by the water that sends out* its roots by the stream. It does not fear when heat comes; its leaves are always green. It has no worries in a year of drought and never fails to bear fruit."* If you have let yourself slip away from worship this summer, your roots may now be too far from the stream. Maybe it's time to pray for a good dousing with *"both autumn and spring rains"* (Deuteronomy 11:14). As every farmer and gardener knows, drought can sneak up quickly and unexpectedly. *"You never miss the water until the well runs dry"* is an old and true saying. Spiritually, it's hard to deal with a crisis, like a family problem, when your soul is dry. The world is always applying the heat at work or at school or, you name it. It will dry you up. Pray for a spiritual shower of blessing.

Dear God, only you can revive my soul. Your refreshment will be welcome and good daily. Amen.

One Year Challenge—Read: Job 13-15

July 25

Building Fences

WHAT IS THIS THING ABOUT FENCES? This area is really into fences. Fencing companies must be doing well. People build beautiful new houses and plan nice lawns and put out attractive shrubbery and then ruin the looks of it all with an ugly fence. I realize that if you have small children or pets you need a fence for their protection and exercise. I know many people would respond to what I have written so far by saying you have to have a fence to protect your beautiful plants from kids and pets. That's true, too! But, so often the fences are but mute reminders of that which separates and divides people. I'm into community and people sharing life together. The privacy fence that shuts me in automatically shuts other people out. It's like that practice in some religions called "shunning" where all the people turn their backs on the rejected person. One of the reasons Jesus came was to break down the barriers that divide people (Ephesians 2:14-15). He desired to create a new type of people, united in Him without any dividing lines. The only real, personal prayer that the Bible records from the lips of Jesus is John 17. The whole point of the prayer is His expressed desire to eliminate division and bring people together. His death on the cross was to that end. He was sent by his heavenly father to take down the wall that sin had built between God and man. Think about what you can do to take down other kinds of walls that divide folks. If you can't take them down, be like David who said, "with my God I can scale a wall" (2 Samuel 22:30). Real love and desire for community will overcome these barriers to our fellowship with one another.

> *Father, will I ever be able to love and trust my neighbors so I don't have to have a fence to protect my space? I long for such a day! Amen.*

ONE YEAR CHALLENGE—Read: Job 16-18

July 26

Without Wax: Real Test of Sincerity

DID YOU EVER HEAR THE DERIVATION OF THE WORD "SINCERE"? It basically means *"without wax."* It's like this: if you have seen old statues or pictures of statues in Greece or even our own Statue of Liberty, you know that the weather erodes away and harms them. Sometimes they crack. Sometimes they get holes. So, many years ago, people thought to try to repair them with hot wax. When the wax got hard, you couldn't see or notice the imperfections. Fine, that worked well, until you had an unusually hot day. You guessed it; the wax melted, and the imperfections were exposed again. So the good statues, those without imperfections, were described as *"sincere"* or *"without wax."* That is such a vital trait. When people sympathize with us or weep with us, are happy with us, smile and speak to us, we want to feel they are *"without wax."* What a disappointment when we find out that what we thought was true friendship doesn't stand *"the heat"* or pass the test of time. Hey, but that works both ways! Are we always sincere? Do we say what we mean and mean what we say? Can folks depend on us to be the same all the time or do we also *"play the crowd"*? Remember in the Bible how Paul accused Peter of insincerity while working with people of different races (Galatians 2:11-21)? In 2 Corinthians 8:8 Paul urges us to prove that our love is sincere. He prayed for God to bless *"all them that love our Lord Jesus Christ in sincerity"* (Ephesians 6:24 KJV). In Joshua 24:14 the man challenged his people to serve the Lord in sincerity or *"faithfulness."* That's another way of saying, *"Don't be a hypocrite, or two-faced."* Resolve today to try to be sincere. Ask God to help you to be sincere, even when it's hot. That's the real test!

> *Father, I would love to pass this wax test. I have gotten used to being insincere since I know others are insincere with me. Deliver me. Amen.*

ONE YEAR CHALLENGE—Read: Job 19-21

July 27

Taking a Gamble

"*SAY IT AIN'T SO, JOE*" was a headline that was repeated over and over again when "*Shoeless Joe*" Jackson and the infamous Chicago Black Sox were exposed for having gambled on baseball games in which they had played (1919). The citizenry was shocked by the idea that gambling should have such a hold on people. If Joe Jackson came back to our world today, he would surely smile at the grip that gambling has on the American public. I recently visited Las Vegas. I discovered that any hour of the day or night a person could gamble on the outcome of something. It is a mania now, out there. Every convenience store makes it possible for you to conveniently gamble. Since that's the current scene, should we be shocked that popular athletes (or anyone) bet on the outcome of games? What's so bad about that? What's wrong with gambling? Many say it doesn't hurt anyone. Again we are in the arena of principle. There is more to "*rightness*" and "*wrongness*" than laws that say "*thou shalt not . . .*" For instance, the Bible condemns covetousness and materialism; gambling is rooted in both of these attitudes (Matthew 6:24-34). How about the biblical instruction that we work and use our possessions for the good of other people (Ephesians 4:28)? And certainly the focus of Jesus in teaching love for God and an equal loving concern for neighbor (Matthew 22:37-40) rules against our desire for personal gain and pleasure at their expense. Chance and luck are not principles to live by today. Trusting in the sovereignty and care of God in our lives (Matthew 10:29-31) is a more fruitful attitude than dancing with Lady Luck. The base egotism in getting something for nothing is destructive in the long run. As for me, I like the sure thing: Jesus (Hebrews 13:8).

O how easily the Devil tempts me Lord. It is because of my natural desire for more money and stuff. I confess that sin now. Amen.

One Year Challenge—Read: Job 22-24

July 28

Tiananmen Square

FOR STUDENTS OF HISTORY, A NEW PLACE has been added to the list of geographical reminders that nothing of value comes cheaply. Remember Valley Forge, Gettysburg, Iwo Jima, Normandy Beach, Corregidor, Pearl Harbor, Tiananmen Square. The last mentioned is the newest and freshest. Because of the speed and excellence of modern communications we watched the oppression, with its massacre, almost as it happened. We sat in on a giant history lesson about freedom and human rights. It has so touched us that many Americans want to memorialize Tiananmen Square in Washington, D.C., the city that contains some of our greatest memorials. History's greatest advances have been carried forward on the backs of those willing to make the ultimate sacrifice. There is an inner imperative that drives many to give all. Isaiah the Prophet caught the vision of what *"might be"* for many people and prayed *"Here am I. Send me"* (Isaiah 6:8). Saul of Tarsus, a rich lawyer and politician, saw the need for people to learn about Jesus and left his comfortable situation for a life of privation and danger and explained it by saying, *"I am compelled to preach. Woe to me if I do not preach the gospel!"* (I Corinthians 9:16). Jesus left the glory place called Heaven and died on a gory place called Calvary because He was committed to His cause (Matthew 20:28). To many onlookers, it does not make sense. To preservers of the status quo, it is foolhardy. To the realist, it is absurd. But for courageous souls, the challenge to realize an impossible dream may only come once in a lifetime, and you dare not let it pass.

> *Thank You, God, for our heroes of history. They challenge us. They inspire us. They tell us that we could do more for the family of mankind. Amen.*

July 29

ONE YEAR CHALLENGE—Read: Job 25-27

Sudden Shock

DID YOU EVER HAVE SOMEONE WAKE YOU UP SUDDENLY and you were so shocked that you jumped? Several times I have gone into a hospital room and the patient was half-asleep and my entering startled them. For a moment they didn't know what was happening. Gratefully, in a case like this, the shock is momentary and mind and body soon return to normal. I compare this to the shocking way Paul, the Apostle said Jesus will make His return: *"for you know very well that the day of the Lord will come like a thief in the night. While people are saying, 'Peace and safety,' destruction will come on them suddenly, as labor pains on a pregnant woman, and they will not escape"* (1 Thessalonians 5:2-3). It sounds like it will be a sudden shock, like the erupting of a volcano, that can't be stopped or controlled. During His ministry on earth, Jesus had much to say about preparedness to avoid the sudden shock. In Luke 12:39,

He said, *"understand this: If the owner of the house had known at what hour the thief was coming, he would not have let his house be broken into. You also must be ready, because the Son of Man will come at an hour when you do not expect him."* Matthew 24:38-39 includes the idea *"in the days before the flood, people were eating and drinking, marrying and giving in marriage, up to the day Noah entered the ark; and they knew nothing about what would happen until the flood came and took them all away. That is how it will be at the coming of the Son of Man."* This means sudden shock—waking up, seeing what's happening and realizing it is not a dream—but real! This will be the climax of history—the greatest day in history. Don't let it slip up on you and shock you.

O God, there have been so many faithful, spiritual giants who challenged me to live for You. There was a beautiful attraction in their lives: Your presence. Thanks! Amen.

July 30

ONE YEAR CHALLENGE—Read: Job 28-30

The Sudden Storm

IT CAME FROM NOWHERE! The afternoon was beautiful and sunny. There was a slight breeze. Everyone was commenting on the delightful weather. Then it happened: suddenly the sky was filled with rain, and hail as big as golf balls fell. People ran for cover and tried to protect their belongings. It came so quickly, with no warning, no time to get ready. You have experienced something like that, I'm sure, or heard something like it described on the evening news. Sudden destructive storms that give no warning are a normal part of nature. There is no way to prepare, we are vulnerable. Let's move this picture from the theater of natural calamity (rain, typhoon, hurricane) to the stage of your personal life. How do you deal with these storms: a discussion that becomes an argument, a rebellious child that goes out of control, serious sickness, or sudden death? These storms of the spirit attack the very fiber of our lives. Can we prepare for these things? YES! Preparing does not mean we can avoid them, it just means having a solid foundation under you so these things do not lead to destruction. *"In this world you will have trouble. But take heart! I have overcome the world"* are the words of Jesus in John 16:33. Surely, you must know that the life of Jesus was bombarded by storms of disappointment: friends deserting, enemies hating, and the like. But none of this defeated him. If we give him control of our life, he can do the same work for us. *"No temptation has seized you except what is common to man. And God is faithful; he will not let you be tempted beyond what you can bear"* (1 Corinthians 10:13). That is not a general statement but a specific word to people of faith in Jesus. Prepare today for tomorrow's storm!

When the storms of life are raging, stand by me, O My God. Sometimes I am very, very fearful. Amen.

ONE YEAR CHALLENGE—Read: Job 31-33

July 31

Crab Grass of the Soul

I WATCH THEM WITH AMAZEMENT, THOSE PEOPLE WHO BATTLE CRAB GRASS. They are patient and determined souls. Crawling around the yard, spade in hand, attacking and digging up this dread enemy of their yard. Do they ever win? Sometimes, temporarily, I suppose. But I see some of the same people doing it every year. There are lots of formulas for battling crab grass, but nothing is as effective as digging it out at the roots. Bad habits and bad attitudes are like crab grass. There are a lot of books and theories on how to clean them out of your life. Some people work long and hard on rooting out the same habit. But since the roots are in the heart, only radical spiritual surgery will do it. James raises the question, *"What causes fights and quarrels among you? Don't they come from your desires that battle within you?"* (James 4:1). Jesus said it in Matthew 12:34-35, *"out of the overflow of the heart the mouth speaks. The good man brings* good things out of the good stored up in him, and the evil man brings evil things out of the evil stored up in him." Self-improvement programs, by themselves, are doomed to failure, if they are mostly cosmetic, dealing only with things beyond the root problems. Those that seriously deal with our "Higher Power" can be helpful, if the person gets on the road to a personal relationship with God, through the only real savior, Jesus. New Year's resolutions always fail because they are like cutting crab grass with your lawn mower and not digging up the roots, the bad is sure to flourish again. Americans seem to always be looking for a quick fix. You don't get rid of crab grass overnight. It took time for it to grow; it will take time to root it out. It's the same with spiritual problems. It will take time for God to completely root out all the old habits, even after an instantaneous conversion. Let Him work it out!

Dear Lord, some of my worst habits seem to be rooted so deep in me, going all the way back to my childhood. Help me to have patience while you root them out. Amen.

OneYearChallenge—Read: Job 34-36

August 1

Strolling on the Beach

IN GENESIS 3, THERE IS THE ACCOUNT OF GOD WALKING IN THE GARDEN IN THE COOL OF THE DAY. It is a beautiful picture, very symbolic! But I ask, *"Was there no beach or oceanside near the Garden of Eden?"* Surely the omnipotent God would have enjoyed a stroll there. Whether at sunrise or sunset, I love to stroll on the deserted beach and watch the waves roll. It speaks so dramatically of God, who creates such beauty. The unceasing roll of waves speaks to me of God's eternal love. It never stops! Sometimes there seems to be a lull between the waves, some waves crest higher than others; isn't that how we experience God's love? Sometimes we think there is a lull and perhaps God has forgotten us; He is so still and quiet. But the waves keep rolling! And the waves cover a multitude of sins, like crisscrossing footprints that scar the beach, trashy picnic leftovers, man-made sand castles and holes that have been dug. Evidence of man's activities are cleared away by powerful waves at night and the morning offers a clean slate on which we start another day. There is beauty, strength, comfort, and peace to be found while walking the beach. A barefoot walk on the beach, with sand squishing through your toes, can sharpen your spiritual perspective. The Psalmist David often mentioned the waves of the sea. Jeremiah said it well in chapter 5, verse 22, " 'Should you not fear me,' declares the LORD? 'Should you not tremble in my presence? I made the sand a boundary for the sea, an everlasting barrier it cannot cross. The waves may roll, but they cannot prevail.' " The perspective from the beach is: If God can handle the waves and calm them (and they do obey him as Jesus illustrated in Matthew 8:26-27) then He can and will bring calm and peace to my life.

Master of the winds and waves, please keep my seas calm. Sometimes I feel like my boat is going to capsize and I will drown. Amen.

ONE YEAR CHALLENGE—Read:
Job 37-39

August 2

Drive-In Church

IN A JOKING KIND OF WAY, A MAN ASKED ME when was our church going to open a drive-in confessional booth. I suppose it is a sign of the times. There are several drive-in churches across the country so confessional booths may be a natural succession. Basically, it's part of a larger problem: the widespread misunderstanding of the word *"church"* in the Bible. If you mention this word today, you just hope you get to explain it! When you say *"church,"* various images come to people's minds. Some think of a building or a place to go, some think of a certain type of worship, some think of a cult or a sect; others think of a particular doctrine or denomination. Although these things may reflect some dimension of church, they are far from the New Testament reality. The biblical word for church means literally *"the called out people."* The church is people—a people who have been called out of something into a relationship with Jesus Christ. Without this personal experience of being called out from a former lifestyle and called into a personal commitment to Christ, there can be no church. Church is not a proxy experience or second-hand experience; it is not an automatic experience; it is a personal decision to leave something to go to someone. That is why church is not just a place to go, but a life experience to share. That's why *"TV church"* or *"drive-in church"* could never qualify; its purpose being to please; non-disturbing, and requiring no commitment. Many people find nothing appealing about the contemporary definitions of church. I believe they would be attracted to church when it is defined in terms of Acts 2:42: *"They devoted themselves to the apostles' teaching and to the fellowship, to the breaking of bread and to prayer."* Read the whole passage! Real church is GREAT!

God, give me the endurance to keep visiting church meeting houses until I find a real church. Plant me in a real dynamic body of believers. Amen.

ONE YEAR CHALLENGE—Read:
Job 40-42

August 3

Laughing at Death

IT IS A STRANGE SPECTACLE! From time to time, in different states and areas of the country, television gives its garish report of people celebrating a death. A group of people is shown gathered outside a prison wall awaiting an execution. They vent their ill-will toward the person about to die. A signal is received from inside the prison that the convict has been killed. Cheers fill the air! People laugh at death! When we read of murder in the newspaper we are shocked and saddened. When it happens to someone we know we are doubly saddened. What is it that causes some to rejoice at the death of another human being? Is it the same feeling that allows some to watch a beating or a rape and not intervene? I seem to hear echoes of *"no one is concerned for me. I have no refuge; no one cares for my life"* (Psalm 142:4). That was David's plaintive cry while caught in a trap of guilt of murder, adultery, and lies. Then I think of Jesus standing on a hill and looking down over a city full of crooks, thugs, criminals (both white- and blue-collar), murderers, etc., and the Bible says Jesus cried out, *"O Jerusalem, . . . how often I have longed to gather your children together, as a hen gathers her chicks under her wings, but you were not willing"* (Matthew 23:37). When Jesus saw people trapped in sin or slaves to sin, he did not laugh at their sin or its consequences. Crime is against God's law first before it is against man's law. It must be punished and it must be punished severely. But it seems to me there should always be a great sense of sadness about a wasted life and wasted opportunities. A society without the ability to show mercy or offer forgiveness is a hard place for all. There is nothing healing for society or the condemned when punishment is a source of celebration. Jesus loves even the worst of us, the same as he loves you, me or Mother Teresa!

ONE YEAR CHALLENGE—Read: Galatians 1-3

> *Dear Jesus, there was no laughter the day You died for us on the cross. Your death once and for all established the value of a human life. Amen.*

August 4

Living for the Moment

IS THERE AN ANSWER to the current outlook of despair that results in addiction, suicide, or meaningless drifting? The answer for some is to go to the other extreme of thought. Plastering their automobiles with stickers like *"Life is a beach,"* they go merrily on their way. Like Pollyanna they see nothing but a good time. Life is a party! Let it all hang out! Go for the gusto! You only go around once! Notice: you don't see this kind of bumper sticker on the cars of senior citizens. They know better. They have already been around once. *"Life is a beach"* does not take life seriously enough. Living for the moment leaves so many permanent scars: permanent paralysis from driving drunk, recurring guilt from having an abortion, broken relations left unmended, institutionalization, and on and on. Let us accept the fullness and excellence of life! The beauty and warmth of summer is especially good for us to be able to experience all that life was meant to be.

Like summer heat, the beach is relatively short-lived. The next tropical storm can wash away the beach sand overnight! Between the extremes of despair and silly stargazing is a solid place to stand, a place of faith in God and commitment to God. It is solid because it recognizes that reality is sometimes very difficult but that there is always a silver lining for every cloud and a daybreak for every night! And waiting confidently for daybreak speaks the challenge of faith. Living life victoriously and meaningfully, even under hardship, is possible for men and women of faith. Paul said, *"I can do everything through him who gives me strength"* (Philippians 4:13), and, *"we are more than conquerors* (of life) *through him who loved us"* (Romans 8:37). Yes, we can all hear the trumpet in the morning. If we dare, by God's strength, we can live life to the fullest!

> *Eternal God, it is so easy for me to get preoccupied with the now. Release me to see the now in the light of yesterday and my hope for tomorrow. Amen.*

ONE YEAR CHALLENGE—Read:
Galatians 4-6

August 5

"Stone Walls Do Not a Prison Make"

RALPH SOCKMAN TOLD OF A TRAIN RIDE he once took. Seated in front of him were two young men. Viewed from the rear they seemed to be looking at the scenery and conversing like the other passengers. Presently it came time for them to leave the train. Then it could be seen that they were handcuffed to each other. As they walked down the aisle, there was a look of humiliation, touched with bitterness. Sockman said he tried to think how he would feel if he were led through a staring crowd shackled like a wild animal that could not be trusted with its freedom. Being a prisoner of the law is indeed a bitter shame. But there is another type of prisoner. He is not shackled or subjected to disgrace like prisoners of the law. He may walk the streets or sit at home without any external restraints. Yet he is imprisoned with bars of his own making. Psalm 142:7 contains the petition, "Set me free from my prison, that I may praise your name." David's spirit was in prison although his body was unfettered in the palace. So it is with many a person—prisoners of their bodies, emotions, pride, habits, prejudices, passions! Jesus came "to proclaim freedom for the prisoners" (Luke 4:18). In the words of Henry van Dyke: "Self is the only prison that can ever bind the soul; Love is the only angel who can bid the gates unroll; And when he comes to call thee, arise and follow fast; His way may lie through darkness, but it leads to light at last." Another poet said, "Stone walls do not a prison make, nor iron bars a cage." Are you feeling trapped? Do you think you are in a rut? Do you ever wonder about being free?

> Why is it, God, that people build prisons for themselves when You made us to be free? Help me to experience today the true freedom of Jesus. Amen.

ONE YEAR CHALLENGE—Read: Ephesians 1-3

August 6

Letting Go

SUMMER MONTHS ARE THE MONTHS OF LETTING GO. High school and college graduations are times of transition in the family when children move to stages of growth toward adulthood and parents are called on to let go. Letting go is very difficult in some families. Some parents are very possessive, some are over-protective, some are experts in control, some are insecure; for many, many reasons it is sometimes hard to just let go. The Bible instructs parents to *"Train a child in the way he should go, and when he is old he will not turn from it"* (Proverbs 22:6). The sense of loss that many parents feel when their children leave the family nest makes it hard to remember biblical instruction. Some parents also entertain self-doubts as to their own effectiveness in raising children and question the readiness of the child to be independent. An apron string or umbilical cord that stretches many miles can be nothing but painful. Young birds only learn to fly in the painful experience of being pushed from the nest. Young adults must have the freedom to fly on their own power also. I am reminded of the wisdom of Hannah (I Samuel 1:27-28) when she let go of her young son, Samuel, to serve the Lord away from home at the temple, saying, *"I prayed for this child, and the LORD has granted me what I asked of him. So now I give him to the LORD. For his whole life he will be given over to the LORD."* It is easier to let go when you know that children are a trust from the Lord. It is easier to let go when you *"bring them up in the training and instruction of the Lord"* (Ephesians 6:4). Perhaps there is some letting go that you need to do today. In prayer, release this person to God.

Hold my hand, Lord, as I walk and try to teach those dear to me about the Christian walk. Guide my steps. Amen.

ONE YEAR CHALLENGE—Read: Ephesians 4-6

August 7

Christ Versus Culture

PATRIOTISM IS A NATURAL! Love of country is instilled in us at an early age. This love is reinforced over and over again through public school education, holidays celebrating our uniqueness in the family of nations, and relatives serving faithfully in our armed services. It becomes so strong a dynamic in our lives, so deeply ingrained, that it becomes difficult for us to be objective. We easily can slide into an *"us"* versus *"them"* mindset among the family of nations. We even certify this with the assurance that God is always on our side, and everything in our culture is always right. To suggest even that America is not a Christian nation sounds like heresy to some of us! To read in the Bible that a Holy God does not agree with any human culture can be disturbing. But that's the way it is! God says in Isaiah 55:8-9, *"my thoughts are not your thoughts, neither are your ways my ways, . . . As the heavens are higher than the earth, so are my ways higher than your ways and my thoughts than your thoughts."* Governments act out of selfishness, looking out for themselves. Relations with other countries are often self-serving; if we only consider the advantage for us, we forget our debt to help others. Jesus Christ always goes against culture, any cultural system. When he talked about his followers being *"the salt of the earth"* (Matthew 5:13), he talked about these Christians using their influence to change the culture. In the community workplace it ought to be perfectly obvious that Christians are marching to be the beat of a different drummer. The reply of John and Peter to those who want to silence their witness about the Savior still applies: *"Judge for yourselves whether it is right in God's sight to obey you rather than God"* (Acts 4:19).

> *Dear Father, when Jesus called His followers "lights in the world" it implied that the world needed light. Teach us that there are insights into human relationships that can only be received from Jesus. Amen.*

August 8

ONE YEAR CHALLENGE—Read:
Psalms 1-5

Being in a Family

IN A FRAGMENTED WORLD WHERE PEOPLE ARE DIVIDED against each other, the church as "the family of God" (I Peter 4:17) holds great promise. Calling each other "brother" and "sister" is rich in meaning (Matthew 12:50). I watched my children grow up loving and caring for one another, helping and protecting one another. Their concern for each other made them go to some effort to include each one in any meaningful activity. As we all spent a week of vacation together this year, I saw that none of these qualities had been lost. I observed my grandchildren living with the same family dynamics. It is easy for the church to learn from the family and the family to learn from the church about relationships. The church should be a loving and caring inclusive body that treats all who enter her doors with equal openness and support. Perhaps one of the reasons many churches are weak today is the loss of a sense of family. Many enter and leave a worship service without a sense of acceptance or that their presence was noticed or made any difference. Many traditional families have "traditions" of favoritism, cliquishness, and division. Families sacrifice unity sometimes over some worthless piece of furniture that someone wanted when the parents died. Many family relations are so distorted by abuse, divorce, materialism, and suspicion that unless these people can see the family modeled by the people of God in the church family, they will never know how to do it. Acts 2:44, 46-47 shows us, "All the believers were together and had everything in common. They broke bread in their homes and ate together with glad and sincere hearts, praising God and enjoying the favor of all the people." Jesus still invites the world "Come, to me all" (Matthew 11:28), and his church should be a receptive family of love where the wandering find refuge.

> *Father, since you are inviting all to come and join your family by means of the second birth, help us not to be afraid. We need to feel at home with You. Amen.*

OneYearChallenge—Read:
Psalms 6-10

August 9

Church Does Work in Mexico

A GROUP OF PEOPLE FROM OUR CHURCH WENT to Mexico to work for God. In spite of language, cultural, economic, social and religious barriers, these people attempted to do a special work for God. Is that possible? Is that presumptuous? In what was their confidence? There was simply a conviction that God had touched their lives and impressed them to go. *"You did not choose me, but I chose you and appointed you to go and bear fruit—fruit that will last"* (John 15:16). Obedience to the Lord takes precedence over all else: *"go and make disciples of all nations, baptizing them in the name of the Father and of the Son and of the Holy Spirit,"* Jesus told us just before he ascended to heaven (Matthew 28:19). He also said in Matthew 9:37-38, *"The harvest is plentiful but the workers are few. Ask the Lord of the harvest, therefore, to send out workers into his harvest field."* You see God is at work trying to redeem the world from the misery of our own making. He calls Christians to be *"God's fellow workers"* (I Corinthians 3:9), and sometimes folks get a once-in-a-lifetime opportunity to sacrifice time, comfort, money, and ease to do a special work for God. It is not payment for salvation; it is an act of gratitude. Salvation is *"not by works"* (Ephesians 2:8-10). In Psalm 2:8 is the challenge, *"Ask of me, and I will make the nations your inheritance, the ends of the earth your possession."* What a privilege—to do something for God that will have an eternal impact! The best memorial most people hope for is a nice granite stone in a neatly trimmed graveyard. God's memorials to His children working with Him are in the lives of the people who have been changed, and their children and grandchildren, . . .

God, You call all Christians to be fellow-workers with You. To be involved in Your work is the greatest challenge I can have. Amen.

One Year Challenge—Read: Psalms 11-15

August 10

The Secret of Happiness

LET'S ASK THE QUESTION ONE MORE TIME: what is the relationship between material goods and happiness? Answer: none! One of the disturbing things about the American celebration of Thanksgiving is all the pompous words about material blessings being a gift from God to make us happy. There is no truth in it. On our church's mission trip to Mexico we worked, worshiped, ate, and shared with some of the poorest people in the world, and some of the happiest. They were poor in material goods but rich in spiritual resources and love. They obviously knew better than we did what Jesus meant when He said *"a man's life does not consist in the abundance of his possessions"* (Luke 12:15). The constant obsession for *"things"* stretches a life to the breaking point. There is no time for people or relationships or developing the inner self. Seeking happiness in *"things"* is really chasing an elusive butterfly.

God made us spiritual beings, not material beings; how did we get so far off the right track? Part of the reason is that Satan has blinded our eyes to spiritual truths and spiritual values. The other part is self-inflicted. In James 1:14, the Bible says *"each one is tempted when, by his own evil desire, he is dragged away and enticed."* Like Eve in the Garden of Eden, people look around at things, instead of fixing their eyes on God, and decide that the things are more important. Unless there is a rebirth experience of spiritual life, the rest of life is spent chasing things, to make for our happiness. In the very beginning of His ministry in that famous Sermon On The Mountain (Matthew 5:1-12), Jesus laid down the guidelines for true happiness and they still work. You don't need any other book or seminar until you try the Bible, God's love letter to you.

Thank You, Jesus, for giving me joy. I have never felt so good in my heart as since I met You. Amen.

ONE YEAR CHALLENGE—Read: Psalms 16-20

August 11

Caring about the Next Generation

THE 1990S HAVE BROUGHT A NEW PROBLEM to society. Now and in the future we will be dealing with the so-called *"crack babies."* Mothers who use cocaine or other drugs during pregnancy are giving birth to children that are already addicted or in some other way permanently harmed. It is strange how men and women can be so caught up in selfish pleasure that they give no thought to what effect it is having on the next generation. I guess that's what comes from living for the *"now!"* The philosophy seems to be: *"If I can just have a good time today, someone else can take care of tomorrow."* I just read a Bible story about this. In 2 Kings 20 is the story of King Hezekiah. He is recorded in the Bible as the man who begged God for fifteen more years to live during a terminal illness. God granted his prayer, but Hezekiah didn't use the time well. Feeling proud, he showed off his great wealth to Babylon's representatives. Then God told him that Babylon would someday take it away and even his children would become slaves. Hezekiah shrugged it off with the thought, *"Will there not be peace and security in my lifetime?"* (v. 19). With a total disregard for the safety and well-being of his children and grandchildren, he satisfied his selfish ego. I believe in individual soul competency before God and that *"each of us will give an account of himself to God"* (Romans 14:12), but that personal freedom is not a freedom to ignore the impact my life has on my children. Adults often try the cop-out: *"I'm not hurting anyone but myself."* We are daily harvesting the results of divorce. Visit a meeting of *"Adult Children of Alcoholics"* and hear stories of one generation's pain pushed on the succeeding generation. You should care about the future.

> *Teach me to care, Lord, teach me to care. Just as I have a debt to godly parents who lived before me, I have a godly responsibility to my children and grandchildren. Amen.*

ONE YEAR CHALLENGE—Read: Psalms 21-25

August 12

Spontaneous Forgiveness

KIDS DON'T KNOW HOW TO STAY MAD. Little ones don't know how to carry a grudge. I've been observing my grandchildren while we were on vacation. They get mad with each other. They get into fights. They say unkind things to one another. They burst into tears. And then they pick up where they left off, playing and getting on with life. It's amazing to me because I'm an adult and most adults don't seem to know how to forget it and go on. Adults remember. Adults carry grudges. Adults say mean things and keep on saying them, especially to other adults. How I wish adults were like children! Conflict is natural. Confrontation is inevitable. Two healthy adults with opinions formed over the years are going to disagree and have differences, even get irritated or angry, defending their ideas. But adults have this extra drive that little kids don't have: the need to win or to come out on top, that won't be ignored. So they don't just drop an issue, they go on and on being upset about it. Maybe this is what Jesus had in mind when he said, *"I tell you the truth, unless you change and become like little children, you will never enter the kingdom of heaven"* (Matthew 18:3). Spontaneous forgiveness is a requirement for Heaven. Right away the expected population of Heaven decreases. If you are mad at someone or holding a grudge or not speaking to a brother or sister, there is no place in Heaven for you. Matthew 5:24 has a little used commandment from Jesus, *"First go and be reconciled to your brother; then come and offer your gift."* *"For anyone who does not love his brother, whom he has seen, cannot love God, whom he has not seen"* (1 John 4:20). Forgive and forget, immediately.

Father, You have forgiven me so much, the least I can do is forgive others. You have already set the example. Amen.

ONE YEAR CHALLENGE—Read: Psalms 26-30

August 13

Tracks on the Sand

WE WERE JUST MEANDERING ALONG THE BEACH after dinner, enjoying a leisurely stroll. Then we were overtaken by a couple who were striding purposefully, their faces set and business-like. Their bare feet made pronounced tracks in the sand and we followed those tracks for a while. But then a wave broke on the beach and the imprint of their walk was gone. I reflected on that: Is the impact of a life to be measured in terms of the washing of the next wave on the shore? Regardless of how important you might think you are, will your influence out-live the next wave? No matter how impressive your credentials may be, will the mark you make in the world outlast the reach of the next wave? How do we make the best of life's short number of days? How do we invest our time and energy in a way that will have a lasting effect? Surely men and women created in the image of God should have a more lasting monument than a two-inch column on the obituary page or a marble stone in a graveyard. The Bible says in Revelation 14:13, *"Blessed are the dead who die in the Lord from now on. Yes, . . . they will rest from their labor, for their deeds will follow them."* Men and women of faith leave a heritage. While faithfully serving the Lord, they are impacting people and influencing lives. For years to come they will have a good effect on the lives of these people. Paul reminded the Corinthian Christians *"that your labor in the Lord is not in vain"* (I Corinthians 15:58). A prayer of Moses mentions lives that have no more influence than dried and withered grass (Psalm 90). Two questions: Where will you spend eternity? What difference are you making in time?

> *O Father, these long days of summer give us extra time to help people and point them to the Truth. Make us sensitive. Amen.*

August 14

ONE YEAR CHALLENGE—Read: Psalms 31-35

Going to Church

How many times have you heard, "I DON'T HAVE TO GO TO CHURCH to be a Christian"? And that's true—if by "Christian," you mean somebody who cooks his meat rather than eating it raw (some folks definition of "Christian"). Or, it's true—if by "Christian," you mean somebody who believes in the ethical teachings of Jesus. Or, it's true—if by "Christian," you mean somebody who believes in the example that Jesus set for mankind. Or, it's true—if by "Christian," you mean joining a church because it's the American thing to do. There are so many different, self-made definitions of "a Christian" that you really have to ask each individual what they mean when they say "Christian." One thing, for sure: there is no New Testament Christianity that is church-less or divorced from church. The very definition of the word from the Bible is: "the called out ones in Jesus Christ." So, if one is called out of something, he is called into something else, which in this case is a body (group) of believers. There is no account in the New Testament of a "Lone Ranger" style, or independent-of-others Christianity. "Believed, baptized, and added to the body" summarizes much of the book of Acts—the beginning of the New Testament church. "Let us not give up meeting together" is a command (Hebrews 10:25). The Bible simply cannot be used to support churchless Christianity. You will have to use another source. The isolated mountain villager who finds a copy of the Bible, reads it and is converted will immediately search to find others of the same heart. The worship, the study, the fellowship, the encouragement that is built into the word "church" forbids a spirit of isolation. "Christ loved the church" (Ephesians 5:25). I love the church too. Do you?

> *Father, what a joy it is to go to a building dedicated to You and meet our other family members. I feel so wanted there. Amen.*

One Year Challenge—Read: Psalms 36-40

August 15

Politeness

ON A MISSION TRIP TO MEXICO, our team was unanimously impressed by the politeness of the Mexican children. Oftentimes, their bodies were dirty and their clothing was sparse, but from the smallest to the largest, they marked their arrival at classes with a handshake and a greeting for every adult. When the class was over, none left without a handshake of gratitude, a kiss on the cheek for the teacher, and a goodbye greeting. It happened daily. It was the lifestyle for these children. Generally speaking, the majority of people born before 1950 in America were raised in the same pattern. *"Always greet your elders politely." "Yes, sir"* and *"no, sir"* were my parent's instructions for relating to anyone older than myself. And even though I carry an A.A.R.P. card today, I still think in those terms. What happened? Except for those in military training, there is little training in showing respect and acting politely.

Politeness is borne from the works of Christian kindness. It is not just a coincidence that the great retreat from the church in the 1950s, that continues today, has spawned a couple of generations that don't understand what it means to be polite. Parents who yell and scream and threaten their off-spring are not good role models of politeness. Basically, we need to recognize that every person we meet is someone for whom Christ died. This should surely breed politeness. Christian love is kind (I Corinthians 13:4) and I find especially direct the command of Ephesians 4:32, *"Be kind and compassionate to one another, forgiving each other, just as in Christ God forgave you."* Jesus exemplified this sensitive attitude of loving respect when He washed His disciples' feet or when He put a child in the middle of a group of religious experts and said that the little one exemplifies the Kingdom.

ONE YEAR CHALLENGE—Read: Psalms 41-45

> *Teach us, Lord, that we are never too young or too old to be polite. Teach us that politeness is Christian kindness in action. Amen.*

August 16

The Pain of Favoritism

How do parents and grandparents get caught up in choosing a favorite child? It has such painful repercussions, that can last a lifetime. Of course, if you are the favorite, you enjoy it a great deal, even though in the long run it may warp your view of life and reality. When parents choose a favorite child they end up with one child that can only do right, and another that can only do wrong, regardless of how hard they try. Some people make it so obvious. I have even heard people say to one child in front of his brothers and sisters, *"You are my favorite."* In Genesis 25, 27 and beyond, we read about the struggle between Jacob and Esau, because Isaac and Rebekah, the parents, had each made their choice of favorite son. With all the trouble it caused Jacob, he didn't learn from it. Jacob's family was torn apart because Jacob picked out Joseph, of all his children, to be his favorite child. There are enough examples for all of us to be aware of the danger. How good it is to know *"that God does not show favoritism but accepts men from every nation who fear him and do what is right"* (Acts 10:34-35). The enemies of Jesus were alert enough to know that He had no favorites. They said, *"we know you are a man of integrity. You aren't swayed by men, because you pay no attention to who they are"* (Mark 12:14). *"God does not show favoritism,"* says Paul in Romans 2:11. There are many Bible verses that focus on God's equal concern for all. *"God so loved the world"*—the whole world, the whole family of mankind—so He made a way for all of mankind to come back into a healthy relationship with Him, through Christ, God's son (John 3:16). The poet said *"in Christ there is no east or west,"* no favored territory.

> *Teach us, Father, that exclusion is a sin. Show us that Christian love is inclusive and accepting of all humans. Amen.*

One Year Challenge—Read: Psalms 46-50

August 17

Seeds of Doubt

IN THE 1980S, THERE WAS THE GREAT APPLE SCARE. Some said the apple crops were sprayed with poison and folks shouldn't eat apples. The seeds of doubt were sown and many apple growers suffered; some lost their farms. The summer of 1991 will be known as the year of the great cantaloupe scare. Someone said they got the salmonella bacteria from cantaloupes. The seeds of doubt were sown and thousands ignored the explanation that the cantaloupe had been left over-night on a salad bar. Many farmers lost their farms and lifetime investments. Seeds of doubt are powerful. Murder by insinuation is committed regularly. Many who would never be guilty of murder by gun or knife think nothing of murdering a reputation or a good name by saying, *"Have you heard?"* or, *"He is a good man, but ..."* or, *"Don't tell anyone I told you this, but ..."* and the like. Relationships can be ruined by seeds of doubt.

Marriages have fallen victim to its power. *"Speaking the truth in love"* (Ephesians 4:15), is the right way to go. Nothing should be said concerning another person unless we know that it is absolutely true. It is easy to determine the truth about people. The easiest is to go directly to the person and ask if what was heard is true. That is true love: a real concern for the other person's family and future. Some people are so crushed by these doubts sown on the field of their character, they may never recover. *"For out of the overflow of his heart his mouth speaks"* (Luke 6:45), is a timely reminder of our spiritual condition, if we get engaged in sowing partial truths about anyone. Words have power, to heal or kill. *"Set a guard over my mouth, O LORD"* (Psalm 141:3) would be a worthy prayer for all of us.

Thank You, God, for trusting me and believing me when I said that I wanted to be your child. Thank You for making me your child. Amen.

ONE YEAR CHALLENGE—Read:
Psalms 51-55

August 18

Faithless or Unfaithful?

WHICH IS WORSE IN GOD'S SIGHT: people who have no faith in God, or people who profess to have faith but do not live according to the faith they profess? I was jolted to attention when I read Jeremiah 3:11 where God said to the Prophet, *"Faithless Israel is more righteous than unfaithful Judah."* There immediately came to my mind all of the people I have met who like to tell you about their religious *"pedigree"* or religious heritage. You have met them: those people who explain their own lack of religion by telling about the uncle who is a preacher or the cousin who is a priest. Or the people who say they don't go to church anymore or read the Bible anymore because they were forced to do so as a child. Have you ever made this kind of excuse? God has an answer for all excuses. When the Apostle James wrote, *"Anyone, then, who knows the good he ought to do and doesn't do it, sins"* (James 4:17), he was dealing with the same issue. We feel pity for the person who has never heard the Word of God but that pity drains away from people who reject God's known commands. Jesus dealt with the Pharisees this way in John 9:41: *"If you were blind, you would not be guilty of sin; but now that you claim you can see, your guilt remains."* How amazing that people could taste *"the goodness of the word of God"* (Hebrews 6:5) and then trash it by ignoring it! If you know yourself to be faithless or an unfaithful believer, the same answer applies in both cases. I refer to 1 John 1:9: *"If we confess our sins, he is faithful (even if we are not) and just and will forgive us our sins and purify us from all unrighteousness."*

You are so faithful, Father, always there when I come with prayers of gratitude or petition. Help me to be faithful to You. Amen.

ONE YEAR CHALLENGE—Read:
Psalms 56-60

August 19

The Indigo Bunting

I REMEMBER THE DAY the Indigo Bunting came. My wife and I like to watch the variety of birds that come to our bird feeder in the back yard. I saw it the first day, just a flash of brilliant blue flying away from me. It was an exciting moment and I told my wife about it, describing what I saw. The next day, while she was home alone, she too got a glimpse—a brief side view. Now we both were excited about what it could be. But we had not seen enough even to search for it in our bird book. Then, several days later, while we sat for dinner, it came again. It perched on the bird feeder and had a leisurely dinner, flitting and hopping from place to place, pecking at seeds while keeping watch. We got to observe it closely. Then it was easy to go to our bird book and learn about the Indigo Bunting. He has been back several times and we are glad every time he comes. I think spiritual discovery is a little like that. It starts with that first flashing thought, or piece of truth brought to your attention. Then you are prompted again, perhaps from a different angle. Finally, the truth confronts you head-on and you recognize its importance, its beauty, its place in what has been missing or misunderstood. Then you can make a personal commitment to it. Read John 1:35-42, and discover one of those situations. John the Baptist calls Jesus *"the Lamb of God;"* a couple of his friends get curious and follow Jesus; He challenges them to come and spend the day with Him. The result: Andrew ends up telling his brother, *"We have found the Messiah."* From then on, Andrew followed Jesus faithfully until he died. Jesus said, *"I am the way and the truth and the life. No one comes to the Father except through me"* (John 14:6). Would you like to consider that closely? You won't forget the day.

God of All Truth, thank You for the exciting journey of spiritual discovery. Whet my appetite for more today. Amen.

One Year Challenge—Read: Psalms 61-65

August 20

"People Days" of Summer

We ARE IN THE *"DOG DAYS"* OF SUMMER. Are *"dog days"* good or bad? Every year at this time I start wondering. Am I supposed to feel better or worse? Is it about people or dogs? Was there a time in history when dogs took vacation in late August? I hear people say, *"I'm feeling like a dog,"* but folks say that the rest of the year also. People sometimes remark about living *"a dog's life."* In this country, that's good (considering we spend more money on dog food than we do on the poor and hungry). Maybe we just ought to leave the poor dog out of it and talk about the *"people days"* of summer. You know, by now a lot of moms, dads and kids are wishing summer vacation was over. Some people are feeling blue and despondent because all of the vacation time has been used up and its back to the old grind for another 11 months and two weeks (nothing left to do but pay off the charge card bills from vacation).

What about the following as an option? Instead of expecting to feel a certain way because of a certain time of the year, let's be realistic. In 2 Corinthians 6:2, we read, *"now is the time of God's favor, now is the day of salvation."* Today is the day of opportunity for you to begin a personal relationship with God or to deepen an existing relationship. In Hebrews 3:13, we are directed to *"encourage one another daily, as long as it is called Today, so that none of you may be hardened by sin's deceitfulness."* As you and I share this in your devotional, God provides a special time-out moment for you to stop and re-evaluate your life today. Regardless of what the calendar or anything else says, will you accept and relish this moment?

> *God, now that You have broken into my thoughts, what do You want to say to me. What should I say to You? Amen.*

August 21

One Year Challenge—Read: Psalms 66-70

August Heat

FOLKS TALK A LOT ABOUT THE HEAT. How hot is it? Some say, *"It's hot as a tin roof."* Others say, *"It's hot as grease in a frying pan."* I heard a weatherman say, *"It's hot as babbitt."* Many say, *"It's hot as Hell."* Now, why would folks say that? The heat of all the things I mentioned are measurable except that of Hell. You can't measure it. There is nothing with which to compare it. We do have the rich man in Hell who asked for someone to dip their finger in water to cool his tongue, because of his anguish in the flames (Luke 16:24). Why do folks make such a comparison? Is it a joke by those who do not take Hell seriously? Is it an unresolved fear that pops out unexpectedly? Or is it just a phrase that means nothing? One thing for sure, Hell is too important a topic to be handled lightly. We have a way of doing that, you know. Nervously, we put down as unimportant issues that have not been resolved. If you believe the Bible is the authoritative Word of God, you must take Hell seriously. You must read the passages that talk about Hell and Heaven. Don't be frightened or alarmed as you read this but go quickly and read Revelation 1:18 where Jesus says, *"I am the Living One; I was dead, but behold I am alive for ever and ever! And I hold the keys of death and Hades."* Regardless of whether you see Hell as literal, symbolic, or parable, it is a word to fill us with fear and dread, and only Jesus can answer that fear. Someone said that we should only speak of Hell with tears in our eyes. It certainly should not be taken lightly.

Forgive me, God, If I treat eternal truths lightly. Surely the eternal destiny of a person is the most important matter of all. Amen.

ONE YEAR CHALLENGE—Read: Psalms 71-75

August 22

Downscaling

THERE IS A SLOW STREAM MOVING through western Christianity that is challenging Christians to *"downscale."* It is not a trend, but perhaps it could be someday. Simply put, we Christians have gotten caught up in a materialistic way of thinking, some even trying to condone materialism and make it acceptable. Remember what Jesus said about materialism in Matthew 5:19-24. In the early 1960s, I attended a Crusade by a famous television evangelist who was selling a book to poor people called, **God Wants Everyone To Be Rich**. That crude distortion of the Bible has now been replaced by slick seminars and weekend retreats where wealthy Christians instruct others Christians on how to get rich, the Christian way. This is a far cry from the Savior who didn't have a place to lay His head (Matthew 8:20). We will never impress the world with the gospel if we must wrap it in expensive clothing and houses. The world will be touched by our getting back to basics *"for Jesus' sake"* (1 Corinthians 4:5-11) or by adopting a simpler lifestyle as more fitting for a spiritual person. We could buy simpler houses, less expensive cars and non-name brand clothing as serious *"downscaling"* efforts, and thereby have more to share with the have-nots of this world. Romans 14:17 says, *"The Kingdom of God is not a matter of eating and drinking, but of righteousness, peace and joy in the Holy Spirit."* Someday, the contemporary church must repent of materialism. Do lavish and ornate buildings that are used for a couple of hours each week honor Jesus? Churches as well as individual Christians need to look at *"downscaling."* Being upwardly-mobile may be good for your bank account but it can be deadening for your spirit. Also, what kind of value system does it teach your children or grandchildren? Try praying about *"downscaling."*

O God, we have been so brainwashed by our culture. We almost think it's un-American to not want to get rich. Help us, Lord. Amen.

ONE YEAR CHALLENGE—Read: Psalms 76-80

August 23

The Failed Coup

I AM SURE THAT MUCH OF FUTURE HISTORY will record the great coup of August, 1991—the Russian coup that failed. The speculation after the coup was unbelievable. Everyone wanted to know, "Why?" The military had theories. Politicians had theories. Every television network hired experts, and they were regularly interviewed on the news programs. But none of them could find a suitable answer. It's amazing, when the answer is so obvious. God did it! With the spread of the Biblical message in the last few years because of "glasnost," thousands of Communists had been converted. Evangelistic teams and missionaries had the freedom to spread the gospel of freedom. When Jesus said "the truth will set you free" (John 8:32), it was not limited to spiritual freedom. Spiritual freedom is the root of all freedoms. A seminary professor prophesied to a group of us students in 1958 that in our lifetime, we would see the fall of Communism in Russia without a shot being fired. Why? Because freedom and democracy are better ideologies than communism. Ideas are defeated by better ideas, not munitions. A God-less humanism pales beside a divinely-planned order of things. Man can work at things but God can accomplish things, especially miracles of freedom: "My times are in your hands" (Psalm 31:15). There is a kind of spiritual blindness in the world. Jesus described it in Matthew 16:2-3: "When evening comes, you say, 'It will be fair weather, for the sky is red,' and in the morning, 'Today it will be stormy, for the sky is red and overcast.' You know how to interpret the appearance of the sky, but you cannot interpret the signs of the times." Be careful to look behind the news to discern the hand of a loving God working out His purpose. Just because the so-called experts don't know, doesn't mean you have to be ignorant.

Father of all history, help us to always look at history to see what You are about. I'm sure we would do less worrying and handwringing. Amen.

One Year Challenge—Read: Psalms 81-85

August 24

Saying "No" with No Base

SOME PEOPLE ARE SO SIMPLISTIC when talking about youth and temptation. If the temptation is to drink, have sex, or do drugs; the answer is to "Just say 'no.'" That's too simplistic; it doesn't even have the ring of sincerity or reality. Society's readiness to grab a slogan betrays a lack of willingness to deal with the real issue. If kids or adults are to refrain from destructive behavior, there has to be a moral base. Self-destruction is a moral issue. People who do liquid drugs, like alcohol, and keep it in the house, or have a cheap view of sex have no basis for moral values to instruct children. There simply has to be an objective, non-changing standard of right and wrong. Cultural values don't work, they always change. Community standards won't work, there is too much fluctuation. Humanism is bankrupt because humans will always slide to the lowest common denominator. Secularism is too materialistic. Hedonism only cares about how something feels. Existentialism only considers the moment. Children coming from these kinds of family systems will shipwreck on the sea of life very young. Some parents take a hands-off, "Let them do what they want" attitude. The Bible warns, "There is a way that seems right to a man, but in the end it leads to death" (Proverbs 14:12). God, in the Bible, has given us a moral base and equipped us to teach our children, if we will accept it. It is so sad when parents try so hard to give their children every material advantage but leave them morally bankrupt. Teach your children the Bible. "These are the commands, decrees and laws the Lord your God directed me to teach you . . . , so that you, your children, and their children after them may fear the LORD your God as long as you live by keeping all his decrees and commands that I give you, and so that you may enjoy long life" (Deuteronomy 6:1-2). Anyone can say "no" with this base.

> Dear God, I am so easily tempted; the world catches my eye and I am distracted from looking at You. Give me light. Amen.

ONE YEAR CHALLENGE—Read: Psalms 86-90

August 25

Good Intentions Fail

I HEARD THIS LITTLE BLURB ON THE RADIO ABOUT A DACHSHUND mother dog that was raising a baby duck along with her puppies. She was very good to the duckling and very protective. She fed it and cared for it. She had the best intentions in the world, but she could never be a good mother for the duckling, no matter how hard she tried. Good intentions are simply not enough. You have probably heard the old saying, *"The road to Hell is paved with good intentions."* This is surely true. How many people do you know who intend to start going to church, read the Bible, pray, or even become a Christian? *"When I get around to it"* is another familiar statement. Have you used it? It reminds me of the time a man displayed good intentions, saying to Jesus, *"I will follow you wherever you go"* (Luke 9:57). Jesus then warned him about the full implications of such good intentions. Good intentions must give way to commitment. Many people like to think about being a Christian or even imagine themselves to be Christians, but never make a commitment. Some will even go to church and join the church and then drop out when they hear the demands of the gospel. Some really think they want to be Christians until they hear the cost of discipleship, then they forget it. Some good-intentioned folks become religious tramps, going from one church to another. So much for good intentions. The call to follow Jesus immediately sifts out good intention from commitment. In Luke 9:62 Jesus declares, *"No one who puts his hand to the plow and looks back is fit for service in the kingdom of God."* The issue is clarified. Honor God today with committed living—no more talk about what you are *"going to do."*

Father, your Holy Spirit is always challenging me to total commitment. Why do I keep wanting to find an easier way? Help! Amen.

ONE YEAR CHALLENGE—Read: Psalms 91-95

August 26

The Beauty of Humanity

I WENT TO MY GARDEN TO PICK PEPPERS. What a beautiful sight! And more beautiful still after I picked them! There were red, yellow, orange, green and mixed colors. The diversity of the colors surprised me. I had never planted this kind of pepper before. And I was picking them at the time of their maturity. They all tasted alike, the compelling beauty was in their variation of colors and shapes. I had to think that God must feel this way when He looks at His human family living together in unity. *"How good and pleasant it is when brothers live together in unity! It is like precious oil poured on the head"* (Psalm 133:1-2). What a pleasant and refreshing experience when different cultures and nationalities get together in unity. Color is no barrier when you look at people from God's point of view. Surely a little pigmentation in the epidermis is not a barrier to oneness. It's so thin! No color of skin is more valuable than any other. The Bible presents a world view: *"God created man in his own image"* (Genesis 1:27). This is describing the whole human family. God doesn't have a favorite color. In the well-known verse of John 3:16, we are told, *"For God so loved the world . . . ."* The world is the whole of humanity. I once heard someone say that Christians should be color-blind. I don't agree. God wants us to look at one another and appreciate how He has made us: different colors and customs and costumes—all making up a beautiful tapestry. Our cultures and environments teach us to be suspicious and fearful of those who are different. That must be challenged and overcome. Can we make this the generation that will read the Bible and accept the message as it is, and not filter it through our cultural biases? Christian love obliterates racial barriers.

It is good to know that every color You created is beautiful to You. Help me to appreciate every color, also. Amen.

ONE YEAR CHALLENGE—Read:
Psalms 96-99

August 27

Handling Conflict

CONFLICT MANAGEMENT IS BIG BUSINESS. Check out the number of volumes in the bookstore. If you are with a major business, you have already attended several seminars. Learning to *"fight fair"* is a big challenge whether at home, school, work, or church. Churches are among the worst at resolving conflict. Much of evangelical church is rooted in conflict; that is, they multiply by dividing in a conflict situation. That's so embarrassing especially when Jesus gave Christians such explicit directions. See Matthew 18:15-17: *"If your brother sins against you, go and show him his fault, just between the two of you. If he listens to you, you have won your brother over. But if he will not listen, take one or two others along, so that 'every matter may be established by the testimony of two or three witnesses.' If he refuses to listen to them, tell it to the church, and if he refuses to listen even to the church,* treat him as you would a pagan." Here is a clear and effective way to handle conflict and get on with the rest of life. Let me suggest that you: (1) Name the issue, (2) Examine the alternatives, (3) Decide your course of action, (4) Act on your decision, and (5) Review the results. Conflict never resolves itself. It takes work by people who refuse to be divided against each other. To deny the existence of conflict and do nothing is to pave the way to destruction for the relationship. When the conflict is resolved, those involved can commit themselves to a healthy relationship and move on to productive living. Keep in mind what Jesus said, *"God blesses those people who make peace. They will be called his children!"* (Matthew 5:9 CEV). That applies to each of us who take His words seriously. To do nothing or refuse to get involved is to be guilty of the sin of omission.

> God of Peace, thank You for settling our conflict with You. Thank You for taking the initiative and coming to us. Amen.

ONE YEAR CHALLENGE—Read: Psalms 100-103

August 28

A Power Encounter

WE RECENTLY HAD ONE OF OUR FOREIGN MISSIONARIES visit our church. He had just finished his first term and came to share with us what the Gospel of Jesus Christ had accomplished. During his presentation, he mentioned *"a power encounter"* that occurred when the good news of God's salvation confronted the belief in animism where he was. It's inevitable when two opposing forces meet: faith versus superstition, belief versus doubt, light versus darkness. There are many descriptive terms for this power encounter. I remember an old Asian man saying that in his chest was a *"battle between a big white dog and a big black dog."* When asked, *"Which dog is the winner?"*, he replied, *"The dog to whom I say 'sic em'."* Think about the many times there has been this power encounter in your own life: the struggle between right and wrong, good and evil. Paul said in Romans 7:21, *"I find this law at work: When I want to do good, evil is right there with me."* He goes on to say that he wants to please God, but evil forces keep trying to pull him back. He concludes in verse 25 that God gives him victory through Jesus. Read Romans 8:37, and I Corinthians 15:57, and hear this praise repeated by Paul. The winner in the inner encounter is always Jesus, if I give Him freedom to fight the battle for me. So many have lost the battle against adultery, homosexuality, gambling, prejudice, lying, drunkenness, speeding, cheating and the like because they foolishly thought they could win the battle against evil alone. When you want to do good, evil personified tightens his grip. But you can be on the winning side. Like the man who was blind said after Jesus restored his sight, *"I was blind but now I see!"* (John 9:25).

You have delivered me, Father, when I had no strength and was powerless to find freedom. I will be eternally grateful. Amen.

ONE YEAR CHALLENGE—Read: Psalms 104-107

August 29

Do Something

"WHY DOESN'T GOD DO SOMETHING? He made the universe. He is all-powerful. He could change things. Why doesn't He?" Heard anyone chastise God lately? Why don't humans do something? Why does mankind allow poverty, famine, racism, and injustice to continue? The question of responsibility is a challenging one. No value comes from affixing blame or asking: "Why this?" "Why that?" Many of us are paralyzed by asking questions like "Why?" The Bible is very clear in saying to Christians, *"faith by itself, if it is not accompanied by action, is dead"* (James 2:17), and, *"I will show you my faith by what I do"* (verse 18), and, *"If anyone has material possessions and sees his brother in need but has no pity on him, how can the love of God be in him?"* (I John 3:17). Just do something. Look around you, see what needs to be done, and do it. Don't debate it. Don't discuss it. If it's obvious, you do it. Don't wait for God to do it. Don't wait for God to get someone else to do it. Do it. Is there poverty near you? You can help. Is there hunger? You can share some food. Is there injustice? You could stand with the oppressed to help balance the scales. Just do it. Christians must make a part of their daily routine being *"salt"* and *"light"* (Matthew 5:13-14). Salt works by coming in contact with what is flavorless. Light works by invading the darkness. Salt and light do what comes naturally for salt and light in the situation. God is not asking the Christian to do anything strange. He is just asking you to imitate your Master who *"went around doing good"* (Acts 10:38). I can't imagine anyone living in such an isolated world where you would have to look for opportunities. They are all around you. Just do it. *"Anyone, then, who knows the good he ought to do and doesn't do it, sins"* (James 4:17).

I am lazy, Lord, I would rather let someone else do all the dirty work. Show me the task, again. Amen.

ONE YEAR CHALLENGE—Read: Psalms 108-111

August 30

Is Anyone Waiting?

As A MINISTER, I SPEND A LOT OF TIME AROUND HOSPITALS. As I pass by the chapel or the surgery waiting room, I always look in to see if anyone is waiting. It is very important to the person having surgery to know that someone is waiting. That gives them a reason to pull through. When a member of our church has surgery, there are usually some people there with the family in the waiting room. Everyone needs to know that there is someone there for them. We all need to know that our well-being is important to somebody. People commit suicide every year because no one is waiting. Have you heard of Henri Nouwen? He wrote a very popular book called **The Wounded Healer**. He once said that if no one is waiting for you, there is no way of surviving. If only one person is waiting, he says, you can make it. As you look at your life today, you may wonder why you are here. Would you consider the notion that it is your privilege to wait for somebody today, or tomorrow. Your being there for them will mean the difference between life and death. There are many widows and widowers, divorced and single folks who have serious reason to wonder if anyone cares. As Christians, we are challenged to *"love one another, for love comes from God"* (I John 4:7). Being there for someone will prove your love. Remember when Cornelius waited for Peter to come and tell him about Jesus and the gospel (Acts 10)? Suppose Peter hadn't loved and cared for Cornelius, he would never have been converted. Did you know God is waiting for you today, if you are not yet a Christian? He is waiting for you to repent, so you won't die separated from him (2 Peter 3:9). Don't disappoint him.

What an encouraging thought, O God, that you are a Waiting Father. I remember how You waited for the Prodigal son to come home. He was so glad. Amen.

August 31

One Year Challenge—Read: Psalms 112-115

The Approaching Harvest

THE EARS OF CORN ARE HANGING FULL ON THE STALK now. The soybeans are waist-high. The tomato vines are heavy with fruit. The pumpkins are getting larger. On the farms we are reminded that harvest time is approaching. It is a beautiful time of the year. It has been planned for, and worked for, and waited for, during all these spring and summer months. The expectations are rich. If you have a rural background, the approaching harvest brings back many fond memories. On God's spiritual calendar for men and women, there is also an approaching harvest time. Much of God's fruit is ripe for the harvesting now. *"You will come to the grave in full vigor, like sheaves gathered in season"* (Job 5:26). Many saints have been growing in their faith for many years and are just waiting for God's harvest. *"man is destined to die once, and after that to face judgment"* (Hebrews 9:27), holds no terror for these faithful children of God. In Hebrews 12, there is a discussion about God's discipline with the conclusion in verse 11: *"No discipline seems pleasant at the time, but painful. Later on, however, it produces a harvest of righteousness."* Yes, God has been cultivating His field and working with His plants and He is anxious to have a harvest of righteous men and women. What about the unrighteous, the weeds in God's field? Well, God said in Matthew 13:30, *"Let both grow together until the harvest. At that time I will tell the harvesters: 'First collect the weeds and tie them in bundles to be burned; then gather the wheat and bring it into my barn.'"* What a positive emotional and psychological (not to mention spiritual) uplift it would bring to our country if the majority had such great expectations about the future. Go to church Sunday for a start.

OneYearChallenge—Read: Psalms 116-119:40

> *Lord of the Harvest, prepare me for that great day when I will meet You face to face. Bless my preparation and its evidence to others. Amen.*

September 1

Teaching and Learning

PEOPLE OF ALL AGES ARE RETURNING TO THE CLASSROOM this month in the pursuit of education. Few people question the value of education today; the majority know it is an absolute necessity. I affirm that public school education is one of the strengths of a democracy. But a person who is educated only with this school knowledge grows up without good values. How can education help a person if it has no moral base? Mastering facts can give one a full head but an empty heart. This was the problem that Solomon was dealing with in Ecclesiastes 12:12, where he warned about books and studying. This is in stark contrast to the teaching of Jesus that is always rooted in the stance of responsibility to God. It is not an accident that Jesus is often referred to as *"Teacher."* Another translation of *"disciples"* could be *"learners."* Contemporary Christianity seems to have lost sight of the hard work of teaching in the church. Churches like to focus on the emotional celebration of worship, but leave the people to learn *"everything that God wants you to know"* (Acts 20:27 CEV), on their own. I too, like to see people jump high when they get religion, but I also want them to know how to *"walk the walk and talk the talk,"* when they come back down to the ground. Jesus took three years to teach twelve men what it meant to be a Christian and they still made mistakes. Can the church do any less today? Can Christian homes wait for the church to teach their children? I think not! *"The things you have heard me say in the presence of many witnesses entrust to reliable men who will also be qualified to teach others"* (2 Timothy 2:2), was Paul's instruction to Timothy. Christian truth cannot be absorbed by osmosis any more than mathematics or science. As you are learning everything you can about God's Word, you must help teach this knowledge and wisdom to others, as Jesus did.

First of all, O God, I pray for a teachable spirit. Then make me a capable learner. Lastly, help me to share this truth. Amen.

ONE YEAR CHALLENGE—Read: Psalms 119:41-120

September 2

A Celebration of Hope

CAN THERE BE A CELEBRATION OF HOPE IN THIS DISMAL TIME? Our times are threatened by clouds of war, international unrest, national political corruption, and local despair from death by drug, drink and domestic disturbance. Can we still have a celebration of hope? Again, the people wonder: *"Watchman, how much longer will it be night?"* (Isaiah 21:11 EB). They ask, *"For how long, O Lord?"* (Isaiah 6:11). *"Where there is no vision, the people perish,"* the Bible says in Proverbs 29:18 (KJV). Let me summarize that if there is no vision of hope, the people certainly will perish. Where can we find hope? What is there to give birth to hope or to bring hope to flower and fruit? I heard of a Christian woman in her eighties who had developed a new way of interpreting the phrase in the Bible, *"[it] will pass"* or, *"[it] will end."* She said that she had lived long enough to know that any bad time that came would pass, and

God would still be on the throne. That's one way of looking at it, but you might still have some long, sleepless nights. How about a hope that is grounded in a living God, and the belief that history is *"His story"*? This is the kind of hope that *"does not disappoint us, because God has poured out his love into our hearts"* (Romans 5:5). God's love and power looks at all of the dismal things that man is doing and defies them to have the final word. *"And we know that in all things God works for the good of those who love him"* (Romans 8:28). A celebration of hope is a faith-inspired celebration. It is grounded in a belief that nothing in this world can take away a Christian's relationship with God, and nothing can rob a Christian of that deep-down, inner joy. Rejoice in the Lord!

Surely, O God, You did not intend for your children to have such heaviness of heart and doubt about tomorrow. O God of hope, bless us. Amen.

ONE YEAR CHALLENGE—Read:
Psalms 121-129

September 3

The Gift of Labor

WE ARE AN INTERESTING PEOPLE WHEN IT COMES TO WORKING. Have you noticed? Folks complain about having to work, or having to work hard. Many radio stations play up this theme on Fridays by talking about *"TGIF"* day— *"thank God it's Friday,"*—and two days of not having to work. How many times have you heard people on Monday morning say, *"It's TGIM* (thank God it's Monday) *day and I get to go to work again"*? Probably never! Yet, working is one of the most important dimensions of our lives; it gives meaning and purpose to our existence. Ask some retired folks and they will tell you how they miss going to work. Even some folks who have won the lottery have continued to hold the job they had before they became rich. Many people who can no longer work suffer emotional and physical problems like impotence, high blood pressure, sleeplessness, etc. We complain too much about our work,

just ask people who can't get a job how important it is. You may have given only a passing thought to the labor holiday, but the symbolic meaning of Labor Day speaks loudly to all of us. The gift of work comes from God. In the Garden of Eden, God gave Adam and Eve the opportunity to work and care for the garden and the animals. Proverbs 16:3 says, *"Commit to the LORD whatever you do, and your plans will succeed."* If you do that, it might give new meaning to Monday through Friday. In Genesis, work was seen as a curse rather than a blessing since humans were in rebellion and disobedience against God. But by the grace of God in Jesus Christ, we can abandon our rebellious spirits, and gratefully enjoy our work as a way to use God's gifts to us.

Father, thank You for the tiredness that comes after a hard day at work, that prepares us for the restoration that is sleep. Amen.

September 4

One Year Challenge—Read: Psalms 130-135

A Word to Calm Troubled Waters

DEALING WITH DISASTERS, both natural and man-made, is a daily event now, whether it is on the local, national, or international scene. A suicide here, a murder, robbery, or rape over there, a public transportation accident, a hate crime and a hazardous substance spill over there. You just know when you get the latest news, there will be something to scare you and push you toward despair. This is the message of today's prophets of doom. Terrorists have their own despicable way of spelling disaster. Fear is all around. Many of us have a feeling of impending doom. Some are snapping under the pressure, and large groups are becoming narcotic dependent, in an attempt to cope. Many schools are canceling trips to our nation's capital and other important cities, thus adding to students' anxieties. Is there a word to calm our troubled waters? Yes. We simply cannot allow ourselves to be paralyzed with fear. We must continue to live normal,

happy, productive lives. Jesus said, *"my peace I give you. I do not give to you as the world gives. Do not let your hearts be troubled and do not be afraid"* (John 14:27). There is a traditional chorus that we Christians sing: *"I have peace like a river in my soul."* That says to me that life for the true believer has a flowing quality, moving along its chosen path. Because it is flowing, it is able to touch many other lives. I spent some time a while back with a man who was held a hostage for 11 months in a foreign country. While experiencing this personal disaster, he discovered a real faith in God and through much prayer was eventually released. A temporary disaster or a long lasting crisis, the answer is the same. Another Christian hymn reminds us, *"I know not what the future holds, but I know Who holds the future."** We must be tender-hearted and helpful to those in disastrous situations. We must trust God and not allow fear to imprison us.

ONE YEAR CHALLENGE—Read: Psalms 136-140

> *In a world shaking with disasters, it is good to know that You have power over disasters, also, Give me peace—please God! Amen.*

September 5

Be Sure Your Sins Will Find You Out

IT'S AMAZING HOW MODERN TECHNOLOGY MAKES SOME PARTS OF THE BIBLE EASIER TO UNDERSTAND. God said that he would not destroy the earth with water again (Genesis 9:15), and that the next time judgment came on the earth it would be by fire. With the warming of the blanket of air around the earth, scientists now sound like evangelists about the earth being consumed by fire. Modern techniques for testing ancient archaeological digs have verified many biblical dates as more accurate than other historical records. My mom used to warn me as a teenager: *"you may be sure that your sin will find you out"* (Numbers 32:23). Like many of her sayings, I didn't take that one too seriously at that age. But now, with all of the giant computer programs linked together between government and business, it is easy to see that Bible truth come alive. If you didn't report some income, it will be revealed; if you ever got a ticket for speeding, it will be revealed. You can lie on your résumé, or about your college transcript, but it's easy for employers to check on you, and have the college send a copy of the transcript. My point is this: if man, by a few inventions can make unheard of or unimaginable things seem simple, why should things be thought impossible for God? Some people jokingly say that there are too many people in the world committing too many sins all the time for God to notice what they are doing. Lulling themselves into a fake sense of security, they roll along through life thinking they will never have to answer for their actions. What a rude awakening is in store for them! No wonder the Bible says that some people will beg for the mountains to fall on them rather than face accountability. The next time you are tempted to make light of your own transgressions, remember: *"each one of us will give an account of himself to God"* (Romans 14:12).

ONE YEAR CHALLENGE—Read: Psalms 141-145

> *Although men devalue one another, You still keep a premium price tag on each of us. Help us not to belittle ourselves with sin. Amen.*

September 6

On Taking a Walk

WHAT ARE THE NON-PHYSICAL ADVANTAGES OF TAKING A WALK? (I don't need to talk about the physical benefits, you read that in the health section of your paper). Well, there is enjoying the beauty of nature, getting to unwind, thinking through some questions, spending quality time with your mate or a close friend, being thankful you have strength to walk, not dreading the after-effects (soreness), and getting to meet some of your neighbors. It would be easy to come up with a really long list. Much of the teachings of Jesus were done while walking; his was a *"walking seminary."* An unhurried walk with people who wanted to know the truth, was the ideal setting for Jesus' teaching. Many personal problems were solved and life directions received while taking a walk with Jesus. As you read the Bible, you see the Christian life described as a *"walk."* You know the old saying, *"Some people talk the talk, but don't walk the walk."* That's where the saying originated. Ephesians 2:2 (KJV) says that before you are converted, you *"walked according to the course of this world,"* but now you are challenged to *"walk in the light, as he* (Jesus) *is in the light"* (1 John 1:7). Romans 6:4, describing believer's baptism says, *"We were therefore buried with him through baptism into death in order that, just as Christ was raised from the dead through the glory of the Father, we too may live a new life."* We are challenged to *"walk worthy of the vocation wherewith ye are called"* (Ephesians 4:1 KJV). If you take the time to think through the challenge of Christians walking, as described in the Bible, the whole Christian message may make more sense to you. No doubt, one of the most challenging walking scenes in the Bible, is when the two disciples were walking to Emmaus after the Resurrection, and Jesus came and walked with them. Later they said, *"Were not our hearts burning within us while he talked with us on the road?"* Try that walk!

> *Father, we don't meditate often enough. Help us to recapture walks with you, like Adam and Eve once did in Eden. Amen.*

September 7

ONE YEAR CHALLENGE—Read:
Psalms 146-150

Earthquakes

THE TREMORS FROM AN EARTHQUAKE ARE POWERFUL AND FAR-REACHING. Those near the epicenter experience immediate destruction of property and perhaps horrible injury and death. Excruciating physical and emotional pain abounds. The shock waves roll outward. Fear and anxiety grip hearts nearby and wherever the news reaches. Relatives and friends far away reel with the impact. Feelings of shock and sympathy stretch across national and ideological borders. A common enemy to humanity has demanded our attention. There is no defense against such disasters. Buildings and highways cannot be built to be earthquake-proof. We stand helpless against the forces of nature; our self-proclaimed strength is suddenly exposed as impotence. Jesus warned us to beware of false teachers of religion who would try to take advantage of situations such as these, who can seize the opportunity to build a following by deceiving some who have become vulnerable (Mark 13:8). Such calamities do not necessarily signal the end of the world. Paul describes these natural calamities in Romans 8:22, "We know that the whole creation has been groaning as in the pains of childbirth right up to the present time." A sin-infected world awaits redemption! Nature, too, revolts against evil, as when the sun was darkened at noonday when Jesus was crucified. Natural calamities are a fact of life. We can try to plan a response before it strikes our area, but we can't avoid nature's worst. I'm not advocating a numb fatalism that says, "What will be, will be," but a spiritual preparation that includes the knowledge that neither "trouble or hardship or persecution or famine or nakedness or danger . . . neither death nor life, . . . nor any powers, . . . nor anything else in all creation, will be able to separate us from the love of God that is in Christ Jesus our Lord" (Romans 8:35, 38-39). The person who says, "God is still in control" affirms their faith as larger than calamity.

ONE YEAR CHALLENGE—Read: Proverbs 1-4

> **Usually, God, we can handle the big earthquakes better than the daily tremors. The daily small quakes unnerve us. Calm us down. Amen.**

September 8

Religious Traditions

WE MAY HAVE BEEN DECEIVED BY A GOOD THING. Early in my life I started hearing that America was a Christian nation. Then I got older and found that the majority of Americans were not professing Christians. Instead, I learned that the founding fathers of America began this democracy on principles gained from the Christian Bible. Today some politicians like to invoke the name of God and religion in their speeches or promote mindless quoting of The Lord's Prayer at public meetings. What really seems to be functioning today is civil religion with a heavy load of religious traditions. There is a kind of tip of the hat to the Almighty, but no one takes Him seriously. For instance, why do people who never go to church or read the Bible or show any inclination toward spiritual things, want to get married in a church building by a minister? Or why do people call a Christian minister to conduct a funeral service for someone who never attended Christian worship or gave any evidence of Christian living? And why do non-Christians celebrate Christmas? Is it custom, or culture, or acted out guilt? I appreciated the honesty of an atheistic couple who sent their children to our Sunday School with the explanation, *"We don't believe a word of it and will tell the children later; but every child growing up in America should have the experience of Sunday School; it's our culture."* Confusing, but at least honest. Maybe that's why the church buses are full of kids on Sunday while the parents sleep. Is the purpose of religion to keep kids out of trouble? We may have become so entrapped by cultural religion that we can't see the real issue. Contrast easy, civil religion to Jesus saying, *"If anyone would come after me, he must deny himself and take up his cross and follow me"* (Matthew 16:24). Different, huh?

Give us wisdom, Dear Father, to sort out culture and tradition from Biblical truth. Help us not to confuse these three things. Amen.

OneYearChallenge—Read: Proverbs 5-8

September 9

Thoughts on Depreciation

"**P**EOPLE DON'T depreciate." This headline caught my eye. I had never thought of this before. Then as I thought of the way people sometimes are treated as things, it seemed to be a timely thought. When you consider the attitude many have toward the aged, you would be led to believe that when people can no longer join the daily work-force and be financially productive, they depreciate to a zero (or negative) value to society. How do we determine personal worth? Is our value always the same or does the value of some increase? When you compare salaries of professional athletes and teachers, what do you think of their value as expressed by their dollars earned? Real worth is not based on physical appearance, or even skill. Ignore what they say in the advertisements for health clubs and clothing outlets. Sure, appearance is important, but true beauty comes from within. Our worth is not assessed according to intellectual accomplishment, social achievement, or economic status. Our personal worth is real, simply because God made us. All products have a trademark. *"Made by God"* is the trademark on humans. That is what makes us unique and very special. In 2 Corinthians 4:16 we read, *"Though outwardly we are wasting away, yet inwardly we are being renewed day by day."* If you are a child of God by the second birth, be glad for what you see in the mirror. You don't have to be like the wicked queen in Snow White who had to get reassurance from her mirror. Even if there are wrinkles, loss of hair, poor functioning organs, don't devalue yourself. God doesn't! Self-depreciation leads to thoughts of uselessness or self-destruction. Age adds the value of experience and looking at things with improved perspective. Every community needs a few more godly grandmothers and grandfathers. Because of Christ, your value increases in the Kingdom of God.

All are precious in Your sight, Heavenly Father. You gave us Jesus to prove our value to You. I am very grateful today. Amen.

OneYearChallenge—Read: Proverbs 9-12

September 10

Room of Open Doors

I PERKED UP MY EARS AT A PHRASE I HEARD on the radio. The speaker said there were some people *"locked in a room of open doors."* I don't know the context of the statement, but it is so descriptive of society. Day by day, people of great potential lock themselves into a lifestyle that is limiting, if not imprisoning them. Many parents are doing it to their children. Some adopt an evolutionary mind-set about humanity and lose their sense of wonder about the universe. Some adopt a materialistic mind-set and lock themselves in money-grubbing self-indulgence, never knowing the freedom of sharing and helping. Some adopt a narrow, fundamentalist view of God and forever restrict themselves from the rich opportunities of sharing faith with folks of other doctrinal persuasions. Some are so pleasure oriented that living only for the moment locks them in to the *"now,"* and they never see the big picture of eternity. How sad to see their offspring so brainwashed! I was in a home discussing the Bible and the things of God with a family, and a neighboring 21 year-old college student listened with fascination. *"This is so great,"* he observed. *"I've never heard any of this before."* How sad that a young college student could be *"locked in a room of open doors."* Some parents are intent on giving their children everything, yet they rob them by not giving them a spiritual heritage. It is no wonder that minds and emotions *"locked in,"* often *"break out"* through alcohol, drugs, violence, sexual exploitation and abuse. Jesus said, *"I have come that they may have life, and have it to the full"* (John 10:10). How free are you? In this day of opportunity for great spiritual freedom and expression, are you still *"locked in,"* refusing to claim the abundant life of Christ?

ONE YEAR CHALLENGE—Read: Proverbs 13-16

Open my eyes, Lord, I want to see Jesus. Then I want to see life from His perspective. Sensitize me now. Amen.

September 11

Dealing with Death

IT IS INTERESTING TO ME HOW THE COMMUNITY REACTS to the death of a child or teenager. Specialists are summoned to the school to be available to talk to kids about death. That's a good thing, if the specialists themselves have come to grips with the question of death and life after death. On the other hand, adults die every day and no provision is made by the community to help adults cope with death. A man loses his wife of 40 years (who also happens to be his best friend), a woman loses her mother who has lived with the family for 25 years, grandparents who raised their grandchildren die, and on and on the list goes. Adults dealing with the death of a loved one are dealing with a tremendous loss—things as severe as any teenager faces. Of course, churches are available (free) and counselors can be found (at a price), but grief often paralyzes people into inactivity. They don't reach out to take advantage of available resources. Job 14:14 begs an answer: *"If a man dies, will he live again?"* Hebrews 9:27 cannot be ignored: *"man is destined to die once, and after that to face judgment."* I do not think death troubles folks as much as what happens after death. Psychological speculations don't help that question! Jesus said, *"I am the resurrection and the life. He who believes in me will live, even though he dies; and whoever lives and believes in me will never die"* (John 11:25-26). It's not like there is a vacuum, and no help is available. The Bible is loaded with truthful answers. We must help people work through cultural superstitions and taboos, and find the helpful truth in God's Word. The best help for children or youths when a friend dies is a set of parents who have their faith grounded in a living Savior.

Remind me again, God, that dying is a part of life—in fact, the climax of life. Help me not to be too busy to prepare. Amen.

One Year Challenge—Read: Proverbs 17-20

September 12

Football Season

YOU CAN ALWAYS TELL WHEN OUR FAVORITE PROFESSIONAL TEAM is playing. It's easier to get a parking place at the shopping center; there are shorter lines at the grocery store (after kickoff), and fewer people are at the video store. People love to watch other people work hard at playing. You've heard the old saying, *"22,000 who need exercise sitting down watching 22 who don't?"* Anyway, football has a big hold on people's lives. Many people love God and love his church and put it first in their lives—unless their favorite team has a home game. Some people read their Bible and pray every night before they go to bed—except Monday night when they are too sleepy after the game goes off around midnight. It is hard for us to avoid contradictions in our lives, to be sure, but let's don't complicate it by placing undue value on that which is meaningless. It's the same problem when Little League parents get angry at their children's games. Keep your priorities in order. Remember the biblical injunction in 1 John 2:15-17: *"Do not love the world or anything in the world. If anyone loves the world, the love of the Father is not in him. For everything* (including sports events) *in the world—the cravings of sinful man, the lust of his eyes and the boasting of what he has and does—comes not from the Father but from the world. The world and its desires pass away, but the man who does the will of God lives forever."* Do those verses prick your spirit to begin some serious self-examination? Maybe you should go back and read them again. Do you hear how the Word is encouraging you? Do we just love the church as part of our cultural upbringing, and therefore, replaceable for a few hours? Or do we love Jesus as Lord of our lives, and therefore, never replaceable? Give priority to the eternal; your pastime can be enjoyed some other time.

Why do I have trouble keeping my priorities straight, dear Lord? I really know what I am supposed to do. Strengthen me. Amen.

OneYearChallenge—Read: Proverbs 21-25

September 13

Dealing with Despair

GREAT PEOPLE ARE HUMAN—that is, we usually find out that they have human flaws. Or maybe, if they have surrendered their humanity to God, they really are great. It shouldn't be hard for the rest of us to identify with the human fallibility of these famous folks. Many so-called *"great"* people today are aloof or plastic—media creations of some advertising firm, but look at King David, a man after God's own heart (Acts 13:22), who exposed his own personal struggles in the Psalms. I was moved as I read Psalm 69:2-3, *"I sink in the miry depths, where there is no foothold. I have come into the deep waters; the floods engulf me. I am worn out calling for help; my throat is parched. My eyes fail, looking for my God."* Every honest person can identify with that, either once in a while or regularly. Despair has a way of driving people down, making the burden of life almost impossible to bear. David had a simple faith in God that was very real. He became King of

the great nation of Israel in its heyday. As the saying goes, *"It's lonely at the top."* This certainly applied to King David and he had many lonely days filled with pressure and problems, but all of this taught him simple lessons on how to deal with despair that are profitable for us. The primary one: take a deep breath and relax on the Lord. Turn your problems over, with a prayer of relinquishment unto God Almighty. Many of the things that plunge humans into despair are totally beyond our control, so we should not let those things devastate us so. Painful and disappointing events cannot be avoided, nor can the occasional attack of despair, but they don't have to be destructive if we will trust the Lord. Long-lasting despair and despondency may be rooted in a physical problem; don't fail to go to your doctor for an examination to clarify your situation. Before you get too far down, ask God to lift you up. Try reading some of David's Psalms. This may be the way out of despair.

> *So many are sick with despair around me; I sometimes feel pulled down. Lift me up again, Lord. Amen.*

September 14

ONE YEAR CHALLENGE—Read: Proverbs 26-31

On Being Childlike

BUT JESUS SAID, *"Let the little children come to me, and do not hinder them, for the kingdom of heaven belongs to such as these"* (Matthew 19:14). It seems that Jesus was busy in his ministry that day. Some ladies came to see him and brought their children. Jesus' helpers wanted to prevent the little children from bothering him, and told the ladies to take the children home. It was then that Jesus made that famous statement. What did he mean, to be like a child? Why is that so important? Why would the converse be a barrier to participating in the kingdom of God? A little child is open and trusting and vulnerable. That's what makes them teachable. They want to learn and so are not fighting back at efforts to teach them. You could contrast the attitude of Jesus' disciples to the attitude of the Pharisees, the religious professionals. They thought they knew it all. Perhaps Jesus wasn't talking about the right atti-tude to enter the kingdom but the right attitude after you got inside? Generally, little children are caring and compassionate, especially to their younger brothers and sisters. Surely it raised a question in Jesus' mind about the effectiveness of the disciples to help anyone, since they were not sensitive to the needs of little children, or children in the faith. To help others certainly demands forgetting your own positions and accomplishments. Humility and helping go hand in hand. These characteristics are strengths, not weaknesses. Probably one of the reasons some people reject Christianity is because they don't see this quality in professing Christians. Some consider it weakness when it actually describes a strength. Don't let our current society sidetrack you on your way to the kingdom. Childlikeness will open your life for all it's God-given potential to be realized.

> *God, make me a child again. I want to be more pleasing to You. Especially give me a childlike disposition. Amen.*

ONE YEAR CHALLENGE—Read:
Philippians

September 15

The Coming of Fall

IT'S ALMOST THAT SPECIAL TIME OF THE YEAR called *"fall,"* or *"autumn."* You couldn't plan it any better. Just the right coolness at night! Just the right warmth in the daytime! The explosion of color is the autumn vegetation's invitation to *"Look at me!"* I love it, don't you? Of course, we all know winter is coming, and we will deal with its difficulties when it comes, but for now, let's enjoy the fall! That hint of color in the trees will dazzle you in a couple of weeks. Indeed, God *"has made everything beautiful in its time"* (Ecclesiastes 3:11). Someone said to me once, *"I never read the paper, there is nothing but ugly stories there."* It's easy to lose our perspective. From up close the ugliness of the back-up on the beltway, the crowded jail facilities, the cancer threats, the broken family, etc., may so blur our vision that we don't see what is all around us. Like a deep sea diver surfacing for fresh air, we need to lift up our eyes several times daily and see the beauty that surrounds us. My grass is greener now than it was in the heat of summer. If everything reproduces accordingly (Genesis 1), we ought to respond to the beauty that God has placed around us. For His beauty, you should *"Worship the LORD in the splendor of his holiness"* (Psalm 96:9). This is not taking the lemons of life and making lemonade, but taking the lemonade of life and enjoying it fully. God is beauty. He created us with an instinctive appreciation of beauty. Cultivate the gift. If you will genuinely appreciate fall's beauty and point it out to someone else, I know you will receive a positive response. Perhaps one of the things David was implying in Psalm 145:15 was the provision of beauty to free the human spirit.

> *Teach me to sing again, O God, the chorus of my childhood: "God made all things beautiful in His time." Amen.*

September 16

ONE YEAR CHALLENGE—Read:
Colossians

Resting

How's your rest? No, this is not a mattress commercial. But it does have something to say about beauty rest. Did you ever hear people say things like, *"I slept but I didn't rest,"* or, *"I wish I had time to rest"*? Rest is important. Some people take medicine or drugs daily to be able to sleep, and hopefully get some rest. Rest is more than sleep. It is the state of a clear mind and a clean conscience allowing the body to renew itself even if it's just with a 15- or 30-minute nap or break, to interrupt the routine of the day. If you have read the Bible very much you know many passages deal with resting. It says that God created the world and then rested from his labors (Genesis 2:2). It was a time to observe all that had happened to that point and say, *"it was very good"* (Genesis 1:31). God not only taught his people the importance of rest but modeled for us how it ought to be done. When you have done your very best with a holy and right purpose, then the reward is being able to say, *"very good,"* and relax enough to enjoy it and recharge. God said we need a day for sabbath, or rest (Exodus 16:23); the human machine can't keep running properly without regular time reflecting on our relationship with the Creator and so find rest. In fact, the Bible even says these times of complete relaxation—letting all our strength down on God, is a foretaste of what Heaven will be like. The challenge of Hebrews 4:1,3 is, *"Therefore, since the promise of entering his rest still stands, let us be careful that none of you be found to have fallen short of it. Now we who have believed enter that rest."* Hell is restlessness! It is tossing and turning and fretting away the hours. Rest is in God.

> *Father, there is nothing as sweet feeling as totally resting all of myself on You. Help me to be able to do it more often. Amen.*

September 17

OneYearChallenge—Read:
Ecclesiastes 1-3

"I was Glad"

ONE OF THE FIRST VERSES I LEARNED from the Bible was Psalm 122:1, *"I rejoiced with those who said to me, 'Let us go to the house of the LORD.' "* This is one of the Pilgrim Psalms. For me and my little friends in Sunday School, it was a challenge to be in Bible study every Sunday and to look forward to it with a joyful heart. To King David, (the author of the Psalm) and his fellow citizens of Israel, it was the description of a pilgrimage (spiritual journey) they made. As an act of spiritual devotion, a trip was made to Jerusalem to worship in the Temple. It took weeks or months of planning and preparation. The long journey on foot, could take several days or even weeks. It was a difficult trip. It was demanding and cost a lot of personal sacrifice, but when the people arrived at the Temple and worshiped God, it was more than worth the trouble it took to get there. There is a joy in a pilgrimage for God: joy in

preparation, joy in the journey, joy in anticipation, and finally, joy in arrival. To stand in the very presence of God in an act of worship stirs and inspires the soul. We have just experienced that in building and entering a new church building. Every week we meet people on a pilgrimage to know God in a personal way. Some travel a long way to find God, some travel only a short way. Some take years, some take weeks, but when they finally arrive and experience worship, there is pure joy. *"I rejoiced,"* David reports. He was invited by his friends to go, and he was glad he did. Maybe you should invite someone to go with you this week, or accept someone's invitation to you? You'll be glad!

> *Father, I feel like I am at home every time I go to a church house. You are always early, always getting there before I do. Amen.*

September 18

ONE YEAR CHALLENGE—Read: Ecclesiastes 4-6

Liars and the Devil

I HAVE TROUBLE WITH LIARS! Sorry, I can't help it. I can deal with most situations that come along, but when someone looks me right in the eye and tells me a lie, it's tough. Why do people do that? Is it human nature? Did your mother teach you to lie? Did you teach your children to lie? No, it came naturally. Kids start at the earliest opportunity. Jesus told some people that when they lied they spoke their father's language (John 8:42-47). Who was their father? The devil! Children of God speak only the truth because God is true and speaks only the truth, and his children copy him. So liars are showing their family heritage! But, that doesn't help me. Knowing that lying comes naturally to some people doesn't help me deal with the problem. It still irritates me, angers me, and hurts my feelings. Jesus had a cure for liars: *"you will know the truth* (himself), *and the truth will set you free"* (John 8:32). There it is—

the only thing that can free a person from a life of lying is getting to know Jesus. He is greater than lies and can defeat them, even when lying is deeply rooted. But still there is the problem, how do we deal with liars? Jesus said, *"pray for those who persecute you"* (Matthew 5:44). Okay, I can try that! Don't give back evil for evil. Love your enemy. Be patient. Be forgiving. Whoa! That's a lot! Yes, because the responsibility always lies with the truth-liver and truth-teller to take the initiative in setting the liar free from lying. Liars are trapped. They dig deeper and deeper holes for themselves. Jesus endured liars and dealt with them patiently. That's the lesson I must learn—like it or not!

God, I don't ever want to tell a lie again. Help me to love the truth and tell it. Amen.

ONE YEAR CHALLENGE—Read: Ecclesiastes 7-9

September 19

Going to Court

From the smallest rural courthouse to our massive metropolitan judicial centers, our court system is busy. The dockets are always full. People spend extraordinary amounts of time in jail just waiting for their trial to be heard. Have you spent any time around a courthouse? It is not a happy place. People stare straight ahead; worried frowns, anger, and tears are all around; rich and poor mingle together; smiles are few. If you have to appear, you want to be prepared and have the best attorney you can get. Visiting the courthouse can give new meaning to 2 Corinthians 5:10, *"For we must all appear before the judgment seat of Christ, that each one may receive what is due him for the things done while in the body."* The seriousness of this verse cannot be overestimated. Each one of us will have our day in court before the only judge that really matters. A man escaped punishment for a serious crime because of a legal technicality. The presiding judge said to him, *"I know you're guilty, you know you're guilty, everyone knows you're guilty. I just want you to remember that someday you will stand before the perfect judge and you will receive what you deserve."* The jails are populated with people who profess their innocence. Many others who are guilty are able to escape the punishment of the court, but again the Bible speaks: *"man is destined to die once, and after that to face judgment"* (Hebrews 9:27). We need to prepare for that great court appearance. We need the best attorney to represent us in that court. There is only one available, according to 1 Timothy 2:5, *"there is one God and one mediator between God and men, the man Christ Jesus."* Have you brought him your case? Go to him. Place yourself on his mercy. This date will be the most important of your life.

Thank You, thank You, Father, that appearing before Your Judgment bar someday will be the climax of a life of preparation. Bless You, God. Amen.

One Year Challenge—Read: Ecclesiastes 10-12

September 20

The Shadows of Yesterday

THE HOUSE WHERE I WAS RAISED IS GONE. After the death of both parents, the place was sold. The investor who bought the farm tore down the buildings. To ride by there today conjures up visions of yesterday. It is a similar story with my in-laws' farm. One by one the buildings have come down except for the main house and a couple of small sheds; all that is there now is a shadow from yesterday. The shadows remind us that the old is passing away. The hymn writer Lyte said, *"Change and decay in all around I see."** Since the old is passing, how do you deal with it? Jesus said, *"Heaven and earth will pass away, but my words will never pass away"* (Luke 21:33). While we deal with the transiency of everything, we have the option of latching on to something permanent. Even those who pursue knowledge have an impossible task. Knowledge is multiplying but the Bible prophecies that *"knowledge, it will pass away"* (I Corinthians 13:8). There is another verse that shines like a beacon through dark clouds, *"Jesus Christ is the same yesterday and today and forever"* (Hebrews 13:8). It is good that the shadows of yesterday do not have to strike fear in our hearts as they remind us of change. *"Nevertheless, God's solid foundation stands firm, sealed with this inscription: 'The Lord knows those who are his' "* (2 Timothy 2:19). Times are no different today than at anytime in history. Every generation has to deal with major events that remind everyone that nothing is permanent. In each generation there have been people who stood on a strong foundation and were not threatened by the transiency. When you anchor your faith in the Eternal Unchanging God, you can live every moment to the fullest. Yesterday has shadows because today has light.

Facing Your light, Father, I see no shadows. Remind me that shadows are for those who turn their backs on You. Amen.

ONE YEAR CHALLENGE—Read: Song of Solomon 1-4

September 21

What's Hiding in There?

I WENT TO A SCULPTOR'S STUDIO TO MEET him personally and learn about his work. To say the least, I was impressed with his ability to take wire and plaster of paris and make a beautiful figure. I was amazed at what could come from common clay, but I was most impressed by what could be sculpted from a piece of wood. On one wall was a life-sized teen-age girl in solid mahogany. It was beautiful! Later as we looked at his storeroom of materials, he showed me an ugly slab of mahogany with the statement, *"In that hunk of wood, a teen-age boy is hiding who will become the companion of the girl."* The thought stayed with me when I left and remains with me. It reminds me of Jesus calling the first disciples with the challenge that he would make them become *"fishers of men"* (Matthew 4:19). Hidden inside of them was a potential that they themselves did not know. It is said that someone asked Michelan-gelo how he could take a shapeless block of stone and sculpt from it something as beautiful as his lovely statue of David. Said Michelangelo, *"It is easy; I just chiseled away what was not needed and there was a statue."* When an ordinary person surrenders his life to Jesus, God can remove what is ugly and unnecessary and something beautiful will come from his work. Such is the Master's touch. A woman reached out to Jesus saying, *"If I just touch his clothes, I will be healed"* (Mark 5:28). Have you looked in the mirror lately? There may be a beautiful person hidden inside of you that has not yet been released. Jesus said he came *"to proclaim freedom for the prisoners"* (Luke 4:18). Jesus was a carpenter rather than a sculptor, but he is the liberator for all of us.

Reveal the good that is hidden in me, O God. The world needs desperately to share it, especially my family. Amen.

ONE YEAR CHALLENGE—Read:
Song of Solomon 5-8

September 22

Youth and Bible Study

ONE OF THE EXCITING EVENTS OF SUMMER IS VACATION BIBLE SCHOOL. Most churches recognize this as a real challenge and opportunity. Many adults have fond memories of time spent in Bible study when they were kids. Some trace their success in life to values learned in this intensive time of studying God's word. What a privilege to teach children the truth of God! I watch their open-minded, wide-eyed response to the gospel and thank God for the opportunity to teach them. What a tragedy that we live in such a pagan time that kids are growing up ignorant of the Bible. It is not surprising that so many teen-agers have trouble with drugs, sex, and alcohol; they have no moral and spiritual foundation on which to build a value system. Jesus is still inviting, *"Let the little children come to me, and do not hinder them, for the kingdom of heaven belongs to such as these"* (Matthew 19:14). Just as the scripture relates that children were drawn to Jesus as by a magnet, so today children who have the opportunity to meet him are drawn to him. Wise mothers are described in the Bible as *"bringing little children to Jesus to have him touch them"* (Mark 10:13). Wise parents and grandparents need to learn from that today; it's still a very good example. Some people treat children the same way they treat minorities: they ignore them and their needs. Jesus made much of children and the quality of childlikeness. In Luke 18:17 he said, *"I tell you the truth, anyone who will not receive the kingdom of God like a little child will never enter it."* Adults reading this should pause to examine their own attitudes about Jesus and the Kingdom, then go tell your child, grandchild, or a friend's child about life in God's Kingdom serving Jesus.

Some of us were so blessed, God, our family taught us the Bible when we were young. Some of us are trying to catch up now. Teach us all, Holy Spirit. Amen.

ONE YEAR CHALLENGE—Read: 1 Thessalonians

September 23

A City of Refuge

THE BIBLICAL ACCOUNTS OF THE *"CITIES of refuge"* (Numbers 35) have fascinating appeal. The idea of showing mercy to *"bad"* people certainly catches one's attention. The story of Cain and Abel illustrates the fact that the man who committed murder committed an offense against God (Genesis 4:10). Having no city of refuge to which he could resort, Cain saw that his fate was inescapable. The biblical book of Numbers reports the beginning of *"cities of refuge."* In the case of an accidental murder, the guilty party could find refuge at God's altar and could be protected from the penalty of his deed. A half-dozen or more cities of salvation were prescribed, near enough to other cities for the law-breaker or sinner to reach. We have no such cities today. The closest thing is the homeless shelter, a place of refuge for people who seem to have no one else to care for them. We leave it to the courts to determine guilt and innocence and to give protection to those who need it, but that does not eliminate the need for refuge. If you follow the New Testament your conclusion would be that the church is the biblical place of refuge. *"Come to me, all you who are weary and burdened, and I will give you rest"* (Matthew 11:28). The inclusiveness of Jesus' invitation should be incarnated in every church so that no one will feel that he or she has no place to turn for solace and salvation. When the church becomes exclusive and caters only to a certain type of people, she strays from the Lord. Jesus is the Ultimate City of Refuge! With outstretched arms, he invites us to find forgiveness for our smallest offenses or grossest sins. You, who for refuge have already fled to Jesus, know what I mean. To the rest, I can only tell you of your opportunity today to find release from your guilt and fear, in Jesus.

When I fled to You, dear God, You received me. I can never thank You enough for the rescue. Thanks. You are so good to me! Amen.

ONE YEAR CHALLENGE—Read: Isaiah 1-6

September 24

The Right Answer

A PASTOR WAS GIVING THE CHILDREN'S SERMON to the little children gathered at the front of the church. He asked, *"What animal is furry and gray, has a big tail, loves to play in the trees and gathers nuts in the fall to eat in the winter?"* All the children were silent. No one answered. Finally, the minister turned to one little boy who regularly attended the church and said, *"Stevie, I know you know the answer. What is it?"* Little Stevie replied, *"It sounds like you are describing a squirrel, but I have been around here long enough to know that the answer to everything is Jesus, so I will say 'Jesus'!"* We smile at the little boy's reasoning while recognizing his grasp on the great truth of the church: *"Christ is the answer."* A skeptic once replied, *"If Christ is the answer, what is the question?"* Just ask the question, there's the answer. One day, a large part of the crowd that followed Jesus suddenly left when he presented the total demands of Christian discipleship. Jesus turned to his disciples and asked, *"You do not want to leave too, do you?"* Peter replied for all of them and said, *"Lord, to whom shall we go? You have the words of eternal life"* (John 6:67-68). Having already searched in all the usual places for life and the meaning of life, they had settled on Jesus because He had real answers to the important questions. That is the key issue. Jesus said, *"I have come that they may have life, and have it to the full"* (John 10:10). The offer stands! I can say with the little boy, *"I've been around here long enough to know the answer to everything is Jesus!"* Seriously, bring your most important question to Jesus right now.

> *Sometimes, God, You must be amazed how we big children keep giving the wrong answer to life's questions when we know the right one. Take away our pride. Amen.*

ONE YEAR CHALLENGE—Read:
Isaiah 7-12

September 25

Wars and Rumors

PEACE IS ALWAYS FRAGILE. It must be nurtured constantly. Because it is such a tender plant, it withers quickly under the hot wind of war and rumors of war. The specter of war haunts humanity. War will never be an isolated event again; our world has become too small. The evening news will be sure that no home will escape the threatening news with all its ugliness. Why so much war? When will we ever learn? Jesus said, *"You will hear of wars and rumors of wars, but see to it that you are not alarmed. Such things must happen, but the end is still to come"* (Matthew 24:6). Wars happen over and over again. James 4:1-2, *"What causes fights and quarrels among you? Don't they come from your desires that battle within you? You want something but don't get it. You kill and covet, but you cannot have what you want. You quarrel and fight."* The Bible aptly describes war as coming from selfishness and self-centered desires.

Isn't that true? Nations, like people, go after things they don't have and egotistically think they have the right to have. War on the world stage will continue. How does an individual live with peace of mind in a strife-torn world? Do you have family or friends directly involved in armed conflict? If so, this is a special concern to you. The peacemaker gives peace to individuals (John 14:27). *"We have peace with God through our Lord Jesus Christ"* (Romans 5:1). *"The mind controlled by the Spirit is life and peace"* (Romans 8:6). A songwriter once said, *"I know not what the future holds, but I know who holds the future and the future is known only to Him."**This knowledge can provide an anchor for your life, a safe haven during the storms of war. Avoid the personal destruction of war through faith in the peacemaker.

> **O God of peace, who brought again from the dead our Lord and Savior Jesus Christ, grant us peace for our every struggle. Amen.**

ONE YEAR CHALLENGE—Read:
Isaiah 13-16

September 26

Nearby Lips, Far Away Hearts

CULTURAL RELIGION MAY YET BE THE DEATH OF AMERICA. We continue to have polls that give positive reports about the state of religion in America, but day-to-day life in our society certainly doesn't validate those reports. You and I know that drug use is up, divorce is up, crimes of violence are up; the actions don't match the survey. A cultural religion is like that, the majority nod their heads in assent but don't act on the facts. So, in a society where there is a white majority, the cultural religions looks a lot like the white social system. Listen to the next political speaker you hear closing his speech: *"God bless you"* or, *"God bless America."* It sounds like a pep rally! Does it mean we want God to bless us Americans, and not bless the rest of the world? Cultural religion always believes that we, of a particular group, are God's chosen, and God will take special care of us. Thinking agnostics see through cultural religion as being empty of personal meaning and stay away from churches. In Isaiah 29:13 the Lord God says, *"These people come near to me with their mouth and honor me with their lips, but their hearts are far from me. Their worship of me is made up only of rules taught by men."* It is easy to talk religious talk. Read the paper—most weddings and funerals are still conducted by ministers of religion. Many of these people don't come near the church otherwise. Their comments about the service often sound like they have attended a Broadway show. Cultural religion looks to be entertained, not challenged about an ungodly lifestyle. Heart religion—that's what God wants—heart religion! Actions speak louder than words. King David prayed, *"Create in me a pure heart"* (Psalm 51:10). If the heart is right with God, actions and speech will validate that truth.

ONE YEAR CHALLENGE—Read: Isaiah 17-23

> *God of Truth, save me from deceitfulness, especially with You. I never want to be a hypocrite. If I am, please convict me, forgive me, and welcome me back. Amen.*

September 27

Where are We Going?

WHAT'S LIFE ALL ABOUT? Where are we going? Is there any purpose or direction to things? Questions like these plague many people. The lack of answers creates anxiety and nervousness. Men and women of faith are not bothered by such issues. Deep inside God has spoken a word and we believe that history is literally *"His story."* *"Now we know that if the earthly tent we live in is destroyed, we have a building from God, an eternal house in heaven, not built by human hands"* (2 Corinthians 5:1). For the person who has decided to trust the Lord, the short time we spend on earth can't be compared to eternity. Jesus said, *"In my Father's house are many rooms; . . . . I am going there to prepare a place for you. . . . I will come back and take you to be with me."* You can read about this in John 14:2-3.. You must admit, it is exciting to imagine: *"For the Lord himself will come down from heaven, with a loud command, with* the voice of the archangel and with the trumpet call of God, and the dead in Christ will rise first. After that, we who are still alive and are left will be caught up together with them in the clouds to meet the Lord in the air. And so we will be with the Lord forever"* (1 Thessalonians 4:16-17). The Bible contains these large chunks of truth about the future, and they create a growing hope in the believer. The hymn of the Southern Baptist Theological Seminary, written by Basil Manly, Jr., has a verse that proclaims, *"We meet to part, but part to meet, when earthly labors are complete, to join in yet more blest employ, in an eternal world of joy."* Best of all, John says, *"we shall be like him, for we shall see him as he is"* (1 John 3:2).

Father, I know Heaven is a wonderful place. You made it. You are there. What a blessed hope we have! Amen.

ONE YEAR CHALLENGE—Read:
Isaiah 24-28

September 28

His Presence

THERE ARE SOME BEAUTIFUL PASSAGES IN THE BIBLE that describe the Lord's presence with His people. They are the kind that give you the *"warm fuzzies"* if you are a believer. Genesis 3:8 says, *"Then the man and his wife heard the sound of the LORD God as he was walking in the garden in the cool of the day."* Then in Exodus 33:11, *"the LORD would speak to Moses face to face, as a man speaks with his friend."* In John 1:14, the Bible says, *"The Word became flesh and made his dwelling among us."* Technically, you call these anthropomorphic, or the attributing of human behavior to the Divine. Nevertheless, they are filled with personal encouragement for the believer. Generally, religions have to do with statues, idols, or pictures that can make no personal response. Religions often are based on fear of an absentee divinity that has great power to harm those who offend him or her or it. One difference in a revealed religion like Christianity is that the Almighty has revealed Himself as ever-present and caring. For instance, in the earlier reference to John 1:14 is the truth that God is not out there (absent) but here, now. He is present and not silent. The great story of the Exodus is that God's presence was always going before the people—the pillar of cloud by day and the pillar of fire by night. God's presence was so necessary that even when the Israelites arrived near the Promised Land, they refused to go up and take possession unless God would go with them (Exodus 33:15). The other side of this is that you can't hide from God, or evade Him. David asked, *"Where can I flee from your presence?"* (Psalm 139:7). That should be a serious consideration also, for those who reject Him. Is this truth helpful to you or scary?

> *O God, my companion—my life would be so lonely without You. Thank You for your Presence. Amen.*

ONE YEAR CHALLENGE—Read: Isaiah 29-34

September 29

Plenty of Toys

I'VE SEEN A CYNICAL BUMPER STICKER. It said, *"When you die, the one with the most toys wins."* Is that why people buy so many toys today for their children? To prove they are winners? My grandchildren have more toys than they will ever use. As I visit homes, I see yards and recreation rooms filled with toys, seemingly forgotten by the children. When December comes, the toy stores add extra staff and extra hours for more business. People stand in line to buy more toys, many of which will be ignored. Children's imaginations run wild. Television brainwashes the child about toys. Parents rush out for new toys to make their children happy. Maybe the idea becomes so deeply ingrained that people grow up with this toy mythology and carry it into adulthood, hence the insatiable desire for things. But what do you do when *"toys"* don't bring happiness? A man shared with me that he bought his wife a house, a car, a stereo, anything she requested, and she still left him. Or perhaps she left because she got all the *"toys"* that were supposed to make her happy, and couldn't stand it when it didn't work? Material things can never fill a spiritual or emotional vacuum. Are you living and working for *"toys"*? A wealthy man ran up to Jesus one day *"and fell on his knees before him. 'Good teacher,' he asked, 'what must I do to inherit eternal life?' "* (Mark 10:17). He had discovered that *"toys"* weren't enough. Notice the self-destruction by suicide and drug abuse of well-known actors, athletes, and other wealthy folks in the limelight. They have discovered that their *"toys"* are not sufficient to give life meaning. Materialism is a dangerous religion. Remember especially during the Christmas buying season, as well as all year long: every effort is being made to convince you that a few more *"toys"* can make a difference in your life. Jesus said, *"a man's life does not consist in the abundance of his possessions"* (Luke 12:15).

ONE YEAR CHALLENGE—Read: Isaiah 35-42

> *What is real? God, what is real? I get deceived often by fast talkers. Show me the real thing. Amen.*

September 30

Washing Windows

THERE ARE LESSONS TO BE LEARNED FROM WASHING WINDOWS. Ask my wife, or me. For one thing, it will improve communication. Sometimes you can't hear, so someone has to make signs or point to spots that still need to be cleaned. Just having to work together (cooperating) is a plus to communication. Isn't it funny how you can wash your side and it looks perfectly clean and you become blind to a very obvious spot, clearly visible when looking from a different angle? Also, some spots get clean before others. Just one swipe and some dirt disappears, other spots demand a lot of elbow grease because they have been there a long time and really hardened. When my wife and I wash windows it usually results in a lot of friendly face-making and smiling and clean windows. The hardest part is getting me started, both with God and my wife! Sometimes, when God and I are working on my life, I feel like a partner in a window washing venture. The results are good and the fellowship is great! Prayer and spiritual self-examination is God's way of window washing. *"Now all we can see of God is like a cloudy picture in a mirror"* (I Corinthians 13:12 CEV). Everything is clouded by my sin. But He gently and lovingly points out the spots (unconfessed sins) and stays with me until it's completely dealt with, not just a one time touch and then forget it. Even a good friend won't always point out your sins for fear of offending you. God is especially good at pointing out the corners where spots are not so obvious. Then the Light shines through and we are called *"out of darkness into his wonderful light"* (I Peter 2:9). Even if the washing demands use of strong vinegar water, I know it's used in love and for my good. Let the Son shine in!

> *Wash me, Lord, make me clean.*
> *Keep me clean every minute.*
> *Give me the courage to agree*
> *with You about the dirty spots.*
> *Amen.*

ONE YEAR CHALLENGE—Read:
Isaiah 43-45

October 1

Where To Go for Help

WELL, I HAD ANOTHER ONE OF THOSE CALLS. It was a prayer request. A crisis had arisen in the life of a family, so they were calling the church for prayer. So what's unusual about that, you ask? These people who wanted prayer never go to church! It's not really unusual, it happens all the time. It's just so contradictory. Why do people who have no time in their lives for God and His church, when trouble comes, they start thinking about God, the minister, and the church? Is it guilt? Fear? Is it the thought that they are being punished for their lifestyle? What is the real motivation for people with *"foxhole"* religion? A similar question comes to mind when a self-described atheist uses the Lord's Name in vain. How can he curse so, when he doesn't believe in God? There seems to be an underlying rule in our society. When in spiritual, physical, mental, marital, or whatever kind of need, call the minister and the church. On the other hand the church and the minister know that once the crisis is solved, you probably won't see these people around the church again, until the next time a crisis arises. Of course, if they are ever disappointed at a time like this, they will often see that as their own answer to their own question, *"What good is God, anyway?"*, and stay away forever. Such a shallow and self-defeating response. So why are Americans like this? Because deep down inside, even if they are rebelling against it, folks know that the church is the ultimate place of care. When no one else does, you can always find a church and a minister who does. Basically, the New Testament church today is the incarnation (fleshing out) of Jesus who said, *"Come to me, all you who are weary and burdened, and I will give you rest"* (Matthew 11:28). Peter said, *"Cast all your anxiety on him because he cares for you"* (I Peter 5:7). The calls will continue. And that's the way it should be. Thank God for the church!

> **God, You thought of everything, even a place of refuge for people in desperate situations. It's no wonder You died for the church to exist. Amen.**

ONE YEAR CHALLENGE—Read: Isaiah 46-48

October 2

The Gift of Smiling

"*SMILING IS THE UNIVERSAL LANGUAGE.*" I've heard that all my life. In recent days I have been convinced that it is true. When my wife and I first went to the Philippines as missionaries and began to study the Tagalong language, there were many things we couldn't say, or understand, so we smiled a lot. If you don't understand, smile. If you can't say what you want to say, smile. I read many years ago that it only takes one-half as many muscles to smile as to frown. What a bonus! I would have exhausted my face muscles if this had not been true. Thank God for the gift of smiling! God said in the Bible, "*A merry heart maketh a cheerful countenance*" (Proverbs 15:13 KJV), or freely translated: "*If you have a smile in your heart, it will shine on your face.*" Well, that's easy, isn't it? When you feel good, you should smile at people. The world has gotten so impersonal, that it seems if you smile at some folks, they are aston-ished, or bewildered. Hey, how about this thought from Proverbs 17:22: "*A cheerful heart is good medicine, but a crushed spirit dries up the bones.*" A frown puts people down. If you already feel bad, and someone looks at you and frowns, you simply feel worse. But a smile is good medicine. It will always help. It says, "*I like you!*"; "*You are acceptable to me!*"; "*I would like to be your friend!*"; "*I want to understand you!*"; "*I'm on your side!*" I picture Jesus as a smiling man. His smile was like a magnet that gave life to His words, "*Come to me*" (Matthew 11:28). A smile is a free gift that you can give to everyone you meet. If they ask where you got it, tell them Jesus gave it to you.

> *Thank You Jesus for giving us a reason to smile. In the Bible You seem to be smiling more than frowning, I need that. Amen.*

ONE YEAR CHALLENGE—Read: Isaiah 49-51

October 3

"Hostages"

THERE'S A NEW WORD IN OUR VOCABULARY now; not really new, but new in frequency of usage. I remember my childhood days, playing cowboys and Indians and taking *"hostages."* But other than that kind of use, Americans just didn't use it much. Now we read it regularly. None can describe the anguish felt by those who are held hostage. Thinking about that brought to my mind the fact that many people are being held hostage by different kinds of terrorists: fear, worry, anxiety about what's going to happen. When you are a hostage, whether there is a terrorist gun at your head or not really doesn't matter. If you don't think this is true, talk to an alcoholic or cocaine or gambling addict or a teenager who has just discovered that she is pregnant or a bookkeeper who is stealing from his boss—hostages one and all, terrorized by their desires and emotions! Some are hostages to their surroundings; they can't buy enough locks to buy inner security. While we are aware of terrorists and hostages who make spectacular news events, I plead for those who live their lives each day in quiet desperation, and no one offers to pay the price of personal involvement that will set them free. Paul remarks about how he was a hostage to worldly success and religious doctrines until he became a prisoner of Jesus (Ephesians 3:1, Philemon 1,9). Of course, that is one of the paradoxes of faith in Jesus, you only become free when you become a hostage or prisoner for Him. Then you can go as an ambassador for Christ and use your keys (Matthew 16:19) that He has given you to set all the other prisoners and hostages free. *"The LORD sets prisoners free"* is the declaration of David in Psalm 146:7. He should know, he was held hostage to guilt for his sin with Bathsheba until pastor Nathan confronted him about it. Only then, as David prayed his confession of Psalm 51, did the good Lord set him free.

Make me sensitive, Lord, to the invisible chains that make hostages of many people. Set them free, I pray. Amen.

ONE YEAR CHALLENGE—Read: Isaiah 52-54

October 4

Dropping Trash on Roads

A NEW BOULEVARD RECENTLY OPENED near our house. My wife and I had been taking our daily walk there during construction. You know what happened the first day it was open? Several people decided to drop bags of trash there instead of at the dump. It was not heavily traveled and they assumed that the police would not catch them. What causes people to do that? What is the motivation that moves a person to take bags of garbage from where he lives and drop them in the public domain? Some people have no respect for their fellow citizen. Some have no respect for the environment and our need to care for it. When Jesus said, *"Love your neighbor as yourself"* (Luke 10:27), He was speaking of our obligation to care for and respect the needs of others. If we are aware of our place in the family of man we cannot live on this crowded earth without being considerate of the needs of other people. Environmental groups are lobbying the government about factories and businesses polluting the earth; they are trying to have an impact on the big picture. It is up to us to teach our children and grandchildren by example how to care for the world's needs. There are some direct words in I Peter 2:16-17: *"Live as free men, but do not use your freedom as a cover-up for evil; live as servants of God. Show proper respect to everyone: Love the brotherhood of believers, fear God, honor the king."* Intricately woven together is love and respect for God and love and respect for our fellow humans, including our leaders. The Bible sums it up pretty bluntly: *"anyone who does not love his brother, whom he has seen, cannot love God, whom he has not seen"* (I John 4:20). That's a powerful statement. If you ever drop litter on the road, why? Pick it up instead.

Remind me again, O Lord, that Christians should be the best citizens and the most sensitive to obeying all laws. Amen.

OneYearChallenge—Read:
Isaiah 55-57

October 5

Uncaring Environment Produces Teen Suicide

AMONG THE TRAGEDIES OF OUR TIME is young people committing suicide. Life is difficult at times for everybody. Life is difficult all the time for some people. What kind of environment is so cold and uncaring as to produce suicide among the young? A few years ago when existentialism was sweeping across the European university scene there followed a wave of college-age suicides. Following the ideas of the philosopher Jean Paul Sarte, who said they could experience how everything in life felt except death, many rushed out to experience death also. Of course they had not yet felt and done everything else. But nowadays it's different; the youth are younger, the despair is deeper. Some, no doubt, take the advice of the rock singer about the *"final solution"* to their problem. But, basically, the kids are not convinced that significant people care about them. Broken homes often produce broken lives.

Parents become so preoccupied with their own happiness that the child is left with no support. A peer group can only mirror a child's unhappiness, not change it. Adults need to think more about kids and care for them, whether they are your children or not. Youth need to be challenged, warned, encouraged, patted on the back, and disciplined—whatever it takes to get across the truth about them: *"You are loved; you are important and have value, no matter how badly you feel about yourself."* The wise writer of Ecclesiastes 12:1 says, *"Remember your Creator in the days of your youth."* That too, is a large contributing factor today; a generation of kids is coming along with no knowledge of God. They haven't rejected God, adults have not introduced them to God and Life (John 14:6). They don't disbelieve God; material minded and success crazy adults have robbed their children of the opportunity to get to know the Truth.

> **Surely, God, suicide must break Your heart. What a great insult to Your love. Make us sensitive to desperate people. Amen.**

October 6

ONE YEAR CHALLENGE—Read: Isaiah 58-60

Enjoying the Beauty of Nature

On A RECENT DRIVE ACROSS VERMONT AND NEW HAMPSHIRE, FOLLOWED BY A FERRY RIDE across Lake Champlain, we were almost speechless at times because of the astounding beauty of the mountains in the fall. Brilliant red and orange with a perfect mixture of evergreens gave a fantastic chorus of praise to God who *"has made everything beautiful in its time"* (Ecclesiastes 3:11). I would join the hymn writer who wrote *"For the beauty of the earth, For the glory of the skies, For the love which from our birth Over and around us lies, Lord of all, to Thee we raise This our hymn of grateful praise."** The fall beauty may be a good time to get your spiritual vision cleared before winter. We get so caught up in the ugliness of the six o'clock news: muggings, bombings, starvation, abuse, racism, the AIDS epidemic, rapes, corruption, etc. Then the weather man comes on with dire predictions of a cold, hard winter.

But here we are in the fall! There is enough beauty to enjoy and appreciate in the natural world to offset some of the other. God trumpets His message in nature, reminding us of His care. In Romans 1:20, Paul said, *"since the creation of the world God's invisible qualities—his eternal power and divine nature—have been clearly seen, being understood from what has been made."* God *"has not left himself without testimony"* (Acts 14:17). David said in Psalm 19:1, *"The heavens declare the glory of God; the skies proclaim the work of his hands."* Gratefully, we are not left with just natural revelations of God's power and might. God has revealed Himself perfectly, incarnated Himself in the God/man Jesus. With that fact, we can doubly rejoice in the beauty of the fall. Prepare for winter with fall praising! How about that?

> *Beautiful things bless my life, O God; they are all treasures for us from Your storehouse. I need the pick-me-up. Amen.*

ONE YEAR CHALLENGE—Read: Isaiah 61-63

October 7

Lottery: "Trick or Treat"

THERE HAS BEEN A BUMPER CROP OF PUMPKINS this year. I like pumpkins, whether or not they have been carved into jack-o-lanterns. I suppose there will be a bumper crop of ghosts and goblins playing *"Trick or treat"* also. Actually, the trick part seems to be long gone. Kids in costume just come to the door and hold up their bags for you to dump in the candy, they don't understand what it means, this *"Trick or treat."* It's just as well! The government has gotten into the act and when a big kid on the block starts playing, everyone should watch out. It's called *"The Lottery."* It seems like harmless fun: *"You have to play to win!"* It's dressed up and given a lot of cute names! A lot of well-known people (already successful and rich) are paid to tell people how much fun they have had playing the game. Then we can look around the corner and watch poor people buying the tickets. *"Trick or treat!"* When I was a kid we would put somebody's cow on their front porch or a wallet on a string and then knock on the door and watch from our observation spot. No one ever got hurt. It was all in fun. Our tricks were simple. But this is serious business, a game that will cost a lot of serious money. Oh, everybody will smile when there is a rare winner. But more people will cry than laugh when rent is not paid and hungry children aren't fed and basic essentials are not provided for families. It's okay for children to play *"Trick or treat"* but it's unseemly for a state government. *"Righteousness exalts a nation, but sin is a disgrace to any people"* (Proverbs 14:34). We should help the poor, not trick them.

> *Father, whom did this "something for nothing" craving come from that makes us do foolish and harmful things? Grant us understanding. Amen.*

ONE YEAR CHALLENGE—Read: Isaiah 64-66

October 8

Debating

DEBATE HAS COME TO BE A POPULAR FORUM FOR EXCHANGING IDEAS again. In past history debate was an important tool in the government process. In fact, even some religious groups have specialized in getting out their particular brand of doctrine through the medium of debate. But we have such a *"winner-loser"* complex that it is hard for us in this culture to appreciate debate. Even the media will make the absurd conclusion that one political candidate won on style, while his opponent won on content. Saying it that way means nobody lost, or more aptly, nobody won. The debate scenario can be deceptive, for it is possible to win the battle, but lose the war, or win the debate, and lose the campaign. If you win the debate what have you accomplished? For instance, what if you debate the existence of God? In a debate scene, the debater taking the negative approach (denying the existence of God) will probably pile up more tangible arguments against, than his opponent can list in the *"for"* column. So, he is declared the winner! What has he gained? He has gained the right to live a God-less existence, while the loser of the debate is joyful in his relationship with the God he could not prove in a debate. As Blaise Pascal, the philosopher said, *"faith has its reasons that reason knows not of."* The Bible doesn't debate the issue, it assumes God and begins with, *"In the beginning God created"* (Genesis 1:1). In John 1:38-39 Jesus didn't ask Andrew if he wanted to debate religion but a more personal question, *"What do you want?"* and followed it with the challenge, *"Come, . . . and you will see."* In debates, there are winners and losers. In a positive response to the challenge to follow Jesus Christ, there are only winners. Drop your arguments, dare to trust him!

> *Some of us, God, are having arguments that we hope we lose. We will be proven lost if we win. Amen.*

ONE YEAR CHALLENGE—Read: 2 Thessalonians

October 9

Three Temptations

"*In the arena of Christian ministry there exist at least three temptations: to shine, to whine or to recline.*" So says David Christie. Let's look at them in reverse order. Many yield to the temptation to "*recline.*" These folks recline on the past, they are spiritually passive. Either reclining on a past when they were "*forced to go to church when I was young,*" or some well-worn excuse about the church being "*full of hypocrites,*" they feel totally released from any type of spiritual responsibility today. Others yield to the temptation to "*whine.*" These folks are a contradiction! Claiming to be religious, they are miserable. They are always complaining; always feeling sorry for themselves; always thinking that God is blessing others more; wringing their hands and moaning, they plod their spiritual path. Then there are those who "*shine.*" As they take their call to ministry seriously, they "*delight greatly in the LORD*" (Isaiah 61:10). They are thrilled to have a personal relationship with Jesus Christ and can't get over the fact that Jesus Christ loves them so much. They like to talk about it, they like to do things to help other people and in doing so "*fulfill the law of Christ*" (Galatians 6:2). They especially like to invite other people to come and share in the wonderful experiences of worship. The Bible likes this figure of shining. In Daniel 12:3, it is prophesied that the righteous "*will shine like the brightness of the heavens, and those who lead many to righteousness, like the stars.*" Jesus used this figure in Matthew 13:43, as the climax of Judgment Day. More appropriate for us today is Matthew 5:16 where Jesus challenges us: "*let your light shine before men, that they may see your good deeds and praise your Father in heaven.*" The Apostle Paul said, "*God is shining in our hearts to let you know that his glory is seen in Jesus Christ*" (2 Corinthians 4:6 CEV). As a child I used to sing, "*This little light of mine, I'm going to let it shine.*" Join Me?

O Loving Savior, I want to shine for You. You are the only light of my life. Help me to radiate light. Amen.

One Year Challenge—Read: Jeremiah 1-5

October 10

Visiting Squirrels

OUR YARD HAS BEEN VISITED several times lately by a squirrel. I hope he comes back. There aren't many trees where I live. In the last place there were lots of trees and lots of squirrels. It was irritating the way they ate the bird food, but squirrels are such good entertainment. They seem so spontaneous and full of life, just filled with vim, vigor and vitality. And they always jump for the higher or highest branch. Did you ever notice that? You know why, don't you? Well, if you jump for the highest branch and miss it, you can always catch a lower branch on the way down. Whereas, if you jump for a low branch and miss it, you are sure to hit the ground, there is no other possibility. Many people could learn from that. Why be satisfied with second best or less than the best you could do? Just like a squirrel, if you jump for a high branch and hit it, you could be in for the ride of your life. I feel that's why Jesus called us to go for the very best: *"Be perfect, therefore, as your heavenly Father is perfect"* (Matthew 5:48). Aim to be the best person you believe God wants you to be. Jesus demanded a total commitment from His disciples, and still does. No half-way response to Jesus will suffice. The seriousness is wrapped up in the warning: *"No one who puts his hand to the plow and looks back is fit for service in the kingdom of God"* (Luke 9:62). A hard saying? No, just a clarification. A squirrel in midair aiming for the highest limb can't suddenly change his mind without disastrous results. Actually, the Christian faith wouldn't be worth much if it didn't demand the best.

> *It is a temptation from the Devil—I know it is—not to give my best to You, O Lord. Don't let me be satisfied with second best efforts. Amen.*

ONE YEAR CHALLENGE—Read: Jeremiah 6-10

October 11

A Beggar is a Beggar

REMEMBER THIS NURSERY RHYME: *"Hark, Hark, the dogs do bark; the beggars are coming to town; some in rags, some in tags, and some in velvet gowns"*? In this day of unmatched plenty, it seems to be an apt description of ourselves to be called: *"Beggars in velvet."* We have so much of everything: more automobiles, more televisions, more radios, more shoes, more bathrooms, and everything else—more than any other people in the world. But yet it seems that something is lacking somewhere. Because we also have more alcoholism, more drug addiction, more crime, more broken homes, more psychiatrist couches than any other people in the world. Could it be that in our velvet attire *"we spend money on what is not bread, and your labor on what does not satisfy"* (Isaiah 55:2)? I wonder if our velvet gowns aren't the best indication that we are basically beggars in this world? In 2 Corinthians 8:9, we have

this answer to our emptiness: *"For you know the grace of our Lord Jesus Christ, that though he was rich, yet for your sakes he became poor, so that you through his poverty might become rich."* Here is the chance for our inward nature to catch up with our obvious outward possessions. It is a terrible thing to have one's pockets full of decaying things and the heart empty of eternal things, don't you think? Could our insatiable desire to acquire material possessions betray something deeper? Is it true that filling an empty life requires more things? Ever notice how in divorce trials the main concern seems to be about the property settlement? A beggar is still a beggar, even in velvet! Tap into the spring of spiritual wealth that is yours from a personal relationship with Jesus Christ. It will make you wealthy even if you hold title to very few physical possessions.

ONE YEAR CHALLENGE—Read: Jeremiah 11-15

> *Teach us again, God, about treasures in Heaven. Many of us get dangerously close to spiritual bankruptcy. Show us the truth. Amen.*

October 12

A Crisis of Confidence

So, WHO CAN YOU BELIEVE THESE DAYS? Do you often feel that people are not giving you the whole story? Do you feel that in times of crisis only? When we discover that we have been deceived on a national basis by the government, does it make us doubt others also? How do you live in the crisis of mistrust? Many marriages are stalemated at a very low level because one person lied to the other. Parent-child relationships often are deadlocked at the level of: *"I can't trust you anymore."* As someone said to me the day I wrote this: *"When you've been lied to so many times, how can you ever trust?"* Can anything be done to relieve the current crisis? Start by being trustworthy yourself. Make a vow to be a person of the *"whole truth and nothing but the truth."* The truth will always stand. You do not have to defend it or apologize for it. If you are always truthful, you can be a good role model for others. If you have children or grandchildren, teach them absolute honesty by word and action. Help to build into our society a core group dedicated to truthfulness. Join a church where hypocrisy and half-truth is not condoned, where people are confronted with the hard demands of living by, and walking in the truth. Commit your life to God's way. He is the truth (John 14:6). In Him is no shadow of deceit or half-truth (I Peter 2:22). *"The truth will set you free"* (John 8:32). You will be free from settling for anything other than the truth. *"Jesus Christ is the same yesterday and today and forever"* (Hebrews 13:8). You don't have to worry that someday you will wake up to find out He lied to you in the Bible. His word is truth. You can build your life on that true foundation.

> *I want to trust You, Lord, I really do. It's just that some days I feel sorry for myself and don't want to trust You or anyone. Amen.*

ONE YEAR CHALLENGE—Read: Jeremiah 16-20

October 13

Forget Grudges: Look to Tomorrow

Do YOU KNOW HAGAR THE HORRIBLE? He has been one of my comic strip friends for a long time. He is getting old, like some of us. In one strip a while back his aging memory served him quite well though. He saw a man he used to hate but now he can't remember why. Now there is a real blessing to aging! Forgetting an old grudge that has been carried too long would be a major breakthrough in many families and individuals. *"Forgive and Forget"* is easy advice to give but it can be hard to follow. To be able to forget a grudge is a real blessing. To have the freedom to forgive and forget is a sublime experience. Many, many people can't forget the past with its hurts and slights, either real or imagined. They are constantly harassed by the happiness and well-being of someone against whom they hold a grudge. Someone said that the best way not to have any enemies is to make them all friends. We will be richer; friends make us feel better, enemies make us feel poorly. The Apostle Paul challenges us when he says, *"Forgetting what is behind and straining toward what is ahead"* (Philippians 3:13). Jesus said, *"If you forgive others for the wrongs they do to you, your Father in heaven will forgive you. But if you don't forgive others, your Father will not forgive your sins"* (Matthew 6:14-15 CEV). He also said that if you approach the altar in worship and suddenly remember there is a bad feeling or a grudge between you and someone else, you should *"leave your gift there in front of the altar. Make peace with that person, then come back and offer your gift to God"* (Matthew 5:24 CEV). Not only should you forget grudges but help others to do the same. The two ladies in the church at Philippi are known because they refused to make up after their quarrel. I speak of Euodias and Synthyche. They were fine women but they had a spiritual blind spot. Forget grudges!

ONE YEAR CHALLENGE—Read: Jeremiah 21-25

> **Thank You for not holding a grudge against me. You had every reason to have one after what I did. Make me a forgiving person. Amen.**

October 14

Cult Temptation

WE ARE SPECIAL, UNIQUE—EACH ONE of us, as different as snowflakes! The Bible says so! God created us that way! It's nothing to brag about or be proud about. We had nothing to do with it. But some of us get a big head anyway. Though we are all special in God's sight, some think they are more special than the rest. People of this kind like to group together or are drawn together. This is cult thinking. A religious group of cult thinkers becomes very exclusive in their thinking. Usually they are centered around some particular doctrine, belief, or opinion that they have drawn from the Bible. Around their area may be groups of them huddled around an audio or video cassette player getting indoctrinated to their special, narrow focus. They struggle hard to maintain their purity against all other teachings. They are very proud that they are the sole possessors of THE truth (or their leader's opinion of the truth) on a particular subject. They espouse that all others are lost and going to Hell, who do not hold to their unique central truths. The ugliest picture of this in recent memory was the carnage in Guyana led by a man named Jim Jones. Today's cults would probably reject any comparison of this image to themselves or their group. But this is an accurate picture of any *"circling the wagons"* against the outside world. My conviction is that it is Jesus—and Jesus only—who gives abundant life (John 10:10), Theories, visions and other professed revelations from Him do not! It is Jesus who is the truth that sets us free (John 8:32), and not the doctrines, speeches, books, or tapes about Him. If we focus on the One who is *"the way and the truth and the life"* (John 14:6), instead of the things somebody said about Him—in humility—we could avoid the temptation of being part of a cult.

Father, I'm glad you said "whosoever will let him come." Thanks for not excluding me. Widen my horizons, I pray. Amen.

ONE YEAR CHALLENGE—Read: Jeremiah 26-30

October 15

Procrastination

HAVE YOU HEARD THE SAYING: *"Today is tomorrow yesterday"*? Have you heard, *"The road to Hell is paved with good intentions"*? Or, *"I'm going to do something about that when I get around to it"*? These are reminders to us of the danger of procrastination. Putting off things that need to be done is a dangerous habit. My own mother put off going to the family doctor for a long time only to discover a rapidly growing cancer, too advanced to be stopped. I grew up in a church where we would sing a song called, *"Why Do You Wait?"* A closing verse of the song goes, *"There's danger and death in delay."** Life's issues are too important to push aside for a more convenient time. In Acts 24:25 is a powerful line. Paul had been discussing spiritual matters with Governor Felix. The governor became very fearful and anxious, and told Paul, *"That's enough for now! You may leave. When I find it convenient, I will send for you."* We have no record of that meeting ever happening.

Tragic results can follow procrastination. In your neighborhood there are people who put off for too long, teaching their children morality, righteousness, and godliness, so now they have a juvenile delinquent in the home. In the 1960s there was a little song called, *"I Wish We Had All Been Ready."*** It dealt with the suddenness and abruptness of the return of Christ to the earth, and so many people being unprepared. Why? Procrastination. Many people today are almost persuaded to commit their lives to serving Jesus, but want to put it off to some unspecified *"better time."* Regretfully, their procrastination will seal their fate on Judgement Day. Friend, if you have read this far, understand 2 Corinthians 6:2: *"now is the time of God's favor, now is the day of salvation."* Commit your life NOW. Don't put off doing anything important, that can and should be done right away. You'll be glad when it's done. That's how we grow.

Forgiving Father, teach me again how to overcome my tendency to put things off until later. Be patient with me; I want to change. Amen.

ONE YEAR CHALLENGE—Read: Jeremiah 31-35

October 16

Prayer or Imagination?

NEWS SOURCES ARE REPORTING A RENEWED INTEREST in prayer, as related to healing. Cynics smile and say that Christians have vivid imaginations, to think that talking out loud to their bodies is going to change sickness. Faithful believers keep on doing what they have always known to do: take it to God. Find any church this week and they will introduce you to several members who were healed by prayer. Every week and all week, we pray for the sick, individually and cooperatively. We share stories of doctors amazement when *"hopeless cases"* are cured, by what even they admit, must be a miracle performed by a supernatural power. In Jeremiah 33:3, we are challenged, *"Call to me and I will answer you and tell you great and unsearchable things you do not know."* When we pray, we link up to God's willingness to share Himself. It's amazing how the media can report as unusual, what true believers have experienced for a lifetime. Hebrews 11:6 is plain, *"without faith it is impossible to please God, because anyone who comes to him must believe that he exists and that he rewards those who earnestly seek him."* We have a solid foundation on which to build our prayer life. Practicing prayer gives us great confidence with God. We all start with small, simple, childlike requests, and gradually grew bolder and bolder. God challenged us to pray more and more. *"Cast all your anxiety on him because he cares for you"* (1 Peter 5:7). No wonder David said in Psalm 55:17, *"Evening, morning and noon I cry out in distress, and he hears my voice."* You can learn to pray. It's not a good luck charm, nor a heavenly slot machine. Here's another invitation: *"Until now you have not asked for anything in my name"* (John 16:24). Because of Jesus, we have direct access to God in prayer.

After giving us Your Son to be our Savior, prayer must be Your next best gift. It's so good to talk with You. Amen.

OneYearChallenge—Read: Jeremiah 36-40

October 17

Bag of Goatburgers and Fries

ONE OF MY FAVORITE COMIC STRIPS became prophetic recently. I don't know if it was intentional, but in **Commander Crock** one of the characters was approaching the huge god-like statue in the desert for a wise message. The statue spoke and said, *"Your sacrifice displeases the gods. They show a lack of effort and commitment."* The man replied, *"What proof do you have?"* And the statue said, *"A bag of goatburgers and fries."** Isn't that prophetic? I mean, it's too true. It sounds like it came from the Bible. In the Old Testament, the people were always being reprimanded for coming to sacrifice to God with crippled animals or lambs with one leg missing or only one eye, rather than their best. Remember when the Prophet Haggai asked the people *"The Temple is still in ruins. Is it right for you to be living in fancy houses?"* (Haggai 1:4 EB). Our actions do betray our words. We talk an impressive *"game"* but then we play by a different standard. Jesus said, *"where your treasure is, there your heart will be also"* (Matthew 6:21). So what have you been offering to God lately, a large *"goatburger,"* (Yuck!) or an offering of real substance and value? Do you offer something you picked up at a spiritual fast-food joint, or, *"your bodies as living sacrifices, holy and pleasing to God"* (Romans 12:1)? Paul calls the latter real and genuine spiritual growth. Some folks go to worship (like the character in the comic strip) but come away empty-hearted. Why? Like the **Crock** god said, *"a lack of effort and commitment."** Simply put: don't wait until Sunday morning to prepare for worship. That's too late! Start now, if you haven't yet. It takes six days usually! Prepare to give yourself to God.

> God, You gave the best when You gave Jesus as our Savior. What a unique gift!! Now I need to give my all to You. Amen.

ONE YEAR CHALLENGE—Read: Jeremiah 41-45

October 18

Preaching: Truth Strained Through a Human Personality

IF YOU GO TO CHURCH, THIS STORY will make sense to you. A five-year-old boy announced to his family that he was going to be a preacher. Since his parents had taken him to church from his infancy, they were not totally shocked by his announcement. The father, guessing that the boy must have had some great spiritual experience recently, asked "Why?" The boy replied, *"Since you are going to take me to church every Sunday anyway, if I am the preacher I can stand up and shout and not have to be quiet."* What is preaching? What are preachers? Why do they do what they do, and why do so many of them get excited while they are doing it? The best definition of preaching I ever heard was *"truth strained through a human personality."* The Bible says about John the Baptist (a preacher), that he was *"a man who was sent from God"* (John 1:6). If you could be sure of that when you listen to a person give God's message,

you could love preachers, right? The most important thing to remember when thinking about the preachers in your life is that *"faith comes from hearing the Good News. And people hear the Good News when someone tells them about Christ"* (Romans 10:17 EB). It is by hearing the Word of God proclaimed that we come to have faith in God. Of course, you can't have faith in a God you do not know, and you can't know God until you are introduced, and that's what preaching is all about. That is the real purpose of preaching and the *"stuff"* of preaching. When preachers start politicking or pushing their own personal *"do's"* and *"don'ts,"* many people stop listening and their minds wander. I have a friend who was greeted every morning at the church office by the church janitor saying, *"Preacher, you got any fresh word from God?"* I like that!

> **Thank You, God, for placing prophetic men and women in the world. I often need their clear, objective insight into my life. Amen.**

ONE YEAR CHALLENGE—Read: Jeremiah 46-50

October 19

Fall: God's Creation

DON'T YOU ENJOY THIS SEASON of the year? About the time you get bored with all the heat and tired of cutting the grass every week, along comes fall. (Forget the leaf-raking, that's later) Look out the windows as you commute to work. Take a walk down the street. Isn't it beautiful with the leaves changing color? The poetic description says God has taken out His pallet and has begun to paint the hillsides in blazing color. In Ecclesiastes 3:1 (KJV) the Bible says, *"To everything there is a season."* In Psalm 104 the Bible says that God made the seasons. Maybe your basic view of life will determine whether you enjoy this season of the year. If you think it's just impersonal and accidental that we have the fall season, you can be a grouch, and grumpy about it. If you see the next few weeks as a heaven-sent interlude called *"Fall,"* you have rich possibilities. The scriptures say that God has made all things beautiful in His time. A lot of the natural beauty has been destroyed. Subdivisions and office complexes don't leave much room for the beauty of the earth. Cement roads and asphalt parking lots don't thrill the heart. That's why many of us try so hard to plant grass and flowers and shrubs in our yard; we keep trying to restore a natural beauty that is being slowly destroyed. Our soul hungers for nature's beauty to counteract the ugly things we humans are doing in the name of *"progress."* The seasons make it easy for us to contemplate the grandeur of God's creation. Surely the fall is a display of His handiwork. The different colors of leaves complement one another in one artistic whole. Feeling crabby? Feeling ugly? Go to the park and look at the leaves. It will help your disposition. Might even make you say, *"Praise the Lord!"* Beauty will do that!

ONE YEAR CHALLENGE—Read:
Jeremiah 51-52,
I Timothy I

> *Creator God, every season has it's special beauty. I don't know which one I love the most. Thank You, Jesus, for helping us to see beauty. Amen.*

October 20

God's Sheep Dogs

I KNOW YOU HAVE CONSIDERED IT BEFORE, but it's such a comfort, let's do it again! The Good Shepherd is described in the 23rd Psalm. It is a favorite scripture of many; the most often quoted passage of scripture at funeral services. In the passage, the Psalmist says, *"Surely goodness and mercy shall follow me all the days of my life"* (KJV). Hence the idea of Goodness and Mercy, the Good Shepherd's sheep dogs who care for the sheep. We know the Shepherd used these dogs to protect the sheep from harm and keep them from straying off and getting lost. How many times in your life did you start to wander off from God, only to be reminded of God's goodness in your life, and you turned back to the straight and narrow path? Romans 2:4 (CEV) explains, *"Don't you know that the reason God is good to you is because he wants you to turn to him?"* How many times in your life have you rebelliously set your face to go away from God, then got into sin and created a miserable situation for yourself? Gratefully, our loving God again reminded you of his mercy, and you turned from sinning, back to God. The broken Prodigal Son in Luke 15 *"hired himself out . . . to feed pigs. . . . When he came to his senses, he said, 'How many of my father's hired men have food to spare, and here I am starving to death!' "* I've watched sheep dogs work, sometimes they bite the sheep and it hurts, but they are going to do whatever is necessary, even if it is painful, to get the sheep back to the safety of the flock. What a reassurance and comfort that is to our wandering lives! I prayed with a man recently who was about to go for open-heart surgery. How good it was for him to know that God's sheep dogs, Goodness and Mercy, were on both sides of the operating room table.

> *You never leave or forsake the sheep, O Great Shepherd of my soul. When I met Jesus it was easier to understand you as a Shepherd. Amen.*

ONE YEAR CHALLENGE—Read: I Timothy 2-6

October 21

Neutralized Believer

ONE OF THE HARD THINGS WE HAVE to deal with sometimes is a *"neutralized believer."* We expect a person to be different when they have said, *"I believe now in Jesus."* The Bible certainly declares that a person who believes in Jesus will be different. Once a person has believed and experienced salvation (Romans 10:9-10), he is free to live life at a different level. He is forever free of demonic control. The devil has no power to take away our salvation. Paul says that God *"has rescued us from the dominion of darkness and brought us into the kingdom of the Son he loves, in whom we have redemption, the forgiveness of sins"* (Colossians 1:13-14). We are forever rescued from death and brought into the Kingdom of Life, but the devil hasn't called off his attacks. He cannot take away our salvation, but he can try to take away the joy of our salvation. John Hunter says the devil is a *"dedicated enemy."* When we were saved, he lost a subject and gained a potential enemy. If we become true soldiers for Christ, we are true enemies of the devil, and he is aware of this fact. It is not in his power to take us back again, but it is in his power to neutralize us, unless we continually resist him. If he can neutralize us and make us ineffective, then he has at least cut his losses. We may be lost to him, but we are no danger to him, and in one sense, no use to God. One of the most effective ways of neutralizing a Christian is to take away the joy of his salvation. Don't let him! A joyless Christian is an ineffective Christian. A joyless Christian is a contradiction. When joy goes so does your personal testimony of the power of your belief in Jesus. Totally ineffective for God means you've been neutralized. Christian, please be alert. Keep a finger on your spiritual pulse.

Father, I want to be effective all the time. I want to bear good fruit and point others to You daily. Use my life. Amen.

ONE YEAR CHALLENGE—Read: Lamentations

October 22

Churches Suffer from Choices

IN MATTERS SPIRITUAL AND RELIGIOUS, CHOICES are demanded. Some of you are old enough to remember the good old days, when choices seemed almost non-existent, compared to today. This was because church was about *"the only game in town"* for average folks. Up until thirty years ago or so, the Sunday *"blue laws"* were still being enforced; very few stores were open on Sunday; a few theaters and ball games were the only amusements. The shopping center didn't compete with going to church. Certainly children's parents didn't have to decide between their soccer league and going to Sunday school. School activities never conflicted with church. There would be no lights on at the school building on Wednesday nights especially, because the churches were holding their mid-week services. Now the church must compete for support from her members. If you go back 35 or 40 years, church business was even easier. The church was still the gathering place for the community, sort of like a religious general store. People went there whether they believed the teachings or not, it was the place to meet and see your friends and go courting. Ah, yes, those were the days for the church! But now, the church building is not the only place to go and not even the most popular. Knowing that we do have more choices to make these days, the words of Jesus become relevant and challenging: *"If anyone would come after me, he must deny himself and take up his cross and follow me"* (Matthew 16:24). Choices must be made. It's time to separate the wheat from the chaff. It's time to see who is merely culturally religious and who is committed. It's time now to find out what's really valuable and important. It's a multiple choice test: *"choose for yourselves this day whom you will serve"* (Joshua 24:15).

ONE YEAR CHALLENGE—Read:
Ezekiel 1-5

> *God, help us as churches never to be captive to the culture. Remind us that culture will never make it easy for Your people. Amen.*

October 23

Helping the Hungry

CHRISTIANS HAVE LOVE for the hungry of the world. But love without action is only sentimental love. Love must be truly compassionate, and moving to action. The Bible encourages authentic, concrete love. *"Dear children, let us not love with words or tongue but with actions and in truth"* (1 John 3:18). We often find it easy to mouth phrases about love in the church house. It is a safe place to say words, because very few churches today near us have hungry and poor people attending. The poor, hungry, and powerless feel out of place in clean, expensive buildings. So, it is safe to affirm loving the poor and feeding the hungry because they are not there to challenge our pious statements. The question is rightfully asked by the Apostle John in the aforementioned passage (v. 17), *"If anyone has material possessions and sees his brother in need but has no pity on him, how can the love of God be in him?"* Open-hearted people are responsive to hunger and do something about it. On the one hand we have a desire to share the abundance of life, while on the other hand we are tight-fisted, protecting what we have, lest some needy person try to take it from us—such is the struggle. As we enter the time of harvest again, it behooves us to take a close look at our attitudes. As good citizens, we can try to get compassionate leaders elected to public office, who will try to coordinate use of our public resources to feed the hungry. Perhaps most important, personally and in our churches, we should strive to be as loving, caring, and helpful as possible with the calling and help of God. We can help cultivate awareness in our churches, and among friends and community, about hunger needs. Then ask God and each other what you should do about it. We can sensitize others as we express our God-given sensitivity to the needs of the poor and hungry.

Lord Jesus, You set an example in always feeding the hungry. Can we do less and say we are true believers? Your Spirit says "no." Amen.

ONE YEAR CHALLENGE—Read:
Ezekiel 6-10

October 24

"Lord, Give me Patience!"

I DIDN'T KNOW THAT I NEEDED PATIENCE so badly, but I must have, for God has had me in the School of Patience for at least twelve months. We have been wanting to build a place for our church to meet—a place to worship, fellowship, and equip the saints to serve. But there are so many permits to secure, plans to be approved, requirements to be met, etc. It takes a long time. If you are a person who is easily excitable and action oriented, boy, you are in trouble! It's not that I haven't prayed for patience. I have! It's not that God doesn't have plenty to give, He does! It's that I pray for patience and forget that I did. But God reminds me, in some not so subtle ways, that I asked for patience and patience is what I need. What areas of your life most need patience? The Bible is loaded with positive challenges to patience. Just sit down, be quiet for a minute, and listen to them: "Be patient when trouble comes" (Romans 12:12 EB); "be patient with everyone" (1 Thessalonians 5:14); "be ... as patient as Christ" (2 Thessalonians 3:5 CEV); "Not ... ; but patient" (1 Timothy 3:3 KJV); "Be patient, then, brothers, until the Lord's coming. ... be patient and stand firm, because the Lord's coming is near" (James 5:7-8). These spiritual tablets are better than any prescription drug you can buy to help you relax. A deep breath and a clearing of perspective will do wonders for your patience. Later today (if you are like me) or tomorrow, you will have to repeat the procedure, but that's good. And that is proof that you are becoming more patient, just in the fact that you have learned to grab perspective back in hand. That building? Oh, we have started construction.

Father, I am comforted to learn that saints of old were often impatient. You helped them; I know there is help for me. Amen.

ONE YEAR CHALLENGE—Read: Ezekiel 11-15

October 25

"Not in My Back Yard!"

IF YOU READ THE PAPER often, or follow local government considerations, you recognize N.I.M.B.Y. as the acronym for *"Not In My Back Yard."* It is a regular barrier erected by communities to protect themselves from undesirable elements: you know, people and activities that would drive down property values. Over the last years people have protested the location of jails, half-way houses, homes for the handicapped, homes for unwed mothers, etc. The list is long. Now joining N.I.M.B.Y.s, are houses of worship. This is not a local phenomenon by any means, all across America religious groups are having a difficult time securing land and building permits. While there has been no definitive study to prove the point, it is said that church facilities cause property values to go down. I am old enough to remember when people moving into a community tried to be sure they were near the community church house. What has happened to make the church meeting-house a *"persona non grata"* in the community? Is the church to blame? When Jesus drove the buyers and sellers and money changers from the temple, he referred to God's word recorded by Isaiah (Matthew 21:13): *"mine house will be called a house of prayer for all people"* (Isaiah 56:7 KJV). Did the church stop being a house of prayer? Did the church become racially and economically selective instead of for *"all people"*? Did the church get too interested in money? Is the community angry at the church because she changed from her New Testament pattern? Does a worshiping group of people put others on a guilt trip? I have more questions about this than answers. I do know this: when this last bastion of morality is absent, there will be no other! Oh, one more thing I know: Jesus said that Hell itself couldn't stop the advance of his church (Matthew 16:18)!

> *O God, You love the church. Christians love the church. Help us to be lovely and attractive again. The world needs us. Amen.*

ONE YEAR CHALLENGE—Read: Ezekiel 16-20

October 26

Forgetting

THEY SAY THERE ARE TWO WAYS TO TELL IF YOU ARE BEGINNING TO GET OLD: the first way is that you can't remember simple things and the second way . . . . I forget just now! So, I now make notes to myself on little scraps of paper, so I can be reminded of what I would otherwise probably forget! Perhaps it would be comforting to the young if only the aging had trouble remembering, but it is a weakness that afflicts many. Spiritual people often forget. The Psalmist, David, has a shocking line in Psalm 106:13 about the Israelites coming out of captivity in Egypt, *"But they soon forgot what he had done."* God had worked many miracles for them in delivering them from their terrible bondage, but they soon forgot and began to complain. Have you ever been guilty of that? God will do a wonderful thing for you or your family or bless you with some special blessing and you soon are heard complaining about God for-getting you and not helping you. The aforementioned David, in another place, challenges his own soul to be alert, *"Praise the LORD, O my soul, and forget not all his benefits"* (Psalm 103:2). This is one of the great reasons why group worship is so important. Alone, it is easy to lose perspective, easy to focus your attention on yourself. Being with a large group in worship can help remind you of God's goodness to you and to your Christian brothers and sisters. It is a great antidote to feeling sorry for yourself, for what you don't have. Yes, all of us need to keep our *"thinking cap"* in good shape to avoid the temptation of forgetting God. When I remember the promise of Hebrews 6:10, that God *"will not forget your work and the love you have shown him as you have helped his people,"* I need to also be diligent in remembering what God is doing for me.

God, remind me daily, however you can, of all the blessings I receive and how I need to live thankfully. Forgive my forgetfulness. Amen.

ONE YEAR CHALLENGE—Read:
Ezekiel 21-25

October 27

The Insomnia of God

I HAD DIFFICULTY SLEEPING the night before I wrote this. That was unusual for me. I must say, I didn't enjoy it. I'm glad I don't suffer from chronic insomnia. But then, I remembered: God has insomnia, and I'm glad. David talked about it in Psalm 121:3-4, *"he who watches over you will not slumber; indeed, he who watches over Israel will neither slumber nor sleep."* God's care is constant. While I sleep, He is awake. Knowing that makes my sleep easy. I remember a little song that said, *"All day, all night, angels watching over me, my Lord."* I knew of a person who suffered from insomnia until reading Psalm 121 and then reasoned, *"If God is staying up all night watching over things, then there is no need for both of us to be awake, so I will just sleep."* Pretty powerful sleeping pill, huh? I think Peter had that in mind when he said in I Peter 5:7, *"Cast all your anxiety on him because he cares for you."* Why lie awake at night tossing and turning when the Lord is willing to take those sleep-killing worries? There is another thought to ponder here. Many people picture God as being totally at ease and relaxed in a Heavenly rocking chair, untouched by this world of ours. Just the opposite is true. God is pained for us. *"His heart is touched with my grief,"** the poet said. Remember there is a cross at the heart of God. God's discomfort at our discomfort brought forth a Savior. *"by his wounds we are healed"* (Isaiah 53:5). Two short observations: the next night you can't sleep, why not talk to God about it, since you both are awake? Second, have you taken the time to thank God for going to such extremes to make peace of mind possible for you?

> *I rest assured in Your care, my King and my God. I relax in knowing that my Heavenly Father always watches over me. Amen.*

October 28

One Year Challenge—Read:
Ezekiel 26-30

Sharing the Gospel

SOME UNKNOWN (TO ME) SAINT said, *"The gospel never has been and never will be primarily informational. The gospel always has been and always will be relational. This puts the mission of the church on Christians who are used by Christ to share the gospel."* If this is true, then all the television programs and the radio programs and all the Christian literature that is being printed will never get the job done in spreading the good news about Jesus. Building a few more church houses may touch a few more people but it will never touch the majority. The quicker we correct this error, the better. Just passing on the historical facts of Christian history is insufficient. I remember a whimsical story about a *"gospel blimp"* that was to rain down pamphlets of Christian information on ignorant people. Even New Testament truth can be taken as nothing more than historical information. You could store it away in the brain without giving any thought to the full implications. Remember how Jesus took twelve men with Him for three years? Read the gospel and watch Jesus use a *"hands-on"* technique of getting to know people's needs and then applying the gospel. *"One size fits all"* may work fine for socks, but the gospel must be personalized. When the *"good news"* makes a difference in your life, the people you rub shoulders with every day will be conditioned to hear what you say about what means most to you. When the Apostle Peter talks about Christians as *"a holy priesthood"* (1 Peter 2:5), it is good to know that the definition of a priest is *"a bridge."* Practically speaking, from a relational point of view, that means people can walk across your life to meet Jesus. Our Christian role is not to beat people with the *"Jesus club"* but to give them a cup of cold water, in Jesus name (Matthew 10:42).

Thank you, Jesus, for all those people who loved me and showed me your love, before I knew to give my life to you. Amen.

ONE YEAR CHALLENGE—Read: Ezekiel 31-35

October 29

Lambs in a Meadow

WHEN PREPARING FOR A FUNERAL service, I always ask the family for a favorite scripture that they would like for me to read. At least nine out of ten of them will request the 23rd Psalm, whether they are church people or not. Little children learn early in Sunday School that *"The Lord is my Shepherd."* It is one of the most dependable pictures we have in the Bible of God as a source of our security. Personally, I'm comforted to think of God providing for my needs and guarding my life. That's why I jump to attention when I read Hosea 4:16, *"The Israelites are stubborn, like a stubborn heifer. How then can the LORD pasture them like lambs in a meadow?"* I remember as a child on our farm how stubborn young cows can be. We sometimes would put a rope about their necks and pull and pull to try to get them in or out of the barn. It was for their own good! Are people like that? Obviously, yes! Lambs taken to the meadow by the shepherd have the best time frolicking and grazing without the threat of danger. This is the way that God wishes to provide for His children. Why would we reject God the way Hosea described? Foolishness? Stubbornness? *"All day long have I held out my hand to an obstinate people, who walk in ways not good, pursuing their own imaginations"* (Isaiah 65:2). In other words, many people who are complaining of being miserable in the world have only themselves to blame. God certainly didn't plan and purpose it that way. *"I have come that they may have life, and have it to the full"* is the offer of Jesus in John 10:10. Look in the mirror, are you stubborn as a heifer or submissive as a lamb? A stubborn heart will never experience peace and serenity from the Good Shepherd.

Father, I can judge others. I see them making the same mistake I made and I wish to help. Give me a lamb-like, sweet spirit. Amen.

ONE YEAR CHALLENGE—Read:
Ezekiel 36-40

October 30

Translating Holy Language

CHURCHES AND CHURCH PEOPLE SOMETIMES GET OUT OF TOUCH with reality. I'm thinking about the use of church language. (Some people even change the tone of their voice when they pray in church, but that's another subject.) Church people often use words that no one understands but church members. For instance, if you had not been in a church service before and you went and you heard the people talk about being *"saved"* or *"sanctified"* or *"justified"* or *"raptured,"* what would you think? Paul clearly cautions the church regarding using unknown tongues (I Corinthians 14:23), because it scares unbelievers, but I think we need to consider the English words we use that confuse the uninitiated. This is not a new problem. When the New Testament began to be translated from Greek, there was a long period of confusion. The scholars were trying to interpret the Greek from a *"classical"* or scholarly point of view. Then the discovery was made that the Greek language of the gospels was common, ordinary *"street-Greek."* It was instantly clear. When God wanted to communicate with us through the Bible, He gave it in everyday language. Folks with a background of evangelical Christianity or sacramental Christianity often use the same words with two different sets of meaning. We are a pluralistic society. The generation of the 1990s doesn't have a Biblical or church background. Many are able to grasp immediately spiritual truths. The language of the church must be clear even to the youngest child. The good news of Jesus must be heard and understood by the heart before it reaches the intellect. Even Jesus touched a man's eyes twice so he could see *"clearly"* (Mark 8:25). The newer translations of the Bible are helpful because they get us out of King James' England into small town America or metropolitan America. The Bible's message is clear and simple; let's keep it so.

Thank God for Immanuel, the God who is with us. We see You, hear You, and You touch us. It's so clear. Thanks. Amen.

ONE YEAR CHALLENGE—Read: Ezekiel 41-45

October 31

The Difference in Fall

NOW WE KNOW THAT FALL IS REALLY HERE. October sometimes deceives us and often teases us, but now we know the reality of fall. No more of those summer-type days; we now settle in for November's specialty. Don't wait three weeks to begin to be thankful. As you make your plans for family celebrations later on this month, plan a month of gratitude. There is so much physical need around the world, even in your own areas, that you have much to be thankful for, regardless how meager your possessions may be. But thanksgiving goes deeper than that. There is thanksgiving for the gift of life. Nothing that we can purchase can compare with the wonder of life. Then we should offer thanksgiving for the gift of eternal life. This is the gift that Paul says is *"indescribable"* (2 Corinthians 9:15)! What a wonderful thought for the believer: spending eternity with God in heaven. Then there is

"thanksliving." (Nope, it's not a typo.) *"Thanksliving"* means living with a thankful heart and grateful attitude. We always focus our attention on what we have received. How about reversing our Thanksgiving focus to giving an abundant harvest of joy to God, a kind of heavenly harvest? November could be a time to celebrate spiritual harvest! Godly men and women could spread the good news of God's salvation and share it with their families and neighbors and fill every house of worship with people seeking to know God better. Generally speaking, church attendance for all denominations is better at this time of the year. We can bring joy to heaven: *"there will be more rejoicing in heaven over one sinner who repents than over ninety-nine righteous persons who do not need to repent"* (Luke 15:7). Let's make heaven glad!

ONE YEAR CHALLENGE—Read:
Ezekiel 46-48
2 Timothy 1

> *Sometimes I forget to thank You, Father. Help me to fix my memory so it will always sensitively remember the Source of my blessings. Amen.*

November 1

Harvest and Sharing

Now that we are in November, plans are being made about Thanksgiving. We are in a harvest-time pattern of thinking. If you have kindergarten or elementary children, their bring-home papers already reflect the season. The rooms and bulletin boards at school are focusing in this direction. It is a good time of year! We ought to make it more practical by sharing our bounty. Many religious people will go to church or synagogue this month and express gratitude to God. But God says that the words of thanks are only part of our responsibility. Praise and worship is completed by action. The Prophet Isaiah, in chapter 58, verse 7) gives us a way to validate our ritual of thanksgiving worship, by asking this question: *"Is it not to share your food with the hungry and to provide the poor wanderer with shelter—when you see the naked, to clothe him, and not to turn away from your own flesh and blood."* He goes on to say in verse 10, *"and if you spend yourselves in behalf of the hungry and satisfy the needs of the oppressed, then your light will rise in the darkness, and your night will become like the noonday."* There is insight here that we need to latch on to: we will be happier if we share. So many Americans are bored, despondent, despairing, depressed, miserable—lives full of things but empty of meaning. God is saying through Isaiah that the way to a meaningful, gloom-free life is to share what you have with other people. This remedy may keep some psychiatrists' couches empty for a few hours. It's worth a try! Instead of getting eaten up with the cancer of greed, selfishness, covetousness, and hoarding, people could find freedom and relief by relieving another's burdens. Losing your black cloud of sorrow by giving a silver lining to someone else will help you live life to it's fullest. Try it!

One Year Challenge—Read: 2 Timothy 2-4

> *Teach me to care Lord. Teach me to share. Help me to test the Bible statement "it is more blessed to give than receive." Amen.*

November 2

The Green-Eyed Monster

WHY DO WE CALL ENVY *"the green-eyed monster"*? I don't know. Perhaps it's because envy is always destructive. The Bible is full of evidence to support this. Cain envied Abel. Joseph's older brothers envied him. Haman envied Mordecai. The Jewish religious leaders envied the popularity of Jesus. King Saul was eaten up with envy toward David. The list is long. Conclusion: deception, destruction, and violence follows every Biblical account of envy. Jesus spoke directly to this evil at the beginning of His ministry. In Luke 3:14, *"some soldiers asked him, 'And what should we do?' He replied, 'Don't extort money and don't accuse people falsely—be content with your pay.' "* Contentment—that's the key. Coming out of the 1980s, we were brainwashed with the idea that we should have everything we wanted and besides, we deserved it. Yes, it's subtle most of the time. We deserve to be treated right and our children certainly deserve the best; it's part of being an American, right? The spirit of this world *"envies intensely"* (James 4:5). We tend to base our self-worth on possessions and accomplishments. This can create a dangerous mind sickness. Envy isolates and destroys fellowship between people. Paul said, *"I have learned to be content"* (Philippians 4:11). It doesn't come easy. It's a sign of spiritual maturity to be able to feel good about other people's good fortune, or their kids doing better in school than ours, or their living in a nicer house. Jesus taught us to pray, *"Give us today our daily bread"* (Matthew 6:11). Just be content with the basic physical necessities, because spiritual values are more important. Paul wrote the young preacher Timothy and said, *"if we have food and clothing, we will be content with that"* (I Timothy 6:8). Your choices: let envy live and be miserable or surrender envy to God and live contentedly.

Father, You give salvation and eternal life freely to all. We are rich in faith, enjoying the favor of God through Jesus Christ. We have enough. Amen.

November 3

ONE YEAR CHALLENGE—Read: Daniel 1-3

Political Speeches

It's good that national political conventions only come every four years. It's difficult to stomach a week of endless political speeches. Television and radio relay the speeches to the masses and then the commentators explain what the speakers were really saying. The warning Jesus gave in Matthew 6:7 about empty prayer words comes to mind: *"And when you pray, do not keep on babbling like pagans, for they think they will be heard because of their many words."* Meaningless speech can be a real pitfall for Christians. Speech is a barometer of spirituality. *"But I tell you that men will have to give account on the day of judgment for every careless word they have spoken. For by your words you will be acquitted, and by your words you will be condemned"* (Matthew 12:36-37), was another warning from Jesus. In the third chapter of James, there is an extended discussion on the proper use of speech. It ends with a warning in verse 9: *"With the tongue we praise our Lord and Father, and with it we curse men, who have been made in God's likeness. Out of the same mouth come praise and cursing. My brothers, this should not be."* Politicians are expected to be talkative and make countless promises that the people don't expect them to keep. *"Empty words"* would be a good description. Christians can't afford that kind of reputation. Paul instructed young Timothy that church leaders *"must not say things they do not mean;"* (I Timothy 3:8 EB) our speech should be consistent with our commitment to Christ. A positive approach is in Colossians 4:6, *"Let your conversation be always full of grace, seasoned with salt, so that you may know how to answer everyone."* After people have talked with you, what kind of taste has been left in their mouths? Hopefully, if a Christian should say, *"Read my lips,"* it could be restated as an affirmation of what God has done in us: *"Read my life."*

ONE YEAR CHALLENGE—Read:
Daniel 4-6

> *Teach me how to talk, Lord. Help me to speak the truth always in a spirit of love. Give meaning to our words. Amen.*

November 4

The Election

HERE WE ARE, READY TO GO TO THE VOTING BOOTH. We have listened and tried to digest all we have heard, unless you are a *"yellow-dog"* Democrat or a *"rock-ribbed"* Republican, and just vote by party affiliation. Now is the time of action. Let's go vote! What? You are not going to vote? It's been a big job to get more people registered to vote and now you say your vote won't matter? You don't think there is enough difference in the candidates to excite you? Whoa! Just a minute. We are talking about responsibility now. Emotion has nothing to do with this, nor party affiliation. If you are a Christian, I appeal to your obligation as a Christian citizen. I don't want to hear: *"All politics are dirty."* Jesus said to *"Give to Caesar what is Caesar's, and to God what is God's"* (Matthew 22:21). In Romans 13:1-7, Paul directs our thinking to our responsibility as citizens. We are not to be so heavenly-minded that we are no earthly good. Pay your dues to the government, show honor and respect to the role of citizen. When Christians don't go to the polling places and vote their conscience and convictions, the way is left for unscrupulous people to be in control. Votes that influence for world peace and anti-war, votes for feeding the hungry and caring for the helpless and anti-isolation, votes for equality and anti-special interest groups, votes for fair and just taxation and against favoritism—these votes ought to be cast. Christian people and people of like-mind must make their influence felt at the ballot box, it is your duty. Use your wonderful citizenship gift. *"And do not let anyone treat you as if you* [or your vote] *were not important"* (Titus 2:15 EB). And remember: if you don't vote, don't complain!

Father, I know that I should be a good citizen. Show me the importance of my witness and influence in my community. Amen.

ONE YEAR CHALLENGE—Read:
Daniel 7-9

November 5

Political Campaigning or Neighborhood Gossip?

BOY, I'M GLAD THE LAST WEEK OF THIS ELECTION IS OVER! *"Only in America!"* Surely, only in America people pay great sums of money to broadcast bad things about someone else. Of course, the broadcasting industry loves it, it overflows their bank accounts. Because the rest of America likes to sit and listen to garbage about someone else? Why are we like that? Does it make us feel better by comparison? Have so many people said so many bad things about us that we can vicariously experience revenge? Do we think mud-slinging is fun? Is a political campaign just a public extension of two people in the neighborhood gossiping over the phone? Like I said, I'm glad it's over. If it's part of the American political process, then we need to surgically remove it. There is enough bad stuff being done on a daily basis without adding to it. There's a lesson in this for us: Jesus said, *"Why do you look at the speck of saw-dust in your brother's eye and pay no attention to the plank in your own eye? How can you say to your brother, 'Let me take the speck out of your eye,' when all the time there is a plank in your own eye? You hypocrite, first take the plank out of your own eye, and then you will see clearly to remove the speck from your brother's eye"* (Matthew 7:3-5). Paul said that if God's people will speak *"the truth in love, we will in all things grow up into him who is the Head, that is, Christ. . . . Therefore each of you must put off falsehood and speak truthfully to his neighbor, for we are all members of one body"* (Ephesians 4:15,25). Wouldn't it be a refreshing experience if the candidates (winners and losers, most of whom acknowledge God's authority) would go back on television now and apologize publicly for all the lies, half-truths, and innuendos they said during the campaign?

> *Forgive me, God, for prejudging people because of what others have said rather than getting to know persons for myself. Thank You for accepting me. Amen.*

ONE YEAR CHALLENGE—Read:
Daniel 10-12

November 6

Quilting a Patchwork Life

A MENTAL PICTURE RECENTLY CAME TO ME THAT SOCIETY IS LIKE a patchwork quilt. Anyone raised in rural America before 1960 can identify with this image. It's amazing how scraps of material can be joined together to make something beautiful and useful! Mind you, it was not easy. I remember the long hours my mother spent quilting. It is not easy either, in the human family, to make something beautiful out of so much diversity. It takes intensity, determination, cooperation, compromise and a host of other *"patches"* to make a community of people beautiful. Paul was once preaching to some very wise people in Athens and pointed out that *"From one man he [God] made every nation of men, that they should inhabit the whole earth; and he determined the times set for them and the exact places where they should live"* (Acts 17:26). It's so sad that today we reap in hostility and division the fruits of our forefathers' rebellion against God. When man broke away from God, he broke away from his fellow man and community was ruined. Sin (rebellion against God) doesn't want a beautiful quilt of people in community. After Adam sinned, the woman he previously described to God as *"bone of my bones and flesh of my flesh"* (Genesis 2:23), became *"The woman you put here"* (Genesis 3:12). If you are out of step with God, you will be out of step with your neighbor. *"If anyone says, 'I love God,' yet hates his brother, he is a liar. For anyone who does not love his brother, whom he has seen, cannot love God, whom he has not seen"* (1 John 4:20). A part of the Great Commandment of Jesus is *"love your neighbor as yourself"* (Matthew 19:19). A political pronouncement or a political party program won't bring the *"quilt"* effect to our society. Only as we confess our egotistical sins to God do we give Him the opportunity of putting our pieces together in a real community.

ONE YEAR CHALLENGE—Read:
Titus, Philemon

> *Make your church a real community, Lord Jesus. Help me to encourage the process and not hinder it. Amen.*

November 7

A Free Ride?

WHAT DO YOU THINK OF PEOPLE WHO ALWAYS WANT A FREE RIDE OR A FREE LUNCH? Are they travelling on someone else's talent? Is their tribe increasing? I meet them fairly often, those people who have nothing to do with the work of God or the people of God until they want to bury someone or marry someone. Their assumption is that the church or the minister ought to be available for them. As I heard one say recently, *"Just because I don't go to church doesn't mean I don't believe in God."* Their reasoning seems to be, *"I have paid my debt to God if I have some vague belief in God ('without obligation,' of course)."* My question is: What if everyone reasoned like this? Where would we find churches? Who would support the ministry? (No minister lives on wedding and funeral fees!) It's the *"free ride"* fallacy. Many people wait for the faithful church folks to provide church buildings and ministers for their use, on demand, even though they take no responsibility at all. Years ago I had a friend who would answer the phone with, *"Go ahead, it's your quarter."* Flippant? Yes! But no more flippant than those who use the facilities of place and personnel provided by others. Is the church just a service provider for the culture at large? Has Christianity been degraded to the status of a *"civil religion"* that has no distinction? There is a lost respect for the church. Is it there to be used (like the park) and keep quiet? Do you use the church, or insult the church, or do you serve the church? Jesus *"loved the church and gave himself up for her"* (Ephesians 5:25). I believe that. That's why I honor the church. Someone said, *"The church is the only institution in the world that exists for the people who don't come."* Loving Jesus means loving His church!

> *Cleanse me, O Lord, of the selfishness that always wants to receive the most valuable things at no cost. Teach me to give. Amen.*

ONE YEAR CHALLENGE—Read: Hosea 1-4

November 8

A Wake Up Call for the Church

I BECAME A TEENAGER IN THE LATE 1940s. I grew up a little more than two miles from my hometown of Fredericksburg, Virginia. It was a totally rural community. There was no church. Most of the neighbors didn't go to church. Most did not adopt Christianity as a way of life but they *"went along"* with Christian values because they didn't want to be different. Their children said the Lord's Prayer at school, they didn't demonstrate to have the stores open on Sunday, and they agreed that America was a *"Christian nation"*. It was easier for that generation to go along with the crowd. Today, Ferry Road, where my home was, is totally urban; subdivisions cover the landscape. *"Christian values"* are no longer automatically accepted. At the place of my youth and the place where I now serve, a wake-up call has been sounded for the church. Wake up! Be relevant. Prove the value of your doctrine in practical ways.

Don't try to force your feelings on us with political clout. The world is no longer willing to *"go along"* with the church. Just notice what a hard time a church has getting a permit to build a building for serving God and the community. Again, it's reveille for the church. She must be *"the salt of the earth,"* and *"the light of the world"* (Matthew 5:13-14) or face extinction. She must let her *"light shine before men, that they may see your good deeds and praise your Father in heaven"* (Matthew 5:16) or lose her right to exist. She must announce with clarity to an antagonistic world that Jesus is the one and only *"way and the truth and the life"* (John 14:6), or get lost in the clamor of voices vying for everyone's attention. Our time is much like that of the first century. In that pagan world, the church had her finest hour. May history repeat herself! Please, God.

Father, it is so sad to see a church close down. It is sad to see a church ignored. Strengthen all lovers of the church today. Amen.

ONE YEAR CHALLENGE—Read: Hosea 5-8

November 9

In The Lord's Hand

EVERY TIME I READ PROVERBS 21:1, I GET ENAMORED WITH IT all over again; *"The king's heart is in the hand of the LORD; he directs it like a watercourse wherever he pleases."* Isn't that an encouraging thought? Can you imagine a person being so sensitive to the Lord's leading? Can you imagine a person being so submissive to the Lord? I like this verse because it describes a very personal and intimate relationship with God. If you give your life to the Lord, of course, your life is in his hand: you have surrendered the control of your life to him. He directs. How about that? We don't have to be beating our heads against the wall trying to determine the right thing to do. We don't have to be pulled in so many different directions trying to please so many people. There is guidance available, Divine guidance, at that. The very idea of God having a plan for your life is super. You are not a "chance" person. You are not just another object on the earth. The universe is not impersonal. A Personal God created you and has a personal plan for your life and you are personally able to discover that plan if you are willing to surrender to the Lord. Confusion reigns in many homes and schools, even churches. *"If a blind man leads a blind man, both will fall into a pit,"* Jesus said in Matthew 15:14. Another translation (EB) of Proverbs 21:1 goes like this: *"The Lord can control a king's mind as easily as he controls a river. He can direct it as he pleases."* The challenge is there for you, sure enough! All it requires is responsiveness on your part. Hear and comprehend John 8:12 as Jesus speaks, *"I am the light of the world. Whoever follows me will never walk in darkness, but will have the light of life."*

O God, I want a sensitive heart. More than that, I want a heart that is sensitive to You. Melt me. Amen.

ONE YEAR CHALLENGE—Read: Hosea 9-12

November 10

Forgiveness

MOST PEOPLE DON'T KNOW THEY ARE QUOTING THE BIBLE when they say, *"love covers a multitude of sins"* (I Peter 4:8). Can that possibly be true? Is forgiveness automatic? Must one always request it? Many people today are longing for forgiveness in order to move on to living the rest of their lives. Life cannot proceed at a meaningful level without forgiveness. The freedom to ask for forgiveness is a great emotional freedom. The grace to grant forgiveness is equal to it. The need to forgive and forget was something Jesus emphasized. *"Peter came to Jesus and asked, 'Lord, how many times shall I forgive my brother when he sins against me? Up to seven times?' Jesus answered, 'I tell you, not seven times, but seventy-seven times' "* (Matthew 18:21-22). He didn't mean to keep counting. It comes from the heart and it means that we are not willing to let anything on earth permanently come between us and another person. Another emphasis on this was made by Paul in Ephesians 4:2 (CEV) when he said we should *"Patiently put up with each other and love each other."* And later on in verse 32 (CEV), he says we should *"be kind and merciful, and forgive others, just as God forgave you because of Christ."* If people do not forgive, they engage in a kind of emotional self-destruction. No person can live a satisfying life while carrying bitterness in their heart against another person. It is really a matter of protecting your own mental health as well as your spiritual condition to take literally Paul's directive in verse 26 (CEV): *"Don't go to bed angry."* Forgive it and forget it! That's clear! Refusing to forgive causes sleeplessness, which causes exhaustion, which causes ineffectiveness in work, school, and family life. You see, it's a downhill trip. To refuse to forgive is to hurt yourself more than the other. There is another angle: *"But if you don't forgive the wrongs of others, then your Father in heaven will not forgive the wrong things you do"* (Matthew 6:15 EB). Accept God's forgiveness and forgive anyone who needs it.

ONE YEAR CHALLENGE—Read: Hosea 13-14, Joel

> *Thank You, Loving Father, for Your wonderful forgiveness. I feel clean now. Use me to help others enjoy this cleansing. Amen.*

November 11

An Eyewitness

IN MY DEVOTIONAL READING on the day I wrote this, I found in the Book of Second Peter, Chapter 1, I read a thrilling idea in verse 16: *"We did not follow cleverly invented stories when we told you about the power and coming of our Lord Jesus Christ, but we were eyewitnesses of his majesty."* Isn't that thrilling? You can't beat the powerful statement of an eyewitness. Let all the doubters and skeptics and cynics have their say, but nothing, absolutely nothing, can take away the testimony of an eyewitness. The gospel story of Jesus is so simple, a little child can understand it. Why? Because Matthew, Mark, Luke, and John are giving an eyewitness account. That's why Christianity has not only survived, but thrived for 2,000 years; you can't beat an eyewitness account. Many people have set out to disprove Christianity by looking for errors in the Bible, but then been converted to the faith. Why? You can't argue with an eyewitness. He knows what he has seen, and can tell you so you know it's true. Peter, raised and thoroughly indoctrinated in Old Testament history, recognized the majesty of God in Jesus Christ. No one had to tell him. No one could take it away from him, even though he was finally crucified, upside down, on a cross. He was an eyewitness. John said, *"That . . . which we have heard, which we have seen with our eyes, which we have looked at and our hands have touched—this we proclaim"* (I John 1:1). No second-hand account here. Eyewitness accounts must be heard. As the ex-blind man said to Jesus' detractors in John 9:25, *"One thing I do know. I was blind but now I see!"* Have you been looking for the truth? Have you been looking at the truth and not seeing it? Ask some of the eyewitnesses for a report. Don't just keep turning it over in your own mind. Look at the real Jesus, NOW, and ask him to reveal himself to you.

Lord Jesus, I thank you for the eye witness who told me what You had personally done for him. His testimony was convincing. Amen.

ONE YEAR CHALLENGE—Read: Hebrews 1-4

November 12

The Trick Play

GENERALLY SPEAKING, PROFESSIONAL FOOTBALL is predictable. Knowledgeable fans have a good idea of what kind of play will be called in a certain situation. Ex-football players, who are now broadcasters, regularly predict what will happen. That's why I was so surprised to see a team on TV use a play that we used forty years ago on the playground. We called it a "trick play;" it was used to give us a sudden and decisive advantage. It was daring! It took courage to execute! It was superb! The church needs something like that! What's happened to the church? Like so many football games, it has become predictable. It's no wonder people don't like to attend. The order of worship never changes, the prayers and the music sound the same, the sacraments or the rituals can be done from memory; what's happened to spontaneity? Some churches that advertise "Spontaneity" actually rehearse it in the same way that I found that the pro team had been practicing for several weeks their surprise trick play. In the New Testament, the church is alive and unpredictable. The church is proactive, moving quickly to take the advantage. It is on the attack. Jesus said this about *"my church; and the gates of hell shall not prevail against it."* (Matthew 16:18 KJV). In the first century they spoke *"to one another with psalms, hymns and spiritual songs"* (Ephesians 5:19). For the modern Christian, the first century may seem like it was full of confusion, but they kept in mind that *"God is not a God of disorder but of peace"* (I Corinthians 14:33). Practice reading the Book of Psalms before you go to worship. *"Enter his gates with thanksgiving and his courts with praise"* (Psalm 100:4). *"I rejoiced with those who said to me, 'Let us go to the house of the LORD' "* Thus proclaimed King David in Psalm 122:1. Worship expectantly.

ONE YEAR CHALLENGE—Read: Hebrews 5-8

> **God of Life, may our worship of You always be alive. Forgive us for the times when we worshiped with a dead spirit! Revive us. Amen.**

November 13

Help for the Hungry

I HAVE TO BRING THIS UP: MOST OF THE WORLD IS HUNGRY. In America, this is the time of year to celebrate plenty. Stacks of bright pumpkins along the roadside in the fall are reminders of the bounty of harvest. The stores and restaurants are all stocked with an abundance of good food. Sensations of Thanksgiving Dinner already float across the mind's eye, nostrils and tongue! We love to eat our fill, but most of the world is hungry. Some shrug and say, *"It's not my fault."* Others piously reply, *"It's God will"* quoting Jesus, *"you will always have the poor among you"* (John 12:8). Regardless of the comment, the fact of hunger remains. The late President of the United States, Dwight Eisenhower, said on April 16, 1953, *"every gun that is made, every warship launched, every rocket fired signifies, in the final sense, a theft from those who hunger and are not fed, those who are cold and are not clothed. This world in arms is not spending money alone. It is spending the sweat of its laborers, the genius of its scientists, the hopes of its children. The cost of one modern heavy bomber is this: a modern brick school in more than 30 cities. It is electric power plants, each serving a town of 60,000 population. It is two fine, fully equipped hospitals. It is some 50 miles of concrete highway. We pay for a single fighter plane with a half million bushels of wheat. This, I repeat, is the best way of life to be found on the road the world has been taking. This is not a way of life at all, in any true sense. Under the cloud of threatening war, it is humanity hanging from a cross of iron."* Jesus said in Matthew 15:32, *"I have compassion for these people; they have . . . nothing to eat. I do not want to send them away hungry."*

> **Often I don't understand myself, O God. I eat and fill myself and seldom think of the hungry or pray for them or feed them. Forgive me. Amen.**

ONE YEAR CHALLENGE—Read: Hebrews 9-13

November 14

Ring Around the Tub

WHERE DO THEY COME FROM? How do they suddenly appear? How do people who use as much soap as we do in this country leave rings in the bathtub? Somebody somewhere ought to find an answer for that. It's amazing! People who bathe once a day still leave a ring around the tub! Maybe this is the problem: rationally, we think we should have no problems. We have such inflated self-opinions, we don't deal with reality. Fact is; in this land of great technological know-how, we still have a lot of *"rings around the tub."* In this bountiful country, 20 million people will go at least two days without food. In this land of huge budgets devoted to sexually transmitted diseases, we have a major health problem while promoting *"safe-sex."* In this generation that put men on the moon, we still have people walking in the mire of racial prejudice and other harmful stereotyping. The list could go on. None of it makes sense. We think we have all the answers. Knowledge was supposed to cure all these ills! *"To know good is to do good,"* they said. No more rings in the tub! But alas, they are still there. Our accomplishments notwithstanding, *"The heart is deceitful above all things, and desperately wicked"* (Jeremiah 17:9 KJV). As an unknown poet once said, *"With the best of efforts, man will just muddle into a muddle."* I hold no part with those who say man is predestined to be evil. God created mankind as a good creation but mankind in rebellion against God doesn't want to submit to God. There is an answer: *"the blood of Jesus, . . . purifies us from all sin"* (1 John 1:7). That is the spiritual cleansing that washes men and women and doesn't leave a tell-tale ring.

> *Cleanse me, O Lord, totally. Make me realize daily that Your death on the cross offers me complete forgiveness. Amen.*

November 15

ONE YEAR CHALLENGE—Read: Amos 1-3

Reading Cereal Boxes

READ ANY GOOD CEREAL boxes lately? The other morning I found myself deeply engrossed in the possibility of a $5 rebate because I was eating the kind of bran flakes that I enjoy. When all of our children were still at home, they used to fight over reading the boxes. I have never been quite sure of why cereal box reading is so popular—short; interesting; good advertising technique; captive audience? Or on the other hand, we could just assume that if you have something you want to say, and say it attractively or enticingly; people will hear your message, or read it. It's like Proverbs 25:11 says, *"A word aptly spoken is like apples of gold in settings of silver"*; it is sure to strike attention. The packaging, the setting—that's it! Look at Jesus, God fleshed-out or God in a package that we could read and handle. The Gospel of John says *"The Word became flesh and made his dwelling among us. We have seen his glory, the glory of the One and Only, who came from the Father, full of grace and truth"* (1:14). Suddenly God can be seen and understood as clearly as a cereal box on the breakfast table. God is now approachable; you can know Him personally. Before Jesus came, many thought God was hidden away. Then when Jesus came, all of a sudden God was the Friend, not the Enemy; the Father, not the sheriff; the Savior, not the poor soul begging a hearing. That's when He caught my eye (and my heart). The attractiveness of the good news of Jesus can be seen in the Bible. It's the best selling book for good reason, and it's as available to you as your favorite cereal! Eat it up, and enjoy!

I am so glad that You came into the world personally. I understand and now I accept the Truth. Amen.

ONE YEAR CHALLENGE—Read:
Amos 4-6

November 16

Pre-Thanksgiving

DID YOU NOTICE THE NEWSPAPERS today? Many stores are having *"Pre-Thanksgiving"* sales. I suppose that is an attention grabber for some stores. I feel like having a pre-Thanksgiving thanksgiving! Would you join me? We may get so busy next week with the holiday celebration that we forget the quiet experience of thanksgiving worship. We sing a little chorus *"Thank you, Lord, for saving my soul. Thank you, Lord, for making me whole. Thank you, Lord, for giving to me thy salvation so rich and free."** Jesus said in John 10:28, *"I give them eternal life, and they shall never perish; no one can snatch them out of my hand."* A conscious awareness of this great truth should save us from much selfishness. We can thank God today for his sustenance of life. He provides our day-to-day needs. (Thank God he doesn't listen to all our foolish wants.) In fact this whole chapter of John 10 is a bubbling spring of thanksgiving possibilities as we meditate on Jesus as the Good Shepherd caring for his sheep. It echoes Psalm 23:2, *"He makes me lie down in green pastures, he leads me beside quiet waters."* These verses can be a real launching pad for thanksgiving. You may have already decided that this year won't be much of a Thanksgiving. You have had problems, your finances have been tight, the sickness or death of a friend may have drained you emotionally, the immediate future doesn't look any brighter; you just don't feel much Thanksgiving. As the old hymn of the church says *"Count your many blessings."*** Start right now. Make a list of things small and large. It may indeed surprise you what the Lord has done for you. By the time Thanksgiving Day arrives you may have a new outlook and attitude. Gratitude is a good corrective attitude.

> *How do I spell "gratitude" this year God? I seem to have forgotten what comes first at this time of year. Save me from fretting. Amen.*

ONE YEAR CHALLENGE—Read: Amos 7-9

November 17

The Empty Nest

FROM TIME TO TIME I HAVE READ articles about the *"empty nest."* As a pastoral counselor, across the years I have tried to help people as they adjusted to this life change. My wife and I have joined the group. Children are a trust from God. We parents are stewards of lives entrusted to us for a short time. Parents who try to hang on to their children and keep them from cutting the apron strings do the child a disservice. On the other hand, children who refuse to leave the nest do the parents a disservice. Leaving father and mother is one of the rites of passage in our culture. It is at this point that a crisis arises: Parents, have you trained your *"child in the way he should go, and when he is old he will not turn from it"* (Proverbs 22:6)? If you have you don't have to worry. Having done your faithful best as a stewardship, you can now return the child back to God with gratitude. Parents, have you developed your rela- tionship with your mate to the point where you can pick up where you left off when the children leave? Dust off the single-minded devotion and joy that you had for each other before the children started coming. Many couples divorce at this point because they only stayed together *"for the children."* If you have submitted yourselves *"to one another out of reverence for Christ"* and loved one another as much as you love yourself (Ephesians 5:21-28), then the future should be very meaningful. The nest is not completely empty. It is emptier, because some birds have flown. Mom and Dad remain to maintain the nest. For even as they have been examples to the young, they must still be examples in growing old and maturity.

Thank You, Father, for Your promise to never leave us or forsake us and to be with us to the end of time. I am comforted. Amen.

November 18

ONE YEAR CHALLENGE—**Read:**
Obadiah, Jonah

Giving People a Chance

I WAS TALKING TO A MAN THE OTHER DAY ABOUT HIS JOB and the company that employed him. He compared himself to his son who had just taken a new job and was doing well. He summed it up by saying, *"They gave him a chance to better himself; my company won't give anybody a chance."* I have wondered since then how many talented people there are in the world who could and would improve their life situation if given a chance. In another light, how many poor or homeless or refugees wouldn't be living on welfare if someone gave them a chance to do better? Or perhaps more personally, how many people are there who are waiting to be your friend and make a big difference in your life if you would give them a chance? There is a wealth of potential inside each human being if just given the chance to come out and develop. That's one of the attractive things about Jesus. He saw potential in people and gave them a chance. *"Follow me and I will make you [to become] . . . ."* whatever the potential of the individual, he or she would be given the freedom to express that potential. Too many times we write people off as hopeless, no-count, lazy, shiftless, undependable; we make a quick observation and judgment, often refusing to reconsider. Jesus saw people not for what they were but for what they could become. He didn't give up on James and John just because they were hotheaded *"Sons of Thunder"* (Mark 3:17). He didn't give up on Mary Magdalene because she was a woman of the streets or on Matthew because he was a cheating tax collector. Give people a chance to be the real people God created them to be. Get to know them, love them, encourage them to do their best, help them; give them a chance. You'll be blessed too.

> *Father, I don't want to consider for a moment what my life would have been without You. Thanks for calling me. Amen.*

OneYearChallenge—Read: James

November 19

Words with Different Meanings

ONCE UPON A TIME, "HOLY" WAS A GOOD WORD. It comes from the Bible. People didn't mind being called "holy." In fact, it was considered to be a great compliment. People who were holy were respected and honored. The word "holy" in Bible language meant dedicated to God, different from the ordinary, a mind set on serving God by serving man. Nothing bad about "holy" so far! Another word that meant the same was "saint," another descriptive word for ordinary people that loved the Lord. Then, somehow, people changed the meaning of "holy" and "saint" to mean perfect. It couldn't be a good word anymore because no one is perfect, or without sin. Unless you are dead! So, who is "holy"? Who is "saintly"? Dead people? Wow, no one wants to be thought of as dead—that's no fun. So the new meaning comes out for these words. It's commonly understood nowadays that if you don't like to have fun, if you are a kill-joy, if you are a square, if you are a wimp—you are "holy." If people see you as a "goody-goody" they might ask you if you are a candidate for sainthood. It's so bad now, in this age of extreme broad-mindedness and "anything goes" philosophy, that calling someone "holy" is an insult. Let's reclaim the word "holy!" Like I said in the beginning, "holy" just means ordinary men and women who have decided to follow the Lord with all their hearts. Paul said, "I urge you, brothers, in view of God's mercy, to offer your bodies as living sacrifices, holy and pleasing to God" (Romans 12:1). I hope someone calls you "holy" this week. What a compliment if it means you have realized Jesus can make your life holy and you have surrendered to Him. If you are experiencing new life now because God's Holy Spirit is permanently living in you, people are already observing saintly actions and attitudes.

> *Until I met You, Jesus, I never dreamed that I could be holy. I like what You saw in me. Amen.*

ONE YEAR CHALLENGE—Read:
Micah

November 20

Contending with Today's Lifestyles

ONE OF THE MOST COMMONLY EXPERIENCED PRESSURES IN A METROPOLITAN area like this is the pull of so many forces on our lives. People claim they are being pulled to pieces; everybody wants a piece of us. Life is frustration multiplied! Dad and Mom are pulled by demands on their time by the office, the church, the family, the softball team, the service club, washing the clothes, picking up kids, doing dishes, dropping off kids, shopping, and on and on. Some parents, especially moms, say they spend so much time in the car they can't get anything else done. And the kids grow up, copying the adults, and try to get involved in as many activities as possible. Where does it end? Too often it ends in the divorce court or the bottom of a bottle; the pressure finally had to blow off somewhere. Caught up in this, how do we reach out to pull all of this together into one unifying pattern? Jesus understood this problem. He said *"The thing you should want most is God's kingdom and doing what God wants. Then all these other things you need will be given to you"* (Matthew 6:33 EB). This followed His explanation to the crowd that they were tearing themselves up with anxiety over the clothes they wore, food they ate, or chasing material security for the future. You see, He said that He came to give abundant life (John 10:10). For those who felt pulled apart He said, *"my peace [unifying purpose for life] I give you. Do not let your hearts be troubled and do not be afraid"* (John 14:27). I believe this sounds a lot better than the lifestyle many are contending with on a daily basis. Jesus can give direction. If He is Lord of your life, *"each thought and each motive is beneath His control,"** said the songwriter. Is your lifestyle stressful? Try letting Jesus control it for a change.

Pull my life together, Jesus, unify me through Your Spirit. Keep me from living wildly. Amen.

ONE YEAR CHALLENGE—Read: Nahum

November 21

Caring about Children

WHEN CHILDREN GET IN TROUBLE or don't act well-adjusted, the community generally is very quick to point an accusing finger at the parents. It may be justified. But what about the rest of us in the adult world? I believe it should be the responsibility of all who have reached adulthood to care for the children. Their mental, emotional, physical, and certainly their spiritual health should be a concern to all of us. It's too easy to pass off the responsibility to someone else. What kind of role model are you for little kids? Let's not think about television stars or athletic heroes; most have long since failed as role models. Let's think about the Tom, Dick, and Mary Adult that live in your neighborhood. The Bible says, *"Train a child in the way he should go, and when he is old he will not turn from it"* (Proverbs 22:6). Training a child demands exemplary behavior. Children learn by imitation and repetition. They imitate adults and repeat adult words and behavior. Remember this old saying the next time you are around children: *"What you are is speaking so loudly, I can't hear a word you are saying."* I've heard adults excuse their drinking habits or excessive lifestyle with, *"I'm not hurting anyone but myself."* That's simply not true; children are watching adult reactions for a key as to how they should react to life situations. Crime and lawlessness is just as much a learned behavior as righteousness and fair-play. The Bible is very *"useful for teaching, rebuking, correcting and training in righteousness,"* said Paul in 2 Timothy 3:16. Christians are especially challenged to care for children. Jesus said, *"if anyone causes one of these little ones who believe in me to sin, it would be better for him to have a large millstone hung around his neck and to be drowned in the depths of the sea"* (Matthew 18:6). What are kids learning from you?

ONE YEAR CHALLENGE—Read: 1 Peter

> *Some of us were "raised up" and some of us were "yanked up," Lord. Will You be a real father to us now? Amen.*

November 22

The Vacant House

VACANT HOUSES STICK OUT! In an area where housing is at a premium, an unoccupied house is very obvious. New houses are being built at a record pace, new developments seem to be springing up like mushrooms. And even in the newer areas, there it is, standing like a sentinel: the vacant house. Many questions flood the mind as to why this house is vacant: A death? A broken marriage? A failed career? A legal battle? . . . ? Boarded up with unkept lawn it reminds us of broken plans and wasted possibilities. It does not echo with laughter; it does not indicate lives being shared; it is muted to tell any encouraging story. So many lives are like vacant houses, and not just the lives stripped bare by drugs and alcohol. So many lives have been stripped of joy and robbed of purpose. So many have been raped of dreams and pillaged of meaning that there is only a blank look and an empty stare. The light of the life has gone out and no one is at home. The reasons for an empty life are just as numerous as the reasons for a vacant house. One house on our street stood vacant for so long! Even though the real estate agent said several successive contracts were placed on the house, none were ever finalized. Its possibilities were untested. There will always be vacant houses, but, thank God, there doesn't have to be vacant, empty lives. The Bible is the record of God's offer to fill the vacuum, the emptiness of life. Jesus said in John 10:10, *"I have come that they may have life, and have it to the full."* Please understand that an empty heart is a vulnerable place for all types of devils and demons to enter. The love of Jesus fills a vacant life.

Fill my cup, Lord, with the water of life. I need the cool refreshment of the water of life. Thanks! Amen.

ONE YEAR CHALLENGE—Read:
2 Peter

November 23

Remember to Be Thankful

"*AND WHEN YOU PRAY, ALWAYS GIVE THANKS*" (Philippians 4:6 EB). Now there's a worthy injunction: "*always give thanks.*" We tend to forget to do that so easily. I sometimes wonder, (I never ask it out loud): is the reason we make such a big thing over Thanksgiving Day because we have such a guilty conscience for doing so little of it all the rest of the time? We get spoiled so easily! We get into an "*I deserve this*" mind-set; so, if I deserve it, I don't have to feel gratitude. A materialistic society can very easily do a number on your thinking. The advertising world feeds your "*I deserve these good things*" point of view. The shock of this media brain-washing came home to me in a conversation with a "*refuse-to-work*" receiver of public welfare checks demanding the best of food because they "*deserve it as Americans.*" When was the last time you heard the media instruct the populace to "*always give thanks*"? "*Always*" and "*thanks*" seem unusual partners at first glance. They don't seem to be a natural couple. One suggests a dynamic sensitivity, the other suggests passive insensitivity. Being thankful is dynamic! It's present tense! It's looking at God's goodness and responding in an affirmative way. "*give thanks in all circumstances, for this is God's will for you in Christ Jesus*" (1 Thessalonians 5:18); "*Give thanks to the LORD, for he is good*" (Psalm 106:1). There is a spontaneity about the Christian experience of Thanksgiving. "*Always*" means "*don't forget to do it*": we are weak and selfish and take blessings for granted. In Psalm 95:2 (KJV), David challenges us: "*Let us come before his presence with thanksgiving.*" Maybe the cure for our occasional thankfulness would be a daily cultivating of our coming "*before his presence.*" How is your continuing thanksgiving? Cultivate it right this minute.

> *My life is filled to overflowing, Bountiful Father. My cup is running over. You have blessed me. Amen*

ONE YEAR CHALLENGE—Read: Habakkuk 1-2

November 24

Thanksgiving Images

IT'S THAT *"OVER THE RIVER AND THROUGH THE WOODS"* TIME of year again! Images of Thanksgiving abound in our heads today: turkey (why did I eat so much?), pumpkin pie (at least I didn't take the whipped cream topping) and grandma's house (do all grandparents give their house a special smell?) Let's list a few images of pleasant things for Americans: November and Thanksgiving, feasting and football, a family and fun; they're all part of the American scene. We don't have to wax nostalgic about these Thanksgiving images. Most of us enjoy them every year. But what about others less fortunate, here and abroad? Actually, these images could spur us on to do something constructive for others. Realizing that even the poorest Americans are rich when compared to the multitudes of the world, we can recognize our responsibility to share. When he was asked which commandment is the greatest, *"Jesus replied: 'Love the Lord your God with all your heart and with all your soul and with all your mind.' This is the first and greatest commandment. And the second is like it: 'Love your neighbor as yourself' "* (Matthew 22:37-39). The horizontal impact of our vertical love for God is great. Love and concern for other people validates our love for God. One is the fruit of the other. One points to the other. It's too bad we often lose sight of that in our land of plenty. Probably there never would have been any need for a Department of Social Welfare or International Aid if we could learn to share. Caring and sharing—that's a Thanksgiving image we need to work on developing. When the church in the New Testament is described as *"These that have turned the world upside down"* (Acts 17:6 KJV), it was partly because they out-loved everybody else. The apostle John challenged the early believers: *"Dear friends, let us love one another"* (I John 4:7). They accepted and lived out that challenge, and what a difference the world could see!

ONE YEAR CHALLENGE—Read: Habakkuk 3, Zephaniah 1

> **Love and family go together in the Bible, God. Devotion to you, and dedication to family and neighbor is so important. Help us to recover and practice these qualities. Amen.**

November 25

Family Gratitude

WE HAVE JUST PASSED ONE OF THE MOST FAMILY ORIENTED celebrations on our calendar. Thanksgiving is really a focus on family in our society. If you weren't involved in the tremendous traffic problems over the Thanksgiving holiday, at least you were aware of them. Families want to get together at Thanksgiving. At Christmas, for many of us, the celebration seems to be more centered on individual families than our extended families, perhaps because we can't afford gifts for that many. What did Thanksgiving do for your family? Was there a lot of joy and sharing this year? Maybe it's because the family has become so fragile in our society that Thanksgiving is a symbol of how we wish it could be all the time. Selfishness is put aside, unity is the goal, and mutual appreciation of what the family has in common is emphasized. The question I want to raise is this: isn't the joy of sharing with family worth the effort all year long? Surely having the house clean and neat was appreciated. Surely the hard work in cooking was appreciated. Surely the efforts made by all to be congenial was appreciated. If the same kind of efforts were made the other 364 days as well, perhaps our statistics of divorce, abuse, separation, run-aways, abortions, and such would decrease instead of always increase. Instead of a nostalgic, sentimental, tear-producing drive back home after the feast, how about a resolution to make family sharing and togetherness a lifestyle? In the Old Testament, Joshua, the leader of Israel, stood before his community and recounted the goodness of God to all of them and then challenged the people to serve the Lord by making a family commitment: *"But if serving the LORD seems undesirable to you, then choose for yourselves this day whom you will serve, ... But as for me and my household, we will serve the LORD"* (Joshua 24:15). History records God's blessing on this family because the whole family served the Lord together. Try it.

Save our splintering families, Lord. Our houses are being divided. Only You can create family oneness. Amen.

November 26

ONE YEAR CHALLENGE—Read: Zephaniah 2-3

Talking or Acting

LAST WEEK EVERYONE WAS TALKING ABOUT THE WEATHER: how bad it was! This week everyone is talking about the weather: how nice it is! Naturally! That's what once made a curbside philosopher observe: *"Everyone is talking about the weather but no one is doing anything about it."* That's true! But on the other hand, what can we do about it? It's beyond us. We have no control! Someone else is responsible. Yes, all I can do is react: turn up the heat, turn down the air conditioning. Sometimes it seems life is lived this way: wait until something happens and then talk about reacting. The man or woman of faith has a different attitude. Life is too short to live by reaction. There is too much to be done to spend my time talking about the state of things. The wise man who wrote Ecclesiastes 9:10 in the Bible said, *"Whatever your hand finds to do, do it with your might."* This is the positive outlook of a man who feels responsible before God. He views life as stewardship. Today has been entrusted to him by God. Just outside his front door is a world of opportunity (or maybe just inside). Time must not be wasted by saying, *"I am only one, there is nothing I can do,"* or, *"The job is too big for one person."* No, while we reason like that, the hungry remain hungry, the cold remain cold, the lonely remain uncomforted, the hopeless remain disillusioned. Of course, I can't do everything, but I can do something. I can't help everyone, but I can help someone. Issues like the weather may be beyond my control, but daily there are dozens of positive things I can do for Jesus! Don't just talk about it, do it!

> *Father, You said I was a co-laborer with You because of Jesus. I had better get up and get to work. Amen.*

ONE YEAR CHALLENGE—Read:
Haggai

November 27

Post-Thanksgiving

SOME FOLKS HAVE TO BE REMINDED to be thankful. They are very agreeable, even congenial about it on that special day when we all are thinking Thanksgiving. What about the day after? That's different. Do we get any carry-over? Sometimes we suffer a let-down. We were excited as we built up for it. Many even attended a Thanksgiving Eve worship service and were sensitive and were thinking praise thoughts as they started the day on Thursday. Friends and family, young and old, helped to make it meaningful. But what of today and tomorrow and the long run? Did you ever consider thanksgiving as a lifestyle? Based on what? Here are some truths from the Bible, our standard: James 1:17 says, *"Every good and perfect gift is from above, coming down from the Father of the heavenly lights, who does not change like shifting shadows"*; or as the Apostle John put it, *"From the fullness of his grace we have all received one blessing after another"* (John 1:16). The day after Thanksgiving has become the biggest materialism day on the calendar. Many stores refer to it as *"Black Friday"* because it is expected to be the biggest money-maker of the year as people begin to celebrate themselves by purchasing Christmas presents. Consumerism runs wild. The spirit of gratitude, so recently celebrated, seems far away. The simple, meager life-style of our Founding Fathers seems very remote. God freely and abundantly gives us a good life and many good things. We need to be aware of that each day. Try this one: *"How can I repay the LORD for all his goodness to me? I will lift up the cup of salvation and call on the name of the LORD. I will fulfill my vows to the LORD in the presence of all his people"* (Psalm 116:12-14). Don't lose your Thanksgiving perspective.

How mellow we would be Loving Father, if we thought "thankfully" all the time! How sweet would be our fellowship! Help us to make it real. Amen.

ONE YEAR CHALLENGE—Read:
Zechariah 1-2

November 28

Cherish the Children

JESUS LOVED CHILDREN. He said, *"Let the little children come to me, and do not hinder them"* (Mark 10:14). Children loved Jesus. As pastor of a church, I want to have that kind of relationship with children. I watched them come to Vacation Bible School. They were so alert and alive, with faces so expectant to learn about Jesus. In the worship time, they sang with true enthusiasm and faith. I looked at them, as I do every Sunday, and prayed and hoped that they would give their lives to Jesus early and avoid a lot of the needless pain that comes from experimenting with evil. Christianity teaches us to cherish the children. In many cultures, children are helpless pawns. They are made slaves of blind religion and selfish governments. Even here in our own country child abuse is at an all-time high. Why and how does a society allow that to happen? The cancer that is eating away at the American home is seen in the way children are treated. *"Latch-key"* and *"throwaway"* kids stand out in public, by their behavior, craving attention. I am just as concerned for the children who are abused and neglected in middle class families. So many children are angry. They strike out in violent acts, gang behavior, disrespect for authority—a society pays a terrible price when it doesn't cherish the children. In I Samuel 1:27-28, we are told that Hannah cherished her boy Samuel so much that she dedicated him to God saying, *"I prayed for this child, and the LORD has granted me what I asked of him. So now I give him to the LORD. For his whole life he will be given over to the LORD."* Did that affect what kind of mother she would be? You'd better believe it! Raise your children in this Biblical value system; you'll bear much better fruit than with conventional values.

Dear God, thank You for our children. Help us to guard our best national treasure diligently. Amen.

ONE YEAR CHALLENGE—Read:
Zechariah 3-4

November 29

Your Reflection

SOME OF THE MEMBERS OF OUR CHURCH CHALLENGED ME the other day with the idea of Christians as reflections. They believe that Christians should be reflections of Jesus. The impact of Jesus should be reflected daily in the Christian life. In the same sense, they felt the church should also be a reflection of Christ. The combined body of believers that make up the body of Christ should be a larger reflection. The reflection may not be the clearest, but it must be a reflection. In 1 Corinthians 13:12, Paul talks about our human limitations that cause us to see Jesus as in a dull mirror or on a piece of polished metal. Still, the reflection is there, and we learn from it. This whole idea made me do some self-examination and also forced me to ask some questions about my church family. Am I reflecting Jesus back to the world in which I live? Is my church in all her activities reflecting the love of Jesus to the community. There is a little prayer chorus that goes, *"Let the beauty of Jesus be seen in me; all of his wonderful passion and purity! O, thou Spirit Divine, all my nature refine, until the beauty of Jesus is seen in me."* This is the same idea as the biblical teaching about your life as an example. In John 13:15, Jesus said, *"I have set you an example that you should do as I have done for you."* Paul challenges in 1 Timothy 4:12, *"set an example for the believers in speech, in life, in love, in faith and in purity."* 1 Peter 2:21 says that Christ left *"you an example, that you should follow in his steps."* When I reflect the person of Jesus Christ, I am an example that people can follow to the source of the True Light. What kind of reflection are you casting?

> *Dear Father, I want to look like you. I want to have a personality and characteristics like you. Make me over in your likeness. Amen.*

November 30

One Year Challenge—Read:
Zechariah 5-6

Thanksgiving to Christmas

THE SONG WRITER PENNED "IT'S A LONG, LONG WAY FROM MAY TO DECEMBER," and I'm sure that's true for people in love. But of greater importance to me and you today is the distance from Thanksgiving to Christmas. The calendar may say it's only a month but reality makes the distance greater. They used to be very close, both were originally religious holidays. Essentially, they were symbolic reminders of God's care and blessing. There are still a large number of Thanksgiving services in churches but basically it has become a national holiday. The government and the community affirms there is a higher power somewhere who feels kindly toward the earth. Recent years have witnessed several public battles over Christmas displays. City governments and courts have agreed that Christmas is a secular holiday of the American culture and that the manger scene and Rudolph the Reindeer and Santa Claus have one and the same meaning. If you protest this merger of the secular and the Christian, someone may think you are a bigot or religious fanatic. But the truth is that both Thanksgiving and Christmas are not fairy tales; these traditions are based on historical record that was written and verified by many witnesses. The accounts of the first Thanksgiving records real people worshiping a real God with heartfelt thanksgiving. The first Christmas was seen by real people who worshipped the real God with authentic thanksgiving. They were very close, not just on the calendar, but in basic meaning. If we separate them too far, we may do ourselves and humanity a disservice. Psalm 95:2 still challenges us to come before God with thanksgiving. Let's do that! And remember that *"when the time had fully come, God sent his Son, born of a woman, born under law, to redeem those under law, that we might receive the full rights of sons"* (Galatians 4:4-5). There is a spiritual bridge connecting Thanksgiving to Christmas.

ONE YEAR CHALLENGE—Read: Zechariah 7-8

> **O Lord, life is so disjointed and fragmented. Through Jesus, help me to see the pattern of Your work and find confidence. Amen.**

December 1

A Gift that Never Stops

RECENTLY I READ AN ADVERTISEMENT ABOUT *"A GIFT that never stops giving."* Know what it was about? A reclining chair that would give rest all year long! I think there are several gifts that you can give this Christmas that will give all year long. How about the gift of praise? Give it to the person, in recognition and appreciation of a job well done, recognizing that God has been glorified. Or you can give the gift of consideration. Put yourself in someone else's shoes and attempt real understanding. Maybe at other times you can give the gift of apology, to say at the right time: *"I am sorry, you are right and I am wrong."* Try the gift of gratitude, Don't forget, especially at this season, to say, *"Thank you,"* and, *"I'm grateful,"* and forget about keeping score about it. Consider about the gift of attention. Put down the newspaper or turn off the television and listen attentively when someone is speaking directly to you. Can you give the gift of inspiration? Seeds of encouragement and hope can be planted in another person's heart. What about the gift of presence? So many people are sick and worried and troubled and lonely and there's no substitute for just being there for them. Jesus offers an eternal gift that keeps giving every day. In John 1:12, the Bible says, *"to all who received him, to those who believed in his name, he gave the right to become children of God."* It is because of His non-stop giving that we have the inspiration to give non-stop gifts. In fact, Jesus said, *"If a person believes in me, rivers of living water will flow out from his heart"* (John 7:38 EB). This is certainly in contrast to the momentary highs of pagan religious or hedonistic experiences. So, while you are giving your gifts, give the gift that never stops giving: the good news of Jesus Christ, THE Savior.

> *Lord, your gift of your Son to this world certainly gives a different perspective on giving. Teach me how to give and what to give. Amen.*

One Year Challenge—Read: Zechariah 9-10

December 2

Visiting the Dump

Like many of you, I visit the county landfill regularly to dispose of trash and drop off recyclables. One unusual part of the place is designated: *"Too Good To Throw Away."* There is always a variety of stuff there. Things that people don't like anymore or don't find useful are abandoned on this spot. Items that have become without value to the original owner, but perhaps in someone else's eyes, *"too good to throw away."* It just impressed me last week that God finds us on the *"too good to throw away"* part of life. Many of us are abandoned by spouse, parents, children, employer and the like who got the best we had to offer and then put us aside. Genesis 2:7 says, *"the LORD God formed the man from the dust of the ground and breathed into his nostrils the breath of life, and the man became a living being."* Made in the image of God, we were in the ideal location to have a relationship with God. But we rebelled and listened to the appeal of Satan and selfish desires, and went to follow him. He used us and tossed us aside after we were miserable. But God saw that we were, *"too good to throw away."* David asks, *"Who is like the LORD our God, the One who sits enthroned on high, who stoops down to look on the heavens and the earth? He raises the poor from the dust and lifts the needy from the ash heap"* (Psalm 113:5-7). So many people are considered worthless and disposable by other humans but God sees us through different eyes. *"Though my father and mother forsake me, the LORD will receive me"* (Psalm 27:10). The dearest person to you in this world may turn on you but the Lord will find you in your abandoned state and save you for future fellowship.

> **Thank you God, for not giving up on me. I am so glad that I was valuable to you. You are so merciful. Amen.**

December 3

One Year Challenge—Read:
Zechariah 11-12

Cooperation

WHAT A DIFFERENCE COOPERATION MAKES! When we were in the process of building a new church building, we relied heavily on volunteer labor. People cooperated in clearing the site, digging the footings, pouring the concrete slab, and other tasks. This continued until the project was completed. What a beautiful sight it is to see people working together! Not only had there been a building and strengthening of human relationships, there had been a tremendous financial savings. Blessings abound from cooperation. Of course, that's the secret of the work of the church, voluntary participation and giving. This is one good thing for the church to model to the community and to the world. There is so much competition in the world and competition breeds division. Someone observed that it is a perverted society when competition draws a bigger crowd than cooperation, for example, the millions that are drawn to the competition of pro-fessional football or boxing versus the number of those same people that are drawn to the cooperative spirit of the church. In Acts 17:6 (KJV) when Paul and Silas, the Christian missionaries, arrived in Thessalonica, their opposition said of them and their Christian brothers, *"these that have turned the world upside down are come."* Who were these people? They were just 12 men who had cooperated with Jesus in launching the Kingdom of God in the world and had now become a mighty force in history. That original genius of cooperation is the birthright of the church today! Let's pray for a community where all of the churches cooperate together all of the time for the glory of God and the good of all the people—not just at Thanksgiving and Easter and Christmas for community services, but all of the time. I Corinthians 3:9 says, *"we are God's fellow workers,"* not competitors. Let competition die, let cooperation live!

ONE YEAR CHALLENGE—Read: Zechariah 13-14

O God, the world is waiting to see Christians get along together and work together. Help me to help my church get involved with the larger Christian family. Amen.

December 4

Oil's Altar

THIS IS A TIME OF YEAR WHEN MANY PEOPLE'S THOUGHTS TURN TO GOD and worship. Generally it is to the God revealed in the Bible. But another god is vying for our attention. Many seem to be preoccupied with the god of oil. The world's attention is focused on the need for oil. The world economy demands it, business and international trade depends on it, and politicians daily remind the world of the important role that oil plays. Many people are even willing to sacrifice the young men and women of the nations on the altar of war for the sake of preserving the place of oil. The stock market fluctuates according to what oil is doing. The prices of gasoline and heating oil and its other derivatives are the subject of many radio talk shows and neighborhood cookouts. The value of oil to human society is debated in the highest levels of government. Is this as it should be? Have we become so dependent on this natural resource that we now talk about its role with religious fervor? It sounds to me like another one of those times where we are worshiping *"created things rather than the Creator"* (Romans 1:25). Our trust and our security is in the Lord who made heaven and earth, not in the military and economic powers that control the oil fields. Because of our materialism as a consumer society, we often lose sight of a true sense of values. Our currency reminds us: *"In God We Trust."* This has perhaps helped deter us from trusting in other would-be gods. Historically, the gods of nationalism, racism, isolationism, anti-communism, humanism (to mention a few) have each tempted us to worship at their altar. *"Blessed is the nation whose God is the LORD"* (Psalm 33:12).

Man-made idols surround us, O God. Save us from the paganism of worshiping any of them. Amen.

ONE YEAR CHALLENGE—Read: Malachi 1-2

December 5

Purple Mountain Majesty

MOUNTAINS HAVE A SPECIAL FASCINATION for most people. We recently were in Southwest Virginia, driving along the Blue Ridge Mountains. Know what? From a distance, they actually appeared to be blue. When Katherine Lee Bates penned our patriotic song, *America the Beautiful*, she eloquently described *"purple mountain majesties."* I guess there was just a little difference of opinion on color. The figure of mountains is used so many times in the Bible. When the Bible wants to portray strength, stability, protection, beauty, even holiness—mountains are often used to symbolize these virtues. *"He [God] has set his foundation on the holy mountain,"* said David in Psalm 87:1. He even calls on the mountains to praise the Lord in Psalm 148:7-9. Since the mountains have been around and seen so much, the mountains are called upon to be God's witnesses against the sins of mankind (Micah 6:1-2). I especially like Psalm 114:6, where the mountains are described as skipping because of the greatness of God. It's outstanding that the God-inspired poet can see things and learn things from the mountains that many of us ignore or refuse to see. Unlike man, the mountains have had only one ultimate embarrassment in history. That was the day some men took the Savior out to a mountain called Calvary and crucified Him (Luke 23:33 NKJV). As if the earth was so offended by that event, an earthquake split the mountain side (Matthew 27:51). Remember the Psalmist said, *"I lift up my eyes to the hills—where does my help come from? My help comes from the LORD, the Maker of heaven and earth"* (Psalm 121:1-2). As beautiful and majestic as the mountains appear, they have no answer for the deep needs of man's soul. Thank God for mountains and the blessings of their beauty. Thank God for Jesus, who died on Mt. Calvary for us.

Dear God, I want to worship you and have fellowship with you. Thank You for being so personal and responsive. Amen.

ONE YEAR CHALLENGE—Read:
Malachi 3-4

December 6

Giving of One's Self

Christmas Club Savings accounts have been cashed in, the first big shopping binge weekend is upon us. Without restraint, affluent Americans will flash their greenbacks and credit cards. Having overindulged on turkey, ham, gravy and pumpkin pie, we now turn our attention to tinsel and such things. Without a second thought, parents will spend hundreds of dollars indulging their children with gifts. With what's left over, they will indulge themselves. So complete is the *"buy, buy buy"* brainwashing that many will follow this pattern of action without a second thought. All that will really be bought from this mind-set will be unhappiness. Money can't buy happiness through over-indulgence because *"a man's life does not consist in the abundance of his possessions."* So, *"Watch out! Be on your guard against all kinds of greed"* (desiring things). In the same context Jesus told about a man who struck it rich and said to himself, *"You have plenty of good things laid up for many years. Take life easy; eat, drink and be merry."* But Jesus observed that the man was a fool (Luke 12:15-20). Surrounding one's self with lots of material things can't hide inner, spiritual emptiness. Maybe that's the obsession of over-indulgence: attempting to fill up an inner vacuum with something that is only an outward covering. Jesus asked *"What good will it be for a man if he gains the whole world, yet forfeits his soul?"* (Matthew 16:26). How about heading toward Christmas with a different approach? Looking for opportunities to help and share? Giving of yourself is the best gift and you don't even have to wrap it. Focus in on spiritual values, giving love and sensitivity, gifts that keep giving all year long. A Bible, a book of poetry, a jar of jelly that you made, a hand-craft you put together, a handwritten greeting, ...

One Year Challenge—Read: 1 John 1-3

Father, why do I withhold myself? Why is it easier to give things than giving myself? Thank You for giving yourself to me and the world. Amen.

December 7

The Fire of God

ONE CHARACTERISTIC OF GOD we don't often think about is the image of God as fire. I don't mean God using fire as a means of judgment as in *"the fires of Hell."* If you have read Dante's description of Hell, you may not be able to think of God in a positive way with the image of fire. There is a beautiful challenge in Hebrews 12:28-29 that says, *"since we are receiving a kingdom that cannot be shaken, let us be thankful, and so worship God acceptably with reverence and awe, for our 'God is a consuming fire'."* Let's look at fire in this positive way— if you have ever sat before a roaring fireplace on a freezing night this will not be difficult. There is comfort and hope in this picture, as well as awe, as we bask in the warmth of God's love and the hope that it inspires in us. Many of us have been challenged repeatedly by the experience of John Wesley who said his heart was *"strangely warmed"* when he experienced the fire of God's love. (Notice the sign out in front of your neighborhood Methodist church.) Fire purges, or purifies. The Bible describes how the dross and impurities are removed from our lives as we are filled more and more with God's holiness. Sometimes we feel that crisis, trial, discipline, sickness, and the like, put us *"out of the frying pan into the fire,"* focusing our attention on God. Fire illuminates. Remember how the children of Israel were led by a *"pillar of fire by night"* (Exodus 13:22) when they crossed the unknown desert after escaping Egypt. In 1 Corinthians 3:10-15, Paul's ultimate challenge to Christians is to remember that the ultimate test of our life of commitment is if it can stand the scrutiny or revelation of God's fire. Is the *"fire of God"* (2 Kings 1:12) a threat or a thanksgiving in your life?

> *Frankly, God, I have not thought of You much in terms of fire. I will try to focus on this truth today. Amen.*

ONE YEAR CHALLENGE—Read: 1 John 4-5, 2 John

December 8

In Authority

IN YOUR DAYDREAMS, WOULD YOU LIKE TO BE A KING, OR AN EMPEROR, OR EVEN PRESIDENT of the United States of America? In our fantasy, we sometimes wonder what it would be like to have so much authority. Whoever does, has such awesome responsibility that the Bible gives us clear instructions on how we should support them. Paul teaches, *"I urge, then, first of all, that requests, prayers, intercession and thanksgiving be made for everyone—for kings and all those in authority, that we may live peaceful and quiet lives in all godliness and holiness"* (I Timothy 2:1-2). In Romans 13:1-7, there is an extended teaching about how Christians are to live under *"authorities."* It says, *"for the authorities are God's servants, who give their full time to governing. Give everyone what you owe him: If you owe taxes, pay taxes; if revenue, then revenue; if respect, then respect; if honor, then honor."* The Bible does not concern itself with political parties.

God is neither a Republican nor a Democrat. Unless we have an anti-God government which denies the existence of God and freedom of religion, we are called to support it, in order to have an orderly society. Each of us has our own idea about how the government should operate. Each has his or her own special interest that he or she would like to see become the law of the land. The only problem with this is that we are often blind to the opinions and feelings of others. So in our kind of democratic society, we are charged with our responsibility to elect fair and moral leaders who will work for the common good. Whether you are a member of the *"moral majority"* or *"moral minority"* or the *"loyal opposition,"* the demands of these times are such that we pray faithfully for those who are in places of authority and encourage them as much as we can. A better country for all will be the result.

> *Forgive me, Dear Lord, for complaining more than I pray, especially concerning those who rule over us. Amen.*

December 9

OneYearChallenge—Read:
3 John, Jude

Peace to You

How badly do you want peace? I'm not talking about world peace now, I mean personally or in your family? Is turmoil a way of life for you? Some folks have known turmoil for so long that peace seems like a fantasy. To have things unified in one's life or having everything going in the same direction would be such a great blessing. Many complain about the feeling of being torn in different directions. In Luke 19, Jesus speaks about the chaos in the lives of the people and even offers an explanation for the problem. In verse 41, Jesus weeps over the city of Jerusalem because there is such turmoil and chaos. Jesus mourns for the people because they seem blind to that which produces peace. Then He proceeds to say in verse 44 that the people didn't recognize their opportunity for peace, or the agent for peace who was right in front of them. The solution to the *"getting my life together"* problem is very simple: discover a living and personal relationship with God through Jesus Christ. In 1 Timothy 2:5, the Bible says, *"there is one God and one mediator between God and men, the man Jesus Christ."* This Great Mediator is able to bring you together with God because He gave His life to make it possible. If your life is going madly in several different directions, don't you think it's time that you took another look at Jesus? He is a peacemaker; He alone is able to give you peace. Does it matter to you that Jesus hurts for you in your turmoil? He is touched by your lack of peace. He wants to give you his peace; not a cheap substitute, but the real thing. Stop listening to worldly peacemakers who can only make promises that they can only hope to deliver. Read the Luke 19 passage again. Don't miss peace because of spiritual blindness.

Often, Father, I do feel pulled in several different directions. My Life seems fragmented! Give unity and purpose, please. Amen.

One Year Challenge—Read: Revelation 1

December 10

Respect for Life

Do you stop for funeral processions? Many people do. When I was a child, everyone did except the rebels against society. I was taught that it was a matter of respect for life to acknowledge that another human being had died. Are people too much in a hurry today or has respect for life been lost? Is this loss of respect for life also reflected in drive-by shootings and gang-style murders and kids carrying guns to school to settle arguments? My Bible still reads, *"So God created man in his own image, in the image of God he created him; male and female he created them"* (Genesis 1:27). We must respect life at every level of society. Are we reaping today, on a personal and community level, what was started when we bombed Hiroshima and Nagasaki? As wars have progressed in horror and body counts go out of sight, have humans lost value? Seeing millions starving on the evening news certainly doesn't seem to increase our respect for life; rather it seems to anesthetize us against human pain. As long as there is no respect for life generally, there will be no respect for life at the abortion clinic or the drug dealer's corner. *"God loved the people of this world so much that he gave his only Son"* (John 3:16 CEV). *"Christ Jesus came into the world to save sinners—of whom I am the worst,"* Paul said in 1 Timothy 1:15. God created human life and gave Jesus to redeem it, so there is no question about the value God has placed on human life. In Psalm 8:5 (CEV), David expresses the unfathomable generosity of our creator, saying to God, *"You made us a little lower than you yourself, and you have crowned us with glory and honor."* Quite a compliment for humans, don't you think? Maybe the real problem is here: when people lose sight of God, they lose sight of the value of God's creation. During the next funeral procession—think seriously.

One Year Challenge—Read: Revelation 2

> *Respect for life covers so many facets of our society. Help me to hear the Biblical message, not the political or popular one. Amen.*

December 11

Perspective

ARE YOU AN OPTIMIST OR A PESSIMIST? You know, when you look at a partially filled glass of water, do you describe it as *"half-full"* or *"half-empty"*? Your perspective will make the difference. Or, in street talk, *"where you are coming from"* will determine your outlook. I heard a variation on this in November. A man was describing his feelings of gratitude and thanks to God for all of his blessings. He described his view as standing on the economic ladder and looking down. He saw so many people less fortunate rather than looking up the ladder and complaining about how many people had so much more. That's a healthy perspective! Remember the song that says, *"It depends on how you look at things"*? Jesus said, *"What good is it for a man to gain the whole world, yet forfeit his soul?"* (Mark 8:36). If you read Matthew's Gospel, chapters 5, 6, and 7 (The Sermon on the Mount), you will have your perspective challenged. If your perspective is totally physical or material, you will miss out on the best that God has for you. You will never smell the roses or admire a sunset because there is no material payoff in doing so. In John 12:29, the voice of God spoke from Heaven affirming Jesus' ministry and *"The crowd that was there and heard it said it had thundered; others said an angel had spoken to him."* What if you had been there? Depending on your point of view, you can be amazed at the glory of God or just see nothing. It's so amazing that some people say there is no God. They can't find Him. And some of the rest of us can't get away from Him! Jesus quizzed Philip (John 14:9), *"Don't you know me, Philip, even after I have been among you such a long time?"* The condition of your heart will control what you see. Check your perspective.

> I need to look with eyes of faith, Father. I want to see things from your point of view and make correct value judgments. Amen.

ONE YEAR CHALLENGE—Read:
Revelation 3

December 12

The Scratchy Pen

WHEN I WAS A CHILD, PEOPLE STILL WROTE WITH FOUNTAIN PENS. I could never do it smoothly. It was worse when all I had was a scratchy pen, one with a point where the ink did not flow evenly, or got snagged on the paper. The finished piece would look very rough and uneven. I recently read about Hannah More, a 19th-century Christian. She wrote about her spiritual penmanship, a source of discouragement for her. She had a low opinion of her spiritual effectiveness. In one of her self-appraisals she wrote: *"God is sometimes pleased to work with the most unworthy instruments. It always gives me the idea of a great author writing with a very bad pen."* Some of you readers have never used a scratchy fountain pen, but I am sure you have used a ball point pen that skips and blots; it leaves your writing not very attractive either. Christian's life stories are written like that; some days the prose is smooth and descriptive but on other days the sentences are disjointed and barely scribbled. Some days our poetry just won't rhyme. What kind of story is God writing with you today? The main question is legibility. Is it readable? You see, even if a pen didn't write smoothly it should still be legible. One should be able to read the message. The Bible instructs, *"Whatever happens, conduct yourselves in a manner worthy of the gospel of Christ"* (Philippians 1:27). Titus 1:15 says, *"To the pure, all things are pure."* When your inner heart and mind are kept pure, the life message you write will be clear and consistent. An occasional misspelled word will not betray the whole body of the message. Even a dirty face can't hide a pure heart. Daily submit your life to the Lord and ask Him to write someone a love letter through you. His hand is not shaky, the writing will be legible.

> *Your love story is so legible, God, anyone can read your writing. When we copy the story, help us to write clearly. Amen.*

ONE YEAR CHALLENGE—Read: Revelation 4

December 13

A Perspective on the Meaning of Christmas

THERE'S AN OLD SONG THAT SUGGESTS, *"YOU GOT TO STOP AND SMELL THE ROSES."* Well, it's not the season for roses, so maybe we could paraphrase it to *"stop and look at the poinsettias"* or Christmas trees or lights. If we keep up this rushing around for the next couple of weeks we will rush right through Christmas and not notice it. Why are we in such a hurry? I know we have a lot to do, or so we think. We get peer-pressured into buying too much and partying too much while our insides cry out, *"Christmas is not supposed to be like this!"* A celebration of the greatest spiritual event in the history of mankind ought to be a blessing and joy-giver to the human spirit. But many don't take the time for it! Slow down. Better yet, stop! Go to your room (or somewhere quiet) and collect your thoughts. Get a Bible. Read Isaiah 53 and Luke 2 straight through. Take a deep breath and get a better perspective on what these next few days are all about. It doesn't make sense at all for professed Christians to lose sight of what this season is all about. Slow down. In Isaiah 30:15, the prophet said, *"in quietness and trust is your strength."* Remember what the angel called the coming baby Jesus in Matthew 1:23? *"Immanuel"*—God is now with us! A deep trust in God's purpose at Christmas will give you the inner peace that will be your strength reserve to call on during this society-induced season of pressure. I have seen the same scene so many times: harried parents or grandparents jerking a child around in a toy store—futile attempts to guarantee the child will have a good Christmas. What a contradiction! We are celebrating the Prince of Peace! Don't miss this special opportunity to experience peace with God. This special gift won't cost you a penny.

Father, don't let me miss Christmas, I will feel so sorry. Open the eyes of my heart. I want to see the glory of Jesus. Amen.

ONE YEAR CHALLENGE—Read: Revelation 5

December 14

God's Giving, Our Example

DID YOU EVER GET THE FEELING THAT EVERYBODY IS TRYING TO GET THEIR HANDS IN YOUR POCKET? There are so many appeals for your money, from the latest fad to the newest *"must have"* item on everybody's Christmas list; it's tough, isn't it? How do you deal with it? There are our regular expenses and now the Christmas expenses plus the calls for charity during this season of the year—whoa! Most people don't want to be selfish or appear selfish. How do we unleash genuine liberality with genuine love? That's a good question. How do we overcome our natural self-centeredness? This season of the year is an opportune time for us to learn. The heartbeat of Christmas is liberality: *"For God so loved the world that he gave his one and only son"* (John 3:16). This is the cornerstone of the Christian faith. If like begets like, then the children of God ought to be liberal in giving, like our heavenly Daddy. The willingness with which God gave his best is reflected in the biblical challenge for us that *"God loves a cheerful giver"* (2 Corinthians 9:7). God's giving is our ideal, God's giving is our example. There is another challenge in Romans 12:8: that all who practice acts of mercy or kindness should do it with a cheerful spirit. Be sensitive to your attitude when you give. Recipients of charity sometimes have a hard time enjoying what they receive because of the attitude of the giver. May I suggest that when you give, don't be in a hurry; spend time with the receiver; get to know about the receiver; let the material gift be an expression of the giving spirit within you. At such times I often try to make myself aware of how I would feel if I were the recipient instead of the giver. The promise of 2 Corinthians 9:6-14 is spiritual blessings in exchange for our liberal giving to meet the needs of others.

> *Father, how did I become so selfish and self centered? How can I learn liberality and unselfishness? Help me, please, this week. Amen.*

ONE YEAR CHALLENGE—Read: Revelation 6

December 15

The Poverty of Affluence

MY ATTENTION WAS CAPTURED BY A HEADLINE: *"The Poverty of Affluence."* As I write this, I live in the suburbs of Washington D.C. In the inner city, people are dying daily with the trappings of affluence on their bodies: expensive basketball shoes, gold chains, fashionable clothes, and a wallet full of bloody money. Yes, this is the poverty of affluence! But it's no different in the suburbs. Suburban youth, with more money than they need, drive expensive cars to all night parties and get high on drugs and booze, finding no real meaning in life. The poverty of affluence—many people have everything but a reason for living! The poverty of affluence affords you the luxury of going to an expensive psychiatrist to tell him how happy you were when you were first out of college and had nothing but a dream. Why do you think some rich people long for the days when they had little and life was simple? The poverty of affluence stands in stark contrast to the poverty of the truly poor. What a joke it was when the Iron Curtain fell and we discovered that the Russian people thought the average American was like those portrayed in the television program, **Dallas**. Many people migrate to metropolitan centers because it is easier to get money there. Many become affluent, then bored with living. Jesus said, *"Do not store up for yourselves treasures on earth, where moth and rust destroy, and where thieves break in and steal. But store up for yourselves treasures in heaven, where moth and rust do not destroy, and where thieves do not break in and steal. For where your treasure is, there your heart will be also"* (Matthew 6:19-21). Do you want to be rich in things or rich in spirit? You can be spiritually rich without being affluent, but you can't be affluent before God with only currency and what it buys.

Father, in some parts of the world I am considered to be rich, in some, I am considered to be poor. What is my heavenly bank balance? Amen.

ONE YEAR CHALLENGE—Read:
Revelation 7

December 16

Songs of Christmas

ACTUALLY, WE TAKE THEM FOR GRANTED, the songs of Christmas. Those of us who grew up in America learned them unconsciously. They were always on the radio; every December at school and church we sang them. We could not help but learn them. Even non-Christians learned them, whether they understood the meaning or not. If Christmas and Christianity gave only the music of Christmas to the world it would be a substantial contribution. Where would we be without this music? Here in America, or in other countries where Christianity is strong, it is signified by its joyful music. Many religions are non-musical or non-singing. There are chants, dirges, and instrumental worship. But it is Christianity that has given the whole world a song for Christmas. Can you imagine what Christmas would be like without hearing the Hallelujah Chorus? The theme of that great song is more about the triumphant reign and rule of Christ as Savior and Lord than about the birth of Christ: *"Hark! The herald angels sing: Glory to the newborn King!"* *"Joy to the world! the Lord is come; Let earth receive her King."** "It came upon the midnight clear, That glorious song of old."*** "Good Christian men, rejoice With heart and soul and voice."**** How could you sing these songs, even if they are good music, without wanting Jesus to save you from your sins? Think about the words of the Christmas carols. They are almost all Biblically based, their messages are laden with Biblical truth. Listen carefully to the words! Let them speak to your heart! In Psalm 40:3, David said God *"put a new song"* in his mouth. That's what I'd say about Christmas carols. Don't get caught in the mindless trap that Christmas carols are just a cultural expression of the season. They are magnificent expressions of pure joy, all based on Jesus!

In my heart a melody is ringing. On my lips, a melody is singing. In may soul, another praise song is forming. All because of Christmas. Amen.

ONE YEAR CHALLENGE—Read: Revelation 8

December 17

A Week Before Christmas

SOME FOLKS HAVE NO EXPECTANCY about Christmas. Unless you have a baby that is going to experience its first Christmas, or you got married this year, you may be thinking this is going to be a typical Christmas. There will be nothing new or exciting; you will work hard, shop hard, cook hard and then be so tired on December 25, that you will not have much expectancy left. Can anything be done to create a fresh attitude at your house? I am reminded of my childhood in the country. As kids, we would find terrapins near the woods. We would try to examine them but they would pull in their heads and close their shell tightly. We tried to pry the turtle's shell open; it wouldn't work. One day my Dad said the secret to getting a terrapin to open up was to place it in an open, warm spot. We tried it and it worked! Soon the terrapin stuck out his head and feet and started moving. People are like that, too. If you create a warm place, they will open up. If they are warmed up with kindness, you don't have to try to force them to open up and be friendly and relaxed. Apply Romans 12:13: *"Share with God's people who are in need. Practice hospitality,"* and also I Peter 4:9, *"Offer hospitality to one another without grumbling."* So much of Christmas preparation tends to be selfish or centered around our immediate family. Helping others or sharing with others can create expectancy. The something *"new"* or *"different"* about this Christmas for you and your family could happen by sharing the love of Jesus with someone who hasn't experienced it fully. With the exception of Easter, this is the most important week on the Christian calendar. Appreciate every moment of it; refuse to get overwhelmed. Ask the Lord to make Christmas fresh every day.

Father, give me a child-like faith again, for the rest of this month. Restore to me anew the meaning of "God so loved the world." I know that will bless me. Amen.

ONE YEAR CHALLENGE—Read: Revelation 9

December 18

Helping the Homeless

IN HIS PARABLE OF THE LAST JUDGMENT, one of the criteria for being blessed by God and received into Heaven for eternity, is having received into your home the strangers and homeless (Matthew 25:35). For many years and in most places in America, this scripture has been read and glossed over. We're tempted to presume that it applies to someone else besides us. It has been used to raise money to support foreign missions work. Third World Christians have never had the luxury of ignoring that verse. Many communities nowadays are being forced to deal with the wandering strangers who have no place to lay their heads. Churches are being asked to open their doors to give shelter to the homeless. Strangely enough, some churches are saying *"no."* They fear the homeless will get their nice building dirty, or they don't want to be distracted from *"saving souls."* What a contradiction! Still the winter stretches out before us and the strangers need a place to sleep other than in cars and dumpsters. Shame on those who talk a lot of religion but then *"sees his brother in need but has no pity on him"* (I John 3:17). There are Christians who say to the poor and hungry homeless, *"God be with you! I hope you stay warm and get plenty to eat"* (James 2:16 EB), but do nothing about these real needs; they only disappoint. What good is that kind of faith that does not act? Individually and collectively we need to take seriously the New Testament program of relief for the needy and helping the powerless. If each church in America adopted one homeless person, it would change many cities. Spend a night in a homeless shelter. Try to sleep on a cot in a room full of strangers with all your clothes on—it's no fun! It can be dangerous if some are mentally ill. I know most won't or couldn't do that. Get involved at some level. Care and work to solve the problem.

> *December could be a good learning time for me. Jesus, if I have your help. You came to help me. Teach me to be a helper to the helpless. Amen.*

December 19

ONE YEAR CHALLENGE—Read: Revelation 10

Winter Weather

THIS COLD WINTER WEATHER creates many problems for us. Nightly I watch the weather news and follow the meandering curves of cold fronts here and there. News clips remind me of the influence of cold weather in shaping many lives. Most people are especially touched by the plight of the homeless during the cold weather. Huddled in doorways, sleeping on steam grates, sipping coffee in all-night restaurants and bus stations; they show us the ugliest pressures of the cold. Deep snow and thick ice and sub-zero temperatures may inconvenience and trouble all of us, but some of us suffer miserably when it is this cold. Just as I wonder how the small birds survive on my bird feeder, I wonder how these homeless people survive. But some have said you can survive the outer cold if there is inner warmth. Those who's bodies freeze have frozen spirits; They've given up and succumbed to the outer cold. Some have confessed to me about feeling cold toward God or their marriage partner or about the future. Some confess no desire to go on living because of this coldness of spirit. In fact, Jesus used the term *"cold"* to describe what will happen at the end of time: *"Because of the increase of wickedness, the love of most will grow cold"* (Matthew 24:12). He is describing how many professing Christians will change because of the persecutions and hardships they experience in their faith. The term seems to always have a sense of foreboding about it. At this cold weather time of the year, both physically and spiritually, I like to remember how Hosea the Prophet described God's compassion toward a cold and unresponsive people: *"My heart beats for you. My love for you stirs up my pity. I won't punish you in my anger. I won't destroy"* (Hosea 11:8-9 EB). Draw close to God today, experience his warmth!

Thank you, God, for warming my cold heart. I was so unfeeling toward people. Your warm acceptance changed me. Amen.

ONE YEAR CHALLENGE—Read: Revelation 11

December 20

Winter Has Come

It HAS FINALLY ARRIVED. AFTER SEVERAL CONFRONTATIONS WITH INDIAN SUMMER, winter has broken away from fall and has taken over the weather scene. There is something foreboding about winter. It carries a threat. Its threat is built on many hazards of past winters. Some fear and dread winter. The Apostle Paul must have had experience with the dreaded cold of winter. At the end of his earthly ministry, he was in prison for preaching the good news about Jesus. He wrote to Timothy (2 Timothy 4:21) and told him what was happening and asked Timothy to come to visit him, and emphasized, *"Do your best to get here before winter."* In winter the days are short and the nights long and cold. Darkness is an easy atmosphere for depression to take root. Before we get too far into winter, it would be good to stock up your spiritual pantry. Many of our great-grandparents had cellars where they stored meat, fruits and vegetables to get them through the winter. The high point of winter for the Christian is the celebration of the birth of Jesus. Are you making special plans to give Jesus a birthday party with a special gift this year? January is a great month for self-examination and making new beginnings in overcoming old problems. February is a month for celebrating love and the great differences love makes in our lives. However you're planning to spend your time this winter, there is some great reading material to help you get the most out of it. David said to the Lord in Psalm 31:15, *"My times are in your hands."* There is a further challenge in Psalm 62:8: *"Trust in him at all times."* As you move into the winter months, consider the spiritual challenge. The pace of life has changed. Be thankful for the change and come to grips with some personal issues. Need help? Meet me in the church house Sunday morning! Welcome winter!

One Year Challenge—Read: Revelation 12

> *I know, O God, that You control the seasons. I know, there are special blessings for me this winter. Make me humble to receive them. Amen.*

December 21

The True Meaning of Christmas

THE **PEANUTS** CHARACTERS had an interesting problem under discussion. It started with a concern for Santa's health; he's overweight and obviously out of shape. Then it got really serious when it was announced that Santa Claus got sick at the department store and was admitted to the hospital emergency room with a heart attack (after being harassed by a little kid.) If you are a parent, you might get asked a serious question by your young child some day, such as, *"is Santa allowed to get sick?"* or *"Does Santa have an assistant?"* How would you answer that? Suppose your Santa Claus doesn't come? Just suppose? Does your Christmas depend upon a person? What if that person gets sick, or dies, or can't come home to visit, or just doesn't call or visit or give you a present? Will you be shattered? Will you be miserable and disappointed? These questions can help you dig down to the true meaning of Christmas: *"God so loved . . . that He gave"* (John 3:16). This is the primary fact of Christmas and the foundation of this celebration. A loving God, who created Heaven and Earth, and all of us, has shown His love for us in a real and personal way. Regardless of the events of the Christmas week, that fact will not change. It will be a stabilizer for you and give you true joy. Add to this, the rest of the verse, that is, *"what"* He gave and you really have a boundless, unchanging source of joy. He gave Himself when He gave Jesus. God gave the best He could give! Giving Himself meant He could have a daily relationship with you. The joy of the Christmas week doesn't depend on a contemporary Santa, but an Eternal Savior who came to give you real joy. Merry Christmas? Indeed! Merry Christmas!

Thank You, God, for changing my calendar and giving me many "red-letter" days to celebrate your love. I'm excited this year. Amen.

ONE YEAR CHALLENGE—Read: Revelation 13

December 22

Tent People

THERE IS AN OLD COUNTRY SONG that says *"this world is not my home, I'm just passing through."* I agree with that; this world is not my permanent address. This is just the place where I pick up my mail. The people of God are like Abraham of old, who *"when called to go to a place he would later receive as his inheritance, obeyed and went, even though he did not know where he was going. By faith he made his home in the promised land like a stranger in a foreign country; he lived in tents, as did Isaac and Jacob, who were heirs with him of the same promise. For he was looking forward to the city with foundations, whose architect and builder is God"* (Hebrews 11:8-10). As the people of God, we are tent people. We are on a journey. We are making a pilgrimage. There will always be a restlessness in our hearts. We will never be totally satisfied on this earth; it simply can't give us what we need. Some people may even think there is a haunted look in our eyes because of this spiritual restlessness. It gives us a different goal. Paul said it this way, *"I press on toward the goal to win the prize for which God has called me heavenward in Christ Jesus"* (Philippians 3:14). Even though Paul was spiritually mature and had *"learned to be content"* (Philippians 4:11), he was never going to be totally satisfied with the material world. Jesus recommended, *"store up for yourselves treasures in heaven, . . . For where your treasure is, there your heart will be also"* (Matthew 6:20-21). So, how far along are you on the journey? Is it getting easier for you to pull up your tent pegs every week and move a little further down the road?

> *Honestly, Father, I am looking forward to seeing the place You have prepared for me. I know I will enjoy it. Amen.*

December 23

One Year Challenge—Read: Revelation 14

" 'twas the Night Before Christmas"

" 'TWAS THE NIGHT BEFORE CHRISTMAS AND ALL THROUGH THE HOUSE . . . ." I don't need to repeat the rest, your mind has already run ahead of my pen as the familiar words were triggered in your brain. But stop a minute: return with me to the first line again: *"the night before Christmas."* Have you ever considered the impact of that phrase? Before Jesus came, there was a spiritual night—darkness, hopelessness, and despair covered the earth. The voice of the Old Testament prophets had been silenced for well over 500 years. There was nothing to light the way for mankind. Ancient religions had been exposed as empty and valueless. Atheism was self-destructive as always. Seneca, a philosopher of the time said of his contemporaries, *"Men need salvation from themselves."* It was the darkest spiritual nighttime! People lived for the flesh and life had no purpose. *"But when the right time came, God sent His Son"* (Galatians 4:4 EB) into the world—when mankind could not stand the darkness any longer. Nearly 800 years before, the Prophet Isaiah had predicted the day when the Messiah (Savior) would come: *"Arise, shine, for your light has come, and the glory of the LORD rises upon you"* (Isaiah 60:1). How great to know the night is over because of Jesus! *"The Light shines in the darkness. And the darkness has not overpowered the Light"* (John 1:5 EB). Strange that *"Light has come into the world, but men loved darkness instead of light because their deeds were evil"* (John 3:19). At this special place in your life, the day before celebrating the birth of *"the light of the world"* (John 8:12) open your life totally to The Light. Enough of darkness and its shadows. Allow The Light to fill your whole person. Be glad that the night before Christmas has been destroyed. Have a bright Christmas!

> *Bless You, Lord, for taking away my night. I feel like Easter morning when I stand in Your light. Amen.*

ONE YEAR CHALLENGE—Read: Revelation 15

December 24

Meaning of Christmas

WELL, IT CAME WITH A RUSH, didn't it? We had 11 months to get ready; now all of a sudden, here is Christmas. We ought to think about it more this year. We may be losing something. Yearly there have been court battles in several states about nativity scenes on public property. The courts have ruled in several instances that this is allowable because the manger scene is no longer a religious symbol, but cultural like Santa Claus, Rudolph, and Jingle Bells. Pardon me, but that is pure baloney! The manger scene is not cultural; it is above culture. In the rush toward a civil religion you may be handed that conclusion, but it flies in the face of history and the Bible. I have always maintained that Christmas (like Easter) is only for Christians and has no meaning outside of a personal commitment to Jesus Christ as Savior and Lord of Life. Why celebrate something you don't believe? Why celebrate the birth of one you reject as Master of your life? This is a pluralistic society, we should accept it as such. Bible-believing, born-again Christians are a minority in the world. Let's accept that and live accordingly! Let's hold dear the things that are dear to us as Christians and not prostitute them to the place where the courts or the press or the educational system can say they are no longer religious symbols, relegating them to a cultural stockpile. All truly objective historians know better. Jesus asked for no special favors. He demanded that people receive Him or reject Him as Savior and Lord. That's why He came! Certainly not for the contemporary celebration of *"me-ism."* Christmas Day says that God came into the world one day as a human being (Matthew 1:23). December 25th is as good as any day to celebrate it. Happy Birthday, Jesus!

> *Father, I refuse to listen to any other voice today except Yours, telling me that You have sent The Savior into the world. Thank You so much. Amen.*

ONE YEAR CHALLENGE—Read: Revelation 16

December 25

Is It a Habit?

As I WRITE THIS TODAY, I WONDER WHY YOU are reading it. Is it a habit? Are you looking for inspiration or the answer to a problem? Are you a secret believer that needs to come out of the closet? Perhaps you wonder why I write this. I am writing this because I believe that God wants to say something to you. He has a word for you, regardless of your life situation. I see this as a seed-sowing ministry. Like Jesus said in the explanation of the Parable of the Sower (Mark 4:3-20), these words fall on different kinds of hearts and get different kinds of responses, depending on the spiritual condition of the reader. Scripture verses are always included on these pages because God has promised to always honor his word (Isaiah 55:11). Long after you have forgotten what I have written, the Spirit of God will remind you of what the Bible has said to you. And since God's word is *"sharper than any two-edged sword"* (Hebrews 4:12 KJV), it is sure to go directly to the place in your life that needs it most. Another reason why I write these words is because many people who, for various reasons don't attend church, still have a hunger for a word from God; they will look for God's message to them in these words, since they will not hear them from a pulpit. You see, the Hound of Heaven (Francis Thompson's description for Jesus) had many ways of trying to get to the human heart. Maybe this page is just another expression of Romans 2:4: *"do you show contempt for the riches of his kindness, tolerance and patience, not realizing that God's kindness leads you toward repentance?"* Listen closely: is God trying to get your attention for something special today? Is there a special word from the Lord that you need to hear? I wonder!

> *God, we have been surprised many times at the places we have met You. Is this moment another Divine Appointment? Amen.*

One Year Challenge—Read:
Revelation 17

December 26

Salvaging Christmas

"CHRISTMAS BLUES." While many people are into their Christmas celebrating, many have slid gradually into a depression. Isn't that strange? What a contradiction! Just two days after Christmas Day, the packages have all been opened, the round of parties is in full swing, and the New Year's celebration planned. And people are depressed? How? Why? For many it is because of tremendously high expectations. There was an unreal hope that all of the problems and pressures of the year would be forgotten or at least pushed into the background for a while. For others it was the realization that glitter and tinsel would not change reality. Life seems to be always passing some folks. Life is running in the fast lane and there is no possible way that they can keep up with the flow. So, we wind up with Christmas Blues. I think it is possible to get out of them today. There is still time to salvage Christmas! First, there needs to be a quiet reflection on the true meaning of the season, (reading the Biblical account of the birth of Jesus would be good). Second, there needs to be a humble and positive acceptance of your personal worth before God and your fellow men. God created and loves you, and you need to believe that you are important to Him. Third, there needs to be a spirit of thanksgiving. Nothing overcomes depression and despair like a grateful heart. A friend of mine said upon arriving home from the Medical Center, *"I thought I had it bad! There are many people in a worse condition than me."* That statement came from a person in a bad situation looking at those in a worse situation. If you are in a basically good situation, you don't have to use a negative comparison. Just thank God for His rich goodness to you, especially *"for his undescribable gift"* (2 Corinthians 9:15). Last, but not least, put off post-Christmas depression by sharing blessings and concerns with other Christians via phone, letter, church or what have you.

> **Help me, Lord, to count my blessings and name them one by one. Help me to Praise You many times today for the birth of the Savior. Amen.**

December 27

One Year Challenge—Read:
Revelation 18

First Hearing: Salvation

IT IS A BEAUTIFUL SIGHT TO SEE and I have been privileged to see it happen several times in my life: an immediate conversion to Christianity the first time a person heard the Good News (gospel) about Jesus. I remember an old man in the Philippines who said, *"All my life I have believed there must be somebody like Jesus and now I know there is."* On our mission campaign into Chalco, Mexico, people who had never seen or read the Bible in their lives, prayed to receive Jesus as Savior and Lord. Such is the amazing power of the gospel! It's too bad that in our communities there are so many people *"gospel-hardened,"* that is, they have heard the gospel so many times and rejected it so many times that they can't hear it anymore with spiritual perception. If only these people could hear it again for the first time. First-time hearers of the gospel are excited to hear it. First-time hearers usually aren't antagonistic to the gospel.

They honestly admit that they have a spiritual vacuum. They have tried and proven ineffective, the world's answers to their search for meaning and purpose in life. They are like the soil Jesus described as *"good soil, where it produced a crop—a hundred, sixty or thirty times what was sown"* (Matthew 13:8). My own feeling is that people locked in the prison of spiritual darkness, go without hesitation for the freedom of Jesus when it is offered. I remember a man in Bataan Province saying, *"If my father could have heard your message, he would have believed too."* If you are a Christian and you want to see a miracle, find someone who hasn't read the Bible and tell them about Jesus. As surely as Peter and Andrew *"At once . . . left their nets and followed him"* (Matthew 4:20), there is the possibility that you will participate in a miracle.

> *Father, many of us were surprised by the gospel. It was almost too good to be true. Thank You for sending people out to speak to those who have never heard about Jesus. Amen.*

ONE YEAR CHALLENGE—Read:
Revelation 19

December 28

Panic Buying

REMEMBER THE EXPERIMENTS OF PAVLOV and his dog? He so trained and conditioned his dog that a ring of his bell could start the animal salivating, thinking that it was about to be fed. Have you noticed how our society has become so trained? If the local weatherman says it is going to snow, droves of people immediately run to the grocery stores to stock up. Lines form early in the morning. Store managers rejoice while attempting to get extra shipments of staples from their suppliers. People who aren't even worried about a little snow will soon find themselves caught up in the herd mentality and join the crowds at the checkout counters. Are you one who responds to panic pressure? Of course, it is only in affluent countries that this can happen. It amazes me that people could get so excited or panicked about a shortage of food but are so unconcerned about the shortage of spirituality in our society. Isaiah 55:2-3 asks, "Why spend money on what is not bread, and your labor on what does not satisfy? Listen, listen to me, and eat what is good, and your soul will delight in the richest of fare. Give ear and come to me; hear me, that your soul may live." Jesus found strength to resist temptation in Matthew 4:4 when he quoted the scripture: "Man does not live on bread alone, but on every word that comes from the mouth of the LORD" (Deuteronomy 8:3). If you stock-up on milk and bread and toilet paper before a hurricane or snowstorm comes, I'm not criticizing you for that, I'm just making an appeal to you to make spiritual preparation now because of the storms of life that are sure to come your way. Don't put off the spiritual needs of life and then panic when life is hanging by a thread. The parable of Matthew 25:1-13 describes five foolish virgins who waited until too late to do their panic buying when the Bridegroom came. It is a lesson about the return of Jesus to the earth. Are you ready to meet Him?

Father, as I near the close of another year, help me to make spiritual preparations for the New Year. Help me to find the Bread of Life very satisfying today. Amen.

ONE YEAR CHALLENGE—Read: Revelation 20

December 29

"You Can't Get There from Here"

YOU HAVE PROBABLY HEARD THE STORY ABOUT THE OLD FARMER trying to explain to a city man how to reach his destination. After trying several ways, he finally gave up. With irritation in his voice he concluded, *"You can't get there from here."* I think this applies to people trying to settle disputes while angry. They are just burning up energy and making themselves more frustrated. Jesus spoke clearly about this as He explained the spiritual base of the Kingdom of God. Remember this? *"You have heard that it was said, 'Eye for eye, and tooth for tooth.' But I tell you, Do not resist an evil person. If someone strikes you on the right cheek, turn to him the other also"* (Matthew 5:38-39). Anger produces a desire to get even—revenge. You can't come to peace and unity of spirit if there is still hostility. Jesus went on to say, *"You have heard that it was said, 'Love your neighbor and hate your enemy.' But I tell you: Love your enemies and pray for those who persecute you, that you may be sons of your Father in heaven"* (verses 43-45). The battle with anger that you fight within yourself must be carried to a different kind of battlefield: a field of non-retaliation or a field of spiritual values. Anger, like all other spiritual dangers, is something that can destroy the person who carries it. It can destroy you and remain a barrier to reconciliation. How bad do you want to resolve that old dispute, or that old hurt feeling? The least you can do is initiate a resolution. Confess to God your part in contributing to the problem and then confess your part to the one you have offended or who may have offended you. I tell you, you can get there from here.

> *What a relief it would be, O Lord, to never have to carry the load of anger again. Forgive me my anger and help me to forgive others. Amen.*

ONE YEAR CHALLENGE—Read: Revelation 21

December 30

End of Year Evaluation

"*CLOSED FOR INVENTORY*" will be appearing on a lot of storefronts for the next week. It's time to look back at this year before looking into next year. What were the debits and credits, the pluses and minuses, the memorable and the forgettable? The Bible marks several of these events: "*I am going to confront you with evidence before the LORD as to all the righteous acts performed by the LORD for you*" (I Samuel 12:7), and, "*Forgetting what is behind and straining toward what is ahead,*" said Paul after evaluating things in Philippians 3:13-14. What do you see as you look back? Regretfully, many look back and see only lost time or wasted years. The past is not a pleasant memory for some folks. Where have you been? What have you accomplished? What have you done of lasting value? If you died today, what good things did you do in the world this year that would out-live your funeral service? Think about it. What kind of investments have you made: in materialism, morality, or ministering? Jesus said, "*Do not store up for yourselves treasures on earth, where moth and rust destroy, and where thieves break in and steal. But store up for yourselves treasures in heaven, where moth and rust do not destroy, and where thieves do not break in and steal* [invest in Heavenly valuables]. *For where your treasure is, there your heart will be also*" (Matthew 6:19-21). What profit do you show for this year? What's the bottom line? Not according to your CPA, but according to God's Book of Life and Death? I know, some people never learn. History will repeat itself for many and next year will be more of this year. But for the wise, this time will bring forth a healthy resolve to live life by a different value system. By the grace of God, as I pause for this time of reflection and inventory, I will live life at a better level. Personal resolve may not do it, but God's grace makes the impossible possible and the undoable, doable.

Loving God, I thank You for giving me another year of life. Prepare my heart right now to live totally for You in the New Year. I love you! Amen.

ONE YEAR CHALLENGE—Read: Revelation 22

December 31

Sources of some quoted material *(designated with asterisks*)*

January 6
When You Can't Come Back, by Dave Dravecky
© Zondervan Harper 1992

January 8
Burdens are Lifted at Calvary, by John M. Moore, © 1952.
Renewal 1980 by J. M. Moore. Assigned to
Singspiration (ASCAP). Division of Zondervan Corp.

January 23
Webster's Third New International Dictionary of the
English Language. © 1993 by Mirriam-Webster, Inc.

January 30
Winnie-the-Pooh, by A. A. Milne, © 1935 E. P. Dutton
Publishers

February 9
When I Survey the Wondrous Cross, by Isaac Watts

March 1
Commander Crock, by Don Wilder © North American
Syndicate, used by permission of the author

April 1
How Great Thou Art, by Stuart K. Hine. © 1953, 1955 by
Manna Music, Inc., Burbank CA 91504

April 2
We Have an Anchor, By Priscilla Owens

April 8
Who Killed Jesus, by Mickey Holiday, © 1970 by
Singspiration, Inc.

April 11
Christ Arose, by Robert Lowry

April 12
*Christ the Lord Is Risen Today, by Charles Wesley, and
others
**Christ Arose, by Robert Lowry
***I Know That My Redeemer Liveth, by Jessie H. Brown

May 14
Known Only To Him, by Alfred B. Smith

May 27
Put Your Hand In The Hand, by Gene MacLelland, © 1977
New Life Records

May 29
Precious Memories, By J. B. F. Wright

June 21
My Country 'Tis of Thee, by Samuel Francis Smith

Sources (continued)

July 4
*My Country 'Tis of Thee, by Samuel Francis Smith
**God Bless America, by Irving Berlin

July 15
The Solid Rock, by Edward Mote

July 18
Near to the Heart of God, by Cleland B. McAfee

September 5
Known Only To Him, by Alfred B. Smith

September 21
Abide With Me, by Henry F. Lyte

September 26
Known Only To Him, by Alfred B. Smith

October 7
For the Beauty of the Earth, by Folliott S. Pierpoint

October 16
*Why Do You Wait?, by George F. Root
**I Wish We Had All Been Ready, by Larry Norman

October 18
Commander Crock, by Don Wilder © North American
　　Syndicate, used by permission of the author

October 28
Does Jesus Care?, by Frank E. Graeff

November 17
*Thank You, Lord, by Mr. & Mrs. Seth Sykes, © 1940
　　Renewal 1968 by Bessie Sykes; assigned to
　　Singspiration, Inc.
**Count Your Blessings, by Johnson Oatman, Jr.

November 21
Take Time To Be Holy, by William D. Longstaff

December 17
*Hark! The Herald Angels Sing, by Charles Wesley
**Joy to the World! The Lord Is Come, by Isaac Watts
***It Came Upon the Midnight Clear, by Edmund H. Sears
****Good Christian Men, Rejoice, medieval Latin Carol,
　　translated by John M. Neale

If you want more copies of this book, and can't find it in nearby bookstores, ask a bookstore to order it, or contact Trinity Rivers Publishing at either of the following:

Internet home page address: http://www.mnsinc.com/trinity

e-mail: trinity@mnsinc.com

U.S. Mail: P.O. Box 209
                                Manassas, VA 20108

Phone/facs':   (703) 330-3262

Cost per book is US$10 (Virginia orders: $10.45, including sales tax)
Shipping charges (per order, 1 or more books): US$4

Notes